The American Bureaucracy

The Nelson-Hall Series in Political Science
Consulting Editor: Samuel C. Patterson
The Ohio State University

The American Bureaucracy

Richard J. Stillman II
George Mason University

Nelson-Hall Chicago

For
Kathleen,
my wife

LIBRARY OF CONGRESS CATALOGING-IN-PUBLICATION DATA

Stillman, Richard Joseph, II, 1943–
  The American bureaucracy.

  Includes bibliographies and index.
    1. Administrative agencies–United States.
2. Bureaucracy–United States.   I. Title.
JK421.S75   1987   353'.01   86-23923
ISBN 0-8304-1052-X

The paper used in this book meets the minimum requirements of American National Standard for Information Sciences—Permanence of Paper for Printed Library Materials, ANSI Z39.48-1984.

Contents

4 Inside Public Bureaucracy   115

5 Outputs of U.S. Bureaucracy   169

"I would remark how rarely additions to the public sector have been initiated by the demands of voters or the advocacy of pressure groups or platforms of political parties. On the contrary in the fields of health, housing, urban renewal, transportation, welfare, education, poverty, and energy, it has been, in very great measure, people in government service, or closely associated with it, acting on the basis of their specialized and technical knowledge, who first perceived the problem, conceived the program, initially urged it on the president and Congress, went on to help lobby it through to enactment, and then saw to its administration."

> Samuel Beer, Presidential Address before the American Political Science Association, "Federalism, Nationalism, and Democracy in America," *American Political Science Review,* vol. LXXII, no. 1 (March 1978).

"The modern state is operated by technicians according to the hierarchical model of administrative management, rather than by equal participants according to a model of deliberation and persuasion."

> Sheldon Wolin, "Reagan Country," *New York Review of Books* (December 18, 1980), p. 9.

"For better or worse—or better and worse—much of our government is now in the hands of professionals. . . ."

> Frederick C. Mosher, *Democracy and the Public Service,* 2nd ed., chapter five (1982).

". . . public administration exists, massively, centrally, and often decisively for our individual and collective lives."

> Dwight Waldo, "A Conversation with Dwight Waldo," in *Public Administration Review,* vol. 35, no. 4 (July/Aug. 1985), p. 465.

"The work of government will henceforth be too vast and varied, the sum of money too great, the details with which it will have to deal too complicated to render it possible to perform without a staff of trained officials, furnished with the usual motives to behave well and make the public service the whole and sole business of their lives."

> Senator Charles Sumner (R, MA.) in offering the first civil service proposal to Congress in 1864 as quoted in the *New York Times* (May 10, 1864) p. four.

Preface

In the recent decades Americans ironically have exhibited intense hostility towards public bureaucracy and, at the same time, increasing dependence upon its services. Certainly government bureaucracy is unloved and unwanted but it also is very much a fact of contemporary life. American government, the society, and its citizens are now dependent upon vast, interconnecting webs of complicated administrative systems, processes, and procedures. In the routine visit to the county hospital and the simple delivery of a personal letter, in NASA's projects putting men and women in space and the National Institutes of Health's long-term projects for discovering a cure for cancer, public bureaucracies are at work. Large, complex administrative machinery, often hidden from public view, carries out these tasks through formal and informal hierarchies of experts using advanced technologies and diverse skills. Public agencies are decisively reshaping our lives, for today and into the distant future, through the public policies they implement, the services they perform (or fail to perform), and the regulations and research they develop. The exercise of this authority over the public and private sectors comes from diverse sources of power, both granted and acquired by public bureaucracies.

The following pages introduce students and general readers to public bureaucracy in the United States and seek to answer such questions as: what is the nature of modern public bureaucracy? How has it grown and acquired such influence over our lives? What are its formal elements? Informal elements? Internal dynamics? External sources of power? The tasks it performs? The impacts on our lives? The ways these outputs are fashioned and made to happen? The major trends in public bureaucracy in the 1980s? And its future?

First and foremost, this book provides an introductory overview of public bureaucracy in the United States for general readers and students new to the field. It assumes no prior background or understanding of the topic. As in any introductory text, some details are omitted in order to paint a broad picture of the whole. Since the topic is large and the literature is vast, further readings are suggested at the end of each chapter.

Second, the book argues throughout that public bureaucracy is now *the core* of modern U.S. government. Although no mention of bureaucracy is made in the U.S. Constitution, the heart of every public function, at every level of government today, depends largely upon the work of public bureaucracies and bureaucrats. For better or worse—or better *and* worse—it is the way public business gets accomplished. Examining how bureaucracy works and influences the directions of public policies will be the principal focus of this book. To use Harold Lasswell's famous phrase, this text looks at how bureaucracy determines "who gets what, when, how." In brief, a study of the whys and hows of bureaucracy as our modern central means of making political choices.

Third, this book approaches the institutions of public bureaucracy as open, dynamic *systems* with the essential elements of inputs, outputs, formal structures, internal dynamics, feedback mechanisms, and environmental influences. Successive chapters are organized around an explanation of the systems' essential features and explore the nature of the bureaucratic system, its components, and their interrelationship with the whole. Review questions and listings of key terms at the end of each chapter further serve to underscore its key points. What a bureaucratic system is and how it can be understood as a dynamic whole will be discussed in the opening chapter.

Finally, this book studies the subject of public bureaucracy from an analytical and descriptive point of view, rather than from an advocacy or prescriptive standpoint. It makes no case *for* bureaucracy, or *against* bureaucracy. The text is written primarily to help students and the general public understand this important and central governing institution and how it affects their everyday lives. Therefore, the author aims to describe public bureaucracy as it is, not as it ought to be. Obviously, this task can be difficult because of the derogatory connotations of the term, "bureaucracy." The reader should be cautioned from the outset that this word is used throughout the text in its neutral, descriptive, and analytical meaning, i.e., as an institution of government. Furthermore, "bureaucracy" is used, to avoid boring repetition, interchangeably in this text with other terms such as "public agency," "executive branch," "government organization," "bureau" and "public enterprise," even though the author realizes all too well that these words do not denote precisely the same meanings.

One last point: this writer might reasonably be asked why he spent the past five years laboring over this book on a subject that many regard at best as "dull" and at worst as "noxious." My reply is to remind the reader of a delightful scene in the *Wizard of Oz* where Dorothy and her companions glimpse the wizard behind a curtain. He is busy running the gears, wheels, and machinery that create the steam clouds and awesome illusions of the magician. Dorothy scolds, "You are a very bad man," to which the wizard replies, "Oh, no, my dear, I'm really a very good man; but I'm a very bad wizard." The underlying premise of this text is very much the same: bureaucracies are not the results of some inherent evil or of "bad men," but perhaps only of *our own* ineffective wizardry. It is hoped that this text will make a small step in the direction of improving our understanding about public bureaucracy—and maybe even our wizardry in dealing with them.

1
U.S. Public Bureaucracy

Introduction

On January 28, 1986 booster rockets carrying NASA's Space Shuttle Challenger exploded. Its crew members, teacher Christa McAuliffe and six other astronauts, were instantly killed. The immediate cause of the accident, according to reports from the investigation of the disaster, was eventually traced to faulty O-Rings, washer-like seals between segments of the solid rocket boosters that few experts thought could become a major safety problem. O-Rings had been used for years on rockets to seal all kinds of rocket joints. They had successfully carried 24 prior Shuttle launches with their crews and payloads into orbit. So why would O-Rings fail on the 25th launch?

As the Rogers Commission investigating the accident would discover, the cause of the tragedy would be well beyond the specific technical problem of a faulty O-Ring. Human managerial dilemmas of the entire NASA organization itself were to blame: i.e., improper inspection of workmanship on Shuttle parts; inattention to the details of installation and maintenance of equipment; lack of adequate control over major contractors who built the boosters; ineffective communications between the farflung NASA operations at the Johnson, Kennedy and Marshall Space Flight Centers; emphasis upon "cost-cutting" over "safety" factors; pressures to maintain flight schedules and "a good PR image." In other words, the NASA *organization as a whole and the way it operated,* as much as the technical flaw of a single part, led to the disaster. In short, a public bureaucracy was flawed.

For better or worse, or better *and* worse, we as a society, like the members of the Challenger crew, are dependent upon various public bureaucracies at times for our lives and livelihoods.

1

Today no institution is more vital to our daily existence and well-being as a nation, a community, a neighborhood, or as individuals. Though we cannot often see it or touch it, public bureaucracy plays a major role, perhaps even a life and death role, in deciding such questions as:

What is the quality of the air we breathe?
How safe are our city streets?
Is the water we drink and the food we eat pure?
Are highways planned and maintained properly?
Will there be parks, playgrounds, and recreation for our leisure time?
How well will the next generation be educated?
Do the aged, infirm, poor, and unemployed receive public assistance?
Are our communities well designed for living?
Where should research next explore—the frontiers of space, the oceans, the land, or the human body?
Will a first-class letter we mail arrive promptly?
Is the U.S. nuclear arsenal controlled and commanded properly?
How safe and healthy are the job sites we work at?
Are doctors, nurses, and hospitals capable of healing the sick?
Or, for that matter, is the hairstylist, tradesperson, or any professional certified to perform work for his or her customers?
Can we be sure the house we live in or the car we drive is well constructed?
Will the U.S. economy—its currency, trade, and fiscal matters—be managed fairly and efficiently?

Public bureaucrats not only perform such jobs but also help to make other critical policy decisions. Indeed, our fate as a nation and people depends upon complicated networks of a vast and pervasive bureaucratic system that, though largely unseen, is central to our lives. Yet these very attributes—pervasiveness, invisibility, and centrality—make public bureaucracy exceedingly difficult to define as a phenomenon. What is "it," if "it" is everywhere?

Public Bureaucracy Defined

No precise definition of public bureaucracy exists, but for the purposes of this text it is defined as *the structure and personnel of organizations, rooted in law, that collectively function as the core system of U.S. government and that both determine and carry out public policies using a high degree of specialized expertise.*

Note that this definition of public bureaucracy contains several elements:

- *structure and personnel of organizations* refers to both the formal and informal attributes of public agencies and the people who are employed in them;
- *rooted in law* means that bureaucracies are ultimately based on written laws, codes and statutes;

- *core system* is a set of elements that together function as the central network for operating the U.S. government;
- *U.S. government* involves the three branches (executive, legislative, and judicial) as well as the three levels (federal, state, and local);
- *determine and carry out public policies* means that the organizations both decide and implement choices in governmental affairs;
- *high degree of specialized expertise* concerns specific professional skills, knowledge, and advanced training to perform bureaucratic work.

The definition above is an analytical, descriptive, and neutral one that identifies public bureaucracy as a central institution in U.S. government. This text explores the topic of public bureaucracy from the standpoint of that definition. However, the word *bureaucracy* often has a highly emotional, negative, *prescriptive* meaning. And here lies the source of much confusion. The word has a double meaning that defines essentially the same phenomenon as something that is *both good and bad*. The double meaning implied in the word *bureaucracy* leads to a number of popular myths and misconceptions about it. This chapter will begin by outlining some attitudes toward bureaucracy and bureaucrats. It will next sketch aspects of the realities of modern U.S. bureaucracy that frequently stand in sharp contrast to our popular beliefs and ideas about U.S. bureaucracy. The rationale and design for this book will emerge from discussion about the myths and realities of U.S. public bureaucracy.

Some of Our Negative Ideas about Bureaucracy

Few things are more disliked in our modern society than bureaucracy; hardly an occupation is held in lower esteem than that of a bureaucrat. Both bureaucracy and bureaucrats are subject to contempt and criticism in both the press and private conversation. "Inefficient," "full of red tape," "big," "unresponsive," "unproductive," "inhumane," and "inept" are frequently among the emotionally charged criticisms regularly leveled at bureaucracy and bureaucrats.

Maybe we hold bureaucracy in such low esteem because of firsthand experiences. Most of us are familiar with standing in long lines at a post office waiting to mail a letter and with filling out long forms for motor vehicle registrations, or for God knows what purposes. Every April 15 we gripe at paying what may seem higher taxes to Uncle Sam in return for fewer and fewer visible public services.

Whatever the cause or source of our perpetual criticisms of those nameless, faceless bureaucrats, these views have become part and parcel of our American folklore. It is no wonder that popular dictionary definitions echo our profound dislike of bureaucracy. *The American Heritage Dictionary*'s definition of bureaucracy reads in part: "numerous offices and adherence to inflexible rules of operation; . . . any unwieldy administration.'' According to *Webster's New World Dictionary of the American Language,* "bureaucracy is governmental officialism or inflexible routine.'' *Roget's Thesaurus* gives equally demeaning synonyms for *bureaucracy:* "officialism,'' "officiousness,'' and "red tape.''

Scholars have likewise damned it. Max Weber, the great German scholar of bureaucracy, was horrified by what he saw as the irreversible trend of "bureaucratization'' in human affairs, and he mourned the concomitant loss of human dignity and freedom: "It is horrible to think that the world could one day be filled with nothing but those little cogs, little men clinging to little jobs and striving towards bigger ones. . . . This passion for bureaucracy is enough to drive one to despair.''[1] The contemporary French scholar Michel Crozier, in *The Bureaucratic Phenomenon,* argues that "the vulgar and frequent sense of the word 'bureaucracy' . . . evokes the slowness, the ponderousness, the routine, the complication of procedures, and the maladapted response of 'bureaucratic' organizations to the needs which they should satisfy, and the frustrations which their members, clients or subjects consequently endure.''[2] The English scholar C. N. Parkinson gained an international reputation by developing his "laws'' of bureaucratic practice; such as, "Work expands to fill the time allotted.''[3]

American scholars have been little kinder over the years. E. Pendleton Herring saw bureaucracies as rigid and run by "special interests.''[4] In his *Bureaucratization of the World,*[5] Henry Jacoby dismally pictures bureaucracy's worldwide spread as the central cause of decline in democratic values. Many of the writings of sociologist Robert Merton focus on the "dysfunctions'' of bureaucracy[6] by cataloguing its various shortcomings and inadequacies in modern life. In *Bureaucratic Government USA,*[7] David Nachmias and David Rosenbloom paint an equally unhappy portrait of the spreading of bureaucratic control over most aspects of life in the United States and the subsequent loss of control by Americans over bureaucracy.

For the most part, politicians echo our critical sentiments about bureaucracy. Both Democratic presidential candidate Jimmy Carter in 1976 and Republican candidate Ronald Reagan in 1980 and 1984 ran against "bureaucracy.'' Both candidates' victories were due, at least in part, to their promises to "cut it,'' "trim it,'' "reform it,'' and "clean it up.'' In future elections, no doubt, similar campaign slogans for the reform of bureaucracy are likely to appear. Politicians mirror our popular disgust. From left to right in the political spectrum, bureaucracy is a target, as reflected by the following popular opinions expressed by the man on the street—"it's the problem with government''; "it's too big''; "full of lame-brained, overpaid pencil-pushers''; "it's where everyone stays on for life''; "it's out of touch with the grass roots''; "it grows relentlessly''; "it produces only red tape''; "it's all-powerful''; "it's inefficient.'' Table 1.1 sums up popular views of the federal bureaucracy—no other institution in society is considered "less well run.''

TABLE 1.1
In which of the following people in government
do you have the most trust and confidence?

Public Responses	% (1987) of Population
Those running the federal goverment	19%
Those running state goverment	22%
Those running local goverment	37%
Don't know	22%

Source: Advisory Commission on Intergovernmental
Relations (Jan. 1987).

In a nutshell, these statements reflect the hostile ideas many people, from august scholars to the man on the street *believe* about bureaucracy. Charles Goodsell summed it up well when he observed: "The employee of bureaucracy, that lowly bureaucrat, is seen as lazy or snarling or both. The office occupied by this pariah is viewed as bungling or inhuman or both. The overall edifice of bureaucracy is pictured as overstaffed, inflexible, unresponsive, and power-hungry, all at once."[8]

But there is another side to the discussion, namely the reality—what is U.S. public bureaucracy actually like? Let's examine some popular myths a little more closely in order to gain a clearer and more accurate understanding of U.S. public bureaucracy. Let's begin our discussion by separating the facts from fiction about bureaucracy. Now, will the *real* bureaucracy please stand up (or step forward)?

Some Myths and Realities about U.S. Public Bureaucracy

Bureaucracy is criticized on television shows, by presidents, the press, the public, and academics. Indeed, almost everyone takes a shot at bureaucracy. It is blamed for a variety of social ills from causing "red tape" to failing to cure cancer. Again, in the words of Charles Goodsell, "Bureaucracy stands as a splendid hate object."[9]

What is bureaucracy in the United States really like? What are its forms and elements? There are, as previously outlined, many popular beliefs concerning bureaucracy, and we might begin this discussion by clearing the air, so to speak, by examining some popular notions about bureaucracy.

Myth 1: "Bureaucracy is the problem with U.S. government" Ask almost anyone about bureaucracy, and the response "It's THE PROBLEM with U.S. government!" comes almost automatically. The presidency, the Supreme Court, and Congress often receive far greater, and more charitable, press coverage than the bureaucracy (though they too have received hard knocks in recent years). Presidents, courts, and Congress are generally associated with what U.S. government is *and* does. These institutions are seen as the places where the *real* decisions and actions of government take place, often for the good of all citizens. But the president is merely one individual; the Supreme Court, simply nine judges; and Congress, only 535 individuals, compared with governmental bureaucracy, which is composed of roughly 16 million federal, state, and local employees. In the words of Carl Friedrich, these people and their organizations form "the core of modern government," for it is here where the bulk of government work gets done—"where the rubber meets the road," so to speak.[10]

Public bureaucracies educate 46 million public school children every day, pass out 3.048 million unemployment checks every week, deliver 10.767 million social security retirement checks every month, maintain 300,456 miles of interstate highways (and another 4 million miles of public roads), run 172 veterans hospitals, serve in 142 embassies and delegations overseas, put astronauts on the moon, handle 110 billion letters and packages every year, register and license 12 million autos, and much more. Whether this work is done efficiently, wisely, or well—or whether it should be done at all—is open to argument. These questions aside, public bureaucracies carry out most of the work of government and so are central to the operations of the U.S. government. Therefore, bureaucracy is not only THE PROBLEM with government; it makes government possible. Bureaucracy is how most things get done in government, and so it is "the core" of governmental operations. It is the way society carries out the purposes of government; the way much of government actually governs and acts in *both* "good" and "bad" ways. Thus bureaucracy creates *both* problems and possibilities for change and improvements in U.S. government as well as for society as a whole. Its effects and influences are profound and two-sided.

At the heart of bureaucracy's influence upon everyday life is its ability to make political choices—sometimes critical life and death choices—for society *and* for all its citizens—to determine, in Harold Lasswell's view of politics, "who gets what, when, how."[11] Government bureaucracies exercise important administrative choices—to decide and act in ways that affect all of us—through essentially four routes, according to Theodore Lowi;[12] i.e., by regulatory activities, redistributive policies, distributive policies, and constituent services.

Regulatory activities concern the making and enforcing of rules and regulations. There is a broad array of regulatory agencies involved with rule-making and rule-enforcing activities such as the Interstate Commerce Commission, which regulates interstate transportation and business practices; the Security Exchange Commission, which regulates securities and stock exchange activities; and the Food and Drug Administration, which ensures the purity of foods and the safeness of drug and medical practices.

Redistributive functions involve the transfer of tax benefits from one group of citizens to another: the Social Security Administration annually transfers billions of dollars from working citizens to retired persons; and state and local welfare agencies transfer billions of dollars from the general population to the poor.

Distributive policies are performed by public agencies that use general revenues to provide goods and services to entire populations, regardless of class or group: police, public schools, and the U.S. Postal Service "distribute" services to everyone.

Constituent services involve the work of those agencies and departments that service government as a whole. A municipal budget office's decision can affect the whole of city government; or the State Department's foreign policy choices can influence the entire nation. These are "constituent-type" bureaucracies.

More will be said in chapter 2 about the nature and scope of these different types of bureaucratic policies and how they affect our lives in the United States. The important point for now is that bureaucracy plays a huge role in the way government works and in determining how society is governed. Hence, bureaucracy creates *both* problems and progress. It can be the source of much good and much ill. It is always a two-edged sword.

Myth 2: "Government bureaucracy is overwhelmingly large and monolithic"   Much of the criticism directed at U.S. public bureaucracy involves its size. "It's overwhelming." "It's too big." "It's overpowering." Statistics are frequently cited to shore up this argument: data that indicate that U.S. bureaucracy is the largest employer in the country, consuming a quarter of the Gross National Product, and that it is the fourth-largest bureaucracy in the world—behind only the U.S.S.R., China, and India in numbers of employees. United States public bureaucracy spends more than a trillion dollars annually. All such data are accurate—but only partly.

United States bureaucracy is not one massive organization but numerous small units, mostly very small ones situated at the grass roots. Actually, as table 1.2 points out, there are over 80,000 U.S. bureaucracies—or, more precisely, 1 federal government, 50 state bureaucracies, and 82,290 local public bureaucracies. As table 1.2 shows, the bulk of public employees work in local bureaucracies with 19,076 municipalities; 16,734 townships; 28,588 special districts; 3,041 counties; and 14,851 school districts. Of these, 30,913 public organizations have *no* full-time employees. And only 1,159 have more than 1,000 employees—and nearly one-third or 493 of these are school districts, which means that the bulk of "big" bureaucracy is in reality made up of very small organizational units located at the grass roots. Many of the big public organizations on the local level are school systems.

But what about the federal level? Approximately two million civilian employees and nearly the same number of military add up to a large and impressive figure, but here, too, as table 1.3 points out, these are scattered throughout 45,431 units with 57.2% of them employing fewer than 4 people. Only twenty-two or .06% employ more than 10,000 personnel. Contra-

TABLE 1.2
Number of U.S. Governments by Type in 1982

Federal Government	1
State Governments	50
County Governments	3,041
Municipalities	19,076
Towns	16,734
School Districts	14,851
Special Districts	28,588
Total	82,341

Source: *Statistical Abstract of the United States
1986*, p.285.

TABLE 1.3
Number of Employees per Unit in Federal Agencies in 1980.

Number of Employees	Total Number Units	Percent of Units in This Size Range
1–4	25,992	57.2
5–9 (P.O. 5–10)	7,017	15.4
10–24 (P.O. 11–25)	5,789	12.7
25–49 (P.O. 26–50)	2,634	5.8
50–99 (P.O. 51–99)	1,502	3.3
100–199	977	2.2
200–299	372	.8
300–499	331	.7
500–999	338	.7
1,000–1,999	218	.5
2,000–4,999	189	.4
5,000–9,999	47	.1
10,000 and up	25	.06
Totals	45,431	99.9

Source: U.S. Office of Personnel Management, and Charles T. Goodsell, *The Case for
Bureaucracy* (N.J.: Chatham House, 1983) p.112.

dicting Max Weber's view of bureaucracy as "overtowering," data show that
even the federal level is composed mostly of small, fragmented organizations.
Chapter 2 will deal with the variety and types of bureaucratic structures in the
United States.

Myth 3: "Bureaucrats are all alike"   We hear talk of the typical bureaucrat, as if bureaucrats were a homogeneous mass of green-eye-shaded under-
achievers or nonachievers. The evidence, however, points to considerable diversity in public bureaucrats; it is impossible to speak of "a typical
bureaucrat." Bureaucrats do many jobs, and so there are many varieties of
public employees. There are over 10,000 government job categories describing tasks such as the policing of roads, the flying of space shuttles, and the
delivering of mail. People engaged in these occupations are individually and
collectively far from being "lame-brains." As figure 1.1 points out, more

FIGURE 1.1
Percentages of White Collar Full-Time Civilian Workers in the Federal Government
by Occupational Group (1981)
Total (1,512,800)

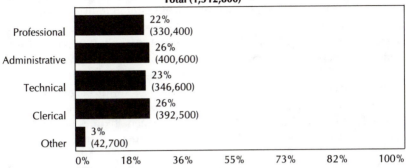

Source: U.S. Office of Personnel Management.

than 45 percent of full-time white collar federal employees work at professional or technical occupations (by comparison, only 10.8 percent of private sector workers are classed as "professionals").

Specifically, the Office of Personnel Management's *Occupations of Federal White-Collar and Blue-Collar Workers* (1981) lists such diverse professional federal jobholders as chaplains (531), economists (5,521), IRS agents (13,876), nurses (35,529), electronics engineers (20,115), attorneys (17,118), museum curators (249), and chemists (7,969).

Increasingly, public employees are highly trained engineers, scientists, dentists, doctors, nurses, biological and physical scientists, mathematicians, teachers, librarians, archivists, accountants, and so on. As Frederick Mosher points out, public service is increasingly "a professional state."[13] Numerous highly skilled blue collar personnel and craftspeople are also employees of the public services. Today, for instance, a firefighter, while he or she may not be categorized as a professional, has to have increasing and specialized expertise in the use of a wide assortment of new techniques and complex substances in order to fight fires in houses, highrises, factories, and offices. Chapter 4 will further describe the professionalization of employees inside U.S. public bureaucracy.

Myth 4: "Bureaucrats stay on forever"   The popular image of a bureaucrat is of someone tenured for life in a comfortable job. The old adage says, once a bureaucrat, always a bureaucrat. Here, too, statistics tell a different story. Public bureaucrats are in reality quite mobile, having turnover rates equal to and sometimes exceeding those of private business. One-fourth to one-sixth of public employees leave government annually. While rates of separation from public service vary considerably from jurisdiction to jurisdiction and according to level of government, in 1980 alone almost 1 million federal employees left the civil service—one-third of all federal workers! Most left voluntarily; only 20,000 were discharged in 1980. Turnover rates at the state and local levels are roughly the same overall, though rates in individual state and municipal bureaucracies, and at various grade levels, differ widely from that figure. Cutbacks at the federal level between 1981 and 1983 varied from agency to agency, as indicated in table 1.4. Even those who remain within a single agency frequently change jobs (averaging only 2.3 years in one slot at the federal level), moving laterally or upward across a wide range of government positions. The point is that unlike the Washington monument, bureaucrats individually and collectively are not permanent fixtures on the landscape. More will be said about their transitory nature in chapter 4.

Myth 5: "All bureaucrats live in Washington, D.C."   The bulk of civil servants are local, not federal, workers—10.8 million are employed by states or localities and therefore are scattered throughout the fifty states. As figure

TABLE 1.4
Staff Changes in Federal Agencies between Jan. 1981 and Sept. 1983

Agency	Sept. 1983	Jan. 1981	Percentage Change
Education	5,226	7,256	− 28.0
TVA	37,181	51,146	− 27.3
Commerce	35,283	48,000	− 26.5
OPM	6,322	8,344	− 24.2
HUD	12,953	17,069	− 24.1
FEMA	2,473	3,259	− 24.1
GSA	29,214	37,010	− 21.1
EPA	11,170	14,088	− 20.7
Labor	18,859	23,495	− 19.7
Energy	17,000	21,168	− 19.7
SBA	5,011	5,886	− 14.9
Transportation	62,174	71,791	− 13.4
NASA	22,534	23,396	− 9.6
HHS	143,097	157,235	− 9.0
EEOC	3,182	3,584	− 8.9
NLRB	2,703	2,950	− 8.4
Treasury	123,574	117,849	− 4.6
FDIC	3,622	3,773	− 4.0
Agriculture	122,786	127,420	− 3.6
Interior	78,621	80,961	− 2.9
DoD (civilian)	32,823	33,393	− 1.7
USIA	7,974	8,095	− 1.5
Postal Service	663,027	664,096	− 0.2
State	23,890	23,525	+ 1.6
VA	236,257	232,168	+ 1.8
Smithsonian	4,689	4,554	+ 3.0
Justice	57,943	55,727	+ 4.0
DoD (military)	983,644	925,323	+ 6.3
NRC	3,486	3,251	+ 6.3

Source: U.S. Office of Personnel Management.

FIGURE 1.2
American Bureaucracy—1950 vs.1984

(% of Federal, State, Local Bureaucrats)

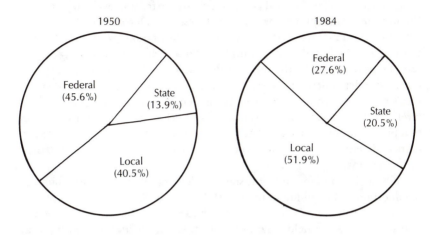

Source: Statistical Abstract of the United States, 1986, p.294.

1.2 shows, local bureaucracy has grown from 40.5 percent (1950) to 51.9 per-cent (1982) of the total number of public employees. Of the total federal work force of 2.7 million civilian and 2.8 million military personnel, as indicated in figure 1.3, only 12.5 percent are stationed in Washington, D.C. Or, put an-other way, 87.5 percent live elsewhere. The distribution of the federal civilian workforce is roughly uniform across the United States, depending upon pop-ulation. Large states such as California and New York have greater concentra-tions by comparison with smaller states. There tends to be a higher concentra-tion of local bureaucrats in state capitals and county seats—as would be expected—but the overall distribution of the bureaucratic work force shows a fairly even spread geographically; hence bureaucrats are hardly removed phys-ically from the grass roots. Indeed, as several studies show, bureaucrats are probably more closely representative of the overall characteristics of the U.S. population than employees of other institutions, such as Congress, labor unions, and big business.

FIGURE 1.3
Federal Employment in Washington, D.C. Area vs. 50 States in Percentages (1980)

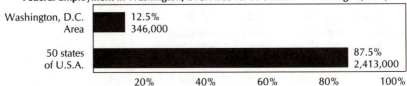

Source: Statistical Abstract of the United States, 1986, p.322.

Myth 6: "Bureaucrats are found everywhere"   As indicated, bureaucrats are found in diverse occupational categories (even private organizations, such as churches and businesses have plenty), but most, surprisingly, are concentrated in just a few fields of government. At the federal level, 70 percent of the workforce is employed by three agencies—the Department of Defense, with 973,100 employees; the Veterans Administration, with 237,700 employees; and the Postal Service, with 667,300 workers. The remaining 30 percent are scattered across the other twelve executive departments and several hundred independent agencies. Only 162,500 work for the Department of Health and Human Services—the major welfare bureaucracy at the federal level. The federal government is increasingly becoming a contracting agency that pumps out monies to get others to do its work. Only in a few fields today, namely defense and law enforcement, do "feds" directly implement their own programs.

Of the 10.8 million full-time state and local employees, 5.3 million work in education; 1.29 million in the health field; 596,000 in police and protective service; only 369,000 in social service and welfare; the remaining 3.3 million work in diverse fields like fire protection, city planning, and highway construction. Thus, the major share of employees in the federal, state, and local bureaucracies are not everywhere but are quite highly concentrated in a few fields—in defense activities at the national level and in education at the state and local levels. Again, chapter 4 will outline in more detail the changing nature of public services in the United States.

Myth 7: "Bureaucracy grows relentlessly"   Actually, the bureaucratic growth rate has been highly uneven, as figure 1.4 shows. In 1930 there were slightly over a half million federal employees and there were about 2.5 million in 1950. During the 20 years between 1930 and 1950, three critical changes forced the quadrupling of federal bureaucracy: hot war and cold war demands caused the formation of new large public bureaucracies (Department of Defense, Veterans Administration, Central Intelligence Agency, Agency for International Development, U.S. Information Agency, National Security Council) and the growth of existing ones. *New technologies* also spawned postwar growth in new agencies (Atomic Energy Commission, National Science Foundation, the air force, Federal Aviation Administration, and Federal Communications Commission). The need for *regulating the economy and dealing with the economic hardship* caused by the Great Depression during the 1930s stimulated the creation of other new agencies (Security Exchange Commission, Farm Credit Administration, Social Security Administration, National Labor Relations Board, and others).

Since 1950, however, the total federal workforce has remained relatively stable at roughly 3 million civilians and 2.5 million military—give or take a few hundred thousand workers. Indeed, the federal employees dropped from 4 percent of the total workforce in 1950 to 2 percent in 1981—or 31 employ-

FIGURE 1.4
Growth of the Federal Bureaucracy

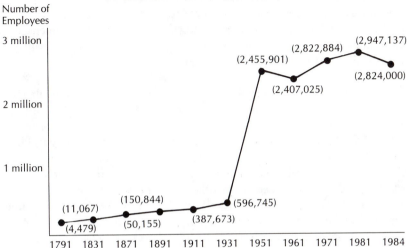

Source: *Historical Statistics of U.S.* and *Statistical Abstract of the United States 1986,*
  p.322.

ees (federal, civilian, and military) per 1,000 U.S. population in 1957, down
to 22 per 1,000 in 1980. During the 1980s the federal workforce dropped in
absolute numbers in many agencies because of President Reagan's budget
and personnel reductions.

Local-level public employment, however, grew from 6 million in 1960 to
10.8 million in 1981. This increase is the result of categorical, block grant, and
revenue-sharing funds that were made available by the federal government
during the past decade. Since 1980 localities also experienced slight employment declines to 10.8 million. The point is that U.S. bureaucracy over the
years has both grown and declined at uneven rates and is not ever-growing.
Moreover, some public agencies expand while others decline. Wartime pressures alone caused marked changes in the size of bureaucracy because of the
changing pressures of defense requirements. Task demands for public services, such as defense, change over time, as does the size of public agencies.
Indeed, some agencies even go out of business entirely. Herbert Kaufman,
who examined federal organization survival rates since 1923, found that 15
percent of public organizations had disappeared, for an organizational death
rate of 27.6 per 10,000 (one-half the death rate for business firms, which
stands at 56.8 per 10,000 businesses). Bureaucracies, then, do die like other
organizations.[14] Furthermore, recent studies indicate that when public bureaucracies grow it is largely because of legislative pressures. According to
Gary J. Miller and Terry M. Moe, bureaucratic growth "depends upon conditions reflecting the way the legislature organizes itself for decision making. In

particular, through the design of its committee system, the operation of rules of thumb, and the adoption of characteristic modes of oversight, the legislature sets the parameters of governmental supply. It is this structure imposed by the legislature that most fundamentally shapes the size of government, the performance of bureaucracy, and the impact of reforms.''[15] Chapter 2 will describe U.S. bureaucracy's growth and change.

Myth 8: "Bureaucracy produces only red tape"   Rules and regulations are part and parcel of every organization, including large and small businesses as well as large and small public agencies. A private doctor must follow the rules—both formal and informal—of his or her profession, just as a public employee must. Whether government has more or less red tape is by no means clear. Certainly there is no clear evidence one way or another. Furthermore, what may be red tape or needless regulation to one person may not be so for another. The Federal Aviation Administration's (FAA) rule banning pipe smoking on airplanes may be both a boon to nonsmokers and a blow to pipe smokers. An annual state-required auto emissions checkup may be a waste of time for an individual driver, but the annual test certainly helps to clean up air and can result in health benefits to an entire community. Securing a municipal business license or a zoning variance to operate a small business at home may well be a headache for the businessperson, but the enforcement of licensing and zoning laws also helps to maintain neighborhood privacy, community attractiveness, and public health. It may well be red tape to require a police officer to read a person his or her rights prior to making an arrest, but it is a very important legal means for protecting individual rights. Red tape can be viewed both ways—as needless bureaucratic rules and regulations and as essential requirements for health, happiness, and security. Much depends on an individual's perspective.

Yet, more importantly, red tape is not the major product of bureaucracy: U.S. bureaucracies and bureaucrats are incredibly diverse, doing many jobs that society deems essential. Some bureaucracies *are* regulatory agencies, such as the FAA, which regulates the airline industry, and the Federal Communications Commission, which regulates the airwaves. Some involve distributive or redistributive services, while others provide constituent services. The list of their activities is long and complex and will be discussed further in chapter 2.

Myth 9: "Bureaucracy is all-powerful and out of control"   While bureaucracy is indeed the core system of U.S. government, as this text argues, in general, individual bureaus and bureaucrats have exercised enormous unchecked power and unfettered influence only for brief historical periods and within specific functional fields. As examples one can cite General Eisenhower's command of the D-Day invasion forces of Europe on June 6, 1944; General MacArthur's postwar occupation of Japan in the late 1940s; Admiral Rickover's development of the nuclear navy during the 1950s; Allen Dulles's direction of the CIA during the 1950s; and J. Edgar Hoover's tenure as the head of the FBI until the early 1970s. Such examples of unchecked bureaucratic power, however, are quite rare and are generally confined to unique individuals with forceful personalities operating in unusual times of stress or crisis. The truth is that power varies enormously from agency to agency and from policy field to policy field. As figure 1.5 shows, some agencies' budgets dwarf the sales of even the largest private businesses. The bulk of U.S. bureaucracy, however, is composed of small, fragmented organizations exercising limited influence over the lives of the general population (see tables 1.2 and 1.3). What effective power do the 450 employees at the American Battle Monuments Commission or the dozen bureaucrats at the Kern County Mosquito Abatement District have over our lives? Not much. But others are powerful, such as the Federal Reserve System, which regulates interest rates and other monetary matters, or, say, a particular state highway department, and they very well may be a source of both political clout and big-ticket public expenditures.

Yet, even these agencies certainly are not all-powerful or out of control, for every public agency operates within the political context of numerous external checks placed upon it by the legislature, the chief executive, the courts, and outside pressure groups. All agencies in government are dependent and interdependent upon a variety of other political institutions for their enabling legislation, annual budgets, personnel authorizations, and policy oversight.

FIGURE 1.5
Three Largest Government and Industrial Organizations by Budget or Sales (1986)

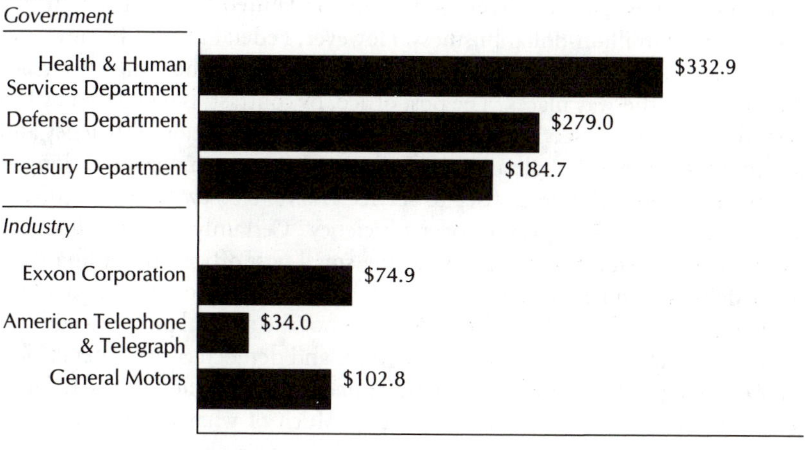

Federal Government

Health & Human Services Department	$332.9
Defense Department	$279.0
Treasury Department	$184.7

Industry

Exxon Corporation	$74.9
American Telephone & Telegraph	$34.0
General Motors	$102.8

Sources: Statistical Abstracts of the United States, 1987, and Moody's Industrial Manual.

None can go it alone. These diverse external checks upon bureaucratic actions will be extensively discussed in chapter 3.

Myth 10: "Governmental bureaucracy is inefficient and wastes resources" The most frequent charge leveled at bureaucracy is that it is inefficient. However, efficiency must be measured against something. Normally it is defined by the achievement of the greatest returns for the least amount of resources or energy expended. As Clarence Ridley and Herbert Simon determined in their classic book *Measuring Municipal Services* (1940), efficiency of public enterprise depends upon what goals or objectives are established and which resources and personal energies are expended. Certainly in the private sector, where the goal is the production of one or more types of goods and services and where the bottom line is quantifiable, profit and loss statements can be relatively good indicators of corporate efficiency or inefficiency. In the public sector, where goals are diverse and outputs are often nonquantifiable, the efficiency of public agencies proves much harder to determine. Is the U.S. Army efficient? It is hard to say, because there is only *one* U.S. Army, and its missions are multiple, frequently nonquantifiable, and certainly not concerned with producing more goods for the least cost. What are the ''returns'' for winning a battle? Or preventing a war? Here, achieving the safety and security of the nation through preventing or winning wars is more important than simply the efficient use of military resources (i.e., counting the numbers of guns fired or bullets used or reducing body counts or weapons costs—to take such logic to the absurd!).

Indeed, efficiency is only one of the goals, priorities, and values of most governmental bureaucracies. Government agencies are often mandated by law to emphasize other values than the bottom line. Take, for instance, the Federal Express Company vs. the U.S. Postal Service. Federal Express pioneered overnight parcel delivery service in the United States. Today it is a thriving multimillion-dollar business. However, Federal Express became successful by selectively servicing high-volume markets, namely big cities, not small, out-of-the-way places. The post office, by contrast, is mandated by law to provide daily mail service to *everyone*, regardless of location. Efficiency and profitability are not the sole aims of the post office, nor can they be, as long as Congress requires the post office to service *everyone equally*. Here equity is emphasized as a clear priority over efficiency. Certainly the postal service could make much more money by closing small post offices, by ending rural mail delivery, and by concentrating solely upon high-volume—and high-revenue—post offices. But neither Congress nor the general public would tolerate such selective service. Fairness, equity, and democracy are other critical values that public agencies must be concerned with, not just efficiency (though efficiency *is* an important value). Much of what government does cannot be measured only by the yardstick of efficiency, because of the multiple values that come into play in the public arena.

But the accusation of inefficiency is usually tied to the problem of wasted resources or, more specifically, wasted monies. No doubt waste can be found in many areas of governmental bureaucracy, especially in budgets with the magnitude of the federal budget, which stands at well over one trillion dollars, and with governmental spending of over one-quarter of the Gross National Product. But increasingly fewer goods, services, and activities are actually being provided and performed by the federal government. One-half of the annual federal budget is today expended on interest payments for the national debt, on direct payments to individuals, such as military pensions or social security benefits, and on direct transfers to others (entitlement programs). One-third of the remainder goes to grants-in-aid to states and localities, and another third goes to other institutions and businesses in exchange for various contracted services. That means that only 5 to 7 percent of the entire federal budget is being used by the government to run its own programs *and to waste at its own discretion!* In other words, a comparatively small amount of the federal budget is discretionary funding used to run civilian agencies. Most federal expenditures are expenditures *mandated* through entitlements, contracts, direct grants, debt servicing, and so on. Limited funds are available for bureaucrats to use for their own purposes—either efficiently or inefficiently! Chapter 6 will discuss some of these factors and their implications and complexities in light of the problems associated with the contemporary bureaucratic system.

Myth 11: "Bureaucrats are unrepresentative of the U.S. population"
The rebuttal to this statement largely turns on the meaning of *unrepresentative*. If the term is used to describe bureaucracy's numerical similarity with the entire U.S. population, then U.S. bureaucrats are probably more representative of the country as a whole than any other institution in U.S. society—Congress, the Judiciary, labor unions, businesses, churches, and so on. But, public agencies vary considerably in the percentages of females, minorities, and handicapped individuals they employ. Some, such as Health and Human Services and the Treasury, exceed those particular groups' percentages in the general population. In 1982 HHS had 65.3% of its workforce made up of females; 34.6% were minorities and 0.99% handicapped; Treasury had 53.8%, 26% and 1.39% in the same categories. Indeed, more than half of some combat units in the U.S. military are made up of blacks (compared to 12 percent of blacks in the entire U.S. population). And some agencies clearly "underrepresent" the total population, as in the case of females (51 percent of the entire population), who are employed by the U.S. Postal Service and the Department of the Interior in percentages of 25 and 32.7 respectively.

These statistics, nevertheless, can be highly deceptive because they tell us little about the *actual* composition of each agency's workforce much beyond very simplistic totals in terms of percentages of ethnic, racial, or sexual identification. As chapter 4 of this text will discuss, each bureau or agency generally reflects the characteristics of the major clientele it serves. The Bureau of Land Management, for example, which manages the federal grazing land in western states, is heavily "stocked" with employees from the West, who are mostly graduates of land-grant agricultural schools, and thus is highly reflective of its principal "users," western cattlemen and ranchers. By contrast, the U.S. Foreign Service within the State Department tends to be dominated by Ivy-League, liberal arts graduates from generally upper-middle-class families, again reflecting the chief characteristics of its clients, namely, international corporations, diplomatic organizations, and foreign governments. The truth is that the *overall* composition of U.S. bureaucracy is perhaps more representative of the population than any other U.S. institution, but particular bureaus and agencies often reflect the peculiar characteristics, traditions, and demands of the clientele they service. More will be said about this subject in chapter 4.

Myth 12: "Bureaucracy is the same everywhere in the world"   The last four decades of rich and intensive research into comparative politics and administration have taught us much about the uniqueness of the U.S. bureaucratic system. According to these studies, none in the world quite matches the U.S. bureaucracy in structure, design, personnel, and controls.

The United States, according to Gabriel A. Almond and Sidney Verba, has a unique "civil culture" characterized by "broad-based pluralism and mass participation," including "communications and persuasion, a culture of consensus and diversity, a culture that permitted change but moderated it." In their words, the United States stands out as "a participant civic culture" by comparison with the rest of the world.[16]

These distinctive features of U.S. political culture mark its bureaucratic system as being distinctive as well in five important ways:

First, whereas continental European bureaucracies tended to be created "overnight," normally by "a great leader" (i.e., Frederick the Great in Prussia or Napoleon in France), the development of U.S. bureaucracy took place gradually over 150 years. The most important effect of such gradualism on public administration, as Ferrel Heady observes: "was that the administrative system was able to take shape feature by feature in a way that reflected the political changes and was consonant with them. Political and administrative adaptations were concurrent and fairly well balanced, but the political theme was dominant. At no time has the administrative apparatus been called upon to assume the whole burden of government because of a breakdown of the political machinery."[17]

Second, the United States, largely because it was and is "a participant civic culture," treated professional bureaucrats throughout much of its history with a contempt uncharacteristic of other nations. In most other societies, working for government is considered a high-status job, but it certainly is not in the United States. Jobs in public bureaucracy carry far less prestige than jobs in the largely private sector fields of law, medicine, and business. As a result, the United States was slow to professionalize its public services and relied heavily upon mass citizen participation to do much of the government work normally assigned to professional careerists in other countries. Not until 1883 did the U.S. Congress pass a civil service law (covering then only 10 percent of the federal workforce), nearly thirty years *after* the British Northcote-Trevelyn Report of 1854 had substantially professionalized their civil service and more than two centuries after the French minister Richelieu had created an intendant system, a rudimentary civil service, for collecting taxes for King Louis XIII. As Frederick Mosher has argued, it was not until the mid-twentieth century that the United States could claim to have a "professionalized civil service,"[18] considerably later than any other western nation. Even today U.S. bureaucracy contains widespread participation by amateurs and volunteers, as will be described in chapter 6.

Third, the structure of U.S. bureaucracy likewise shows remarkable differences from that in the rest of the world. The bureaucracies in most other countries operate with uniformly structured ministries that are clearly differentiated from the legislature and responsible to top-level elected officials, who in turn are responsible to an elected parliament. Top ministerial posts are political, but just a rung below them are permanent senior civil servants who run ministry affairs over the long term. In the United States, on the other hand, executive departments, again as Ferrel Heady notes, are "the major entities but included in the executive branch are a plethora of regulatory commissions, government corporations and other units. Decisions as to executive reorganization as well as many other matters about their operations are basically legislative matters."[19] In the United States, furthermore, relationships between the senior political officials and permanent careerists in agencies are often highly ambiguous. They are very often temporary, fluid situations leading to what Hugh Heclo calls "a government of strangers."[20]

Fourth, much of the development of western bureaucracies is based upon class lines, often rigid ones that allow little mobility between different classes inside bureaucracies. The British Civil Service is divided into three major classes—clerical, executive, and administrative (in ascending order of class "eliteness" and functional responsibilities). The French have their highly meritocratic "grands corps," drawn largely from their elite civil service training academy, Ecole National d'Administration. Germany divides its civil service into lower, medium, and higher classes. The United States operates its bureaucracy without an apparent class system. There is no "Oxbridge" or "Grands Corps" tradition in this country. Certainly there is a hierarchy of officialdom imposed by a government service (GS) rating structure, but securing a GS slot is based upon open, competitive exams that are practical, specialized, and directly related to the ability to perform specific tasks necessary for fulfilling the duties of the post. Task, not class, is the chief determinant of personnel assignments in the system. Thus the U.S. bureaucratic system reflects a far greater degree of vertical mobility than others. If there tend to be rigidities inside the U.S. system, they run horizontally—perhaps for obvious reasons there may be fewer personnel transfers between agencies than elsewhere in the world, though this has not been empirically verified.

Fifth, on the whole, European bureaucracies remain much more closed, prone to secrecy, and controlled from the top down than those in the United States. As Brian Chapman and James B. Christoph point out, in Great Britain and on the Continent, the attention of civil servants is focused on the political minister in charge of the department as "the key political referent in their lives as officials."[21] The political ministers set policy and speak to "the outside world." Loyalty from subordinates is expected. Ministerial responsibility, coupled with hierarchical loyalty to the person at the top, is the chief way of securing administrative control. By contrast, control over the U.S. bureaucracy issues from diverse sources—legislature, judiciary, chief executive, other agencies, outside special interests, internal rules, procedures, and professional norms. United States bureaucratic involvement in policy-making processes is prized, even rewarded, which leads to considerably more openness and participation by bureaucrats in what most foreign observers would regard as "the political arena." As Wallace Sayre remarks, "The American civil servant who earns high and lasting prestige in his society is usually one who most completely breaks the mask of anonymity and becomes a public figure."[22] As a result, the U.S. system is less "closed" and more "noisy"than its European counterparts and even third world and communist bureaucracies. Controls are also exercised less from the top down and more from the bottom up, from the inside to the outside, and from the outside to the inside.

In sum, U.S. bureaucracy is very different from bureaucracies in other parts of the world. Most other bureaucracies, as Sayre remarks, opt for "a more orderly and symmetrical, a more prudent, a more cohesive and more powerful bureaucracy," whereas the United States has chosen instead "a more internally competitive, a more experimental, a noisier and less coherent, a less powerful bureaucracy within its own governmental system, but a more dynamic one."[23]

What sources have created this unique U.S. system? What are the varieties of its "experimental" forms? Its less coherent arrangements? Its "less powerful" but "more dynamic" functions and roles in society? Its distinguishing features? These questions will be discussed in the next chapters.

What Is U.S. Public Bureaucracy?

Some basic patterns and contours of U.S. public bureaucracy emerge from the foregoing discussion. Puncturing some of the popular myths and describing some of the major realities of U.S. bureaucracy tell us a good deal about its basic attributes. To characterize briefly its salient features, U.S. public bureaucracy:

- is made up of roughly 80,000 separate units rather than one massive whole;
- is a heterogeneous variety of organizations, some large, like the Department of Defense, but most quite small, employing relatively few people;
- is broken up among federal, state, and local levels, with the bulk of public organizations found at the local level;
- is sometimes expanding in size and sometimes contracting;
- is geographically distributed fairly evenly across the nation;
- performs a variety of central functions deemed useful or necessary by society: the bulk of the federal bureaucracy is defense-related while much of the local level is heavily education-oriented;
- consumes a major share of the Gross National Product, though increasingly at the federal level these monies go for "contracting-out" services with only 5 to 7 percent of bureaucratic work done in-house;
- is made up of several thousand occupational categories containing increasingly professional employees;
- is neither "all-powerful" nor "out of control" but very much dependent, bounded, and controlled by several institutions such as legislatures, courts, elected chief executives, and other agencies as well as by special interests and political groups outside government;
- is hard to measure in terms of its efficiency or inefficiency because of unique, nonquantifiable outputs and diverse goals, purposes, and activities;
- is highly representative of the U.S. population though particular agencies reflect salient features of their specific clientele groups;
- is very different from other public systems in the world because of its fragmented and diverse structures, its experimental nature, its political participation, and its gradual development;
- is involved with "core functions" in government, particularly in making decisions involving four kinds of critical functions: regulative, distributive, redistributive, and constituent;
- along with Congress, the president, and the courts is actively engaged in the entire spectrum of duties and responsibilities of public policy making and the governing of the United States.

In brief, U.S. public bureaucracy is composed of fragmented, heterogeneous, dispersed, fluid, professionalized, and "localized" organizations that come in numerous and diverse shapes and sizes and have varied powers and purposes and exercise various degrees of influence over the lives of citizens. United States public bureaucracies stand at the very heart of the policy-making and governing processes, for along with Congress, the presidency, and the courts they actively engage in shaping and making public policies affecting the lives of all Americans.

Why Study U.S. Public Bureaucracy?

Precisely because U.S. bureaucracy stands at the very heart of the governing processes and influences the ways we live, work, and act, bureaucratic institutions are worth knowing about. Students of U.S. government devote considerable attention to the study of the legislative processes and to an examination of how the presidency influences decisions in government and how the courts use their interpretative functions to affect lives and livelihoods. But frequently the most critical element of bureaucracy's role within U.S. government is neglected or mentioned only in passing. A typical U.S. government textbook devotes only a few pages, if that, to bureaucracy's roles and influences, while the presidency, the Congress, and the Supreme Court may be given several chapters of commentary, description, and analysis. Although those institutions attract more attention from the media, a well-rounded understanding of governmental processes also necessitates a study of bureaucracy. Bureaucracy is not merely the passive, routine implementor of the laws enacted elsewhere in government. It is not a machine. It is an active partner in the political processes and as such is involved in deciding "who gets what, where, when and how." Understanding how these decisional processes work, why they work the way they do, the manner in which they affect our lives, and their possibilities for change and reform is not only intellectually satisfying, it is a basic step to becoming knowledgeable about how modern U.S. government operates.

Further, bureaucracy is an increasing source of employment. Knowing about possibilities for employment in this area and about the setting where many work today—the possibilities and constraints of working within U.S. public bureaucracy—will be helpful to those thinking about careers in this field.

For those who never will set foot in a public agency, it can be useful to know about bureaucracy. Few professionals, businesspersons, or unions are unaffected today by a government agency's licensing, policing, regulation, contracts, or prohibitions. We all, sooner or later, for better or worse—or for better *and* worse—are influenced by the activities of U.S. public bureaucracy. It is to our own advantage to know how public bureaucracy works. It serves our self-interest to be as informed as we can be about this subject, which is so vital to our lives and livelihoods.

How This Text Approaches U.S. Public Bureaucracy

Several years ago Stephen Bailey wrote a delightful essay in *Public Administration Review* entitled "A Structured Interaction Pattern for Harpsichord and Kazoo."[24] His essay was partly whimsical, partly autobiographical, and very much true to life. In essence, it recounted a day in the life of a political science professor (Bailey) who suddenly found himself elected mayor of Middletown, Connecticut. During the day, Professor Bailey taught the *theory* of

U.S. government, in which he often stressed its neat, rational, ideal format. At night he served as the part-time leader of a midsized, complex municipality. As its chief administrator, he regularly had to cope with the messy, often irrational difficulties of dealing with irate citizens who did not get their garbage picked up or snow removed and with city hall employees who wanted better pay. By day, Bailey could be the detached outside observer (the harpsichord approach to viewing government); by night he often found himself being the "artful improvisor" on the inside (the kazoo approach to government).

Bailey's article stressed an important point: things look different from the inside of municipal bureaucracy than they do from the outside. This is not to say that one view is necessarily superior to the other. A general, theoretical overview is essential to a grasp of the panorama of bureaucracy, whereas the insider's perspective is equally useful in appreciating the hard realities of government and in sensing that the parts of the whole do not always fit neatly together.

This book is different from others on bureaucracy. It will attempt to capture *both* dimensions of U.S. bureaucracy—the big picture as well as the reality of its operations. Each chapter will discuss an important theoretical component of U.S. bureaucracy based upon a systems model—the grand view from the outside. Each chapter through numerous examples will relate how the theoretical elements discussed *actually operate.* An attempt will be made to appreciate both the theoretical and practical realities of U.S. bureaucracy *and* how both dimensions interrelate. In this manner, students will be exposed to both the theory and practice of U.S. public bureaucracy—the view from outside *and* from within.

What theoretical model is most useful in gaining a sense of the whole from the outside? What model will provide an overview of the structure and a framework for analysis? How can we make sense out of the whole as well as the parts?

While there are numerous approaches to the study of bureaucracy, this book will utilize a systems perspective to guide the general discussion of U.S. public bureaucracy. What is a systems model? Why utilize this methodological framework? Basically, a systems model provides an effective way of viewing the whole as well as the parts and how they interrelate. Systems models are utilized in many fields—engineering, medicine, physics, and chemistry and in economics and the other social sciences—as a tool for understanding the components of a field and how these components of a system work together and interact as an ongoing process. Some systems models are highly complex and methodologically quantified, such as those purporting to describe how the entire U.S. economy operates, but a simplified, nonquantifiable systems model will suffice for illustrating how U.S. public bureaucracy works. This systems model will include, as figure 1.6 illustrates, a discussion of: (1) the forms of bureaucratic institutions and the sources that gave rise to U.S. bureaucracy; (2) the environment within which these units operate and the basic inputs into the bureaucratic system that are the chief sources for agency

FIGURE 1.6
Government Bureaucracy as a System

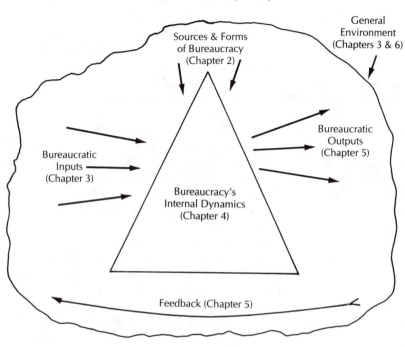

The Future of the
Bureaucratic System (Chapter 7) 27a.

growth, decline, and stability; (3) the internal conversion processes or the elements and activities inside bureaucratic structures by which inputs are turned into outputs; (4) the outputs (goods, services, and activities) of bureaucracy and the manner by which these various inputs are "fed back" into the general environment; and (5) the operation and future of the bureaucratic system as a whole and its relationships to society's future.

Each of the next six chapters will examine one of the aforementioned elements of U.S. public bureaucracy. Chapter 2 will look at the rise of U.S. bureaucracy—the sources, structures, and variety of public bureaucracies in the United States. What gave rise to U.S. bureaucracy? What are its various kinds of organizations? What are the contemporary forms and functions through which U.S. public bureaucracy operates today? Its formal policy-making roles? Its formal processes?

Chapter 3 focuses upon the major types of inputs into bureaucracy: what is the general environment of public organizations? What are the major sources of growth, decline, and stability? How do contemporary socioeconomic factors, political actors, and institutional processes influence the future of every public agency?

Chapter 4 looks inside bureaucracy: its basic internal structures, subsystems, major groups, and the political and professional elites that direct its activities and outputs. How does each of these elements influence the work that public agencies perform in society?

Chapter 5 examines the types of bureaucratic outputs and their feedback in the environment: what are the major products of U.S. bureaucracy? How are these produced? What gamesmanship is involved? What are the institutional forces and the political situations that support or impede these outputs? How do these outputs influence our lives?

Chapters 6 and 7 will view the present and the future of U.S. bureaucracy from the standpoint of the overall bureaucratic system. What are the major trends influencing bureaucracy in the 1980s? What forces strengthen or weaken its role and institutions in society? Given the contemporary dynamics of the bureaucratic system, how can bureaucracy tomorrow best be made to serve and be responsive to the public interest? What will ensure that it is controlled by the citizenry and responsible to its citizens?

Summary of Key Points

Public bureaucracy plays a central role in governing the modern United States, and it therefore has been described throughout this chapter as "the core system of U.S. government." It decisively determines important policy questions in U.S. life today and is the chief institution for implementing those policy choices. However, bureaucracy, even though it is pervasive and critical to running our society, often cannot be seen, recognized or easily comprehended. Partly for these reasons many myths surround its purposes, structure, and activities. Several of these myths have been examined and exploded in this opening chapter, such as the myths that state that bureaucracy is "too large," "out of control," "produces only red tape," and so on. From this discussion about bureaucratic myths emerges bureaucracy's general modern characteristics as well as a systems model for comprehending its elements and its totality. The following chapters will discuss these major elements of the bureaucratic system and how public bureaucracy operates today as the central system of U.S. governance.

Key Terms

myths about bureaucracy
bureaucratic system
fragmented organizations
public professionals
policy-making roles
public vs. private bureaucracy
bureaucratic waste

turnover rates
red tape
external bureaucratic checks
core system of U.S. government
bureaucratic efficiency
inputs and outputs of the system
external environment

Review Questions

1. How would you describe the major characteristics of U.S. bureaucracy? Its actual practice and operation?
2. What are some of the popular notions or "myths" about bureaucracy you have expressed or heard expressed in discussions with friends, family, and others?
3. What are the sources of these opinions? Are these beliefs well founded?
4. In general, can you describe in what ways U.S. public bureaucracy plays a central role in society?
5. Based on your reading of this chapter, how do you define public bureaucracy?

Notes

1. As quoted in Reinhard Bendix, *Max Weber: An Intellectual Portrait* (NY: Doubleday, 1960), p. 464.
2. Michel Crozier, *The Bureaucratic Phenomenon* (Chicago: University of Chicago Press, 1964), p. 3.
3. C. N. Parkinson, *Parkinson's Law and Other Studies in Administration* (Boston: Houghton Mifflin, 1957), p. 16.
4. E. Pendleton Herring, *Public Administration and the Public Interest* (NY: McGraw-Hill, 1936), p. 10.
5. Henry Jacoby, *The Bureaucratization of the World* (Berkeley: University of California Press, 1973), p. 32.
6. Robert K. Merton et al., *A Reader in Bureaucracy* (NY: Free Press, 1952), p. 6.
7. David Nachmias and David H. Rosenbloom, *Bureaucratic Government USA* (NY: St. Martin's Press, 1980), p. 18.
8. Charles Goodsell, *The Case for Bureaucracy* (NJ: Chatham House, 1983), p. 2.
9. Ibid., p. 14.
10. Carl J. Friedrich, *Constitutional Government and Democracy,* 4th ed. (Waltham, MA: Blaisdell, 1968), p. 38.
11. Harold Lasswell, *Politics: Who Gets What, When, How* (NY: McGraw-Hill, 1936), p. 7.
12. Theodore Lowi, "Four Systems of Policy, Politics and Choice," *Public Administrator Review* 32 (July/Aug 1972), pp. 298–310.
13. Frederick C. Mosher, *Democracy and the Public Service,* 2d ed. (NY: Oxford University Press, 1982), chapter 5.
14. Herbert Kaufman, *Are Government Organizations Immortal?* (Washington, DC: Brookings Institution, 1976), pp. 73–77.
15. Gary J. Miller and Terry M. Moe, "Bureaucrats, Legislators, and the Size of Government," *The American Political Science Review* (1983), p. 320.

16. Gabriel A. Almond and Sidney Verba, *The Civic Culture* (Princeton: Princeton University Press, 1963), p. 8.
17. Ferrel Heady, *Public Administration: A Comparative Perspective*, 3d ed. (NY: Marcel Dekker, 1985), p. 207.
18. Frederick C. Mosher, *Democracy and the Public Service*, 2d ed. (NY: Oxford University Press, 1982), chapter 5.
19. Ferrel Heady, *Public Administration*, p. 209.
20. Hugh Heclo, *A Government of Strangers* (Washington, DC: Brookings Institution, 1977). Heclo's entire book relates to this theme and the problems it raises for U.S. government.
21. As quoted in Ferrel Heady, *Public Administration*, p. 214.
22. Wallace Sayre, "Bureaucracies: Some Contrasts in Systems," *Indian Journal of Public Administration*, vol. 10, no. 2 (1964), p. 228.
23. Ibid., p. 223.
24. Stephen K. Bailey, "A Structured Interaction Pattern for Harpsichord and Kazoo," *Public Administration Review* 14 (Summer 1954), pp. 202–204.

Further Readings

The term *bureaucracy* has eighteenth-century French origins: *bureaucratie*, apparently from the woolen cloth (burel) used to cover writing desks; thus the term for the place of such activity—bureaus, or, more broadly, bureaucracy. For an interesting review of the history of the idea of bureaucracy, read Martin Albrow's *Bureaucracy* (1970).

Serious scholarly study of bureaucracy began in this century largely because of the work of the German scholar Max Weber (1864–1920). His fragments of writings on this subject were published posthumously and did not become widely available in the United States until after World War II via such books as H. H. Gerth and C. Wright Mills (eds.), *From Max Weber* (1946), and Reinhard Bendix's *Max Weber: An Intellectual Portrait* (1960). Marianne Weber's biography of her husband, *Max Weber: A Biography* (1975), provides an especially good review of his life and ideas.

Taylor Cole and Carl Friedrich's *Responsible Bureaucracy* (1932) was probably the first book published in the United States with *bureaucracy* in the title and that heavily drew upon Weberian thinking. During the postwar era sociologists in particular studied this subject extensively with numerous fruitful results. See especially Peter M. Blau and Marshall W. Meyer's *Bureaucracy in Modern Society*, 2d ed. (1971) and Robert K. Merton et al., *A Reader in Bureaucracy* (1952) as worthy heirs of Weberian traditions.

The postwar literature in public administration, though not titled as books on bureaucracy, contains several distinguished and diverse contributions to our understanding of bureaucracy. Included in this literature are:

Herbert Simon's *Administrative Behavior* (1947); Dwight Waldo's *The Administrative State* (1948); Fritz Morstein Marx (ed.), *Elements of Public Administration*, 2d ed. (1959); Paul Appleby's *Policy and Administration* (1949); John Gaus's *Reflections on Public Administration* (1947); Harold Stein (ed.), *Public Administration and Policy Development* (1952); and Frederick C. Mosher's *Democracy and the Public Service*, 2d ed. (1982).

Political science literature of the last two decades also has produced a varied, rich, and distinguished literature on bureaucracy that includes Anthony Downs's *Inside Bureaucracy* (1967); Graham Allison's *Essence of Decision* (1971); Harold Seidman's *Politics, Position and Power*, 4th ed. (1986); Francis E. Rourke's *Bureaucracy, Politics, and Public Policy*, 3d ed. (1984); Donald P. Warwick's *A Theory of Public Bureaucracy* (1975); Peter Woll's *American Bureaucracy*, 2d ed. (1977); Gary L. Wamsley and Mayer N. Zald's *The Political Economy of Public Organizations* (1973); Kenneth Meier's *Politics and the Bureaucracy* (1979); Douglas Yates's *Bureaucratic Democracy* (1982), and David Nachmias and David H. Rosenbloom's *Bureaucratic Government USA* (1980).

Several excellent essays on this topic are found in Francis E. Rourke (ed.), *Bureaucratic Power in National Politics*, 3d ed. (1978). Also helpful are Norton Long's "Bureaucracy and the Constitution" as well as his other writings on the topic, all found in his book *The Polity* (1962); Dwight Waldo's "Bureaucracy," in *Collier's Encyclopedia* (1962); Alfred Diamant's "The Bureaucratic Model: Max Weber Rejected, Rediscovered, and Reformed," in *Papers in Comparative Administration*, Ferrel Heady and Sybil L. Stokes (eds.) (1962); James Q. Wilson's "The Rise of the Bureaucratic State," in *The Public Interest* (Fall 1975); Richard Schott's *The Bureaucratic State* (1974); and Gary J. Miller and Terry M. Moe's "Bureaucrats, Legislators, and the Size of Government," in *The American Political Science Review* (1983). Harold Laski's essay "Bureaucracy" in the *Encyclopedia of Social Sciences*, vol. 3 (1930) is dated but still well worth reading.

For the best comparative examination of modern bureaucratic systems see Ferrel Heady's *Public Administration: A Comparative Perspective*, 3d ed. (1985).

The most witty and disparaging view of bureaucracy remains C. Northcote Parkinson's now-classic *Parkinson's Law and Other Studies in Administration* (1957). For two good replies to this point of view, see Marshall E. Dimock's *Administrative Vitality* (1959) and more recently, Charles T. Goodsell's *The Case For Bureaucracy* (1983).

Some of the great "classics" of literature that can tell us much more than most social science texts on this topic include: Norman Mailer's *The Naked and the Dead* (1948), James Gould Cozzens's *Guard of Honor* (1948), James Jones's *From Here to Eternity* (1951), and Herman Wouk's *The Caine Mutiny* (1951).

2
The Rise of U.S. Bureaucracy

The Growth and Emergence of
  Organized Functions of Government
  Bureaucracy
General Characteristics of the Rise of
  U.S. Bureaucracy: Gradualism,
  Experimentalism, Majoritarianism,
  and Complexity

Forms, Functions, Policies, and
  Processses of Contemporary
  Bureaucracy
Summary of Key Points
Key Terms
Review Questions
Notes
Further Readings

The United States did not always have much of a bureaucracy. Nor did it need one. When the United States began in 1789 as a "new nation," the population was under 4 million (compared with over 240 million today). The average American was a farmer. Nine out of ten people lived directly off the land (now less than 5 percent are farmers). Given the social simplicity and rural autonomy of 1789, few demands were made upon government. No autos meant that no roads had to be built, no drivers' licenses granted, no taxes raised for these purposes. There were no telephones, airlines, or television stations to regulate. No sewage, water, or utilities were provided for homes. Nor were clean air, pure food, and good public health then considered "essentials." Compulsory education through high school was unheard of. Geographic isolation of the "first new nation" prompted little need for a standing army, navy, and air force to defend "global American interests"; nor were there orbiting space shuttles, lunar landings, COMSAT weather satellites, social security retirement benefits, and medicare/medicaid protection. There was no need of a big bureaucracy to provide such services.

Now our 240 million population is sixty times larger, more heterogeneous, more technologically dependent and interdependent, making greater and more complex demands upon government for a wide variety of goods and services. In particular, urbanization increased dependence upon government activities. In 1789 New York City had a population of 33,000; today it contains more than 8 million people, bringing enormous new demands upon municipal government for basic services. Fire, police, schools, welfare, zoning, water, sewage, and housing are just a few "basics" required by modern urban life. A complex social environment today tends to promote the development of complex bureaucratic services.

The Growth and Emergence of Organized Functions of Government Bureaucracy

Much as the hull of a ship gradually acquires barnacles, the United States acquired its bureaucratic institutions and services gradually as layers upon layers of responsibilities were added over the course of two hundred years. Different types of social pressures spawned, over a long time, bureaucracy's organizations. These new bureaucratic services or tasks were added gradually and unevenly. Sometimes the buildup of these public bureaucracies was so slow as to be imperceptible; sometimes it was quite swift. First, the basic core bureaucratic service functions were created at the start of the new nation's existence; second, those involved with national economic development evolved in the nineteenth century; third, service-oriented tasks came about in the late nineteenth century; fourth, the rise of regulatory agencies and government corporations services developed in the progressive period of the early twentieth century; fifth, surges in social service organizations arose during the Great Depression; sixth, the development of the large standing defense establishment appeared during World War II and the postwar Cold War era; and seventh, new forms of staff services as well as state and local bureaucracies grew throughout the twentieth century (see figure 2.1). Each of these basic types of bureaucratic organizations will be examined in turn.

Creation of the Basic Core Service Functions

At the inception of the U.S. government in 1789, little bureaucracy was needed. Nevertheless, a few public agencies were necessary. Congress created the first executive departments to perform the essential core service functions. Core tasks are those which every nation (or state or municipality) develops in order to be a nation (or state or municipality). The United States set up five units in 1789 to carry out these core functions: the State Department to conduct its external affairs with other nations; the War Department and later the Navy Department (now combined into the Defense Department) to provide protection from threats from other nations; the Treasury Department to collect revenues, pay bills, settle accounts, and establish broad economic policies; the Attorney General's Office (now the Department of Justice) to represent legal cases and offer legal advice to the president and his Cabinet; and the Postal Services Department to run the national mail system, which was and still is essential for internal communications (the U.S. Postal Service now operates as an independent government corporation).

As indicated in figure 2.2, the *department* (with the exception of the Office of the Attorney General, which became a department in 1870) was the key bureaucratic building block from the start. It was the basic organizational arrangement for providing critical national services, and departments

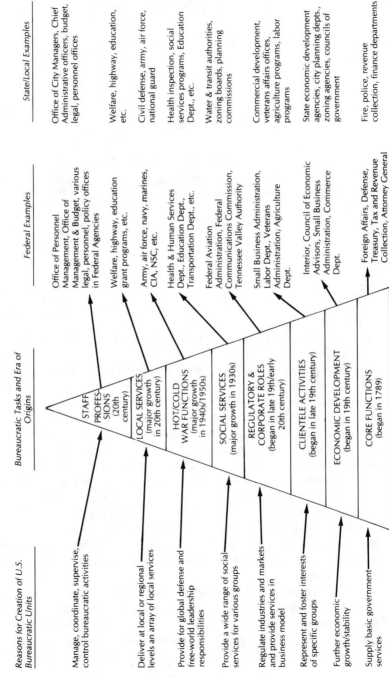

FIGURE 2.1
Modern U.S. Bureaucracy

Reasons for Creation of U.S. Bureaucratic Units

Manage, coordinate, supervise, control bureaucratic activities

Deliver at local or regional levels an array of local services

Provide for global defense and free-world leadership responsibilities

Provide a wide range of social services for various groups

Regulate industries and markets and provide services in business model

Represent and foster interests of specific groups

Further economic growth/stability

Supply basic government services

Bureaucratic Tasks and Era of Origins

STAFF PROFESSIONS (20th century)

LOCAL SERVICES (major growth in 20th century)

HOT/COLD WAR FUNCTIONS (major growth in 1940s/1950s)

SOCIAL SERVICES (major growth in 1930s)

REGULATORY & CORPORATE ROLES (began in late 19th/early 20th century)

CLIENTELE ACTIVITIES (began in late 19th century)

ECONOMIC DEVELOPMENT (began in 19th century)

CORE FUNCTIONS (began in 1789)

Federal Examples

Office of Personnel Management, Office of Management & Budget, various legal, personnel, policy offices in Federal Agencies

Welfare, highway, education grant programs, etc.

Army, air force, navy, marines, CIA, NSC, etc.

Health & Human Services Dept., Education Dept., Transportation Dept., etc.

Federal Aviation Administration, Federal Communications Commission, Tennessee Valley Authority

Small Business Administration, Labor Dept., Veterans Administration, Agriculture Dept.

Interior, Council of Economic Advisors, Small Business Administration, Commerce Dept.

Foreign Affairs, Defense, Treasury, Tax and Revenue Collection, Attorney General

State/Local Examples

Office of City Managers, Chief Administrative officers, budget, legal, personnel offices

Welfare, highway, education, etc.

Civil defense, army, air force, national guard

Health inspection, social services programs, Education Dept., etc.

Water & transit authorities, zoning boards, planning commissions

Commercial development, veterans affairs offices, agriculture programs, labor programs

State economic development agencies, city planning depts., zoning agencies, councils of government

Fire, police, revenue collection, finance departments

31

FIGURE 2.2

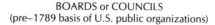

BOARDS or COUNCILS
(pre–1789 basis of U.S. public organizations)

Equality of participants (lacking
single head, hierarchy chain of
command, specific functional
assignments)

DEPARTMENTS
(post–1789 federal departmental structure)

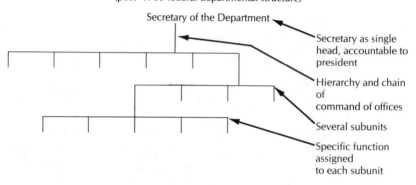

Secretary of the Department

Secretary as single
head, accountable to
president

Hierarchy and chain
of
command of offices

Several subunits

Specific function
assigned
to each subunit

still remain the basic organizational building blocks at federal, state, and local levels.

Why? Largely because the founding fathers had had several unhappy experiences throughout the Revolutionary War in conducting administrative business with councils, boards, and legislative committees. These had proved to be slow, unresponsive, and irresponsible. General George Washington, as commander-in-chief of the Continental Armies during the Revolutionary War, continually complained about the inability of these committees to reach agreements and to decide and act expeditiously on critical military matters. When Washington became president, it was no small wonder that he, along with others in Congress who had experienced similar frustrations, instituted departments that were responsible to a single chief executive. The founding fathers had learned one bitter lesson from the Revolution—i.e., some*one* should be held responsible for doing the work of government, and the department format, they saw, was the most effective organizational model to facilitate that end.

The departmental head would be called a secretary (following the British model) and would be appointed, with the consent of the Senate, by the president and would serve at his pleasure. It was this last point that stirred the only real debates in Congress relative to the formation of these early departments. Some representatives argued that only with the consent of the Senate should the president be able to remove Cabinet officials, but the arguments of Congressmen James Madison (Virginia), Fisher Ames (Massachusetts), and others won out. They stressed the need for executive accountability for departmental affairs. One individual, the president, should be held responsible for executive affairs, and thus the president, not Congress should be entrusted with the power to remove his key assistants. For a period after the Civil War, the Tenure of Office Act of 1867 restricted presidential powers of removal, but since the Supreme Court decision reached in *Myers vs. the United States* (1926), the president has been given an essentially free hand in removing political appointees.

While small and informally run, the early departments were created to perform specific tasks, as evidenced by their enabling legislation, that were vital to the nation's well-being. The tasks at hand involved the basic work of the new nation. In short, defense, diplomacy, and functional necessities stimulated the creation and subsequent structure of these first bureaucracies. The State Department was established to conduct foreign affairs, maintain embassies and ambassadors abroad, and advise the president on international policies. Thomas Jefferson, the first secretary of state, not only managed diplomatic affairs but had multiple, often unrelated duties (as is the case today with many Cabinet secretaries). He was in charge of issuing copyrights and patents, minting currency, and taking the national census (largely because of Jefferson's interest in these subjects and because no one else wanted to assume responsibility for them). All this Jefferson performed with the assistance of just one chief clerk, seven assistant clerks, and one messenger.[1]

The War Department supervised at first both the army and navy, but in 1798 the navy "spun off" into a separate department in order to prepare for the then-expected naval warfare with Great Britain. Here is an early example of how a crisis precipitated the formation of a new, independent department; in a similar fashion nearly two centuries later, in 1977, the Energy Department, forged from bits and pieces of several smaller agencies, came into existence because of a national energy crisis. Like the State Department, the War and Navy departments were small operations, having few ships, less than 4,000 soldiers, and only eighty civilian employees. The following account by a prominent foreign visitor of his meeting with secretary of war James McHenry in 1796 gives a sense of the informality of these departments' daily operations.

> The government officials were as simple in their manners as ever. I had occasion to call upon McHenry, the Secretary of War. It was about eleven o'clock in the morning when I called. There was no sentinel at the door, all the rooms, the walls of which were covered with maps, were open, and in the midst of the solitude I found two clerks each sitting at his own table, engaged in writing. At last I met a servant, or rather *the* servant, for there was but one in the house, and asked for the Secretary. He replied that his master was absent for the moment, having gone to the barber's to be

FIGURE 2.3

The development of every bureaucracy is rooted in specific public laws approved by the legislature and establishing its missions, structure, and personnel

PUBLIC LAW 96–465—Oct. 17, 1980

94 STAT. 2071

Public Law 96–465
96th Congress

An Act

To promote the foreign policy of the United States by strengthening and improving the Foreign Service of the United States, and for other purposes.

Oct. 17, 1980
[H.R. 6790]

Be it enacted by the Senate and House of Representatives of the United States of America in Congress assembled,

Foreign Service
Act of 1980.
22 USC 3901
note.

SECTION 1. SHORT TITLE.—This Act may be cited as the "Foreign Service Act of 1980".

SEC. 2. TABLE OF CONTENTS.—The table of contents for this Act is as follows:

TABLE OF CONTENTS

Source: PL 96–465, 94 STAT. 2071—Oct. 17, 1980.

shaved. Mr. McHenry's name figured in the State Budget for $2,000, a salary quite sufficient in a country where the Secretary of War goes in the morning to his neighbor, the barber, at the corner, to get shaved. I was as much surprised to find all the business of the War Office transacted by two clerks, as I was to hear that the Secretary had gone to the barber's.[2]

While informality was a characteristic of early departmental activities, pronounced differences between the departments were even then apparent. The Treasury Department, partly because of the vigorous personality and leadership of Alexander Hamilton, was given the broadest mandate and widest latitude in its original enabling legislation: "to digest and prepare plans for the improvement and management of revenue"; "to superintend the collection of the revenue"; "to execute such services relative to the sale of the lands belonging to the United States"; and "to perform all such services relative to the finances."[3] And indeed Hamilton exercised broad, sweeping powers in his efforts to raise and collect new sources of national revenues, supervise and direct disbursement of funds, control public debts, and create a national bank. He even drew up the first economic blueprint of national economic growth in his *Report on Manufacturers*. As is also true today, personalities and intellectual capacities of leaders combined with the departmental legal authority and day-to-day responsibilities create wide variations *between* government organizations, even if they can all be broadly defined as departments.

The attorney general, as noted earlier, was different in that his authority was represented by an office, not a department. Until well into the nineteenth century, attorneys general were part-timers. They acted more or less as legal advisors to presidents and as chief litigators for the United States. This tradition continues to this day. Recent attorneys general have been close personal friends, indeed personal attorneys, of presidents they have served—witness two recent appointees, Griffin Bell and William French Smith. Early attorneys general were expected to continue their private legal practices to support themselves. The same was true for local postmasters who worked for the postmaster general. They were also unsalaried and were expected to charge customers for services (a tradition that also holds true today in an altered form, since the U.S. Postal Service is now an independent government corporation and is expected to be a self-supporting enterprise).

For the most part, these core service functions—diplomacy, national defense, finance, legal advice, and internal communications—with minor variations remain today core service functions of U.S. bureaucracy, but with one important difference. Each federal department that performs these basic tasks has multiplied its scope, activities, and size enormously over the past two hundred years.

Figure 2.4 shows the State Department's present organization. It is a far cry from the way it was in Thomas Jefferson's day when it had eight clerks, one

FIGURE 2.4

Department of State

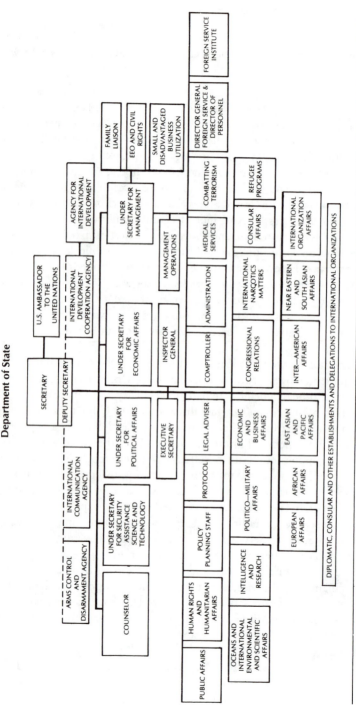

Source: *The United States Government Manual 1984-85.*

messenger, and twenty-five agents! Today State's bureaucracy comprises more than 30,000 persons, staffing 142 embassies around the world, and representing the United States in over 50 international organizations and at more than 800 international conferences annually. The tasks that figure 2.4 shows are only the very "tip of the iceberg" of State's incredibly complex functional responsibilities. Many of these tasks were not even conceived of in 1789. They include descriptors like "combating terrorism," "human rights," "refugee programs," "international narcotics matters," and "international organization affairs." The same expansion of roles and responsibilities has taken place in other core departments—Treasury, Defense, Justice, and the Postal Service. Though these departments' activities have greatly enlarged, as in the case of the State Department, their basic structures remain much the same as when they were first organized—i.e., having a cabinet secretary in charge, a chain of command, a hierarchy and functionally differentiated activities, and some responsibilities that do not fit in clearly with their overall basic missions.

National Economic Development in the Nineteenth Century

The first governmental organizations in the United States were created to service the essential core functions of the new nation and were organized in the form of departments and offices. But the nineteenth century saw the emergence of other organizational arrangements. The Interior Department, the only federal department created between 1789 and 1889, was established in 1849 to foster domestic growth and national development. This was the era of rapid westward expansion. As the population shifted west, a new department was necessary to serve new national needs. Proposals to create a "Home Office," along the lines of a British Home Office (essentially a department for domestic affairs), had repeatedly been raised since 1789. However, local pressures to resist federal involvement in this area, coupled with the worries of a growing bureaucracy (even then), had blocked any moves in this direction until 1849, when the need for greater coherence and policy direction became imperative. The Interior Department emerged as an amalgam of bits and pieces of several other agencies then in existence—all involving domestic concerns: Bureau of Indian Affairs (from the War Department); Military Pensions (from War); Patent Office (from State); Census Bureau (from State), and Land Office (from Treasury). Note that the bureau became the organizing principle at Interior. Interior's scattered and somewhat unrelated collection of domestically oriented agencies with a mix of names containing the words *bureau* and *office* remain to a large extent its basic pattern and mode of operation to this very day.

Some of the old functions are still important at Interior (see figure 2.5), such as the Bureau of Indian Affairs or the Bureau of Land Management (formerly Land Office), but many new functions have been added, including the

FIGURE 2.5

Department of the Interior

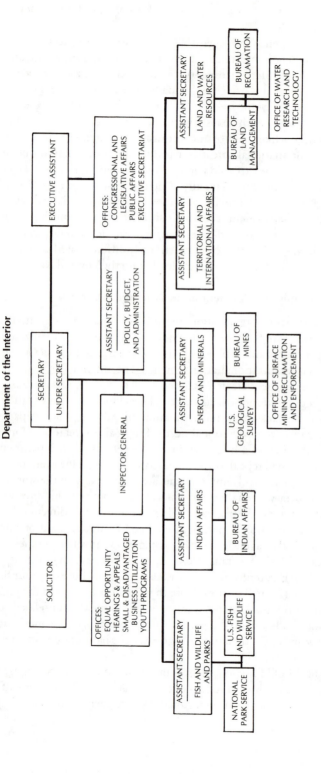

Source: The United States Government Manual 1984-85.

38

Bureau of Mines, for the inspection of mines and enforcement of safety rules; the National Park Service, for running the national parks; and the U.S. Fish and Wildlife Service, devoted to the protection and improvement of fish and game. Many more functions that were not even envisioned in 1849 are now included in Interior, such as the Ocean Mining Administration.

While the domestically oriented and service-directed tasks have greatly expanded at Interior, its original coupling of disconnected, hodgepodge tasks remains intact. What this organizational pattern created, unlike the original core service departments, was a greater degree of subunit autonomy within its structure (the name *bureau* may therefore designate a greater degree of subunit independence). Generally, oversight from the Cabinet secretary or president of, say, the Land Office within Interior (now the Bureau of Land Management) was less evident even from the start because of the "pulls" of congressional subcommittees and interest groups. Again, this historic pattern holds true today. Even now a president or a secretary of Interior often finds it difficult, if not impossible, to impose long-term policy direction and coherence on diverse Interior service functions such as parks, recreation, wildlife management, resource management, and Indian affairs. Particularly as these domestic functions develop strong domestic constituencies, bureau fragmentation and independence increase.

New service functions were also added to old-line departments in the nineteenth century, along with other varieties of organizational designs. The Civil War and its aftermath forged a diversity of new public activities. The War Department added the Freedmen's Bureau (1866) to aid newly freed slaves; the Treasury added the Internal Revenue Service (1866), the Controller of the Currency (1863), and the Secret Service (1865)—all formed to supervise the collection of revenue and the regulation of currency. The attorney general became an officer with Cabinet rank in 1870 and was put in charge of the Justice Department to handle growing numbers of post-Civil War civil suits, legal controversies over natural resources and taxes. The Justice Department's subunits were called *divisions;* e.g., the Civil Division and the Tax Division. Why this occurred and why their chiefs were called assistant attorneys general is unclear, though here as elsewhere the pressures of dealing with problems resulting from national growth and development fostered new service functions and an enlarged bureaucracy. Bureaucratic institutions grew quickly in the late nineteenth and early twentieth centuries. But note how the new names utilized to distinguish the subunits in bureaucracy varied widely; e.g., *bureau, service, controller,* and *division.* Each term denoted important subunits within major departments performing specified public tasks, yet the names varied principally because of different departmental traditions. *Divisions* were utilized, for instance, to designate Justice's subdivisions, but not elsewhere. Historic accident and unique departmental traditions caused the multiplication of subunit names and variations of U.S. organizational patterns.

An important deviation from the standard organizational pattern occurred with the creation of the Smithsonian Institution in 1846. In 1829 the will of James Smithson of England bequeathed to the United States his entire estate, "to found at Washington, under the name of the Smithsonian Institution, an establishment for the increase and diffusion of knowledge among men."[4] Congress wanted to accept the gift, but the purpose of the grant did not fit neatly into any of the existing departmental activities. Consequently, Congress created the first independent government agency in the form of a "foundation," vesting control of this agency outside the traditional executive branch chain of command by giving it to the Smithsonian Board of Regents. The board is composed of the chief justice, the vice president, three U.S. senators, three House members, and nine private citizens. The Smithsonian Institution began an important trend of bureaucratic autonomy, for today there are more than sixty independent agencies operating outside the thirteen traditional federal departments (see figure 2.6). Some are quite large, like the Veterans Administration (VA), with a $26-billion annual budget and 20,000 employees. The VA operates autonomously from regular executive departments because Congress and various veterans' groups have insisted that it maintain its independence (largely to facilitate congressional and interest group control of the VA's affairs). Other independent agencies, like ACTION, which consist of a loose collection of voluntary agencies such as the Peace Corps, Job Corps, Foster Grandparent Program, Volunteers in Service to America (VISTA), and the Drug Use Prevention Program, are quite small by comparison, with only a few thousand employees and a $200-million annual budget. ACTION's independence set a historic precedent. President Kennedy emphasized at its inception that the Peace Corps' mission should be distinct and separate from such traditional diplomatic agencies as the State Department. Traditional international agencies like State have never wanted to merge with ACTION.

The Clientele Service Functions

The latter half of the nineteenth century saw the formation of distinctly new forms of U.S. bureaucracy. These responded in large part to new pressures and requirements of society. As Richard Schott has observed, "Whereas earlier federal departments had been formed around specialized governmental functions (foreign affairs, war, finance and the like), the new departments of this period—Agriculture, Labor and Commerce—were devoted to interests and aspirations of particular economic groups. Their emergence testified to the growing specialization and occupational differentiation occurring in American Society."[5] In Schott's view, the growing and powerful economic blocks of interest groups in the late nineteenth and early twentieth centuries spawned new and powerful bureaucracies catering to specific clientele service needs.

FIGURE 2.6

The Government of the United States

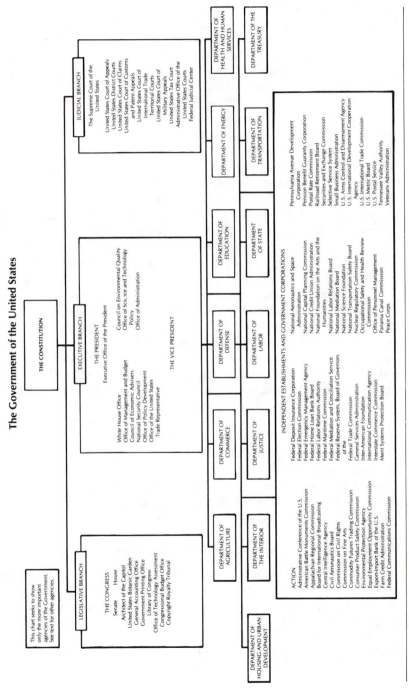

Source: *The United States Government Manual 1984-85.*

41

The largest and most powerfully organized clientele group of this era was made up of farmers. Three-fourths of Americans at the time were living off the land. The U.S. Department of Agriculture (USDA) was created in 1862. It was at first headed by a commissioner, who then assumed full Cabinet status in 1889 as a departmental secretary. The USDA was established in the same year Congress passed the Morrill Act, which granted land for agricultural colleges to western states, and the Homestead Act, which opened public land to homesteaders. As Leonard White points out, these acts and the USDA "were the three major statutory foundations of federal agricultural policy for nearly a century."[6] At first the functions of the USDA were principally research and education. Development of new farming techniques and dissemination of these methods throughout the country were its early departmental priorities. As the charter of the USDA outlined, its initial goals were "to acquire and diffuse among people useful information on subjects connected with agriculture," "to conduct practical and scientific experiments," and "to appoint persons skilled in the natural sciences pertaining to agriculture."[7] The USDA was a federal bureaucracy that, quite unlike core departments such as State, which saw to the needs of the nation as a whole, catered directly to the needs and interests of a single group, farmers.

Today, although less than 5 percent of Americans live on farms, the USDA has grown into one of the largest federal departments because it conducts a variety of agricultural service functions considerably broader and more pervasive than those outlined by the original charter. As figure 2.7 indicates, over the years the activities of the USDA have expanded into economic forecasting, nutritional programs, food stamps, consumer services, rural development, international affairs, natural resources, and environmental protection. Note how the original scientific and educational programs of the department are now headed only by a director, not an assistant secretary, signaling their relative decline in importance within the overall scheme of current departmental activities. Also, while the USDA's clientele is still predominantly the farm population, the department serves many other groups, such as consumers, international markets, and environmentalists. The number of the USDA's "clienteles" has multiplied during the last century, as have its functional tasks.

The Rise of Regulatory Agencies and Government Corporations

The late nineteenth and early twentieth centuries saw the development of two other forms of governmental bureaucracies outside the traditional departmental structures: regulatory agencies and government corporations. Regulatory agencies have been viewed by some as "the fourth" or "hidden" branch of government because they play such powerful, yet unpublicized, roles in shaping policies and agendas. Much of the growth of regulatory bureaucracies

FIGURE 2.7

Department of Agriculture

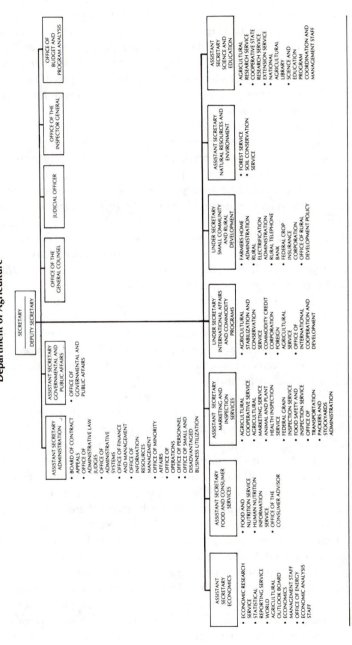

Source: *The United States Government Manual 1984-85.*

43

was, like that of earlier types of federal bureaucracies, the result of new societal needs for public services.

The basic social fabric of the United States was rapidly changing in this era. By the end of the nineteenth century, huge corporate structures, "the trusts," began to control, even monopolize, large segments of markets as diverse as oil, steel, railroads, and other manufacturing enterprises. Trusts had become able to control markets and rig market prices by the late 1800s. Both their enormous economic size and political influence precipitated vigorous demands from the public, particularly western farmers and small businesses, that checks be placed on trusts' unrestrained powers.

Government responded with two measures to control these giant corporations. First, trusts were smashed by legislation. The aim of the Sherman Anti-trust Act of 1890 was to break up these large trusts by assigning new enforcement powers to the Justice Department. Second, regulatory commissions created permanent legal machinery to oversee and regulate corporate trust activities. Independent regulating began at the federal level in 1887 with the Interstate Commerce Commission (ICC), which was set up to regulate railroad rates, then a major economic issue for western farmers. The monopolistic practices of many railroads servicing the West and Midwest had "squeezed" many farmers, who, in turn, demanded government action. Help came in the form of this new type of bureaucracy, the ICC.

The ICC was modeled on early state regulatory commissions. Three-, five-, or seven-person boards were given legal autonomy and political independence (at least in theory) by being placed outside the formal executive departments. These boards were given quasilegal and executive powers to regulate prices in specific economic markets to curb monopolistic and unfair practices by industrial giants.

Today, almost a century after the creation of the ICC, there are several regulatory commissions. While these commissions regulate a diverse number of economic fields, they have the same independence as the ICC. They now constitute a major and influential part of federal bureaucracy. Some of them are: Federal Aviation Commission, Federal Communications Commission, Federal Home Loan Bank Board, Federal Maritime Commission, Federal Power Commission, Federal Reserve Board, Federal Trade Commission, Interstate Commerce Commission, National Labor Relations Board, Securities and Exchange Commission, Consumer Product Safety Commission.

Figure 2.8 shows an organization chart of the Federal Trade Commission, which was established to regulate broad areas of trade practices. Note that its format is essentially the same as the ICC's (though its staff and budget are much smaller). In the words of Professor Marver Bernstein, such commissions involve "location outside an executive department; some measure of independence from supervision by the President or a Cabinet Secretary; immunity from the President's discretionary power to remove members of independent commissions from office."[8] It should be added that while Con-

FIGURE 2.8

Federal Trade Commission

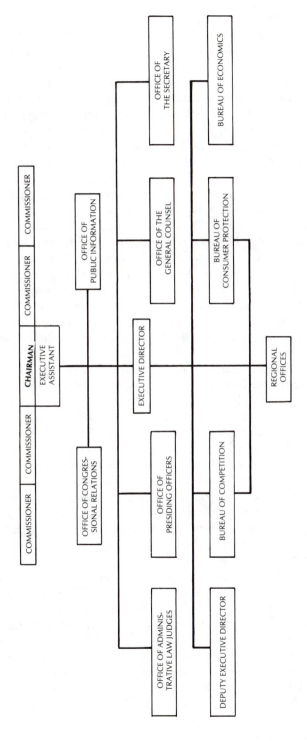

Source: *The United States Government Manual 1984-85.*

45

gress has given many regulatory powers to independent commissions, over the years it has also assigned many regulatory functions to regular departments. For example, under the Packers and Stockyards Act of 1921 regulatory functions were assigned to the secretary of agriculture rather than to the Federal Trade Commission. Regulatory activities today are carried out by many executive departments, and not only within independent commissions. Again, historic accident rather than deliberate design frequently determines the location and degree of authority assigned to bureaucracy by Congress.

The Progressive Era also saw the creation of another important form of public bureaucracy: the government corporation. As Harold Seidman, a well-known scholar in this field, has written, the government corporation was "essentially an empirical response to problems posed by increasing reliance on government-created business enterprise and business-type operations to accomplish public purposes,"[9] The government corporation was modeled on the private corporation. It had a board of directors, which was given a degree of independence from civil service rules and annual budgetary processes in order to enable it to carry out its corporate activities with greater flexibility in personnel and finances. The corporate format was especially appealing because it *did not* look like, nor was it called by any name resembling, "a public bureaucracy." It was, rather, "a corporation." Given the strong appeal of business values—i.e., values associated with efficiency, economy, and effectiveness—throughout U.S. history, such labeling was highly attractive to the electorate and its representatives. Business values were especially popular during the Progressive Era (the "city manager plan," which modeled local government along business lines, was also created at that time).

The corporate model was an effective device for implementing new programs with speed and efficiency. Government was being asked to perform many new public services. The public wanted these tasks done quickly and efficiently. New roads, schools, and utilities were needed. The government corporation therefore found favor precisely because it could execute these new tasks expeditiously and effectively. When the U.S. government purchased the Panama Railroad Company from the French Canal Company in 1904, a government corporation (the first one) was created to operate the canal railway. It was notably successful in aiding the building of the canal. Over one hundred government corporations since 1904 have been established to undertake a wide variety of public tasks—from COMSAT, which operates communications satellites, to the Tennessee Valley Authority (TVA), which provides power, irrigation, recreational facilities, and economic development to the Tennessee Valley. Like regulatory commissions, government corporations, at least in theory, are isolated from politics through the appointment of bipartisan directors with overlapping terms. Such neutrality and independence is an important factor in government corporations' flexibility in decision-making and long-term planning capability, especially in fiscal matters, personnel appointments, and capital planning. This rationale was used by President Nixon in 1970 when he proposed to transform the U.S. Postal Service from an executive department into a government corporation. This change was necessary, according to Nixon, ''to free it from partisan political pressure'' and to ''improve its economy and efficiency.''[10] The ''corporate'' form of the post office, and of many other public service organizations as well, is considered a preferable means of delivering services to the public.

Figure 2.9 shows the U.S. Postal Service's corporate format; many other organizations are modeled along much the same lines. Some of them are: St. Lawrence Seaway Development Corporation, Government National Mortgage Association, Commodity Credit Corporation, Federal Crop Insurance Corporation, Federal Home Loan Corporation, Federal Deposit Insurance Corporation, Export-Import Bank, Overseas Private Investment Corporation, and Rural Telephone Bank. As their names signify, they perform many kinds of specific tasks for the public, generally along the lines of those performed by private business. Their work constitutes a major share of federal activities but is largely a ''hidden'' dimension of government bureaucracy.

Surges in Social Services in the New Deal and the Great Society

As James Q. Wilson has written, much of our modern bureaucracy is a result of ''majoritarian surges of popular demand for more government activity''[11] in the Progressive, New Deal, and Great Society eras. By popular demand, the Progressive Era brought into existence new varieties of regulatory and governmental corporations, yet the greatest source of civilian growth in U.S. bureaucracy occurred during the New Deal in the 1930s and the Great Society in the 1960s. Both eras ushered in new, diverse types of social service bureaucracies.

The New Deal stimulated unprecedented numbers of bureaucratic services. This was largely in response to an economic crisis—the Great Depression—that gripped the United States in the early 1930s. In 1933, 14 million Americans were out of work—one in four workers. In that same year, 5,000 banks closed their doors and industrial income fell from 85 to 37 billion dollars. Industry was at a standstill; breadlines formed; bankruptcies were common. The average of fifty industrial stocks on the New York Stock Exchange dropped from 252 to 61 between 1929 and 1933. Franklin Roosevelt was inaugurated as president on March 4, 1933. With vast support from the electorate and Congress, he moved quickly to set up a broad array of programs to cope with the economic disaster. The Federal Emergency Relief Administration (1933) was established to direct grants to localities for the support of poor and unemployed persons; the Civilian Conservation Corps (1933) put thousands of young men to work planting forest lands; the Farm Credit Administration (1933) extended farm loans and agricultural credit to bankrupt farmers; the Federal Deposit Insurance Corporation (1933) established protection for bank depositors; and the Works Progress Administration (1933)

FIGURE 2.9

United States Postal Service

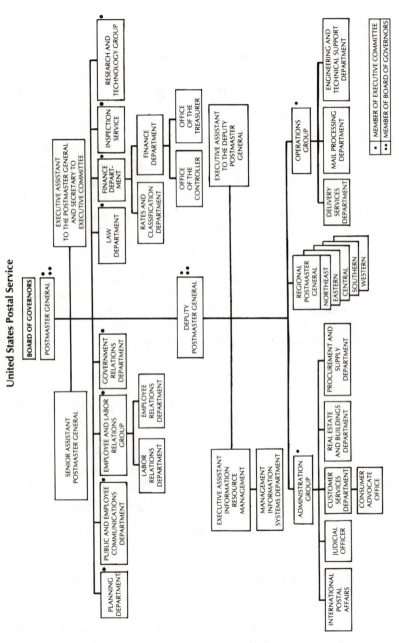

Source: The United States Government Manual 1984-85.

48

hired many men and women to build roads, schools, airports, and hospitals. Many other new public agencies were formed to deal quickly with the problems and impacts of this harsh economic emergency.

Most of the measures enacted in Roosevelt's first term were considered temporary. In his second term, however, many permanent public bureaucracies to alleviate or eliminate future economic crises like the Great Depression were created. The social security system created a mandatory retirement benefit program for workers as well as unemployment compensation and welfare programs for the blind, the handicapped, and dependent children, administered through the Federal Security Agency (1939). The Fair Labor Standards Act (1938) established a minimum wage and maximum work hours, and the National Labor Relations Act (1935) created a national system for labor-management collective bargaining that exists to this day. Another New Deal public agency, the Federal Crop Insurance Corporation (1938), established a system of minimum base prices for farmers—parity payments—that guaranteed farmers minimum base prices for their produce in depressed market years. Through the Rural Electrification Administration (1935), electric power was brought to many isolated households; and the Farm Security Administration (1937) sought to improve the health, safety, and working conditions of farm laborers. These and many other new social services added enormously to the size and scope of the federal bureaucracy. As figure 2.10 shows, the United States developed a large, permanent bureaucracy to carry out these New Deal tasks.

If the New Deal concentrated on finding ways to put people back to work and to provide both ''welfare basics'' to millions and economic stability to various sectors of the economy, the Great Society in the 1960s sought to ex-

FIGURE 2.10
Growth of Federal Bureaucracy, 1932–1950

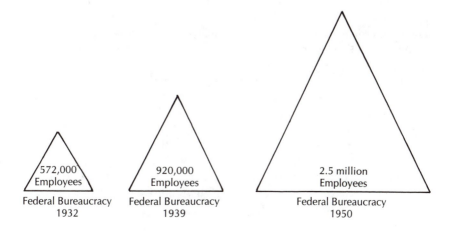

572,000 Employees
Federal Bureaucracy
1932

920,000 Employees
Federal Bureaucracy
1939

2.5 million Employees
Federal Bureaucracy
1950

tend and expand the scope of these social programs to many areas that had been neglected by the New Deal. After the death of President John F. Kennedy on November 22, 1963, President Lyndon Johnson launched the Great Society, a vigorous new expansion of social service programs. The Medicare Program, for example, established in 1966, guaranteed medical insurance for the aged; the Office of Economic Opportunity (1964) administered ''the war on poverty'' through various new programs that required ''the maximum feasible participation'' of the poor; the Department of Housing and Urban Development in 1965 brought together several existing urban-oriented federal agencies and several new ones such as the Model Cities Program, within a new Cabinet-level department, to attack problems of housing and urban development. The Department of Transportation was established in 1966 to coordinate and target mass transit and general transportation policies for the entire nation; several regional commissions, such as the Appalachian Regional Commission, were created to deal with specialized regional economic and social needs. Further, the Great Society saw the rapid expansion of numerous grants-in-aid and categorical programs for the support of specific public programs for hospital, school, and highway construction, largely administered with matching funds through state and local public bureaucracies. Many of these programs are still on the books today.

Hot War/Cold War Defense Organizations

The unique geographic isolation of the United States combined with its historical liberal opposition to standing professional military forces made large defense bureaucracies both unnecessary and unwanted for the first 150 years of its history. Even the large, bloody battles of the Civil War and World War I were waged mostly with temporary volunteer ''citizen soldiers,'' not with professionals.

All this changed in World War II. The geographic isolation of the United States suddenly disappeared as military threats came to its doorstep. Japan attacked Pearl Harbor on December 7, 1941. Declarations of war from Hitler's Germany and Mussolini's Italy followed. These powerful totalitarian regimes, combined with new arms technology and the weakening of western democracies such as England and France, thrust onto the United States new responsibilities for defending its own interests as well as those of the free world. Overnight new defense agencies became necessary to plan, coordinate, mobilize, and administer the U.S. war effort. Twelve million men and women served in the armed services during World War II, and between 1941 and 1945, 147 new bureaucratic units were established by powerful new institutions, such as the Office of Price Administration, which planned and directed the overall war economy, and local draft boards. As figure 2.10 points out, this war-related activity caused the greatest jump in the overall size of the federal bureaucracy in U.S. history.

After the war many of these new bureaucratic entities, such as the Office of Price Administration, were abolished, but many others remained because of continued threats from the Soviet Union and other communist regimes. The Cold War, which sometimes turned hot in out-of-the-way places such as Korea, meant that during the 1940s and 1950s defense readiness and preparedness were considered a high priority. Large, permanent public bureaucracies were created because of these new long-term defense requirements. The Department of Defense (DoD) was established in 1947 through the merging of the War and Navy departments and the creation of a new subunit, the air force. The National Security Act, which created DoD in 1947, also established the Central Intelligence Agency to collect, coordinate, and disseminate foreign intelligence information vital to U.S. security needs (see figure 2.11). Foreign aid to friendly and neutral nations became an indispensable and undisputed part of U.S. strategic defenses. Military aid, offered to allies in substantial amounts during the 1940s and 1950s, was channeled through DoD's Military Area Assistance Group. Nonmilitary aid was dispensed through the Economic Cooperation Administration (ECA), which in 1961 became the Agency for International Development (AID). ECA and later AID sought to strengthen friendly and neutral countries economically, socially, and politically through a variety of grants, loans, and technical assistance programs.

Cold War defense programs spilled over into domestic issues and public programs. The need to harness science and scientific talent to serve the nation's Cold War needs became a vital preoccupation during this period. The Manhattan Project created the atomic bomb, which had brought a swift and dramatic end to hostilities in World War II, but after the war Congress was faced with the awesome task of controlling the future use and development of atomic energy. To this end, the Atomic Energy Commission was created in 1946. Basic and applied research was fostered and stimulated through a new grant system that Congress set up in 1950 through the National Science Foundation (NSF). NSF, an independent agency with its own staff of scientific panels whose function was to approve grants for scientific research, became an important new avenue for stimulating research capabilities in universities and private research laboratories. NSF maintained the independence of scientists within their "home" institutions while fostering research into "potential defense spinoffs" through extensive grants and other assistance. Direct links with scientific knowledge and defense department priorities during the 1940s and 1950s were further enhanced by the growing practice of "contracting out" for services to universities, not-for-profit "think tanks" such as the Rand Corporation, and large numbers of private businesses.

Similarly, Cold War pressures to keep pace with the Russians launched the National Aeronautics and Space Administration (NASA) in 1958. The U.S.S.R.'s launching of Sputnik in October 1957 brought the United States overnight into an accelerated and extended space race with the Soviets. NASA

FIGURE 2.11

Central Intelligence Agency

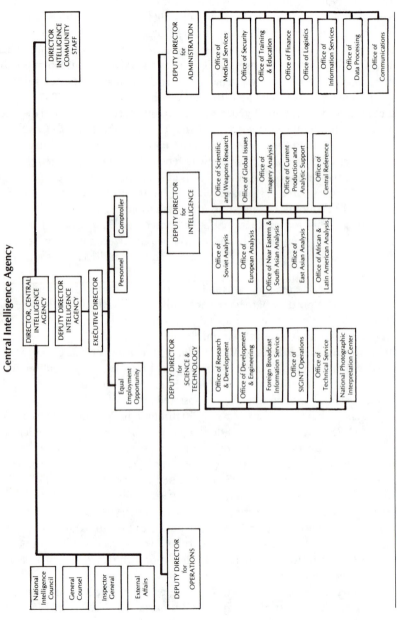

Source: Central Intelligence Agency

throughout the 1960s, and even today, is designated as the "lead" agency in this effort to explore regions beyond the earth. NASA's role and prominence grew largely as a response to Cold War threats from the Soviets; just as AID's, the CIA's, the Atomic Energy Commission's, and NSF's did. Indeed, the spillovers and spinoffs into domestic programs from Cold War concerns were so numerous that it is difficult to describe them all succinctly. For example, the National Defense Highway Act (1955) created a vast, 100-billion-dollar-plus highway program, perhaps the largest public works program in history, stimulated and promoted in part by "defense" concerns (as the legal title of its enabling legislation indicates). The National Defense Education Act of 1958 fostered an influx of loans and grants for mathematics and science education in high schools and colleges. This act was prompted by fears that the United States was falling behind the Soviets in these fields. External threats or fears of external threats to the United States have been a major enduring source of the formation, growth, and maintenance of many postwar public bureaucracies and government programs.

Staff and Local Service Functions

The rise of bureaucratic institutions in the twentieth-century United States spurred the concomitant growth of new layers of bureaucracies to oversee, coordinate, plan, and manage government. One of the earliest staff mechanisms created for these purposes was the General Staff. It was set up by Congress in 1903, upon the advice of Elihu Root, then secretary of war, to better plan and coordinate military activities and to prevent the repetition of the logistical calamities of the Spanish American War. Further, the Budget and Accounting Act of 1921 created an executive budget and added the Bureau of the Budget (first operating under the secretary of the treasury and later within the Executive Office of the President—EOP) as a key instrument for fiscal and budgetary planning. This act (perhaps *the* most critical contribution to federal bureaucracy's development) established the General Accounting Office to provide independent auditing oversight and controls.

The Brownlow Commission Report in 1937, which was the first major study of the organization of the presidency since 1789, recommended to President Franklin Roosevelt a substantial increase in staff assistance for the president. EOP has since grown into a formidable bureaucracy in its own right. Today EOP is the "staff arm" of the president. It consists of several thousand employees, many of them long-term careerists, and comprises a number of powerful policy advisory organizations (see figure 2.12). Some of them are: the Office of Policy Development, which advises the president on domestic policy issues; the National Security Council, which advises on international and defense issues; the Council of Economic Advisers, which set macroeconomic policies; the Office of Management and Budget, which develops the

FIGURE 2.12

Executive Office of the President

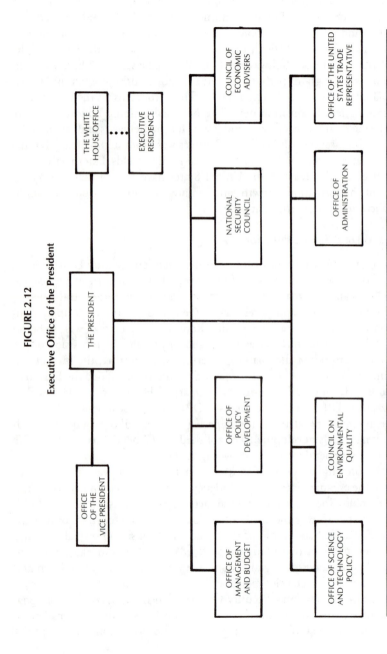

Source: The United States Government Manual 1984-85

annual executive budget; and the Council on Environmental Quality, which assists in developing national environmental policies.

Staff bureaucracies have further proliferated in each of the thirteen federal executive departments, so that reporting to each Cabinet secretary are many large, specialized offices providing legal advice, policy analysis, personnel and budget recommendations, and much more (refer to the foregoing figures). Congress also has added enormous ''overhead staffs'' to its legislative advisory and planning capacities. For example, the Congressional Reference Service provides documentary and data reference for congressional activities; the Congressional Budget Office provides budget and economic advice to Congress; the Office of Technology Assessment helps legislators to plan, evaluate, and anticipate future impacts of technology upon U.S. society; the General Accounting Office, already mentioned, is an important source of fiscal and programmatic oversight. Whereas two decades ago Congress had 5,000 employees, it now has more than 40,000 staffers (more than some federal departments, such as the State Department, which has 30,000 employees). Even the judicial bureaucracy has grown rapidly over the last fifteen years. Ironically, members of Congress, who have been the most vocal critics of federal bureaucracy, are part of the fastest-growing bureaucracy since 1970.

Furthermore, more than 1,500 advisory boards and 120 commissions at the federal level report to either the executive or legislative branches, or both, and provide government with a wide array of technical, expert, or lay advice. Most are small and staffed with temporary personnel, but some have important duties and exert strong influence on government. For example, the Advisory Commission on Intergovernmental Relations, through its staff expertise and coordinative role, is immensely important in charting the future course of federalism and urban policies.

Concomitant with the growth of staff services at the federal level has been the rise of local and state bureaucracies during this century. Throughout much of the nineteenth century, local bureaucracies were limited or nonexistent. Most Americans lived on farms or in small towns where private businesses or voluntary cooperation were the chief routes for getting things done—hence volunteer fire brigades, locally ''raised'' schools, church-supported charities for the poor, aged, and infirm, and privately built and run transit systems, utilities, and housing.

Urbanization, new technologies, industrialization, and demands for new and improved public services brought a rapid growth in state and local bureaucracies throughout the twentieth century. State and local bureaucracies developed around the necessity for core functions, such as police and safety services. Continued economic development, regulatory functions, and corporate forms such as housing and transit authorities added new tasks. Educational needs in particular spurred the development of local public bureaucracies throughout this century. The urbanization and industrialization of the United States in the early 1900s created the need for an educated workforce and for improved training opportunities. State compulsory education laws enacted largely in the twentieth century required, in turn, the development of massive, complex local education systems to educate the young from kindergarten through high school. State-supported universities and colleges became commonplace by the 1960s. The popularity of the automobile stimulated state highway construction and the establishing of licensing and vehicle facilities and programs. After the Great Depression, state and local welfare bureaucracies, funded increasingly through federal grants, replaced voluntary sources for aiding the poor. Fire and police services expanded in size, scope, and sophistication in response to new technological requirements and to demands for better public protection. Federal categorical grants to localities, combined with block grants and revenue sharing enacted in the 1970s, funneled more fiscal aid to states and localities, spawning the rapid growth of these bureaucratic institutions in a wide variety of areas. Mass transit systems, for example, are found in many medium-sized and large municipalities, thanks to various amounts of discretionary and categorical grants from the federal government (mainly from UMTA, Urban Mass Transit Administration). Food stamps also are locally administered but, for the most part, are federally funded (from the USDA programs). As table 2.1 indicates, since 1950 the most sizable increases in public employment have occurred at state and local levels. Further, much like the federal government, state and local bureaucracies have developed large staffs—"budgeters," "personnelists," and lawyers, as well as expert and lay advisory boards and commissions—to oversee and manage their activities.

As figure 2.13 shows, the formal executive departments as well as the many staffs, commissions, and boards of federal bureaucracies are mirrored in local bureaucracies. Local bureaucracy also has core agencies (fire and police functions), economic development activities, social service agencies, even regulatory and corporate enterprises (zoning and planning boards and housing and transit authorities). These tasks, like those at the federal level, have grown over time and have been sustained both by environmental needs and bureaucratic inertia. More will be said in the next chapter about the specific inputs that foster growth and changes within individual bureaucracies. Later chap-

TABLE 2.1
Total U.S. Bureaucracy Workforce, 1950–82

	Employment (millions)		
	1950	*1982*	*Total Increase*
Federal Civilians	2.1 (45.6%)	2.9 (27.6%)	+.8
Military	1.5	2.1	+.6
State	1.1 (13.9%)	3.7 (20.5%)	+2.6
Local	3.2 (40.5%)	9.4 (50.9%)	+6.2
Total	7.9 (100.0%)	18.1 (100.0%)	+10.2

Source: Statistical Abstracts of the United States, p.294.

FIGURE 2.13

Organization Chart of a City Government

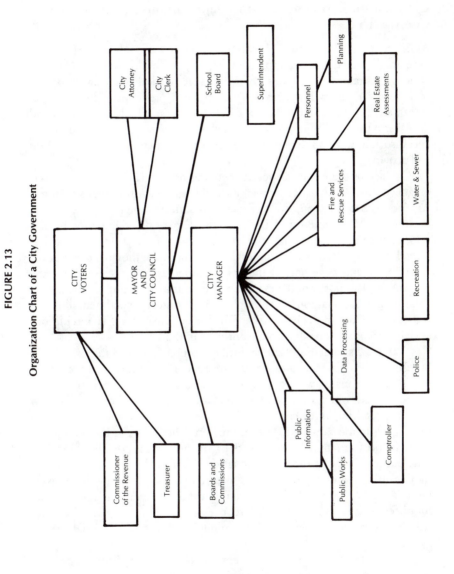

ters will also dwell upon the recent trends in the 1980s affecting bureaucratic organizations.

General Characteristics of the Rise of U.S. Bureaucracy: Gradualism, Experimentalism, Majoritarianism, and Complexity

As this chapter has underscored, U.S. bureaucracy was not built overnight. It developed gradually, without plan, over nearly two hundred years of history, although, as table 2.2 indicates, there were seven critical periods where spurts of bureaucratic growth occurred: Washington's presidency, the midnineteenth century, the Gilded Age, the Progressive Era, the New Deal, World War II and the Cold War, and the Great Society, where new national experiences, such as war and depression, fostered new demands for public actions and activities.

In each of these eras, however, there was no standard format for public organizations. Rather, there was considerable diversity in formal structures. Americans have been remarkably experimental in creating new types of organizations to fulfill various functional needs. Perhaps no other nation has developed such a wide range of bureaucratic forms—from steeply hierarchical formal executive departments under the strict control of the chief elected official (a president, governor, or mayor) to autonomous agencies outside the structure and authority of the executive branch and exhibiting comparatively "flat" organizational forms. Throughout U.S. history, experimentalism has certainly been one of the hallmarks of the rise of bureaucracy. That tradition, as chapter 6 of this text describes, continues in the 1980s.

Table 2.2 also demonstrates a third important feature of the rise of U.S. bureaucracy: its majoritarian sources. The bulk of U.S. bureaucracy, contrary to the belief of many, was not caused by pressure groups. Rather, there were specific periods when strong surges of majoritarian influence overrode special interests, resulting in the creation of public organizations that promoted national goals in the name of the public interest. The Federalist Era saw the demand for the formation of "the core departments" of the executive branch to carry out the work of "the first new nation." Similar "majoritarian surges" significantly expanded governmental programs during the Progressive, New Deal, World War II and Cold War, and Great Society eras, though certainly for different reasons and with different results. Only throughout the nineteenth century were bureaucratic innovations largely caused by special interest rather than majoritarian surges.

Finally, throughout nearly two centuries in the life of bureaucratic institutions, an increasing complexification of the entire system can be observed. Each succeeding wave of "majoritarian surges" formed a new layer of complexity, which in turn increased the size and diversity of the entire administrative system. Much of the general public's frustration with modern-day bu-

TABLE 2.2
Rise of U.S. Public Bureaucracy Since 1789: 7 Critical Eras

Key Period in Bureaucracy's Development	Public Demands & National Requirements	Major Source of Political Support	Sample Types of Public Agency Est.
Federalist Era 1789–1802	Est "Core Functions" of U.S. Government	Early Nationalism & Federalist Party	State Dept, War, Treasury, etc.
Mid-nineteenth century	Nation-state economic development	Jacksonian-Democratic-Whig parties	Interior Dept. & various public works projects
"Gilded Age"—late nineteenth century	Assistance for farmer, labor business	Special interest pressures of agriculture, labor & business	Clientele depts. of agriculture, labor and commerce
Populist & progressive eras of late nineteenth & early 20th century	Regulation of business & new form of public action	Progressive reform led by presidents Theodore Roosevelt & Woodrow Wilson	Regulatory agencies (FTC, ICC, etc.) and Government corporation (Panama Canal Authority, etc.)
New Deal in 1930s	New social regulations and services for coping with Great Depression	Democratic party led by President Franklin Roosevelt & New Deal coalition.	Regulatory units like Farm Credit Administration or Federal Deposit Insurance Corp. and new social services like Social Security adm.
WW II and Cold War Era in 1940s	Global defense requirements	Wartime and postwar national consensus for strong defence	DOD, CIA, NASA, AID, etc.
"Great Society" 1960s	"War on Poverty" & vast new social programs	President Lyndon Johnson and Liberal-Democratic Coalition forged in 1964 election.	HHS, HUD, DOT & various new poverty and social programs like Head Start, VISTA, Medicare, etc.

reaucracy may well be caused by a lack of comprehension of such diverse, complex institutions—their functions, structures, or purposes. Understanding these institutions is, of course, the subject of this text.

Forms, Functions, Policies, and Processes of Contemporary U.S. Bureaucracy

How do the formal elements of U.S. bureaucracy appear today? Table 2.3 summarizes most of the basic forms of present-day federal, state, and local-level bureaucracy. Altogether, these forms represent a composite of two hundred years of U.S. bureaucratic development. The range today, as Harold Seidman notes, is "staggering" and "defies classification."[12] It is a product of gradualism, experimentalism, majoritarianism, and complexification. Who knows for sure whether some of these units can even properly be termed public bureaucracies? For instance, the Rand Corporation, which is a publicly funded, legally chartered private organization, occupies a twilight zone between public and private bureaucracy. Some public bodies are essentially publicly funded but are run like private corporations, as are many local "special district governments." Are these "public" or "private" bureaucracies?

TABLE 2.3
Major Forms and Functions of U.S. Bureacracy

Bureaucratic Form	Examples of Form	Major Functions
Executive Department (all levels)	State Department Education Department Defense Department	Principally implement tasks assigned, with some advisory and regulatory duties
Executive Offices of President, Governor, or Mayor (all levels)	Office of Management and Budget, National Security Council, Council of Economic Advisers	Principally advisory roles for chief executive
Foundations (mainly federal level)	National Science Foundation	Promotion of research through grants; some advisory roles
Institutions and Institutes (mainly federal)	Smithsonian Institution, National Cancer Institute (HHS), Foreign Service Institute (State), Institutes for Environmental Research (Commerce)	Promotion of research-in-house & through grants; education & teaching function
Independent Agencies (all levels)	ACTION (headed by one person) CIA (headed by one person) Veterans Administration (headed by one person), Merit Systems Protection Board (committee governed), Transportation Safety Board (committee governed)	Perform a wide variety of executive quasi-judicial; quasi-legislative and advisory functions *outside* formal executive departments—either single headed or committee governed
Commissions on Claims (mainly federal)	Indian Claims Commission Forerign Claims Settlement Commission	Largely judicial functions
Regulatory Agencies (all levels)	Interstate Commerce Commission Federal Trade Commission Nuclear Regulatory Commission	Largely regulatory functions

TABLE 2.3—Continued

Bureaucratic Form	Examples of Form	Major Functions
Government Corporations (all levels)	Tennessee Valley Authority U.S. Railway Association Federal Prisons Industries, Inc. Federal Crop Insurance Corporation St. Lawrence Seaway Development Corporation	Carry out a wide variety of functions either within an executive dept. or independent of the executive branch; may be mix public-private ownership
Boards, Councils, and Committees (all levels)	Federal Regional Councils Federal Records Council Water Resources Councils	Largely coordinative and advisory duties
Advisory Bodies (all levels)	National Historical Publications Commission Advisory Board of St. Lawrence Seaway Development Advisory Council on Vocational Education	Advisory group of primarily private citizens but legally constituted permanent bodies
Intergovernment Units (all levels)	Advisory Commission on Intergovernment Relations Great Lakes River Basin Commission Ozarks Regional Commission Local Council of Government	National and regional planning, coordinating, and advisory bodies
Joint Executive-Congressional Units (all levels)	Migratory Bird Conservation Commission Advisory Commission on Low Income Housing	Primarily advise both legislature and executive
Legislative Organizations (all levels)	General Accounting Office State Auditor County Auditor	Primarily advisor, research & oversight role for legislature
Special Districts (local only)	School District Water & Sewer District Fire District	Performs a wide range of county and municipal services independent of general government
Private Organizations, funded and set up by government (all levels)	Rand Corporation Institute for Defense Analysis MITRE Los Alamos Labs County Hospitals	Independent units funded almost entirely by government and chartered by governor to perform specific types of contractual service
Public Organizations, privately funded with mixed public-private directorship & highly autonomous (all levels)	Federal Reserve Board Corporation for Public Broadcasting Legal Services Corporation	Autonomous public units, largely privately supported, with a wide variety of tasks

Equally problematic are their functional assignments. As table 2.3 also illustrates, many serve traditional executive roles, carrying out tasks assigned by the chief executive and approved by the legislature and judicial branches, although some fulfill entirely quasi-judicial or quasi-legislative functions. The Indian Claims Commission, for example, acts much like a court. Independent regulatory commissions, such as the Interstate Commerce Commission, have quasi-legislative roles in that Congress has granted to them significant authority to make rules, an essentially legislative function of government. The traditional view that public bureaucracies perform only "executive functions" is wrong. Most agencies are involved in the work of all three branches of government—executive, legislative, and judicial.

The policies that are promulgated as a result of these activities have been well summarized and classified by Theodore Lowi in a four-cell matrix.[13] Lowi sees public sector outputs of administrative units as the making of public policies that *actually* force things to happen to people or groups of people throughout society. Public organizations are not only purposeful but also perform actions that legitimately require actions or inactions on the part of either individuals or the whole environment. The policy outputs of government are unique by comparison with other private or nonprofit organized outputs, according to Lowi, because public agencies have the ability to coerce actions on the part of others. Such coercion may be *immediate* (throwing criminals in jail) or *remote* (administering a sales tax to every customer in an entire state). Lowi uses the polar dimensions of individual vs. environment *and* immediate vs. remote coercion to develop a four-cell matrix in which he summarizes the four basic varieties of public policy outputs of all governmental organizations (see table 2.4).

First, *regulative policies* involve both immediate and individual-oriented outputs of government units, such as ICC actions to stop unfair market competition by businessmen or FCC and Federal Drug Commission (FDC) actions to eliminate fraudulent advertising, or Immigration and Naturalization Service (INS) enforcement of immigration laws, or the Drug Enforcement Agency's efforts to combat illicit drug activities. By contrast, *redistributive policies*, according to Lowi's matrix, are immediate but influence society only as a whole. The Federal Reserve Board (FRB) establishes its bank reserve requirements and prime rates, causing, in turn, general inflationary or deflationary trends throughout society. The administration of the progressive income tax by the Internal Revenue Service (IRS) redistributes monies from one group of citizens in society to another, which affects the entire nation.

TABLE 2.4
Varieties of Policy Products of Public Bureaucracies

	Individual Effects	Environment Effects
Immediate Coercion	Regulatory Policies, e.g., ICC, FCC, FDA, DEA	Redistributive Policies, e.g., Federal Reserve Board, Internal Revenue Service, Social Security Administration, Federal Housing Administration
Remote Coercion	Distributive Policies, Veterans Administration, Agriculture Department, Department of Energy, National Science Foundation	Constituent Policies, e.g., Defense Department, State Department, Justice Department, Office of Management and Budget

The Social Security Administration (SSA) likewise redistributes monies from younger workers to pensioners, affecting all Americans.

Third, *distributive policies* are those public outputs that are remote *and* individual-oriented. Tariffs influence buying habits of individual consumers but are usually administered far from where these consumers live and work. Similarly, direct government subsidies to industry or to particular social groups, such as farmers or veterans, are distributive forms of public policies, according to Lowi. Finally, the fourth cell of Lowi's matrix contains *constituent policies,* which are both remote and aimed at all of society. DoD's policy outputs are, for the most part, in this category; i.e., defense of the national interests against foreign enemies. No one group of Americans gains more or less (at least in theory) from preserving national integrity, freedom, and liberty. Yet the work of DoD is remote from the daily life of the average citizen.

Obviously, real-world public agencies do not always fit neatly as pure types within the Lowi four-cell matrix. Many agencies promulgate multiple types of public policies at the same time. DoD, for example, may be primarily involved in defending the nation, but it is also very much engaged in distributional and redistributional policy making via its huge $300 billion-plus annual budgets. The EPA regulates air, water, and land quality in the United States, though it also acts to distribute grants to state, local, and private organizations and therefore is very much engaged in distributive policy making. The Department of Agriculture (DoA), which was founded as a clientele department to serve the needs of farmers, can properly be viewed as a distributive agency, but it also regulates the entire food chain to ensure the health and safety of Americans. Most agencies thus contain a mix of Lowi's categories.

However, the formal processes that are found within public agencies that produce these policies depend upon the dominant policy activity of an agency as is indicated in table 2.5. Each variety of policy-making activity tends to have associated with it distinctive internal formal processes and procedures essential for carrying out these policies. As one would expect, regulatory policy-making bodies involve highly legalized internal processes, often associated with the legislative or judicial branches of government, rule making, adjudication, law enforcement, and investigation/review processes. Constituent services require more traditional forms of managerial processes to carry out tasks for their agencies: program development, program implementation, policy revision, program review, and evaluation. Redistributive bureaucracies contain normally a mix of legalistic and managerial processes (adjudication, policy development, program implementation, and advisory). The internal processes of distributive organizations, as one would expect, focus upon those processes that relate directly to the distribution of benefits, publicly sponsored research activities, information gathering and dissemination, and advisory processes. Policy activities, therefore, significantly influence, even determine, the type of formal internal processes found in every agency.

Much of this chapter traced the development of the formal structures of

TABLE 2.5
Major Formal Processes of U.S. Bureaucracy

Major Types of Formal Processes Involved in Agency Policy-making Roles	Agency by Type of Policy Products			
	Regulatory	Distributive	Redistributive	Constituent
	Rule Making — Quasi-legislative process of est. agency rules for agency jurisdiction that covers everyone	**Distribution of Benefits** — Specific distribution of cash, goods, services to groups, individuals, state or local government with or without restrictions	**Adjudication** — Determination of whether or not individual can receive benefits that are due under law	**General Program Development** — Designing new programs to meet constituent service needs
	Adjudication — Quasi-judicial of charging violations of agency rules & effects only single case one at a time	**Public Sponsored Research** — In-house or contracted programs for research and development on distributive programs	**Policy Development** — Creation of new proposals to change or readjust distribution of goods and services to individuals	**Program Implementation** — Carrying out specific legislative statutes and executive orders mandating service activities
	Law Enforcement — Quasi-executive function of selected application of laws and rules to groups and individuals	**Information Gathering and Dissemination** — Collect, process and send out data and information to groups and individuals involving benefits	**Program Implementation** — Carrying out of specifically mandated activities according to legislative standards	**Policy Revision and Creation** — Creation or redesign of policies affecting program activities through advice to legislatures and executive
	Investigation & Review — Process of examining complaints to see if merits remedying as well as review regulatory actions in order to revise or change rulings	**Initiation of New Programs** — Assists in development of new goods or changes old ones for distribution of benefits	**Advisory Processes** — Assisting legislative and executive branches in programming new legislation, revising or proposing new laws, particularly using legislative clearance process	**Program Review and Evaluation** — Examination and investigation of programs in order to improve or change actions of agency.

modern U.S. bureaucracy. What *really* shapes bureaucracies' directions and impacts upon society for the most part comes from a variety of informal inputs from the outside. These bureaucratic inputs will be the subject of the next chapter.

Summary of Key Points

This chapter outlined, in brief, the historical development of U.S. bureaucracy. A variety of societal demands over the past two hundred years contributed significantly to the growth of diverse types of bureaucratic institutions. At its creation in 1789 the United States required the formation of the first core functions to conduct diplomacy, wage war, mint currency, and so on. Western expansion brought about new bureaus and agencies, like the Interior Department, to cope with the country's internal economic/social development. Clientele agencies, such as the Agriculture, Commerce, and Labor departments, arose in the late nineteenth century as responses to specialized needs and pressures of important occupational interest groups. At roughly the same time, regulatory agencies and government corporations were created to protect the public interests in new policy areas and were organized with new types of administrative authority. The greatest increases in the size and scope of U.S. bureaucracy occurred as a result of the Great Depression of the 1930s, the defense requirements of the 1940s and 1950s, and the Great Society in the 1960s. Local bureaucracies mirrored the federal model in forms and functions and specialized in providing social services at the grass roots. Because of the surge in federal block grants, categorical aid, and revenue-sharing programs, public bureaucracy in states and localities grew rapidly in the 1960s and 1970s. Gradual growth, experimental design, majoritarian surges, and complexity, coupled with the inertia of bureaucratic institutions, sustain the size and scope of U.S. bureaucracy. United States bureaucracy comes in a variety of forms—executive departments, agencies, bureaus, regulatory commissions, government corporations, boards, and many others. Despite the popular view, there is no *one* typical bureaucracy or bureaucrat in the United States today.

Key Terms

core functions
clientele agencies
regulatory agencies
government corporations
executive departments
staff agencies
Progressive Era

New Deal
Cold War Era
Great Society
constituent policies
distributive policies
redistributive policies
quasi-judicial/quasi-legislative
   functions

Review Questions

1. Why did the United States have little in the way of a bureaucracy until the twentieth century? What were its major organizational forms until the twentieth century?
2. What key factors prompted the growth of bureaucracy in the twentieth century?
3. Why did diverse forms of bureaucratic organizations develop in twentieth-century America?
4. How can we generalize about the overall development of U.S. bureaucracy?
5. What is meant by bureaucratic policy making? How is policy making related to internal agency processes?

Notes

1. Leonard D. White, *The Federalists: A Study in Administrative History* (NY: Macmillan, 1948), pp. 22–23.
2. Ibid., p. 147.
3. Frederick C. Mosher (ed.), *Basic Documents of American Public Administration, 1776-1950* (NY: Holmes and Meier, 1976), pp. 36–38.
4. *The US Government Manual* (Washington, DC, 1980), p. 733.
5. Richard L. Schott, *The Bureaucratic State: The Evolution and Scope of the American Federal Bureaucracy* (NJ: General Learning Press, 1972), p. 9.
6. Leonard D. White, *The Republican Era, 1869-1901* (NY: Macmillan, 1958), p. 232.
7. Ibid.
8. Marver H. Bernstein, *Regulating Business by Independent Commission* (Princeton: Princeton University Press, 1955), p. 130.
9. Harold F. Seidman, *Politics, Position and Power,* 2d ed. (NY: Oxford University Press, 1975), p. 254.
10. House Document, pp. 91–313.
11. James Q. Wilson, "The Rise of the Bureaucratic State," *The Public Interest* (Fall 1975), p. 90.
12. Harold F. Seidman, *Politics,* p. 236.
13. Theodore Lowi, "Four Systems of Policy, Politics, and Choice," Inter-University Case Program, Case No. 110 (Syracuse: 1972), p. 27.

Further Readings

Students can learn much by reading Leonard White's now-classic four-volume history of the growth of U.S. bureaucracy: *The Federalists* (1948); *The Jeffersonians* (1951); *The Jacksonians* (1954); and *The Republican Era* (1958).

Shorter but equally distinguished works include: Matthew A. Crenson's *The Federal Machine* (1975); Frederick C. Mosher's *Democracy and the Public Service,* 2d ed. (1982); and Robert H. Wiebe's *The Search for Order, 1877–1920* (1967). Useful interpretative pieces can be found in Richard Schott's short piece, *The Bureaucratic State* (1972), James Q. Wilson's "The Rise of the Bureaucratic State" in *The Public Interest* (Fall 1975), as well as Herbert Kaufman's "Emerging Conflicts in the Doctrines of Public Administration," in *American Political Science Review* (1956).

For more advanced theoretical conceptions of the rise of bureaucratic institutions, read Stephen Skowronek's *Building a New American State: The Expansion of National Administrative Capacities, 1877–1920* (1982); Don K. Price's *America's Unwritten Constitution* (1983); E. N. Gladden's *A History of Public Administration,* two volumes (1972); Ernest Barker's *The Development of Public Service in Western Europe, 1660–1930* (1944); Martin Albrow's *Bureaucracy* (1970); Brian Chapman's *The Profession of Government* (1959); Sidney H. Aronson's *Status and Kinship in the Higher Civil Service* (1964); Michael Walzer's *The Revolution of the Saints* (1975); A. D. Lindsay's *The Modern Democratic State* (1943); H. H. Gerth and C. Wright Mills (eds.), *From Max Weber* (1946); Alfred D. Chandler's *The Visible Hand* (1977); Dwight Waldo's *The Administrative State,* 2d ed. (1984); Theodore Lowi's *The End of Liberalism,* 2d ed. (1979); Martin J. Schiesl's *The Politics of Efficiency* (1977); Otis L. Graham's *Toward a Planned Society* (1976); Samuel P. Huntington's *American Politics: The Promise of Disharmony* (1981); and Fritz Morstein Marx's *Elements of Public Administration* (1946).

Serious students of bureaucracy should examine primary materials— executive orders, congressional acts, and official reports—as found in Frederick C. Mosher (ed.), *Basic Documents of American Public Administration, 1776–1950* (1976) and Richard J. Stillman's *Basic Documents of American Public Administration Since 1950* (1982).

For an outstanding reference book containing well-written short essays on the development of many individual government agencies, see Donald R. Whitnah (ed.), *Government Agencies* (1983). Look especially at the references in this book for other useful books and essays on these agencies' development. The annual *U.S. Government Organization Manual* is an equally important reference book.

One should not neglect several excellent books on the growth of particular U.S. governmental sectors and units: Thomas K. McCraw's *Prophets of Regulation* (1984); Frederick C. Mosher's *A Tale of Two Agencies* (1984); Samuel P. Huntington's *The Soldier and State* (1957); Larry Berman's *The Office of Management and the Presidency, 1921–1979* (1979); Jane S. Dahlberg's *The New York Bureau of Municipal Research* (1966); Barry Karl's *Executive Reorganization and Reform in the New Deal* (1963); Frederick C. Mosher's *The GAO* (1979); Paul Van Riper's *History of the United States*

Civil Service (1958); Stephen Ambrose's *Upton and the Army* (1964); Martha Derthick's *The National Guard in Politics* (1965); Otto Nelson's *National Security and the General Staff* (1946); Robert Cushman's *The Independent Regulatory Commissions* (1941); and Richard J. Stillman II's *The Rise of the City Manager* (1974). There are many others that are also cited in the Donald R. Whitnah text cited above.

3
External Forces Shaping Modern Bureaucracy

The General Environment of U.S.
    Public Bureaucracy: First-Level Inputs
Socioeconomic Factors: Second-Level
    Inputs
External Political Actors: Third-Level
    Inputs
Major Institutional Actors: Fourth-Level
    Inputs

Basic Patterns of Inputs Surrounding
    Bureaucracy
Summary of Key Points
Key Terms
Review Questions
Notes
Further Readings

George Will recently observed that ''government generally is a dance, a minuet, of small minorities.'' He might have said much the same thing about public bureaucracy: ''It's generally a dance, a minuet, of special interests around government agencies.'' This chapter will examine this ''dance.'' More precisely, this chapter explores the large variety of external forces shaping modern U.S. bureaucracy. What is the general environment of public bureaucracies in the 1980s? What are the major inputs that shape U.S. bureaucratic agencies? The external sources of their growth? Stability? Decline?

It is not easy to differentiate *external* forces from *internal* factors that affect every administrative unit. Modern public agencies are made up of multiple offices, layered one upon another. Historically, this layering occurs as new units are added to older ones or as old ones subdivide responsibilities. For example, the Federal Bureau of Investigation (FBI) was established as an autonomous agency thirty-eight years after the Justice Department was created in 1870. Today it is a subunit of the Justice Department; therefore, from the standpoint of the Justice Department, the FBI is an internal unit. But from the perspective of the director of the FBI, the department is external to the bureau's operations. Similarly, at the local level, the fire department as a distinct agency is normally created *after* the incorporation of a municipality and is inside, or internal to, a city government. But from the vantage point of the fire chief, the city is external to its operations.

The perspective or organizational standpoint from which one views a bureau, office, or agency determines whether forces are considered internal or external to its operations. The emphasis in this chapter, however, will be to point out the major external factors that shape the future of every unit of bureaucracy at the federal, state, and local levels. External inputs are the powerful forces influencing every agency's growth, continuation, or decline. These inputs can determine the fate of a local police department or a state welfare office or a federal regulatory agency. Because of their importance to an agency's future, these inputs should be carefully examined.

As figure 3.1 indicates, the external forces "dancing around" every public bureaucracy can be divided into four types. First is the general environment, consisting of the broad milieu of U.S. values, constitutional structure, and functional requirements. This general environment is the most fundamental and long-term factor, for it shapes the general context within which all U.S. public organizations operate.

Second, the socioeconomic factors involving specific shifts in population, technology, and the economy directly affect the growth, stability, and decline of individual bureaucratic institutions. These socioeconomic inputs influence the types of services and levels of services bureaucracy performs for a society. Socioeconomic forces create "the market" for public services rendered by government bureaucracy. In short, they determine the overall task demands and levels of resources available for bureaucracy.

The third level of input consists of political forces. These are the major external political groups and interests surrounding public agencies. They may be created and fostered by the socioeconomic factors, or they may be autonomous and independent of socioeconomic factors. They include public opinion, clientele groups, media coverage, public interest groups, and power

FIGURE 3.1
External Forces Shaping Public Bureaucracy: Four Type of Inputs

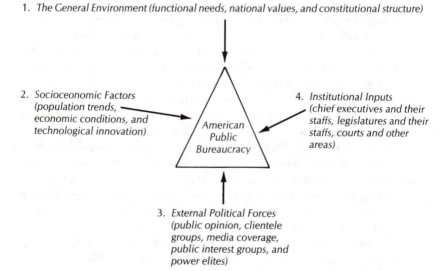

1. *The General Environment (functional needs, national values, and constitutional structure)*

2. *Socioceonomic Factors (population trends, economic conditions, and technological innovation)*

American Public Bureaucracy

4. *Institutional Inputs (chief executives and their staffs, legislatures and their staffs, courts and other areas)*

3. *External Political Forces (public opinion, clientele groups, media coverage, public interest groups, and power elites)*

elites. All these in various yet critical ways influence an agency's survival, stability, and decline.

The fourth level, institutional inputs, come from within government and involve institutions nearest and most directly influential to the bureaucracy itself: chief executives and their staffs, legislatures and their staffs, courts and judges, as well as other offices, agencies, bureaus, and departments at every level of government. Often the political level of inputs registers its influence upon bureaucracy through this institutional level. Nonetheless, institutional inputs are often most immediately germane and necessary to any bureaucracy's survival, especially in regard to establishing the goals to be accomplished, budget appropriations, personnel levels, laws and rules, top leadership, and the formal/informal degrees of independence or dependence.

While the general environment and the three levels of inputs—socioeconomic, political, and institutional—will be discussed separately, in reality they rarely act separately. Rather, they ''dance'' in concert with one another. Changing public opinion may stimulate media coverage, which in turn may cause legislative action or reaction regarding an individual public agency. Further, levels and the patterns of inputs change within different situations; therefore, not all the forces outlined here influence *every* bureaucracy. Some forces influence any given agency more than others; some come into play while others do not, depending on the time, place, and circumstances. Much, therefore, depends on the relationship between the actual situation and the special amalgam of external factors that may affect any one particular bureaucracy. The nature of these inputs, how they shape the future of public organizations, and their basic forms and configurations of power are the central questions addressed in this chapter.

The General Environment of U.S. Public Bureaucracy: First-Level Inputs

Public bureaucracy operates within the general environment of U.S. society, and within this particular milieu (see figure 3.2) three important and constant factors surround bureaucratic institutions: persistent functional needs of society, fundamental national values the American people hold near and dear, and the constitutional structure of government within which public bureaucracy operates.

The Functional Needs of Society

In Chapter 2 we learned that U.S. public bureaucracy grew up to service the essential functional needs which persist to this day.

Core Functions. The purpose of bureaucracy is to perform very essential core functions of government, such as diplomacy, defense, and internal security at the national level; and police, fire, and other functions at the local level.

FIGURE 3.2
Societal Environment—First-Level Inputs

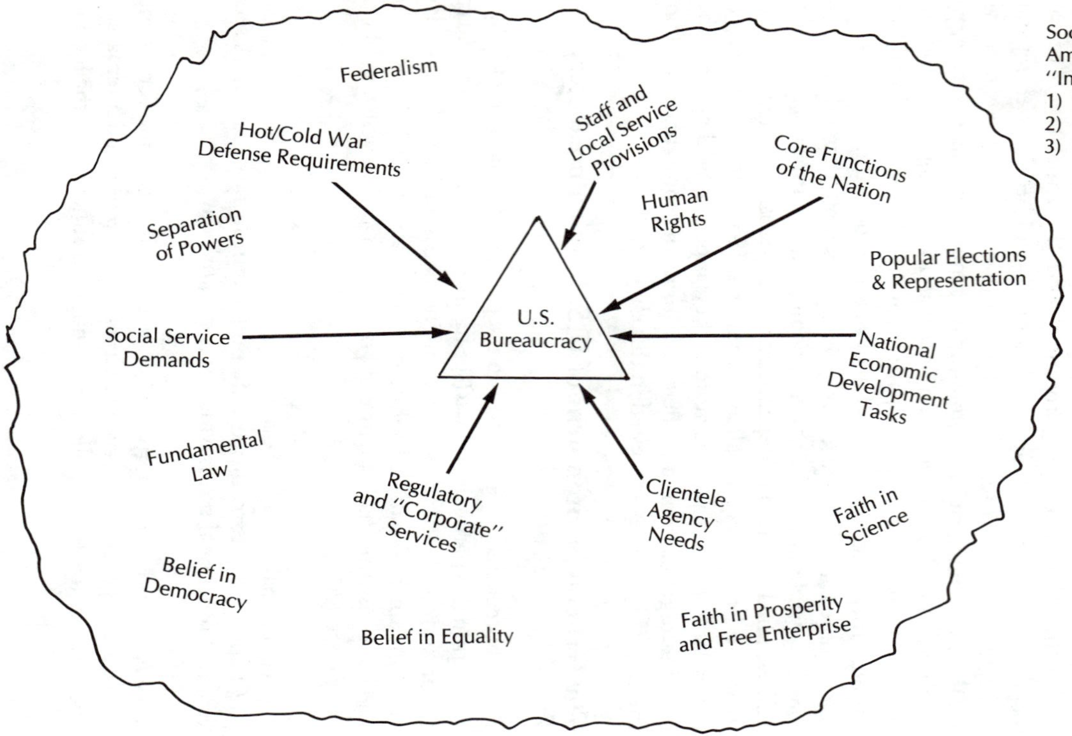

Core Functions
of the Nation

Popular Elections
& Representation

National
Economic
Development
Tasks

Faith in
Science

Staff and
Local Service
Provisions

Human
Rights

Clientele
Agency
Needs

Faith in Prosperity
and Free Enterprise

U.S.
Bureaucracy

Federalism

Hot/Cold War
Defense Requirements

Regulatory
and "Corporate"
Services

Belief in Equality

Separation
of Powers

Social Service
Demands

Fundamental
Law

Belief in
Democracy

Societal Environment—Includes Complex
Amalgam of Three Elements of
"Inputs" to all Public Agencies:
1) Functional needs of society
2) National values of Americans
3) U.S. Constitutional structure

72

National Economic Development Tasks.   The economic requirements necessary to build a nation and provide for industrial growth and prosperity are considered equally fundamental in modern society. Today this remains a major functional activity of several units of bureaucracy, such as the Council of Economic Advisors and the departments of Commerce and the Interior.

Clientele Agency Needs.   Since the late nineteenth century, the major function of U.S. bureaucracy has been to represent the needs, concerns, and interests of key diverse occupational and social groups within government.

Regulatory and Corporate Services.   Regulating the national economy and performing many types of activities through public corporate enterprises also remain fundamental functions of government.

Social Services.   Particularly since the Great Depression of the 1930s, bureaucratic agencies have assumed a variety of important social service tasks, including the care of the aged, the infirm, the poor, the unemployed, and the homeless.

Global Hot and Cold War Requirements.   Since World War II, the U.S. position of leadership in the free world has created important and enduring bureaucratic tasks involving international organizations, defense capabilities, and foreign diplomacy.

Staff and Local Services.   The managerial responsibilities of running large and complex bureaucracies are sources of its further development and of the provision of various local services at the state, county, and municipal levels of government.

National Values

Behind these constant demands upon bureaucracy are important fundamental national values peculiar to the United States, within which bureaucracy operates. These values and structures are critical to the shaping of contemporary bureaucracy. Some of the major civic values are worth outlining in brief:

Belief in Democracy.   Faith in democracy, freedom, and popular participation as a basis of government are considered fundamental to the heritage of the United States. The democratic ideal is a deeply ingrained tradition. It makes its impact upon bureaucratic institutions in numerous ways, from the public's insistence upon specific devices for control of bureaucracy to the broader conceptions that public bureaucracy should ultimately serve ''the people'' and ''the popular will.''

Belief in Equality.   Like democracy, equality is also a basic belief of Americans, stemming from Jefferson's ringing statement in the Declaration of Independence that all men are created equal. Much of the work today within bureaucracy is concerned with promoting equality and equity. Human services must be provided for *all* Americans; thus the means must be found by which bureaucratic institutions can better and more equally deliver their services to every American.

Faith in Prosperity and Free Enterprise.   American culture has largely been shaped by commercial enterprises. Over the years the United States has maintained a strong commitment to the promoting of material prosperity through the free enterprise system. "The business of America is business," a U.S. president once commented, and U.S. bureaucracy today is deeply involved with as well as committed to the promotion of business and national prosperity. Indeed, U.S. bureaucratic institutions (i.e., the government corporation) have been shaped in the corporate model because of the popularity of business ideals.

Faith in Science.   Science, scientists, and scientific methodology are also fundamental ideals. These ideals hold a special place of honor, bordering almost on religious devotion. Partly this devotion to science is based upon the belief that science and scientists can advance material progress and democratic ideals. For whatever the reasons we believe in science and scientists, public bureaucracies are deeply bound up with promoting science, scientists, and scientific techniques in numerous ways that will be discussed in following chapters.

The U.S. Constitution

The general environment within which the U.S. bureaucracy operates has also been shaped by elements of the U.S. Constitution.

The Fundamental Law.   The U.S. Constitution itself serves as the fundamental law for the United States. It sets forth the purposes and basic framework of government and also stresses that the government should be rooted *in law*. Indeed, the basic construct of public bureaucracy is itself framed in laws, rules, and statutes.

Separation of Powers.   Basic to the Constitution is the "scatteration of power" through the vertical division of constitutional authority into three separate branches: executive, legislative, and judicial. This division of power has posed special complexities and dilemmas for U.S. bureaucracy since it fragments bureaucracy's structures, activities, and oversight.

Federalism.   The federal Constitution further divides power horizontally among the federal, state, and local governments, thus giving some degree of institutional autonomy to each level of government. This concept "scatters power" in order to prevent concentration of authority and to safeguard human liberty. Like the concept of separation of powers, the federal design of the U.S. Constitution adds further complexity and unique dilemmas to U.S. bureaucracy.

Protection of Human Rights. The first ten amendments to the Constitution, the Bill of Rights, extend basic liberties to every citizen, such as the freedoms of speech, the press, and religion and the right to due process. These basic protections place limits upon what bureaucracy can and cannot do to individuals, thus further complicating bureaucratic tasks. The Bill of Rights requires that bureaucratic activity hold the rights of human beings as a high priority, even, at times, higher than the needs of society as a whole.

Periodicity of Popular Elections and Representation. According to the Constitution, democratic elections must be held at two-, four-, or six-year intervals. This constitutional requirement provides the avenue for popular participation in governmental affairs as well as the major mechanism for popular oversight of government. Popular elections are also a chief source of top leadership—elected *and* appointed—of public bureaucracy. These elections also create complex issues involving the changing relationships *between* popularly elected officials and permanent bureaucratic officials.

It is important to recognize that the three elements of functional needs, national values, and constitutional structure make up a unique and complex general environment, within which public bureaucracy operates. This environment directly shapes what bureaucracy can and cannot accomplish. Specific bureaus, agencies, and offices are also influenced by socioeconomic, political, and institutional factors.

Socioeconomic Factors: Second-Level Inputs

As Max Weber, one of the great scholars of bureaucracy, once pointed out, bureaucratic institutions arose first under conditions of sufficient populations, particularly urban populations, combined with a "monied economy."[1] Concentrations of people who trade with currency rather than barter are fertile soil for the development of bureaucratic institutions. While Weber was taking "the grand world view" to explain the rise of bureaucracy during the early Roman empire, in fifth-century China, and during the late Middle Ages in Europe, much the same could be said today about U.S. bureaucracy. Bureaus, agencies, and departments are fundamentally dependent upon socioeconomic conditions to set the levels of demands placed on these institutions.

Three factors in particular are important for creating market demand for bureaucratic services and institutions. First are population shifts. Rising or declining populations as well as different demographic mixes of classes, especially income classes, determine to a large extent the levels and types of bureaucratic services rendered and institutions required. Second, economic conditions are critical. The GNP (all goods and services produced in the nation), regional economic growth or decline, increasing or decreasing tax/revenue bases, and general levels of employment, inflation, and interest rates either encourage or retard bureaucracy's development. Finally, technological innovation is a vital element. Much of modern bureaucracy is a response to new technology which must be regulated or accommodated by infrastructure (roads, railroad tracks, telephone poles, and the like). The speed of technological innovation and the kind and quantity of technology developed can decisively influence the growth or stagnation of public bureaucracy.

The following three types of socioeconomic factors involving population shifts, economic changes, and technological inventions can combine in the following ways to influence the future of particular bureaucratic institutions.

Regional/National Socioeconomic Growth Situations: Or High Task Demands

Many sunbelt and western cities and states have experienced enormous growth in the last decade or more. Populations have grown rapidly; their regional economies have boomed as industries moved south and new ones have opened their doors; jobs became plentiful, attracting more people to these areas. In certain areas of California, Texas, and Florida the rapidity of technological innovation by computer, space, and aircraft firms has been an important factor in promoting this economic boom. Workers and their families have moved from the North to the South and West for jobs, and retirees have gone South for the warmth and rest. Population growth, economic expansion, and technological innovation have created strong market demands for public services provided by governmental bureaucracy. Roads and schools are needed; water and sewage facilities and utilities must be built; planning, zoning, and other public services considered essential to industrial and community development are necessary. Local bureaucracies have had to expand to cope with the needs of population growth, industrial expansion, and technological change. The "boom town" or "boom region" syndrome creates, in turn, revenue and tax surpluses that finance very real demands for more public services, particularly social services, physical infrastructures, and economic regulation, which must be supplied by government bureaucracy.

Socioeconomic boom periods generate bureaucratic expansion for the nation as a whole. One such era was the post-World War II period in the United States. Economic conditions—low inflation rates, favorable trade and budget surpluses, and strong growth rates—all provided adequate budget resources for funding the large defense and foreign assistance programs described in the last chapter. Population expansion, particularly the postwar baby boom, stimulated nationwide needs for improved educational, recreational, highway, and housing facilities. These services came to be provided by large federal departments, such as Health and Human Services, Housing and Urban Development, Transportation, and many others. The automobile, computers, television, mass transit, and other such modern conveniences created needs for new public agencies.

Think about the effect of the car on bureaucracy. In the postwar United States, the automobile necessitated the paving of hundreds of thousands of miles of federal, state, and local roadways; caused the out-migration of millions of people to suburbia, which in turn caused the creation of numerous local governments; necessitated massive and complex state regulatory machinery to license vehicles as well as to control the environment. The state highway patrol was also a product of the automobile age. There are many other indirect spinoffs from the development of the auto (some claim even the postwar baby boom was promoted by the backseats of autos).

It is difficult, if not impossible, to sort out exactly which variables are more or less critical to bureaucratic growth. Generally, new bureaucratic activities are stimulated by one or more of the following socioeconomic factors: (1) an expanding population with new needs for services; (2) a changing demographic mix, such as a baby boom, that creates particular demands for new types of public goods and services; (3) a growing revenue and tax base fueled by an expanding regional or national economy. Growing economic bases permit more and better social services; (4) little or no inflation and low interest rates that allow for adequate capital formation and infrastructure development by public agencies; and (5) technological change and scientific innovation spurring the development of public works projects (i.e., highways) or of government regulations (i.e., the Federal Communications Commission's regulation of radio or television frequencies).

Socioeconomic Stability: Constant Bureaucratic Task Demands

Under stable conditions, bureaucratic growth may be limited or nonexistent. Regions or cities where the economy is relatively stable, the population unchanging, and technological innovation constant create markets where demands for bureaucratic services vary little. In small towns, in some suburban communities, and even in some regions where the population-economy-technology variables are stable, few new sorts of public services are needed or demanded. The prime emphasis may well be on keeping the costs of government down and the size of bureaucracy constant. If there is no rapid increase in total numbers of people, there are no new demands for new bureaucratic services. If there is no changing demographic cohort of populations, such as a baby boom, there are no sudden new requirements for specific public services for particular groups of citizens. If there is no jump in consumer incomes, there are no new wants and demands on bureaucracy and no enriched tax and revenue bases for rendering such services. If there are no new technological innovations, no demand for government intervention is stimulated. Under such stable socioeconomic conditions, in a small town, for example, the city government may simply concentrate upon "keeping its doors open" and do little else. The municipal bureaucracy of an affluent, stable suburban community or region concentrates on providing good schools, roads, and safe and quiet streets, at reasonable costs, emphasizing *no* growth in total size of government. The community's goal is efficient, effective, and stable public services and an environment that fosters an unchanging community lifestyle. Hence, there are few new demands for more public tasks and public agencies. This same situation can hold true for state- or regional-level bureaucracies as well.

The United States has rarely, if ever, experienced prolonged eras of socioeconomic stability. Change has been a major part of its history. But some federal activities have experienced stable task demands because of relatively stable socioeconomic conditions surrounding these agencies. The U.S. Battle Monuments Commission, in charge of taking care of battle sites, has been relatively stable in size, except in wartime. Many other public agencies also have few new task demands to stimulate their growth. They thus remain stagnant in activity and static in size.

Socioeconomic Decline: Reduced Task Demands

A declining socioeconomic situation can have two very different effects upon bureaucratic institutions. At the national level, but not at the state and municipal levels, a precipitous socioeconomic decline can be a driving force for rapid expansion of bureaucratic institutions because of the U.S. government's ability to incur massive deficits. The Great Depression prompted massive increases in federal expenditures for a wide range of new social services, primarily to alleviate the chronic unemployment and impoverished social conditions of the 1930s. Such "pump-priming" or "countercycle expenditures," based upon New Deal experimentation and Keynesian economic doctrines, increased federal expenditures to offset industrial unemployment and economic decline. "Pump-priming" throughout the 1930s also fueled a dramatic and unprecedented jump in size, scope, and intensity of bureaucratic activities.

At the state and local levels, where such fiscal policy of countercyclical expenditures is impossible or prohibited by strict local/state debt limitations and revenue ceilings, the reverse generally occurs under declining socioeconomic conditions (except where federal help is provided). For example, during the late 1970s and early 1980s, the frostbelt regions of the United States experienced just such a downturn. The "oil shocks" of the 1970s—a tenfold jump in oil prices, from less than three dollars to over thirty dollars per barrel—produced a rapidly rising double-digit inflation rate. Industrial productivity slowed. Some sectors of the economy, such as northeastern smokestack industries—steel, rubber, and autos—were particularly hard-hit by foreign competition, which caused some plants to slow down production or, in some cases, to close altogether. Unemployment jumped to nearly 11 percent of the total work force. Massive out-migrations to sunbelt states occurred in the late 1970s and early 1980s as people sought work and better living conditions.

FIGURE 3.3
Socioeconomic Forces Influencing Bureaucracy

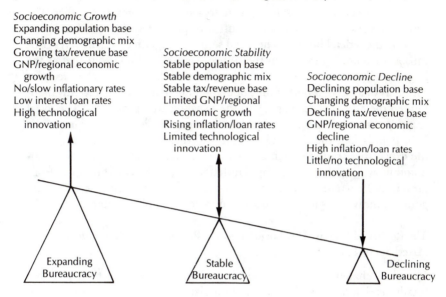

The direct effects of declining socioeconomic conditions in many frost-belt states in the late 1970s and early 1980s brought about sharp cutbacks in state and local public services. Population declines created less need for bureaucratic services; industrial slowdowns and plant closings dried up regional and local revenue bases and taxing powers; technological innovation slowed or shifted elsewhere. Such socioeconomic declines were translated into bureaucratic reductions that in some frostbelt states became quite severe.

In Massachusetts, for example, hard hit by the economic downturn, voters in 1978 passed Proposition 2¹/₂, which slashed property tax revenues from 8 to 2¹/₂ percent of the market rate, cut excise tax revenue, held regional authorities to 4 percent budget increases, and eliminated binding arbitration for police and fire personnel. The direct impact of Proposition 2¹/₂ was a loss of 20,000 public service jobs at the local level and 8,000 at the state level. Bureaucratic services were reduced across the board. Massachusetts residents either did without some public services or were asked to pay for others that had been performed free of charge or at little cost. Similar cutbacks occurred elsewhere in the frostbelt states, although how the cutbacks were handled and their degree of intensity varied widely from state to state and locality to locality.

George E. Peterson and Thomas Muller, Urban Institute scholars, assert: "There can be little doubt that substantial population loss compounds the fiscal pressure on city governments. Population decline tends to bring an automatic loss of tax-raising capacity; corresponding economies in city expenditures are much more difficult to achieve.[2] In these situations local bureaucracy is frequently forced to contract.

The federal level is not immune to socioeconomic pressures, either. The early 1980s saw federal social service cutbacks, prompted in part by fiscal pressures on the federal budget. The social security program especially faces critical socioeconomic pressures in the future. Figure 3.4 points out that as the large baby boom cohort grows up, the total population ages. The executive summary of a recent report of the Population Reference Bureau recently highlighted the effects of such aging on the social security program: "The social security system is in poor financial health in part because of the aging of the U.S. population, the changing face of the American household, improved life expectancy, earlier retirement, large increases in benefits, and slow economic growth combined with rapid inflation."[3] These factors prompted Congress in 1983 to raise social security taxes and to delay benefits to certain categories of individuals in order to save the system from bankruptcy.

The Reality of Present-Day Socioeconomic Pressures upon Bureaucracy: A Mixed Set of Futuristic Influences

In reality, changing socioeconomic factors create mixed effects that neither totally accelerate nor shrink bureaucratic size. A recent Cabinet Council on Economic Affairs report on shifting socioeconomic trends in the United States over the next ten to fifteen years points out that "the changing demographics will have positive overall effects on the economy, but the necessary adjustments may be difficult for specific sectors and individuals."[4] Among the many probable effects on bureaucratic activities cited by the report are:

The decline of the youthful population will make our ability to maintain all volunteer armed forces difficult over the next few decades;

To attract the diminishing pools of young people, military wages may have to be increased by 12 percent in 1995 to compete with higher real wages paid in the private sector;

Decline in the number of young workers will lessen the need for job training and other federal programs targeted at employment for the young;

As the overall school-age population declines by 1995, some schools will be shut, but greater percentages of students will be minorities and immigrants in center cities, creating substantial local needs for specialized educational training;

Today, 25 percent of federal outlays go to the aged. But as the United States "grays," this number could increase to 32 percent by 2000 and to 63 percent by 2025, putting increasing pressures on social security, medicaid, medicare, and other programs for the elderly;

As the population matures, productivity and savings rates generally go up, causing positive effects on tax revenues, interest rates, and credit markets, all sources of possible government revenue;

FIGURE 3.4

U.S. Population Age-Sex Pyramids: 1960–90

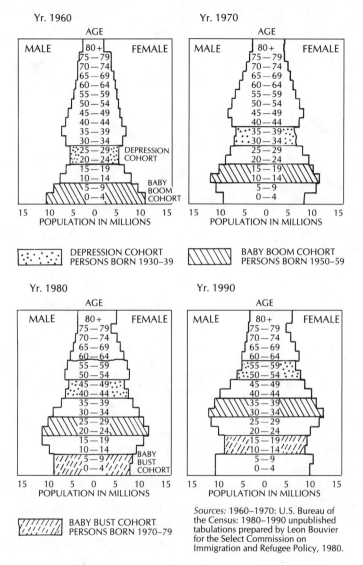

As the population ages, there will be greater pressures for increased varieties of social services and retirement systems;

As the youth cohort (18–25) in the population declines, so will crime, auto accidents, and the student population, resulting in less demand for police-related services, public hospitals, and public educational institutions;

Leisure time activities, particularly recreational services for the elderly and retired, will increase as the population matures;

FIGURE 3.5
Influence of Socioeconomic Factors on Bureaucracy

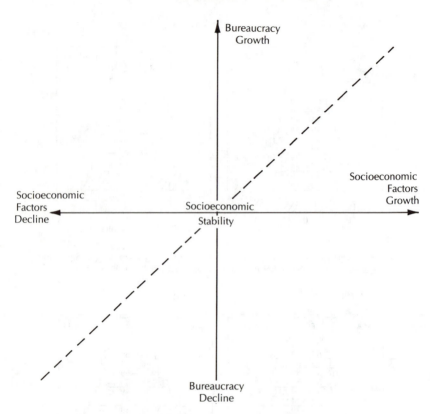

As family formation rates decline because of the decline in the number of youths and the increase in the number of elderly, fewer single-family homes and more apartment and condo dwellings will be needed, thus shifting community governments' emphasis in urban planning and development.

No doubt such predictions are highly speculative and open to challenge, but what is clear from such forecasts is that socioeconomic factors can have many major unforeseen and often contradictory influences upon bureaucratic institutions.

External Political Actors: Third-Level Inputs

The third level of inputs are external political actors that significantly shape the purposes, processes, and actions of bureaucracy. External groups can be highly visible, vocal, and immediately attentive to what public agencies do or don't do. As figure 3.6 indicates, they can be divided into essentially two groups—supporters and opponents of agencies. For the most part, neutral po-

FIGURE 3.6
Supportive/Opposing Political Forces Surrounding Bureaucracy

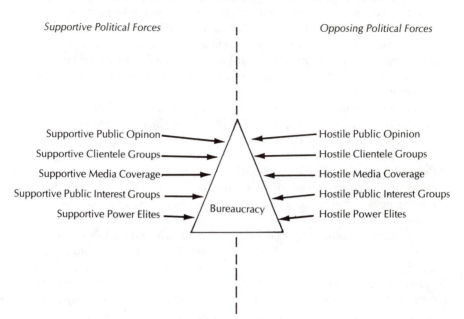

Supportive Political Forces   *Opposing Political Forces*

Supportive Public Opinon ——→ ←—— Hostile Public Opinion
Supportive Clientele Groups ——→ ←—— Hostile Clientele Groups
Supportive Media Coverage ——→ ←—— Hostile Media Coverage
Supportive Public Interest Groups ——→ ←—— Hostile Public Interest Groups
Supportive Power Elites ——→ ←—— Hostile Power Elites

Bureaucracy

litical groups make no significant impacts upon public agencies (though their lack of involvement can indeed give others latitude for taking action).

Administrative organizations do not exist in a vacuum; that is, without some degree of this external public support or hostility exercised either directly upon the agency or through intermediaries such as lawyers and lobbyists. At the widest level, public support (or hostility) is registered upon agencies by public opinion as reflected in polls, surveys, or a barrage of angry letters to an agency head; by contrast, the most direct and explicit pressures on bureaucracy may be from specific powerful clientele groups that surround many agencies. For example, veterans groups like the American Legion and the Veterans of Foreign Wars have vital stakes in the operations of the Veterans Administration. Other external political actors include the media (newspapers, radio, television), public interest groups (Common Cause and Ralph Nader's groups), power elites (often informal but highly powerful networks of influential citizens and advisors, such as consulting firms, contractors, and special counsels). This chapter will examine the specific types of critical inputs each of these makes upon bureaucratic processes and institutions.

Public Opinion

Generally public opinion is too transitory and amorphous to have much influence on the typical public agency. Most agencies simply do not operate in the direct gaze of the public eye. How many citizens care about the County Records Management Office or the Federal Property Resource Service? Most do not even know of their existence. John Q. Public is frequently too busy, too ill-informed, or too uninterested to pay much attention to administrative matters that are frequently technical, arcane, and obscure. As Walter Lippmann wrote, "It is not fair to expect too much of the common man. . . .the public will arrive in the middle of third act and will leave before the last curtain, having stayed just long enough perhaps to decide who is the hero and who is the villain of the piece."[5]

Public opinion expresses itself at the polls every two or four years after highly charged political campaigns. Public opinion directly influences the selection of legislators and chief executives, but rarely does it pay direct, sustained attention to specific administrative actions. But this is not to suggest that public opinion *never* involves itself with bureaucracy. Like a great unseen presence, it exerts tremendous strength at certain moments—perhaps only fleeting ones—creating enormous pressures on particular administrative activities.

Generally, public support or hostility is triggered by three factors: first, a dramatic event such as the disaster at Three Mile Island in 1980 or the U.S.S.R.'s launching of Sputnik in 1957 can evoke a strong and immediate public demand for new or increased bureaucratic activities—better nuclear regulation in the former case and increased funding for U.S. space projects in the latter. A catastrophe like the deaths of 240 marines in Lebanon in October 1983 prompted severe public criticism and resulted in new military efforts to protect U.S. soldiers' safety, eventually leading to the marines' total withdrawal from Lebanon by February 1984.

Second, certain highly visible agencies have over the years made special efforts to curry public favor and develop positive public images. The FBI and the U.S. Marine Corps throughout much of their recent histories have paid particular attention to generating favorable coverage from the media. Their PR efforts in the long run pay these agencies rich dividends, especially in recruitment of personnel and budget allocations. The marine corps' annual Toys for Tots Program and spit-and-polish drill teams help maintain overall public confidence, which then can be translated into legislative support for their activities.

Third, public support can be prompted by long-term external needs. It is no accident, for example, that Los Angeles developed one of the earliest and strongest air pollution control programs in the nation. Beginning shortly after World War II, Los Angeles initiated local air pollution controls because of growing popular support for clean air. Air pollution abatement still remains a high priority for people living in Southern California; and it is therefore a vital concern of local government. Public perceptions, however, can swing rapidly one way or another as external threats increase or decrease. Figure 3.7 shows how over the past three decades public support for defense expenditures has generally coincided with actual increases in defense appropriations. In 1952,

FIGURE 3.7
Public Opinion & U.S. Defense Budgets

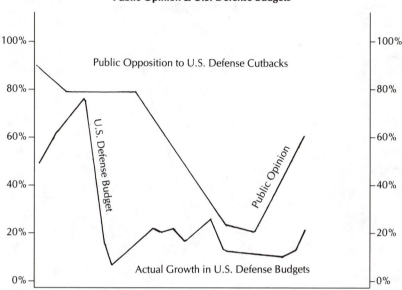

in the midst of the Korean War, 80 percent of the U.S. public opposed cuts in the defense budget, which then grew by almost 60 percent. By contrast, in 1972, as more and more Americans wanted their government to withdraw from Vietnam, only 25 percent of the public opposed defense cuts, and the defense budget grew little. In 1982, 60 percent of Americans opposed defense cuts. New concerns about defense preparedness arose largely because of events such as the 1980 Iran hostage crisis and President Reagan's 1980 political campaign promises, and in 1982 the defense budget grew 20 percent. Sharp swings in public opinion over defense issues have, over the long term, directly affected trends in defense budget allocations and the size and quality of the entire defense establishment.

The Media

A similar situation in the 1980s is illustrated in figure 3.8, which shows that as the AIDS epidemic spread, it attracted more media attention and public outcry. As a result, the federal appropriation for AIDS research was rapidly increased by Congress. Like public opinion, the media ignore much of the work of administrative units in government. Except for large-city papers like the *New York Times,* the *Washington Post,* and the *Los Angeles Times,* and public radio or television news, the media give only fleeting attention to administrative agencies. The exceptional heroism of local firefighters in putting out a

FIGURE 3.8
Federal Budget Appropriations for AIDS Research and Deaths from AIDS

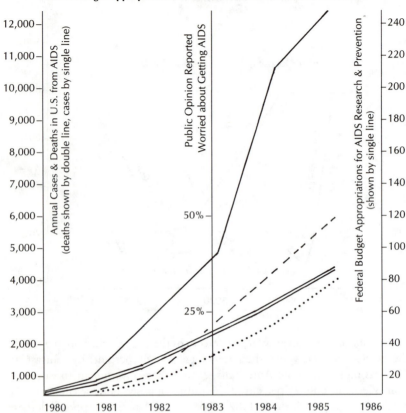

Federal Expenditures for AIDS Research Has Climbed as Reported Cases and Deaths from AIDS Attracted Attention from the Media and the Public in the 1980s

═══ Deaths from AIDS
─── Reported Cases of AIDS
- - - Public Reported Worried about Getting AIDS
······ Federal Budget Appropriation for AIDS research and prevention (in millions of dollars)

three-alarm blaze or a governor's education budget may be highlighted, but the media cover most bureaucratic work with little depth or detail. Why? There are many contributing factors.

First and foremost, the media are in business to sell advertising space, newspapers, and air time. Thus the media are often compelled to cover news that is of interest at the moment. A popular superbowl game thus preempts a report on an obscure regulatory agency or on a budget allocation, even though the latter events may have far-reaching and more profound effects on everyday life. Further, tight deadlines, poorly trained and poorly paid reporters, and limited space, combined with uninformed or careless readers, diminish interest in administrative details that are often boring and complex. All these factors serve to limit, distort, or simplify coverage.

Other factors influence coverage as well. Norton Long once told the story of a New York City mayor who, after returning from a whirlwind European vacation, was badgered by the press to tell about what he had learned on his trip. Trying to make his trip seem important and productive, he said, "I was impressed with the antinoise campaign in Paris." This gave the reporters something to write about and got the mayor off the hook. But the editorial staff at one paper was having a slow day and needed a story to generate copy. So they picked up the antinoise idea and even brought out a special edition of the paper with a headline, "Mayor Favors Anti-Noise Campaign." Soon other city papers took up the hue and cry for an antinoise campaign, and before long city agencies were mobilized to carry out just such a crusade—all because the mayor had to think of something fast off the top of his head to tell local reporters who needed something to print on a slow day.[6]

While this story points out that media coverage can indeed be trivial, episodic, and lacking in depth, the media can nonetheless influence administrative activities by: (1) creating new problems for agencies to solve where none had previously existed or had not been perceived as important—e.g., a municipal antinoise crusade; (2) helping to direct or redirect the existing priorities of departments or agencies through editorials, "the slant of the news," and the intensity of coverage of certain issues or events; and (3) giving sustained support or criticism to public programs and thus influencing *how* these bureaucratic programs are delivered, as well as when, where, and to whom they are delivered—again through the intensity and slant of coverage.

As Brookings scholar Walter G. Held has noted, different media are important to different agencies, depending on the markets served by particular media: "Bureau leaders in the Department of Agriculture are less concerned with efforts by the *New York Times* to affect their decision making than with the editorial views and interpretive reporting of the newspapers in the farmbelt and in rural communities because the *Times* is oriented to the urban dweller rather than toward those in rural areas. On the other hand, the bureau leaders in the State Department find the *Times* of considerable significance when it attempts to influence decisions in international affairs."[7] Indeed, specialized publications like *The American Hunter,* published by the National Rifle Association, or *Today's Education,* prepared by the National Education Association, while not having wide daily circulations can target enormous *and sustained* special interest pressures on particular agency decisions.

By contrast, a highly rated television investigative news program like "60 Minutes" can bring about a brief but sometimes overwhelming public reaction to an agency's actions or inaction. A recent story on "60 Minutes" about a young black man imprisoned in Dallas for a robbery he did not commit brought about his immediate release by the governor. But whether the story will have any long-term impact on the administration of Dallas's criminal justice system is open to doubt. Neither "60 Minutes" nor its viewers can sustain long-term interest in the complicated and difficult details of criminal justice administrative reform.

Clientele and Special Interest Groups

Perhaps the most important and influential external political influences upon agency activities are clientele groups. Special interests surround every agency and try to convince the administrative organization to act, indeed that it has a *duty to act,* in the interests of the clientele group it serves. The National Co-operative Milk Producers once told its membership about the duties of the Agriculture Department:

> Eleven months from now the people will go to the polls. They will decide important issues. One of the greatest issues which farmers will help decide will be on the question of who controls the Department of Agriculture. We believe that the organized farmers of America will demand of both political parties that they will provide a reconstituted Department of Agriculture to serve agriculture. Other Departments of Government serve the groups for which they are named. The Department of Agriculture today is not being permitted to function for farmers. We call for definite pledges on this great fundamental issue.[8]

While they are often not as blatant in their appeals for special help, most special interest groups have a similar view of government departments, a view that may be characterized as narrow, self-servicing and self-promoting. Only at their own peril can agencies ignore such special interests, for they are vital to the survival of agencies in most cases. Or, as Herbert Simon, Victor Thompson, and Donald Smithburg wrote: "For some administrative organizations there are groups within society whose support, working through their representatives in the legislature, can guarantee the survival of the organization against almost any odds and whose opposition, in like fashion, is tantamount to the death of the organization or at least considerable modification of its objectives and methods."[9]

As one would suspect, the clientele groups surrounding any government organization vary considerably according to the nature and purposes of the agency. Farm groups are keenly interested in the work of the Department of Agriculture; businessmen in that of the Commerce Department; organized labor in the Department of Labor; pilots and airline companies in the Federal Aviation Administration, and so on.

These clientele groups' power and influence over public agencies have fascinated political scientists and sociologists for many years. In one of the earliest and now-classic studies of this subject, *TVA and the Grass Roots,* by Philip Selznick, the author describes the development of the TVA, a New Deal program to develop the Tennessee Valley region by means of building dams for hydroelectric power, flood control, and recreational activities. The TVA became a model for many government-sponsored regional developments. Yet, as Selznick's study shows, the TVA's success really came from the development of its "administrative constituency." The TVA worked hard and effectively to nurture and develop this regional support, what Selznick called "informal cooptation—a relation of mutual dependence develops, so that the agency organization must define its constituency and conversely."[10] In many respects, the TVA's clientele group was an ideal one to nurture, develop, and "coopt" because first and foremost it was supportive of TVA activities. The TVA showered numerous economic benefits and privileges on the region.

Support from clientele groups, however, is not always there. Sometimes agencies face large and powerful hostile groups. The National Rifle Association (NRA), for example, has one of the largest and most effective lobbies in Washington. Working on behalf of gun owners and hunters, it has consistently fought—and effectively curbed—its chief regulatory agency, the Bureau of Alcohol, Tobacco and Firearms, by keeping this bureau's budget small, its personnel demoralized, and its leadership on the defensive (in 1981–1982 the NRA very nearly succeeded in demolishing the bureau entirely).

While basic clientele support or hostility is critical to an agency's prosperity, the size and location of the clientele group are important factors as well. The TVA has a ready-made regional constituency that includes almost everyone in the Tennessee Valley. The same is true of another regional agency, the Los Angeles Department of Power and Water (DPW). This is perhaps the most influential public organization in all of southern California because of its captive constituency made up of every consumer of water and power in southern California. Because of its ability to supply its constituents with cheap, plentiful water and electrical power, it has had tremendous influence over the growth patterns and economic development of the region, particularly in determining urban planning, patterns of land use, zoning, rights of way, and water distribution. The DPW has made many enemies in the process of using its influence, but its firm, wealthy, concentrated base of clientele support has permitted it to have its own way on most critical issues. A geographically dispersed clientele can be equally influential if its component groups are numerous and strategically situated. Nearly every town, large or small, contains, for example, a veterans' hall, an American Legion post, or clusters of reserve or retired military personnel. These dispersed veterans groups can have powerful effects on veterans' agencies at the state and federal levels, ensuring protection of veterans' privileges and military interests. Particularly they can aggressively support representatives in Congress or the state legislature who are favorable to their programs and administrative units of government.

Third, not only are size and location critical, but the level of intensity of the economic, organizational, and political resources that clientele groups can bring to bear on an agency is vital to their influence and effectiveness as well. For example, the concentrated economic-political wealth of the region has been used repeatedly to influence the future of the TVA. A sizable voting block of regional members of Congress combined with their strategic positions (Senator Howard Baker, minority and majority leader of the Senate for several years) kept alive for a decade the TVA's multibillion dollar Clinch River Breeder Reactor project in the face, even, of strong presidential opposition. In the summer of 1982 a prosperous but small political lobby, the American Bankers Association, was able to mobilize savers across the country to defeat the proposed Internal Revenue Service dividend and interest withholding legislation, which would have closed a major loophole in the tax code and saved the government billions of dollars. The combination of wealth, expert legal advice, and effective media presentation has been instrumental in stopping government action. For example, contrast the clout of a bankers' lobby with that of a group of welfare mothers with little money, little time, and little organizational talent. The latter combination makes for a weak and ineffective lobby at the federal, state, and local levels.

Fourth, the autonomy of an agency has a direct bearing on the ease or lack of it with which a clientele group gains access to an agency. It is no accident that the TVA or the Veterans Administration remain independent agencies. Their powerful clientele groups generally find this independent organizational status preferable, since independent agencies are generally more open and available to interest groups than agencies that are sandwiched among hierarchical layers of federal, state, or local executive departments that are often—though not always—subject to greater executive oversight.

Indeed, clientele groups sometimes support reorganization in order to attain greater political influence over public agencies. The National Education Association (NEA) secured Jimmy Carter's campaign pledge and later his presidential support for setting up a separate Department of Education in 1979. In part, the NEA sought this new federal department as a means of gaining greater influence over policy making. At the Department of Health, Education and Welfare, the NEA had to jockey with a broader array of special interest groups for policy-making authority.

The number of clientele or special interest groups is estimated to be more than 4,000 in Washington alone; they are equally numerous in state capitals. They come in many shapes and sizes, some being no more than names on stationery letterheads. Depending upon the level of government, their influence over an administration varies in strength. A gay rights group exercises little influence over Congress, but it has a lot of political clout in cities with large gay populations, such as San Francisco. Other clientele groups, such as the AFL-CIO, comprise several million members and exercise enormous political-economic impact on Congress but may be ineffective in some public agencies that have little or no union membership or in some of the six right-to-work states, where compulsory unions are prohibited. Inputs and influences of clientele groups on bureaucratic institutions at the federal, state, and local levels are therefore extraordinarily diverse. These groups aid the election of friendly legislators, lobby for budget increases, sponsor favorable legislation, and secure higher personnel ceilings and favorable policy decisions from elected chief executives. They push for the expansion of existing programs or for the starting up of new administrative activities in their interest. But their inputs may be vast in some agencies and negligible in others, depending on their focus—the NRA may care a lot about guns but about little else.

There are also less obvious clientele inputs into agency actions. As Francis Rourke notes, "One of the major advantages that the support of interest groups have for an executive department is the fact that such groups can often do for a department things that it cannot very easily do for itself."[11] An army, navy, marine, air force officer, or noncommissioned officer on active duty, for example, cannot directly campaign for more divisions or air wings, but the Retired Officers Association or Air Force Association or Boeing Corporation can speak out on these topics. They actively wage media campaigns, hire lawyers and lobbyists to lobby Congress, leak favorable information to the press, and support election campaigns of "good candidates." Military personnel on active duty are prohibited from such activities.

The risk, on the other hand, as figure 3.9 points out, is that when an agency has one (or a few) big sponsoring clientele group, its activities come under so much scrutiny that it has little room to maneuver and can become what some have termed a captive agency. In other words, an interest group can have so much power over an agency's activities that it almost entirely controls the agency's destiny. By contrast, several strong, supportive groups may very well enhance an agency's flexibility, freedom of choice, and autonomy. If several groups surround an agency, the agency can selectively choose its supporters according to *its* interests and not be a captive to any single interest group. Conversely, weak interest group support may mean a weak bureau with either limited or wide autonomy. The size of an agency relative to its surrounding interests has a considerable influence over its autonomy also. No single business enterprise, not even General Motors, can match the annual 300-billion-dollar budget of the Department of Defense. DoD has, therefore, a greater degree of flexibility in dealing with General Motors, by comparison with, say, a city bureaucracy in Pontiac, Michigan, a town in which GM's plant operations dominate Pontiac's life (the economy and future of Pontiac are intimately connected with and dependent upon General Motors' activities there).

"Good Government" or Public Interest Groups

Good government groups purporting to promote the public interest have operated for some time at the local level. Today, moderate-sized communities have several hundred civic organizations promoting "the good of the community," and even the smallest towns have one or two groups that are at least nominally interested in community welfare. Some civic associations with small memberships specialize in relatively narrow fields or even on single

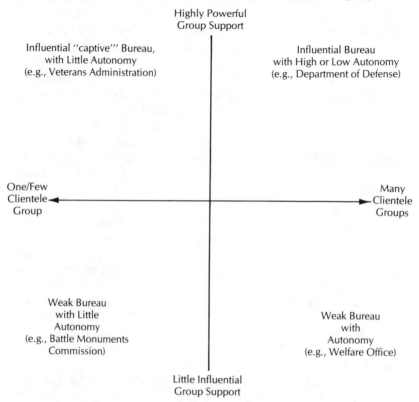

FIGURE 3.9
Relationship between Numbers and Size of Interest Group Support and Agency Power

Highly Powerful
Group Support

Influential "captive'" Bureau,
with Little Autonomy
(e.g., Veterans Administration)

Influential Bureau
with High or Low Autonomy
(e.g., Department of Defense)

One/Few
Clientele ◄─────────────────────────► Many
Group   Clientele
                                     Groups

Weak Bureau
with Little
Autonomy
(e.g., Battle Monuments
Commission)

Weak Bureau
with
Autonomy
(e.g., Welfare Office)

Little Influential
Group Support

themes, such as taxpayer associations that perennially call for reduced government spending. Other associations have broad agendas for reform and attract a cross section of individuals. The League of Women Voters, for instance, acts as a lobby for "good government" causes. Many public interest groups may indeed be only "letterhead organizations" that operate with little more than post office mail drops, but others are well financed, have large memberships, and are highly visible in local, state, and federal activities.

Reformers have long been visible on the national level as well, but powerful and well-staffed public interest groups sprouted at the national level only during the 1960s. In this era John Gardner set up Common Cause, and Ralph Nader, Public Citizen, whose principal aim was to promote "the common cause" and "the public good." In the 1970s conservative "good government" groups, such as the Heritage Foundation and the American Enterprise Institute, emerged as powerful and well-organized forces. Staffed with eager, aggressive volunteers and a small cadre of professionals, these groups on the right, left, or in the center work full-time at fact finding, research, position taking, and generating publicity over a wide range of public issues. The use of computers, mass mailings, television, and other high-tech innovations in the 1980s has made these groups highly influential forces in shaping public policies at all levels of government. Normally their emphases at both the local and national levels are directed at legislative activities; that is, at influencing legislation and supporting sympathetic candidates.

But executive departments are not immune to their activities. First, much of these groups' activities involve monitoring executive agencies—collecting facts, publicizing wrongdoing, researching actions. Nader's organization is composed of several units, many devoted exclusively to exposing federal agencies' wrongdoings, researching their actions, and serving as "watchdogs." Nader units such as the Health Research Group, the Tax Reform Research Group, and the Critical Mass Energy Project aim at having input into government agencies. Nader's Visitor's Center arranges tours through many agencies to help publicize bureaucratic activities to interested citizens and visitors to Washington, D.C.

Second, these groups have played important legal roles in prodding executive agencies to litigate against industry. Nader's Raiders were instrumental in getting the Food and Drug Administration to ban certain unsafe food additives and in getting the Department of Transportation to tighten auto safety standards. They pushed hard for the EPA investigation into the problems of acid rain and for the clean-up of ethylene dibromide. Nader's organizations successfully petitioned the Civil Aeronautics Board to require nonsmoking sections on airplanes. They have been instrumental in prodding regulatory agencies to provide consumer groups with continuous representation in agency rule-making processes.

Third, these groups are not only confrontational but also cooperative; in some cases they actually do research for public agencies that the agencies cannot do for themselves. Some localities regularly rely upon Chambers of Commerce to collect and evaluate economic data for the community and region. Local chapters of the League of Women Voters often provide forums for the discussion and debate of salient administrative issues and opportunities for local public administrators to "educate" the public on particular issues. At the national level such respected institutions as the Council on Foreign Relations and the Brookings Institution are important sources of facts, public information, and policy analysis that are utilized by many federal agencies. Their services can be contracted-out for training agency personnel or doing important studies that can influence fundamental agency actions. This type of advisory service is becoming an increasingly strong influence over bureaucratic activity.

Fourth, public interest groups can further aid bureaucracy by advocating policy positions. PTA groups at the local level argue for educational policies that education officials frequently are not able or are unwilling to openly advocate themselves. Environmental groups at the national level often become spokespersons for "good causes" that employees of the EPA cannot openly advocate.

Finally, in some cases these groups actually take over and run agencies. Jill Claybrook, one-time director of Nader's Congress Watch, was appointed by President Carter in 1977 to head the Highway Safety Administration. Dozens of the Heritage Foundation's policy specialists were channeled into the White House and numerous federal agencies after Reagan's election in 1980. Their transition papers and personnel expertise were key factors in directing Reagan's presidency. Indeed, these public interest groups have increasingly become the "shadow cabinet" of U.S. government (serving as convenient places for out-of-power public officials to live, work, and criticize the incumbents).

Power Elites and Informal Advisors

At every level of government there are informal leaders and advisors who also make important inputs into bureaucratic operations. On the national level it may be "wise old men" such as former secretary of state Henry Kissinger who are asked to lead a commission on Central American policy and therefore on an ad hoc basis advise the State Department on its Central American policies, or such as Robert Strauss, a powerful lawyer-lobbyist, who as former head of the Democratic National Committee can informally exert influence on public agency activities through numerous friendships and connections. Lawyers and lobbyists especially serve this role in municipalities and state capitals as well as in Washington, D.C. Strauss once spoke of himself as "a Washingtonian insider: You're sort of like an animal in the jungle. As you learn to move around the jungle, you develop a sense of trouble without knowing it's there. In Washington, I think I can sniff out the sides and dimensions of a problem."[12] Through his long, intimate acquaintance with the inner workings of Washington and his ties to money and influence as a partner in one of Washington's largest law firms (Akin, Gump, Strauss, Hauer and Felt), Strauss can inform his clients about key government decisions that have affected or will affect them. He is not only a source of insider tips but can also directly pressure agencies for favorable decisions on behalf of his clients. He can even secure the appointment of friends within key agencies, departments, and offices. As Strauss points out, a lot happens on the basis of these informal friendships with "people who run with me and I run with, and trust me, as I do them. We've been involved together over the years; we all ended up in the same orbit."[13].

On the local level, the "court house gang" or "East Side club" can exert these same types of pressures upon local bureaucracies in numerous hidden yet important ways. The extent of their power, however, varies considerably from city to city. As Edward Banfield found in Chicago when Richard J. Daley was mayor, the mayor and the Democratic Machine were clearly in charge of local government. They could decide upon or ratify almost every matter that went on in local agencies.[14] By contrast, in the classic study *Who Governs?* Robert Dahl paints a very different portrait of New Haven's power structure under Mayor Richard Lee.[15] There power elites were fluid, open, and ever-changing; and who got involved was largely dependent upon the issue at hand. In short, New Haven's power elites were "pluralistic." No single group dominated the city government, but, rather, different individuals and groups became involved as issues and events changed. New Haven's power elite was neither uniform nor evident and thus had less clear or sustained influence inside city hall.

Whether power elites are open or closed, static or changing, concentrated or pluralistic depends to a great extent upon the locale and its peculiarities. Location determines, in other words, who they are and how they operate and what leverage they exert upon administrative organizations. In some places they may not even be able to fix a single parking ticket; elsewhere they might run the entire bureaucracy from behind the scenes. Floyd Hunter in his classic power study of Atlanta, *Community Power Structure,* found this to be the case in that city: "The [power] structure is a dominant policy-making group using the machinery of government as a bureaucracy for the attainment of certain goals coordinate with the interests of the policy-making group."[16] While Hunter's methodology remains controversial, his views of Atlanta's informal yet influential "hidden" power elites were probably correct, at least at the time of his study.

Local "influentials" may be propelled dramatically upward to the national scene. President Carter's staff from Georgia exercised considerable influence in formal bureaucratic posts (for example, the Office of Management and Budget's director, Bert Lance) and also in informal ones. President Reagan's "California Kitchen Cabinet" served in much the same role in the 1980s. Some of its members, such as Edwin Meese, Charles Wick, and William French, headed important federal organizations, while others exercised influence from informal advisory positions on the outside. Increasingly, wives of U.S. presidents seem to serve in this outside but very real and powerful advisory capacity, as Rosalyn Carter and Nancy Reagan have demonstrated recently.

On the whole, power elites exercise their influence through informal friendships and ties with government officials they work with, know, or grew up with. They can get friends appointed, remove enemies, thwart the careers of others. Through their superior knowledge of the rules of the game, they also can access bureaucratic data, knowledge, and inside bureaucratic processes. Further, they can more aggressively assert their rights, prerogatives, and privileges involving government services, perks and benefits. This assertiveness stands in sharp contrast with the attitudes of the lower class individuals that Gideon Sjoberg, Richard Bryan, and Buford Farris studied: "The lower

class person stands in awe of bureaucratic regulations and frequently is un-
aware that he has a legal and moral claim to certain rights and privileges. More
often, however, it is the lack of knowledge of the system's technicalities and
back stage regions that is responsible for the lower class person's inability to
manipulate a bureaucratic system to his advantage."[17]

Finally, as Hugh Heclo has recently observed, on the national level these
power elites frequently exert influence through chains of "issue networks."[18]
From behind the scenes, they fund and build conservative think tanks like the
Heritage Foundation which originally was developed by a conservative beer
magnate, Adolph Coors, or those for more liberal groups; for example, the
Brookings Institution, traditionally a home for out-of-power Democrats.
These issue-advocating groups, foundations, associations, and institutions
can exert powerful influences at the national level. They also, as has already
been pointed out, set policies for public bureaucracy and increasingly are a
source of its top administrative leadership.

Major Institutional Actors: Fourth-Level Inputs

The first three levels of inputs to U.S. bureaucracy exert influence on bureaucracy from outside the government. The fourth level involves the critical inputs to bureaucracy from within government. These are the governmental institutions surrounding every public agency, office, department, and unit of
executive bureaucracy—elected or appointed chief executives and their staffs,
legislators and their staffs, courts and other offices, agencies, bureaus, and
departments. Because of their frequently immediate proximity to public bureaucracy and their various influential inputs, they are perhaps the most important influences on growth, stability, and decline of an administrative organization. As figure 3.10 shows, their inputs can be either supportive or hostile
to an agency.

Chief Executives and Their Staff Inputs

Most units of U.S. bureaucracy report to an elected chief executive. In the
federal government, it is the president of the United States; in a state, it is the
governor; and at the local level, it is the mayor. Political appointees at all three
levels of government can also be the chief executives to whom an agency, bureau, office, or administrative unit reports. Normally, each of these chief executives, elected or appointed, has a very considerable staff that provides
budget, personnel, and legal advice to their chief executive. A bureau within
a major federal department might very well confront several levels of these
overhead executive staffs. For instance, the director of the Bureau of Land
Management within the Interior Department must deal with several levels of
chief executives and their staffs—an assistant secretary for Land and Water
Resources; the secretary of Interior and his staff; and the president and the
executive office of the president. A simple budget or personnel request would

FIGURE 3.10
Supportive/Hostile Institutional Forces Surrounding Bureaucracy

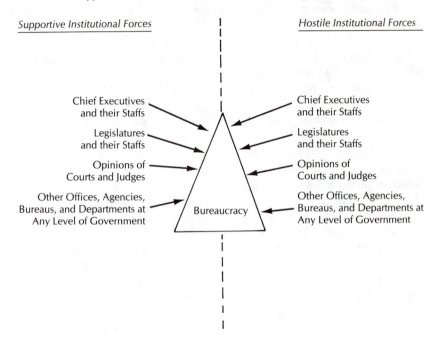

have to be okayed upward through these staff levels, at times making for a lengthy and detailed review process. Opposition—or a veto—at any level may block the bureau's request. The same may be true within large state or local governments. Several executives and hierarchical staff levels exist through which an agency or bureau must report.

In the years since the Brownlow Commission Report (1937) stated that "the president needs help," EoP has grown into a bureaucracy of formidable proportions. Today EoP has thirteen separate offices and over 1,600 employees, who exercise enormous influence over a wide range of budgetary, personnel, and policy fields within the executive branch. Indeed, other executive departmental staffs have become so large that they often do not speak with one voice. The Office of Management and Budget, for example, might work to cut the Department of Defense's budget while the National Security Council, also a part of EoP, might be working to increase it. EoP's Council on Environmental Quality may actively work for an Environmental Protection Agency regulation while EoP's Council of Economic Advisers may oppose it because of its economic consequences. Thus executives and their staffs can make diverse and sometimes contradictory demands upon the same agency.

What sorts of specific key inputs do they make relative to public bureaucracies?

First and foremost, chief executives and their staffs establish broad policy mandates and priorities for public organizations. Presidents, governors, and mayors are elected as chief executives to do something. Their party platforms and campaign statements are full of promises (well over 600 were on record in 1976 for Jimmy Carter and 250 for Ronald Reagan in 1980). Normally these are broad promises, not necessarily specific details about a particular bureaucracy; e.g., Reagan's pledges to "cut taxes," "strengthen defenses," and "cut government social programs." However, the year after Reagan became president these pledges were translated into very real changes in the federal bureaucracy—i.e., expanded defense budget and programs, severe cuts in social programs, plus an overall three-year federal tax reduction, which in turn increased pressures for deeper cuts in social programs.

President Reagan, as have most presidents since John F. Kennedy, relies upon transition team task force reports in formulating the direction of the new administration. Transition teams study every federal agency in some depth in order to provide explicit policy directions to various agencies. They are also instrumental in building the cadre of their new leadership within bureaucracy. For example, read the following principal recommendation to then-governor Ronald Reagan on May 19, 1980, from a senior consultant to his campaign, M. Peter McPherson, then a staff member at the Heritage Foundation, regarding what the Republican candidate should stress for the U.S. foreign aid program: "The United States foreign aid program should be changed to emphasize self-help and technology transfer rather than resource transfer. Studies have shown a higher 'rate of return,' for 'investments in the self-help/technology transfer programs.' "[19]

After the 1980 election McPherson became a top political appointee at the Agency for International Development and spent much of his time promoting just that policy recommendation for AID. McPherson's appointment demonstrates a second important input of chief executives to bureaucracy: namely, in hiring, firing, promoting, rewarding, and punishing personnel. A president of the United States appoints the top 1,600 executive branch officials; a medium-sized state governor, maybe 200 or more cabinet and sub-cabinet level officials; and a middle-sized community mayor, normally far fewer. These appointed agency heads and staff officials are crucial to an elected executive's ability to shape and control the bureaucracy. They link the candidate's campaign potential with the office holder's actual performance. Normally, at the start of their terms, chief executives give these appointments their greatest care and attention. Joseph Califano, Jr., for instance, in his book *Governing America*[20] describes how making key personnel appointments was his first priority after his appointment as President Jimmy Carter's new secretary of Health, Education and Welfare. Califano could select 200 of 150,000 employees at HEW. He gave priority to those "who shared his philosophy of government at HEW'' and could bring skills that would complement his own. His appointment of Hale Champion, for example, as the deputy secretary, or number two man, was based upon Champion's reputed ability to implement HEW's programs at the state level, his administrative toughness, and his sense of humor, which Califano felt he needed at HEW. Champion, Califano later reflected, was a wise choice and one for which he, Califano, was much praised. But personnel appointments can become sources of great difficulties. Califano was criticized most severely over his appointment of a personal staff cook in the secretary's own executive dining room during a period when President Carter was preaching austerity in federal government spending. This appointment became an early source of scandal that dogged Califano with unwanted publicity until the cook was dismissed.

Not appointing personnel, though, can be useful as well to a chief executive. President Reagan's failure to appoint key agency heads for several months in social service departments such as Education, Health and Human Services, and Housing and Urban Development, weakened these agencies' abilities to defend themselves against the new administration's determination to cut their budgets and thus proved to be a highly effective strategy for implementing Reagan's overall philosophy and agenda. On the other hand, his appointment of James Miller III to replace Michael Pertshuk as chairman

FIGURE 3.11
Political Appointees Selected to Key Posts in the Administration Is an Important Way a President Controls the Direction of Bureaucracy

The Choices of Top Economists to Guide National Economic Policies at the Council of Economic Advisors & Federal Reserve Over the Last 3 Decades Have Reflected Presidential Ideological and Party Commitments

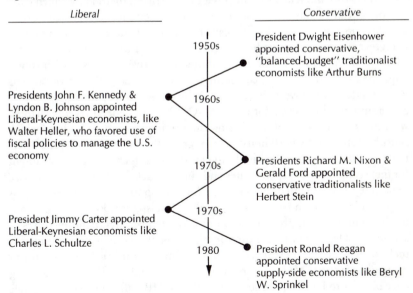

Liberal   *Conservative*

1950s — President Dwight Eisenhower appointed conservative, "balanced-budget" traditionalist economists like Arthur Burns

Presidents John F. Kennedy & Lyndon B. Johnson appointed Liberal-Keynesian economists, like Walter Heller, who favored use of fiscal policies to manage the U.S. economy — **1960s**

1970s — Presidents Richard M. Nixon & Gerald Ford appointed conservative traditionalists like Herbert Stein

President Jimmy Carter appointed Liberal-Keynesian economists like Charles L. Schultze — **1970s**

1980 — President Ronald Reagan appointed conservative supply-side economists like Beryl W. Sprinkel

of the Federal Trade Commission decisively moved that agency away from regulatory activism.

Chief executives can direct the activities of bureaucracies through their personal involvement with their administrations. An activist mayor like former William Schaefer of Baltimore, Maryland, toured his city daily and then wrote memos to various city agencies about such jobs as picking up the trash here, fixing that broken schoolyard swing, cutting down a dead tree limb there, checking on a complaint over in that neighborhood. His frequent comment was, "If I can see it, why can't you?" But more often, especially in larger federal bureaucracies, chief executives cannot "eyeball" problems but must rely upon their appointees and staffs to exercise procedural direction and management oversight of bureaucracies. Particularly in the Reagan administration, the Office of Management and Budget (OMB) under David Stockman increasingly sought to exercise this "micromanagement" of agency operations through OMB's policy procedures. OMB staffs have established detailed procedures to control bureaucratic actions of subordinates. A bureau chief that requests, for instance, policy changes that require legislative action forwards his request through OMB, which, in turn, indicates: (1) that it has no objection and that therefore the agency can proceed with its proposal to Congress; (2) that it opposes the proposal and that therefore the agency cannot proceed; or (3) that the proposal is in accordance with the president's program and will have the full and active support of the president. Similarly, at the departmental level, various personnel including legal, budget, and management staffs exercise much the same policy oversight and "signoff" of actions of subordinate units.

Allocating monetary resources is a fourth critical method by which chief executives can exercise their influence over public bureaucracy. The Budget and Accounting Act of 1921 first gave to presidents the authority to present Congress with an executive budget. Most state and local governments have followed the practice of submitting annual executive budgets, which is perhaps the most direct way of controlling the bureaucracy. Executive budgets give presidents (or governors or mayors) the ability to set spending priorities and adjust funding levels for agencies. OMB at the federal level is charged with this responsibility of developing the president's annual budget, which must be approved by both houses of Congress. President Reagan quite effectively in 1981 used the executive budget process as his chief policy instrument for increasing defense expenditures and cutting back funding to social service departments and regulatory agencies. With supporters in Congress he was largely able to sustain these cuts in funding levels. Also, Reagan's emphasis on drug enforcement programs was implemented through rapid increases in the Justice Department's funding levels. Over the years various budgetary techniques such as Performance Budgeting, Planning, Programming-Budgeting System, Management by Objectives, and Zero-based Budgeting have been introduced by presidents and their OMB staffs precisely to improve oversight and control of funds to ensure that they are allocated in accordance with presidential policies. The budgetary devices have been used with various degrees of success at the local level as well.

Other important methods of bureaucratic control by chief executives include: the power to reorganize—Congress has granted presidents limited powers to reorganize executive agencies; control over agency litigation—the Justice Department approves appeals and interprets statuatory laws for federal agencies; control over whether or not to enforce laws—these decisions are also carried out by the Department of Justice.

In general, stopping or vetoing agency actions is easier than getting them started, as President Carter discovered early in his administration:

> Even the President of the United States, with the august power of that imposing office can be overwhelmed by the incredible obdurateness of the organization. *The New York Times* relates how, after assuming office, Carter detected mice in the Oval Office; the very focal point of the presidency. He called the General Services Administration who then came and handled the matter. Shortly after Carter continued to hear mice, but worse, one died in the wall and the stench was quite noticeable during the formal meetings. However, when he again called the GSA, he was told that they had carefully exterminated all the mice; therefore, any new mice must be 'exterior' mice, and exterior work is apparently the province of the Interior Department. They at first demurred but eventually a 'joint task force' was mounted to deal with the problem.[21]

Agency action can be stymied not only by bureaucratic inertia and overlapping or confused jurisdictions but also by overlapping or confusing signals from the administration itself. An OMB directive may differ from that of a departmental secretary, assistant secretary, deputy assistant secretary, and so on. Rarely do all these multiple levels and their many staffs speak as one. A recent proposal by the secretary of the navy for recommissioning old battleships was supported by the secretary of defense but opposed by the DoD deputy secretary and OMB's director, thereby providing divided leadership on this issue. In such circumstances, what is a subordinate agency to do? Walter G. Held writes that in these cases, "bureau leaders . . . must be able to assess the importance of the various and often conflicting communications coming from the power structures in the presidential line of influence, which do not necessarily follow the organizational chain of command. The decision to respond favorably, to be inactive, or to take actions offsetting communications they judge to be harmful to the programs for which they are responsible is critical and requires the development of special skills."[22]

Legislatures and Their Staff Inputs

The creation of agencies and their continued survival ultimately depend upon legislative bodies—Congress at the federal level, state legislatures for those agencies in state government, and in counties or cities, county boards of supervisors or city councils. Public bureaucracy at every level is ultimately a crea-

ture of the legislature and dependent on the legislature for its survival. Although most elected legislators are all too prone to "damn the bureaucracy"
on the campaign trail, they, in fact, provide the legal mandate for its existence
by establishing not only its basic missions but also in many cases its fundamental organizational structure, staffing patterns, work rules, wage rates, top
appointees, procurement procedures, accounting and auditing requirements,
methods for citizen access to administrative information and various informal
inputs into agency activities, and much more. In constitutional theory the executive and legislature are separate units, but administrative units in reality
are significantly interdependent and interconnected with legislative decisions.

On these and most other matters, however, Congress rarely acts as a
whole body, for as Robert S. Lorsch points out, "Congress has become so pon-
derous that it can hardly act on a significant legislation except under threat of
calamity or force of overwhelming political pressure."[23] Rather, as Woodrow
Wilson said nearly a century ago, "Congress at work is Congress in Committees."[24] Much the same is true for state legislatures and city councils; their
work is done largely in committees. And it is in the committees and subcommittees of the legislature that the major inputs for bureaucracy are generated,
decided on, and enacted.

At the federal level this process is a highly fragmented one. There are
over 250 committees and subcommittees in the House and Senate, with numerous overlapping and competing influences. In practice, in any one executive unit or policy field there are several legislative committees and subcommittees with jurisdiction over a federal agency.

The annual funding requests of DoD, for example, are decided by the
House and Senate Appropriations Committee (with the House reviewing
first). The House and Senate Budget committees set the total budget ceiling
as well as the ceiling for each functional area, such as defense. The House and
Senate Armed Service Committee reviews the policies, programs, and activities of each agency in DoD and authorizes specific commitments for funding
these choices. The House Government Operations and Senate Governmental
Affairs committees examine how closely DoD agencies conformed to congressional mandates in performing their tasks and spending their funds. Here
alone, eight committees and a large number of subcommittees are involved
with the work of DoD. And there can be many other overseers as well: the
House and Senate's Rules committees schedule hearings on defense issues;
the House and Senate's Foreign Affairs committees involve themselves in
overseas matters affecting the military, and the House and Senate Judiciary
committees are concerned with many of DoD's legal matters.

A fragmented, particularistic, and specialized committee and subcommittee system leads to fragmented, particularistic, and specialized legislative
inputs into federal bureaucracy. Except for controversial matters like funding
for the B-1 bomber or the Panama Canal Treaty, Congress rarely addresses a

problem as a body. Congress generally accepts the decisions of its committees. The resulting inputs are frequently mixed and contradictory ones that chief executives and their staffs, offices, agencies, and bureaus must learn to read.

The system leads not only to diverse inputs but also to bureaucratic conservatism and favoritism toward key committees and their members. In 1979, for example, the Pentagon proposed closing Fort Monroe, an antiquated army base in Hampton, Virginia. The fort is a relic from the War of 1812 and actually has a moat around it. It now has little use, and shutting down the base could save taxpayers $10 million annually. But Senator Paul S. Trible, Jr. (Rep.–Va.), in 1982 the ranking Republican on a House subcommittee overseeing military facilities, inserted language in that year's appropriations bill barring the closing of Fort Monroe until the Pentagon had put together a detailed "socioeconomic impact statement" on how the closing of the base would affect the surrounding community. He challenged the Pentagon's estimated cost savings from its closure and secured the requirement that DoD would have to dig up and preserve all the historic artifacts in and around Fort Monroe before opening the base to the public as a kind of museum. This would cost an estimated $30 million, thus making it more expensive to close the base than to keep it operating. Fort Monroe remains today an active military base.[25]

Administrative leaders thus keep a watchful eye on the personalities and the particular constituent interests involved in congressional committees and subcommittees that oversee their organizations. Shifts in these personalities or in committee jurisdictions can significantly alter what happens to a given agency. Administrative agencies are also attentive to key members of these committees and their staffs, because the role and influence of congressional staffs have grown enormously over the past decades. Staffs not only are a source of technical advice to committee members, they also draft the bills that affect agencies and increasingly have provided key political appointees inside agencies through sponsorship by powerful House or Senate members. Furthermore, since 1970 large influential congressional oversight organizations, such as the Office of Technology Assessment and the Congressional Budget Office, have been established, and others such as the General Accounting Office and the Congressional Reference Service, have greatly expanded their oversight activities. As Louis Fisher, a noted scholar on this topic, writes: "The growth of agency and congressional staffs has placed a heavy strain on traditional techniques of legislative oversight and the dependence on good-faith agency efforts. Congress now has the resources to delve more deeply into administration. As the gap between the branches widens, because of staff build-up and turnover, Congress is less able and less willing to rely on customary methods of control. Oral agreements are being replaced by committee report language, which is giving way to statutory directives."[26]

Congressional oversight may indeed be shifting from informal to formal controls as Fisher suggests, though the formal controls exercised by legislators—particularly by committee and subcommittee members—over

FIGURE 3.12

**The Power of Members of Congress to Initiate and Conduct Investigations of Bureaucracy
Is a Key Legislative Power in Exercising Oversight Control of Federal Bureaucracy**

STROM THURMOND, S.C., CHAIRMAN

CHARLES McC. MATHIAS, JR., MD.   JOSEPH R. BIDEN, JR., DEL.
PAUL LAXALT, NEV.   EDWARD M. KENNEDY, MASS.
ORRIN G. HATCH, UTAH   ROBERT C. BYRD, W. VA.
ROBERT DOLE, KANS.   HOWARD M. METZENBAUM, OHIO
ALAN K. SIMPSON, WYO.   DENNIS DeCONCINI, ARIZ.
JOHN P. EAST, N.C.   PATRICK J. LEAHY, VT.
CHARLES E. GRASSLEY, IOWA   MAX BAUCUS, MONT.
JEREMIAH DENTON, ALA.   HOWELL HEFLIN, ALA.
ARLEN SPECTER, PA.

VINTON DeVANE LIDE, CHIEF COUNSEL AND STAFF DIRECTOR
MARK H. GITENSTEIN, MINORITY CHIEF COUNSEL

United States Senate

COMMITTEE ON THE JUDICIARY
WASHINGTON, D.C. 20510

February 16, 1983

The Honorable Charles A. Bowsher
The Comptroller General of the
    United States

Dear Mr. Bowsher:

Last October the Attorney General announced the formation of
12 Drug Enforcement Task Forces in addition to the South Florida
Task Force. These Task Forces will put additional resources in the
fight against illicit drug trafficking.

I would like GAO to assist us by gathering information on the
overall planning and management of these Task Forces. Such information
should include:

--how Task Force locations were selected, and what agencies were
  involved in the planning and development of these sites;

--how the Task Forces will coordinate their work with the drug
  enforcement activities of DEA, FBI, Coast Guard, Customs,
  Organized Crime Strike Forces, and U.S. Attorney Offices, and
  what role will be played by the Law Enforcement Coordination
  Committees;

--how the Task Forces will be organized, staffed, administered
  and funded;

--how much of the overall Task Force plan was based on the
  South Florida Task Force effort;and

--how Task Force efforts will be evaluated and whether an
  accurate data base was avilable from which to measure the
  success as outlined by Congress in the report language for the
  appropriation of these task forces.

This material will be very useful in reviewing the success of
these task forces in striking a blow against organized crime and drug
trafficking. I would appreciate my staff being kept informed of your
progress.

Sincerely,

Joseph R. Biden, Jr.
United States Senate

Source: GAO Report on Drug Enforcement Task Forces (1983)

bureaucracy at every level of government have been the primary contemporary means of making legislative inputs into the administrative processes. Summing up, these methods include: (1) establishing the organizations and their basic frameworks through legislation; (2) creating personnel policy covering a wide variety of areas: wages, classification of positions, hours, leaves, working conditions, and so on; (3) conducting investigations of particular agency activities and policies; (4) either formally advising administrative units as part of oversight commissions or informally advising their chief representatives through committee and subcommittee hearings and investigations; (5) fixing budgets and appropriations annually; (6) requesting casework or enacting private bills that require agencies to perform specific tasks for congressional constituents; and (7) passing resolutions and laws specifically requiring agency action or inaction on certain matters. All add up to powerful legislative sources of influence.

Judicial Inputs

The historic 1803 *Marberry vs. Madison* (1 Cranch 137) decision by the U.S. Supreme Court gave the courts authority to review executive decisions. Today federal and state court oversight of executive activities is a well-established tradition. The activities of bureaucrats and bureaucracy at all levels of government come under regular court scrutiny—and the scope of judicial review of administrative activity has expanded enormously since the 1960s. This growth has been fueled by three elements: first, the rapid increase in numbers of lawyers (particularly activist lawyers, such as Nader's Raiders, who are willing to take on "good government causes"); second, increasing numbers of activist judges willing to expand the scope of judicial oversight by hearing and deciding on novel matters with new local interpretations; third, the growth of public-interest law firms, store-front legal services for middle-class citizens, and government-sponsored legal services for the poor (such as the Legal Services Administration). These organizations have given many people their first opportunity to challenge bureaucracy in the courts.

Wider citizen access to courts results in more court cases against bureaucrats. Today educators, police, prison officials, social workers, and many other bureaucrats regularly and increasingly find their behavior challenged and regulated by court decisions. While normally these involve individual cases affecting bureaucratic clientele, at the extreme courts have taken over the operations of entire bureaucracies. This was apparent in numerous school busing cases during the 1960s and 1970s when an activist judge, Frank Johnson of the U.S. District Court in Alabama, directly supervised the state's prisons, mental health programs, and highway patrol for several years. As Donald L. Horowitz, currently a research scholar at the Smithsonian Institution, has commented: "The frequency of litigation challenging governmental actions, especially in the federal courts, has increased," while "the scope of the exception to judicial review of matters committed to agency discretion has been steadily narrowed."[27]

While there are few administrative areas that courts have not ventured into, most often their influence tends to be: first, episodic and particularistic—that is, immediately concerned with remedying the administrative problem at hand, i.e., police brutality, rather than with setting broad, enduring administrative standards and policies; second, courts more often than not are hostile to administrative activity, normally indicating what bureaucrats cannot do, as in cases involving, for example, unfairness to welfare recipients. In brief, courts are good at vetoing bureaucratic actions but poor vehicles for laying down effective methods for carrying out administrative services; third, court decisions tend to be legalistic, i.e., based upon rules, legal reasoning, and precedent rather than attempts to cope with administrative reality and complex issues, as is illustrated by the finding that, for example, "the personnel test was not fair to minorities under the Civil Rights Act." In short, courts reason from *the* case or the law, thus making their administrative inputs hard to transfer elsewhere. Finally, court decisions tend to be based on limited staff resources, analysis, and data (few courts have much staff), which also restricts their inputs to bureaucracy. For example, a remedy to the problems of Oakland's fire department selection procedures may not be applicable to New York's.

What impact, then, do courts have on the administrative process? While sometimes it can be quite dramatic, as in the case of *Brown vs. the Board of Education* (1953), which led to desegregation of the entire U.S. school system, courts, according to one authority

> Function on a basis that is too intermittent, too spotty, too partial, too ill-informed for them to have a major constructive impact on administrative performance. They can stop action in progress, they can slow it down, and they can make it public (their exposing function has been too little noted). Perhaps most important, they can bring moral judgment to bear, for moral evaluation is a traditional judicial strength. But courts cannot build alternative structures, for the customary modes of judicial reasoning are not adequate for this. . . . nor can they interpret complex or specialized data, to secure expert advice, to sense the need to change course, and to monitor performance after decision. Courts can limit the discretion of others, but they find it harder to exercise their own discretion where that involves choosing among multiple, competing alternatives.[28]

In short, courts can and do have inputs into bureaucracy, but these tend to be restricted to individual cases that lawyers, judges, and juries decide upon on an ad hoc basis.

Other Offices, Bureaus, Agencies, and Departments Inputs

While courts may have weak long-term influences over administrative units, other bureaus, agencies, departments, and offices do have considerable control over their futures. As Herbert Kaufman has noted: "Every agency has natural enemies as well as natural allies."[29] The success of almost every action that an agency undertakes is dependent upon help from other agencies. No agency is entirely self-sufficient largely because of the functional division of authority by legislative bodies involving any policy field. Congress, for example, authorizes the Internal Revenue Service within the Treasury Department to collect taxes but authorizes the Tax Division within the Justice Department to prosecute tax law violators. Further, Congress has established the Council of Economic Advisers (CEA) within the White House to evaluate overall federal spending and revenues, which means that the CEA (along with the Treasury and other agencies) may recommend changes in tax policies. This situation creates considerable potential for both cooperation and rivalry.

A particularly intense conflict can ensue when agencies are given similar mandates. For example, the Bureau of Reclamation and the Army Corps of Engineers have been involved with water projects that have created agency rivalry. On the local level police and fire departments sometimes clash over common public safety assignments or limited budgetary resources. Diametrically opposite philosophies create long-term rivalry, as with the EPA's ''pro-conservation'' ethos as opposed to Interior's generally ''pro-development'' outlook.

Particularly in the 1980s, cutbacks are common at many levels of government, and these reductions generate fierce conflicts between bureaus. Again, citing Kaufman: ''The federal treasury is not bottomless and they all draw from it. Some therefore gain at the expense of others. When the federal revenues increase rapidly, the conflicts are minimized. When they do not, the conflicts can grow very sharp. The economic assistance vis-à-vis domestic requirements, or city-oriented agencies versus agricultural and rural agencies, for example, are exceedingly divisive.''[30]

Public agencies are in continuous competition with other government organizations over their missions, resources, autonomy, and clientele. Much like nations in the international arena of world politics, they engage in a struggle to survive, learning to forge alliances for mutual support and protection in order to fend off attacks from competitors and enemies. In an unstable and shifting political environment where the stakes and outcomes are important, there can be room for considerable conflict. But often there is also the possibility of cooperation. At the local level, for example, city police, the county sheriff, the state highway patrol, and federal law enforcement agencies pool their data and engage in informal and formal cooperation on a wide range of law enforcement cases. At the national level, federal agencies assigned to tackle an important problem often cooperate with one another. The recent AIDS epidemic has brought together, for example, public health units at several levels of government in a combined effort to find a cure for this killer disease.

Basic Patterns of Inputs Surrounding Bureaucracy

What sense can we make out of the welter of inputs described in this chapter that perpetually dance around public agencies at every level of government and determine their directions and destinies? Are there discernible patterns of inputs? In brief, how can we sum up the discussion in chapter 3?

FIGURE 3.13

DEPARTMENT OF EDUCATION

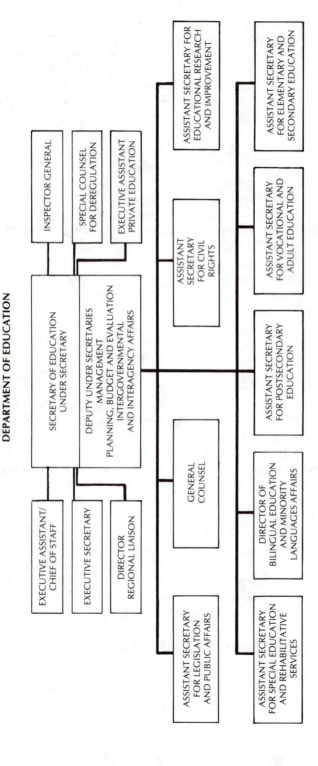

Source: U.S. Government Manual, 1985–86

One thing that should be clear is that inputs affecting agency actions come from many sources. Every public organization is influenced by diverse forces. The dynamics of the U.S. political landscape is pluralistic, pushing and pulling public agencies in many directions. The typical public agency sits in the midst of this fray involving four levels of inputs—i.e., general environment, socioeconomic impacts, and political and institutional forces.

Further, these forces do not affect any two agencies in exactly the same way. Situations vary widely from agency to agency. Inputs affect various parts of even a single agency in diverse and complex ways. For example, the support for or hostility to the major administrative units of the Department of Education exhibits an enormous variety, depending upon which major program one looks at: elementary or secondary education, civil rights, special education, bilingual education, and so on. Each program has a cluster of different interests and forces that surround it and influence its work. Generalization is therefore risky.

Perhaps the most appropriate summary of the seemingly infinite configurations of inputs into public agencies is figure 3.14, which depicts the basic possible patterns of these configurations along a continuum of a two-dimensional plane. The entire plane of the figure is influenced by first-level inputs from the general environment as indicated in the top right hand corner. Level 3 and 4 inputs, political and institutional forces, are shown on the vertical axis. These run from intense attention from numerous groups to near neglect. On the horizontal axis are shown level 2 inputs, socioeconomic forces impacting decisions, ranging from broad, critical inputs to limited and unimportant ones.

On the top left are shown those agencies that have large attentive audiences and large and important socioeconomic impacts. The Federal Reserve Board, which plays a powerful role in regulating the U.S. economy, and the Department of Health and Human Services, which pours vast amounts of money into social programs, exemplify such bureaucracies and their inputs. It is a highly complex, fluid situation, dependent upon a great diversity of inputs, akin to the situation described by Hugh Heclo's concept of "issue network." In the middle of the figure are those agencies with more limited audiences and socioeconomic impacts, such as the Veterans Administration and the Interstate Commerce Commission. These operate within a more customary "classic iron triangle" configuration of inputs, primarily from congressional oversight committees and particular special interest groups. At the extreme bottom right of the figure are shown those agencies, such as the Battle Monuments Commission, that attract little, if any, political or institutional attention because of their limited socioeconomic impact. They do their work routinely, free or almost free of outside control and with limited influence on outside socioeconomic affairs.

Most agencies, however, fall more or less within the center range, in which the "classic iron triangle" arrangement is the norm. Figure 3.15 graphically demonstrates just such an arrangement. In this illustration, an executive bureau—the Peanuts and Tobacco Section of the Price Support Division within the Agricultural Stabilization and Conservation Service of the U.S.

FIGURE 3.14
Influence of Four Levels of Inputs upon Public Bureaucracy—Summary of Impacts

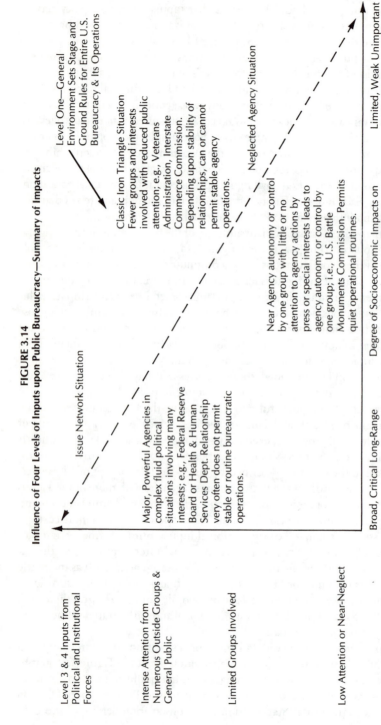

Level 3 & 4 Inputs from Political and Institutional Forces

Intense Attention from Numerous Outside Groups & General Public

Limited Groups Involved

Low Attention or Near-Neglect

Issue Network Situation

Major, Powerful Agencies in complex fluid political situations involving many interests; e.g., Federal Reserve Board or Health & Human Services Dept. Relationship very often does not permit stable or routine bureaucratic operations.

Near Agency autonomy or control by one group with little or no attention to agency actions by press or special interests leads to agency autonomy or control by one group; i.e., U.S. Battle Monuments Commission. Permits quiet operational routines.

Level One—General Environment Sets Stage and Ground Rules for Entire U.S. Bureaucracy & Its Operations

Classic Iron Triangle Situation Fewer groups and interests involved with reduced public attention; e.g., Veterans Administration, Interstate Commerce Commission. Depending upon stability of relationships, can or cannot permit stable agency operations.

Neglected Agency Situation

Broad, Critical Long-Range Impacts

Level Two—Socioeconomic Impacts on Agencies

Degree of Socioeconomic Impacts on Regional, National, World Affairs

Limited, Weak Unimportant and/or Short-term Impacts

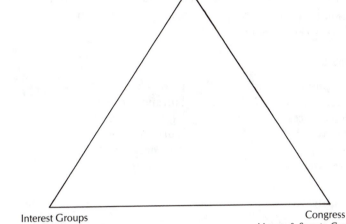

FIGURE 3.15
Classic Iron Triangle Situation

Executive Bureau
Agricultural Stabilization &
Conservation Service, Price
Support & Loan Division,
Peanuts & Tobacco Section,
U.S. Dept. of Agriculture

Interest Groups
Various Tobacco Growers
Associations & Representatives

Congress
House & Senate Committee on
Agriculture; House & Senate
Subcommittee on Tobacco &
Peanuts

Department of Agriculture—takes its marching orders, for the most part, from special interest groups made up of tobacco growers and House and Senate subcommittees concerned with oversight of these affairs.

Summary of Key Points

Every government bureaucracy is surrounded by several external forces that influence its survival, growth, and decline. In this chapter the general environment of bureaucracy as well as three other levels of external pressures were outlined. Socioeconomic factors are the broadest, most pervasive of these external influences. Examples of these factors are population size, shifts in demographic groups, levels of economic activity, technological innovations, and the like. External political actors make up another level. Examples are public opinion, clientele groups, media coverage, and power elites. Yet another level consists of institutional actors within government, such as chief executives and their staffs, legislators and their staffs, courts and other offices, agencies, bureaus, and departments. These external factors come into play and prominence depending on the issue and situation at hand. Some do not get involved at all. The degree of involvement and level of intensity of inputs for any administrative organization depend on the circumstances and the situation. Several may push and pull in opposite directions simultaneously. They may work to promote and perpetuate the organization—or to decimate it.

Generally speaking, though, the patterns of inputs influencing public bureaucracies can be depicted as a continuum, as illustrated by figure 3.14. On opposite extremes are "Issue Network Situations" and "Neglected Agency Situations," within which agencies must function. The more customary position is at the center, the classic iron triangle arrangement of inputs that influence agency actions.

Key Terms

general environment	power elites
socioeconomic factors	bureaucratic inertia
institutional forces	legislative oversight
political forces	judicial review
clientele groups	issue networks
good government groups	iron triangle

Review Questions

1. What factors in the general environment shape U.S. bureaucratic institutions and the behavior of bureaucrats?
2. What are the distinctions between the four levels of inputs—general environment, socioeconomic, political, and institutional?
3. In your view, which ones are the most influential, and why?
4. Why does this chapter argue that the critical legislative inputs to bureaucratic institutions come from committees and subcommittees? Why are these inputs often diverse and contradictory?
5. What are "iron triangles" and how do they differ from "issue networks"?

Notes

1. For an excellent discussion of Max Weber and his views, read H. H. Gerth and C. Wright Mills, *From Max Weber: Essays in Sociology* (NY: Oxford University Press, 1946), particularly the introduction and essay on bureaucracy.
2. George E. Peterson and Thomas Muller, "The Economic and Fiscal Accompaniments of Population Change," in Brian J. L. Berry and Lester P. Silverman, *Population Redistribution and Public Policy* (Washington, DC: National Academy of Sciences, 1980), p. 110.
3. From an executive summary, "The U.S. in the 1980s: Demographic

Trends" (Washington, DC: Population Reference Bureau, Inc., 1980), p. 16.

4. As cited in the *Washington Post*, January 22, 1984, p. G7.

5. Walter Lippmann, *The Phantom Public* (NY: Macmillan, 1925), p. 77.

6. As recounted in Norton Long, *The Polity* (Chicago: Rand McNally, 1962), p. 48.

7. Walter G. Held, "Decision Making in the Federal Government: The Wallace S. Sayre Model," as published in Frederick S. Lane (ed.), *Current Issues in Public Administration*, 2d ed. (NY: St. Martin's Press, 1982), pp. 38–55.

8. As cited in V. O. Key, *Politics, Parties and Pressure Groups*, 4th ed. (NY: Thomas Y. Crowell, 1958), p. 744.

9. Herbert A. Simon, Donald W. Smithburg, and Victor A. Thompson, *Public Administration* (NY: Alfred A. Knopf, 1950), p. 384.

10. Philip Selznick, *TVA and the Grass Roots* (Berkeley: University of California Press, 1949), p. 145.

11. Francis E. Rourke, *Bureaucracy, Politics and Public Policy*, 2d ed. (Boston: Little, Brown, 1976), p. 50.

12. James Conaway, "The Artful Persuader," the *Washington Post Magazine* (November 7, 1982), p. 13.

13. Ibid.

14. Edward C. Banfield, *Political Influence* (NY: Free Press, 1961).

15. Robert A. Dahl, *Who Governs?* (New Haven: Yale University Press, 1962).

16. Floyd Hunter, *Community Power Structure* (Chapel Hill: University of North Carolina Press, 1953), p. 102.

17. Gideon Sjoberg, Ricard A. Brymer, and Buford Farris, "Bureaucracy and the Lower Class," *Sociology and Social Research* 50 (April 1966), p. 47.

18. Hugh Heclo, "Issue Networks and the Executive Establishment," in Anthony King (ed.), *The New Political System* (Washington, DC: The American Enterprise Institute for Public Policy Research, 1978), pp. 87–124.

19. Unpublished transition memo from M. Peter McPherson, senior consultant to the presidential campaign of Governor Ronald Reagan, May 19, 1980, p.1.

20. Joseph A. Califano, Jr., *Governing America* (NY: Simon and Schuster, 1981), chapter 1.

21. *The New York Times*, January 8, 1978, p. 29.

22. Walter G. Held, *Decision Making,* p. 9.

23. Robert S. Lorsch, *Democratic Process and Administrative Law* (Detroit: Wayne State University Press, 1969), p. 12.

24. Woodrow Wilson, *Congressional Government* (Boston: Houghton-Mifflin, 1885).

25. Dale Russakoff, "Grace Panel Finds Pork Barrel Overflowing," the *Washington Post* (January 10, 1984), p. A3.

26. Louis Fisher, *The Politics of Shared Power: Congress and the Executive* (Washington, DC: Congressional Quarterly Press, 1981), p. 109.

27. Donald L. Horowitz, "The Courts as Guardians of the Public Interest," *Public Administration Review* 37 (March/April 1977), p. 150.

28. Ibid.

29. Herbert Kaufman, *Are Government Organizations Immortal?* (Washington, DC: Brookings Institution, 1976), p. 15.

30. Ibid.

Further Readings

A wealth of literature is available on the external environment and its influences upon U.S bureaucracy. Three classics on this subject are E. Pendleton Herring's *Public Administration and the Public Interest* (1936); David B. Truman's *The Governmental Process* (1951), and Emmette S. Redford's *Democracy in the Administrative State* (1969). More recent treatments of this subject are: Francis E. Rourke's *Bureaucracy, Politics and Public Policy*, 2d ed. (1976); Harold Seidman's *Politics, Position and Power*, 4th ed. (1986); Lawrence C. Dodd and Richard L. Schott's *Congress and the Administrative State* (1979); and Louis Fisher's *The Politics of Shared Power* (1981). Also Paul Appleby's *Big Democracy* (1945); William W. Boyer's *Bureaucracy on Trial* (1963); Charles S. Hynneman's *Bureaucracy in a Democracy* (1950); Norton Long's *The Polity* (1966); Don K. Price's *The Scientific Estate* (1965); E. E. Schattschneider's *The Semi-Sovereign People* (1960).

There are several excellent case studies involving these issues, including: Stephen K. Bailey's *Congress Makes a Law* (1950); Raymond A. Bauer, A Ithiel De Sola Pool, and Lewis Anthony Dexter's *American Business and Public Policy* (1963); Daniel M. Berman's *A Bill Becomes a Law*, 2d ed. (1966); James W. Davis, Jr.'s *Little Groups of Neighbors* (1968); A. Lee Fritschler's *Smoking and Politics*, 2d ed. (1975); Philip Selznick's *TVA and the Grass Roots* (1949); Arthur W. Maass's *Muddy Waters—The Army Engineers and the Nation's Rivers* (1951); and Herbert Kaufman's *The Forest Ranger* (1960).

Several useful essays on interest groups and their influence on government are found in Allan J. Cigler and Burdett A. Loomis's *Interest Group Politics* (1983). John Gaus's *Reflections on Public Administration* (1947) offers an especially good treatment of the relationship of general environment to public administration. For a more current view of this subject from a comparative perspective, read Ferrel Heady's *Public Administration: A Comparative Perspective*, 3d ed.(1985). One should not overlook the rich case studies exploring this subject that are available through the Inter-University Case Program, PO Box 229, Syracuse, NY 13210.

4
Inside Public Bureaucracy

Once a young aide to President William Howard Taft kept repeating the phrase "machinery of government" while briefing the president. Taft, so the story goes, became exasperated and turned to a friend and whispered, "My God, the man actually *believes* government is a machine!"

Taft had it right. United States government, especially its bureaucracy, is not an automated assembly line, devoid of human beings, lifeless and machinelike. Quite to the contrary, our public bureaucracy is composed of identifiable clusters of individuals who work and act in influential ways inside the bureaucracy. Each of these subsystems shapes the broad outcomes of bureaucratic institutions. Each competes for power and influence over its particular bureaucracy. These human subsystems perform different tasks in government. Through diverse strategies they aim to achieve different goals with different stakes or outcomes for bureaucracy. Each serves vitally important functions within bureaucracy and significantly determines in various ways what bureaucracy does or does not do and how well it performs these functions. The size and influence of each of these human subgroups vary considerably from agency to agency and locale to locale. Yet many public organizations contain several of these subsystems. Some public operations have all five subsystems, which jockey with one another for influence and status.

The boundary between each of the subsystems is not always clear. They tend to overlap with considerable gray areas between them. Subsystems in different agencies do not always exhibit the same exact dimensions, proportions, or precisely similar characteristics. Nor are all five groups necessarily found in every agency. Sometimes only one or two are represented. In other words, these subsystems are fairly open, fluid, and adaptive to differing organizational contexts and situations. They are also fundamentally *human and political, not machinelike in behavior.* Subsystems do have certain important similarities and differences in their roles, power, status, functions, activities, and influence within public organizations. This chapter will examine the special values, features, outlooks, missions, and roles of each subsystem within organizations and particularly how they affect the outputs of every agency from the inside. Brief descriptions of these five subsystems follow.

Political appointees are those individuals who serve without tenure and whose appointments are based often, though not always, upon political ties or party loyalties.

Professional careerists are various groups of personnel with specialized expertise in specific fields. Positions occupied by these groups are usually based on advanced professional training. This subsystem offers lifetime careers and stresses "rank-in-person" rather than "rank-in-job."

Civil service generalists are usually nonprofessionals who operate under general "merit concepts." Characteristics of this subsystem are tenure, rank-

FIGURE 4.1
Internal Dynamics of America's Public Bureaucracy as Five Subsystems

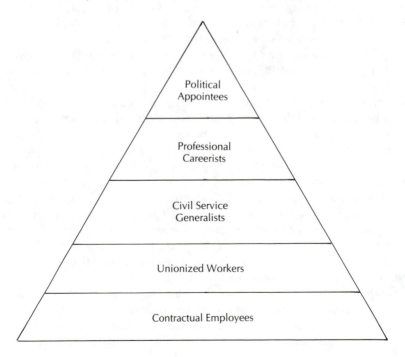

Political
Appointees

Professional
Careerists

Civil Service
Generalists

Unionized Workers

Contractual Employees

in-position, and "classified" hierarchies of positions based upon tasks and responsibilities.

Unionized workers are blue collar and, increasingly, white collar workers whose employment is based upon negotiated contracts between union representatives and management within the jurisdictions they serve.

Contractual employees are untenured workers whose employment with government is directly or indirectly governed by various contractual agreements negotiated with individuals, private firms, nonprofit organizations, and universities for rendering specific services for a limited or specified time. They are not governed by civil service rules nor do they work under union contracts.

The Political Appointee Subsystem: The Birds of Passage

Most political appointees fill the top-level policy-making posts within federal, state, and local bureaucracies. These men and women serve in government without tenure, holding office at the pleasure of the chief elected official, who hires them, promotes them, or dismisses them. At the federal level, political appointees make up a fairly small group, with only about two thousand appointed directly by the president and another four thousand appointed by his subordinates. The number varies considerably in state and local jurisdictions. In some regions where there is no civil service system—particularly rural county governments or the few remaining machine-run cities—virtually all government jobs are handed out on the basis of party loyalty or political patronage. Today, however, most cities and states follow the federal pattern in reserving only top-level policy jobs for political appointees, who serve at the pleasure of a governor or mayor. Particularly in "reformed" or "clean" city and state governments, these posts are few and limited to only the very top levels.

TABLE 4.1
President Reagan Makes 3,925 Political Appointments

Type	Number
PAS[a] positions in cabinet departments	276
PAS positions in independent agencies and regulatory commissions	286
Full-time ambassadors	150
Judges, U.S. marshals, U.S. attorneys	950
Part-time PA[b] and PAS	2,263
Total	3,925

a. PAS = presidential appointment requiring Senate confirmation.
b. PA = presidential appointment not requiring Senate confirmation.
Source: Presidential Personnel Office and Executive Clerk of the White House.
Data and Information is drawn from John W. Macy, Bruce Adams, J. Jackson Walter (eds.), *America's Unelected Government: Appointing the President's Team* (Cambridge, MA: Ballinger Publishing Co., 1983), p. 6.

Within federal bureaucracies, in particular, appointees' lack of tenure limits the length of their employment. The average federal political appointee serves only twenty-two months in office. Hugh Heclo has rightly observed that they are "birds of passage"[1] who recognize from the start that they will not be around for very long. The most they can look forward to is a four-year term, and if a president is reelected (and they are lucky) they *might* be reappointed for longer periods—though that is rare. Transience is their only common trademark. Most, therefore, set their sights and adapt their behavior for the short range by recognizing that if they are to accomplish *anything* in their jobs, they must move quickly. Short-term horizons, limited goals, and quick results tend to characterize their actions. This tendency among political appointees also probably characterizes state and local appointees within jurisdictions where there is a competitive party system. But elsewhere, if the top jobs have little or no turnover, political appointees can look forward to longer tenure in office, thus shifting their time horizons to somewhat longer perspectives.

Generally, though, appointees' job uncertainty means that they have to have another position, outside of government, to fall back on in case they fall out of favor or out of office (a good possibility given the hazards of these untenured posts today). Hence, many political appointees at the federal level are drawn from prestigious law firms or are on leave from big businesses or universities. The pool from which they are drawn is thus quite small and tends to be, but is not always, confined to upperclass individuals who can afford a short time away from their regular lines of work. This qualification also tends to drastically limit the social characteristics of political appointees to white, urban, middle-aged males with advanced educations and ambitions for high-status careers.[2] While President Jimmy Carter attempted to recruit greater numbers of women and minorities into these posts, the bulk of political appointees even in his administration in the late 1970s, and of Ronald Reagan's in the 1980s, was largely drawn from this very small pool, which has changed little over the course of the twentieth century. Political appointees at the state and local levels, particularly as one moves closer to the grass roots, represent much more diversity in talent, training, income, and background. Generally, there is greater heterogeneity and better representation of social groups at lower governmental jurisdictions, though there is by no means a pure popular representation even there.[3]

While there are several prominent examples of political appointees whose faces reappear in government, usually at higher levels of bureaucracy when their party assumes office (George Shultz, Arthur Burns, and Caspar Weinberger crop up repeatedly in Republican administrations, and Harold Brown, and Joseph Califano in Democratic ones), most political appointees have limited backgrounds in government. Very few serve repeated spells in government; few work for more than one administration. Few survive election turnovers in the executive branch. Many simply do not want to stay more than a few years in office, nor can they, because of pressing outside professional or business commitments. Yet most are *drawn from and return to related fields of endeavor*. Western ranchers, businesspersons, and lawyers have tended to occupy the top slots at the Department of the Interior because of their prolonged involvement with western public lands; just as defense contractors, former military officers, and business executives have long been recruited to top political slots at DoD. And most return to these jobs afterwards. Thus different bureaucracies tend to draw their political appointees from different occupational-economic sectors of society as well as from different regions primarily because of these appointees' prior experience with the tasks and activities of the agency. An appropriate ''track record'' in the policy concerns of the

FIGURE 4.2
The Five Rings of Political Appointees in U.S. Public Bureaucracy

Elected Chief Executives President, Governor, & Mayor

''The Inner Cabinet''—The Top Cabinet Positions

Other Heads of Major Departments or Agencies in the Cabinet ''Outer Cabinet''

Major Deputies, Asst. Secretaries, or Heads of Noncabinet Agencies

Political Staffs in Agencies, Advisors, Bureau Chiefs, Regional Directors

Quasi Political-Career Personnel such as S.E.S. Personnel

agency, and the correct party identification, and especially policy positions that are in accord with the chief executive's, are important qualifications for such appointments.

Their specific policy roles in bureaucracy can be conceived of as loose-jointed, concentric rings that emanate outward from the office of the elected chief executive—a president, governor, or mayor. The most powerful appointees are those who occupy leadership roles within the major Cabinet-rank departments, sometimes referred to at the federal level as the inner Cabinet. The inner Cabinet is composed of the secretaries of Defense, State, and of the Office of Management and Budget, as well as senior noncareer or career ambassadors to major governments, such as the Soviet Union. These individuals are responsible for the operations of the largest public agencies (like DoD) and subsequently have powerful policy agenda-setting functions (like OMB). Similarly, inner Cabinets, made up of those closest to the governor or mayor and exercising major policy-organizational tasks, are found at state and local levels as well, though their titles differ. Inner Cabinet members at the federal level are often at the White House with the president or are representing their agencies before Congress. They are responsible for setting—and defending—the major policy priorities of the president and the agency they represent. They also exert the overall leadership within their particular organization, appoint numerous political personnel within the organization, and represent it before the media and special interest groups. Their most important function within government is to translate the campaign platforms and promises of the elected officials into administrative actions of major policy-administrative importance to the chief executive—the president, governor, or mayor. In short, they serve as linchpins between election-night rhetoric and actual institutional performance.

Most elected chief executives are well aware of the importance of this group of men and women and give a good deal of consideration to their selection. (Appointees normally also require confirmation by the Senate at the federal level and approval by legislatures of state and local governments.) A successful track record in government or in large, complex organizations is a critical requirement. For example, Harold Brown became secretary of Defense in the Carter administration but only after having served as secretary of the air force in President Johnson's previous Democratic administration and afterwards having headed California Institute of Technology. George Shultz, secretary of State in Reagan's Cabinet, held prior posts in the Nixon administration as secretary of Labor and director of OMB. He later served as president of the BECTAL Corporation, a large California-based multinational construction company. While their loyalty to the president and his program must be unquestionable, these appointees normally have not been highly visible or active in his previous political campaigns, aside from preparing briefing papers or holding ad hoc advisory roles. Knowledge of the job, its policy issues, ability to be "team players," and competence at running a major organization are generally preferred in order to make the president look good and to implement his programs within and throughout the bureaucracy.

The next ring, or the outer Cabinet, is composed of men and women who see the president (or governor or mayor) less frequently but nevertheless hold Cabinet rank (also normally requiring Senate or legislative confirmation). They are frequently charged with running a major public agency such as the Department of Housing and Urban Development or the Department of Corrections at the state level. They are a rung below the inner Cabinet in *informal* power and status only, for their legal titles and prerogatives are normally much the same as those of their counterparts in the inner Cabinet. Indeed, they may have many of the same responsibilities, such as directing a large department, providing its leadership, setting its policy agenda, defending it before Congress, and so on. Because the work of their agencies is considered of less priority, they see the president less frequently, are involved in fewer of the major policy meetings, and are given, on the whole, less attention by the White House than inner Cabinet members. This is not to say that they or their work is unimportant. What they do is simply of less, but sometimes only slightly less, urgency to the success or failure of the administration. Generally, they do not decide major war/peace or prosperity/depression issues. Hence, they are less visible to the public eye, or for that matter, to the president's.

The third level is generally termed the sub-Cabinet. It is composed of deputy secretaries, assistant secretaries, and administrative heads of major non-Cabinet agencies and bureaus. These individuals also occupy important policy-making posts, and sometimes highly sensitive and critical ones, such as that of deputy attorney general in the Department of Justice, who is normally responsible for the daily management of the department's activities, or of the assistant secretary for International Security Affairs in the Department of Defense who is charged with shaping broad strategic policies within DoD. These men and women are generally more specialized in particular fields of expertise than the inner or outer Cabinet members. While they may have had a variety of experiences and backgrounds in government, business, law, or the professions, their training and work experiences tend to be more appropriate to the positions that they occupy. They have also usually had considerable experience handling political issues related to these offices and are expected to take positions on these issues in accordance with the president's overall priorities.

For example, Robert F. Burford, director of the Bureau of Land Management in the Reagan administration, before his appointment to this post had been a long-time Colorado rancher and Republican speaker of the Colorado

TABLE 4.2
Salaries of Top Federal Political Officials

Position	Salary 1985	% Increase Since 1970
U.S. President	$200,000	0
Cabinet Officers	$ 80,100	33.5
Deputy Secretaries & Heads of Major Agencies	$ 69,800	64
Assistant Secretaries, General Counsels	$ 67,200	77
Directors of Major Units of Agencies	$ 63,800	77

Source: Statistical Abstracts of the U.S.

House of Representatives. He had also been one of the leaders of the "sage brush rebellion," fomented by a group of westerners who strongly backed President Reagan's election in 1980 and were vitally concerned with federal land policies. And Dr. Everett Koop, surgeon general of the U.S. Public Health Service in the Reagan administration, was previously a practicing Philadelphia surgeon. He was also politically active in the national antiabortion campaign and an early Reagan supporter.

Given the increasing proliferation of special interest groups that watch closely these sub-Cabinet appointments and their pronouncements (discussed in chapter 3), key sub-Cabinet officials, at least during the last few years, are often drawn from the ranks of special interest groups and return to these after government service. Democrats tend to draw their appointees from left-leaning policy groups, while Republicans draw theirs from think tanks, legislative staffs, and policy-advocate groups on the right-wing.

Yet some scholars, such as Thomas P. Murphy, Donald E. Nuechterlein, and Ronald Stupak, have argued that the influence of this group of appointees over the policy-making process has declined in recent years, because of its increase in number.[4] For example, in 1924 the Department of the Interior's top-level appointees included one departmental secretary, three administrative assistants, and three assistant secretaries. By contrast, today this group includes one departmental secretary, several dozen on his immediate staff, one deputy secretary, six assistant secretaries, nine deputy assistant secretaries, and nineteen bureau directors or agency administrators. Though as a collective group, their prominence and power has on the whole increased in recent years; a modified Gresham's law operates here; i.e., increasing numbers of political appointees at this sub-Cabinet level drive down their individual influence over policy decisions. Put simply: a call from an assistant secretary does not mean what it once did.

The fourth group of appointees encompasses a wide variety of advisors to the secretary and directors of agencies and bureaus. Like the previous level of appointees, this level has expanded enormously in the past two decades as secretaries brought in their own people to help run their departments. At the federal level these assorted political appointees do not require Senate confirmation, so for the most part their ranks have grown without legislative oversight and control. Few, however, are active politicians or were closely involved with the election campaign of the chief executive. Most are more directly identified with the professional or policy issues of the agencies where they work. Many have had personal ties or friendships with their immediate supervisors. They are generally reputed to be experts in the field of law, business, or education and may have actually been drawn from the ranks of the civil service. Some have known or worked with each other before or fought the opposition party together over the very sets of policy issues they are now actively administering and formulating.

FIGURE 4.3
President Reagan's Political Appointment Process

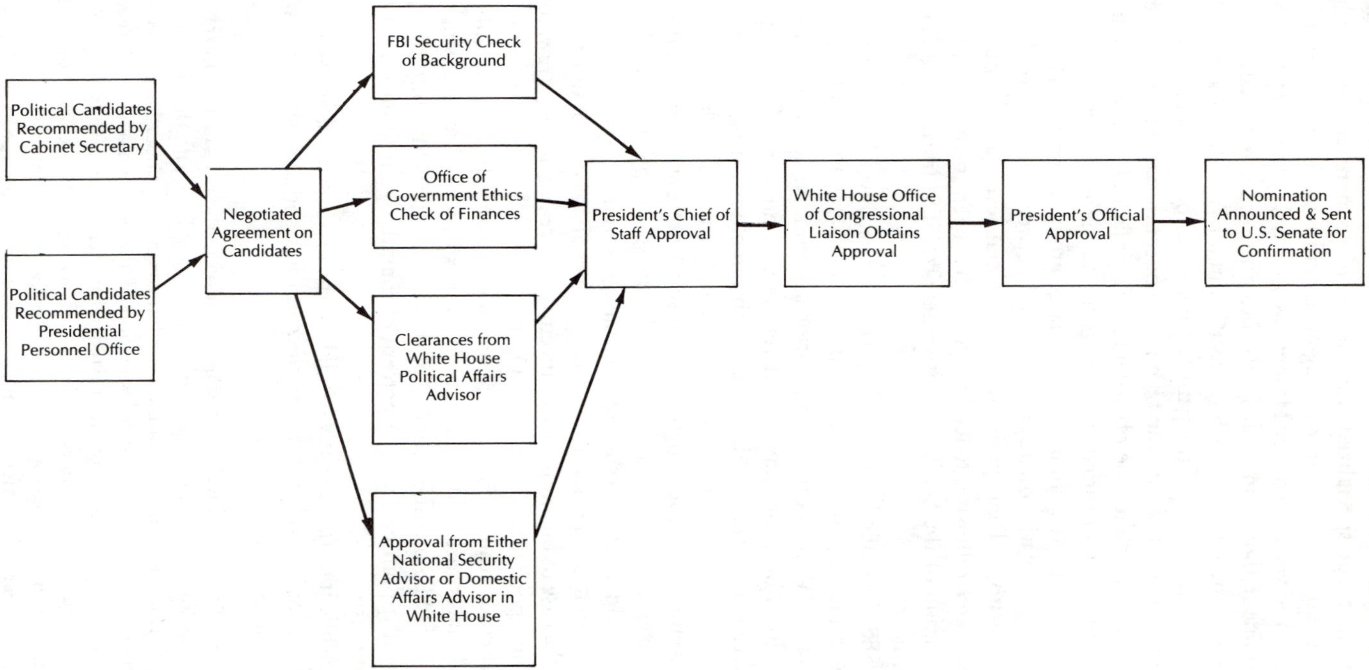

Political Candidates Recommended by Cabinet Secretary

Political Candidates Recommended by Presidential Personnel Office

Negotiated Agreement on Candidates

FBI Security Check of Background

Office of Government Ethics Check of Finances

Clearances from White House Political Affairs Advisor

Approval from Either National Security Advisor or Domestic Affairs Advisor in White House

President's Chief of Staff Approval

White House Office of Congressional Liaison Obtains Approval

President's Official Approval

Nomination Announced & Sent to U.S. Senate for Confirmation

Source: *Government Service*, Report of the Business Roundtable, October 20, 1981, p. 9.

Compared with appointees at other levels, these men and women are the most expert and specialized, and they are often more willing to push forward the interests of their particular agencies and resist political intrusions from others. And yet as Frederick Mosher has observed of these appointees: "Some are eminent figures in their fields, often principal representatives and defenders of the services which they superintend. Yet their stance differs from that of the members of the permanent services below them. They *can* be replaced or their situations can be made so uncomfortable as to induce them to resign or at least alter their behavior."⁵ Their lack of tenure is the heavy stick that ensures their ultimate responsiveness to higher circles of appointees.

Finally, there is an increasingly large group of individuals in public bureaucracy today who occupy a limbo-land between quasipolitical and nonpolitical territory. Their position at the federal level (and in more than two dozen states following federal practices) has been institutionalized through the creation of the Senior Executive Service (SES) in the 1978 Civil Service Reform Act.

SES developed a new category of upper-level administrators that is formed from supergrade officials in grades GS–16, 17, and 18 and in Executive Ranks IV and V, in which position assignments and pay are determined by political decision makers and yet are also protected by the civil service rules (career officials in SES have the option of retreating to GS–15 grades). The rationale for creating SES came mainly from argument that improved management in government could result from greater mobility of its top executives. It was argued that like in business, the president and top executives should be able to shift senior managers from one post to another more easily than the hide-bound civil service rules allowed prior to 1978. Further, as in the case of business, bonus incentives were provided for rewarding outstanding performances in SES. On the other hand, unsatisfactory performances could cause removal or replacement in SES. By law, the bulk of these individuals must be drawn from the ranks of the civil service, since only 10 percent of SES members (or 822 of the current 8,593 SES employees) can be political appointees, and 45 percent of their designated slots must be filled by careerists.

While it is still too early to tell how the newly created SES system is actually functioning today, Chester Newland has perhaps best summarized insiders' views about SES:

> The SES survived well the test of transition to the Reagan administration. Independent research, however, indicates problems with the SES, extending from the Carter administration but continuing under Reagan. For example, "a longitudinal investigation of the SES, among employees in grade levels 13 and above in five federal agencies, reveals that after the first two years virtually none of the major objectives of the architects of the SES are perceived as having been met." Furthermore, some systematic, objective research indicates that negative conclusions about SES are based on

general experience and are widespread: that federal managers perceive that SES appointments are somewhat more political in nature; that newly appointed members of the SES did not have skills appropriate for the positions they had assumed; and "a shift away from merit system principles."[6]

Early indications therefore seem to suggest that the SES is made up of careerists whose work and roles are increasingly being politicized, though they have several trappings of professional careerists and protections of the general civil service.

To sum up the influence of the political appointee subsystem: First, while these individuals occupy the highest, most prominent posts within public organizations and serve as linchpins between campaign promises and bureaucratic performance, they are a highly diverse, fragmented, and transitory group with little cohesiveness.

Second, their influence within bureaucracy depends upon the policy positions they hold, the length of their government service, their connections with top elected officials, their own personalities, their support from outside groups, the immediate tasks at hand, and whether these lend themselves to imminent solutions. Generally, as one moves up the hierarchy of political officials to the inner Cabinet, these individuals have the most generalized backgrounds, and must deal with the broadest, most critical policy issues. They also exercise the widest, most influential policy roles inside public bureaucracy, if their tenure is long enough and their external support adequate to the performance of the tasks at hand. Here at the top the political winds blow the fiercest; the "turf battles" are the most intense, and the stakes are the highest.

Third, as one moves down the hierarchy of these political officials toward those of quasi-political status, greater degrees of specialization are found as well as more identification with the programmatic goals, tasks, and issues within the agencies they serve. They are less generalist in outlook and more concerned with pushing narrower policy agendas, which often means they are less interested in and responsive to their own chief's reelection priorities.

Fourth, sharp turf fights over policy issues therefore ensue frequently between these various levels of political appointees, largely because of the different perspectives built into their hierarchical roles. Here is where pitched policy battles frequently occur and are resolved. In the pecking order of appointees, those at or near the top push agendas that are broader and more responsive to the chief executive's agenda, while those lower down tend to be more programmatic and responsive to the priorities and issues of the particular agencies in which they work.

Fifth, while the subsystem of political appointees is highly fragmented, these tend to cluster into networks in which those near the top have close personal ties, even long friendships, with the chief elected official (though not necessarily with each other, nor are they necessarily active in his political campaigns). Those on the lower rungs tend to be experts in particular fields and to have personal networks that run downward into the agency and outward into various external support groups associated with an agency's mission.

Sixth, what draws all appointees together and keeps them loyal and responsible, at least to some degree, to the elected official's policy agenda (and makes them a distinct bureaucratic subsystem) is the fact that they can be removed or transferred at any time by a president, governor, or mayor. Fear of losing a job can be a powerful incentive to stay in line with the top-level agenda, or at least to refrain from stating opposing views in public. Recent history has demonstrated that publicizing opposition views is highly dangerous to personal survival in this subsystem. The departures of Walter Hickel in the Nixon administration, James Schlesinger in Ford's, Joseph Califano and Michael Blumenthal in Carter's, and Alexander Haig and Martin Feldstein in Reagan's are all reminders of the primary importance of loyalty to the boss at this level and of the hazards inherent in bucking the party line.

However, in this constantly shifting world of personnel and goals, as Norton Long pointed out, determining to whom one is loyal and what one should accomplish become difficult if not impossible tasks. This level in bureaucracy is an ambiguous world in which appearances frequently count more than on-the-job practices. Participants thus spend enormous amounts of time posturing and posing in order to appear to do the correct things for the right people and taking readings and soundings to find information about their own status and about the intentions of others. The closed door, an invitation to the right party, the frequency of meetings with the superior, and the seating arrangement at the conference table often signal more than the untrained eye can perceive or the written document explain. Hard-driving, ambitious men and women, even with considerable experience and exposure, become quickly frustrated and disillusioned with the confusion and pretense inherent in this subsystem, as autobiographies of recent incumbents such as Alexander Haig *(Caveat)* or Joseph Califano *(Governing America)* testify. Policy activity at this level of bureaucracy is very much like the greased pole competition at the old-fashioned county fair, where few, if any, climb to the top and reach the prize. The way up is slippery, uncertain, and treacherous, often crowded with many other frenzied competitors. There are no sure rules for success. And the prize, once reached, is often temporary, of little value, and hardly worth all that fierce competition and furiously expended energy. Many leave disillusioned and despairing about what they have done or failed to do. Good luck rather than personal skills often decides outcomes.

The Professional Careerist Subsystem: Permanent Clusters of Powerful Experts

Professor Samuel H. Beer has said that U.S. society is governed by "technocratic politics" in which specialists with in-depth training and experience in different fields of government have assumed the duty of charting the course of various public organizations. As Beer argues:

I would remark how rarely additions to the public agenda have been initiated by the demands of voters or the advocacy of pressure groups or the platforms of political parties. On the contrary, in the fields of health, housing, urban renewal, transportation, welfare, education, poverty and energy, it has been in very great measure, people in government service or closely associated with it acting on the basis of their specialties and technical knowledge who first perceived the problem, conceived the program, initially urged it on the President and Congress, went on to help lobby it through to enactment and then saw to its administration.[7]

Some scholars, including Zbigniew Brzezinski, have called the phenomenon "the technotronic age"; Don Price calls it "the scientific estate"; for Daniel Bell it is "the post-industrial age"; for Guy Benveniste, "the politics of expertise."[8] But whatever term is used to describe the role of experts within government, the professional strata, a subsystem below that of political appointees, is now recognized by many scholars as a significant influence over the activities of modern public organizations. As Frederick C. Mosher has perceptively written, "For better or worse—or better and worse—much of government is now in the hands of professionals (including scientists). The choice of these professionals, the determination of their skills and the content of their work are now principally determined not by the general government agencies, but by their own professional elites, professional organizations and the institutions and facilities of higher education. It is unlikely the trend toward professionalization in or outside government will be reversed or even slowed."[9]

The development of professional control over the inner dynamics of U.S. bureaucracy came slowly and in piecemeal fashion, mostly in the twentieth century. Some agencies, such as DoJ, have since their inception been dominated by lawyers, but professionally trained lawyers with LL.B. degrees, steeped in learning, responsive to the American Bar Association's policy concerns. Specialists in highly diverse elements of the law did not appear at DoJ in any sizable numbers until the New Deal in the 1930s. Military officers held the top army posts from the time the War Department was established in 1789, but even throughout most of the nineteenth century officers were poorly trained and politically motivated amateurs with little or no technical competency (except for those trained as engineers at West Point).

The modern generalist-professional cadre of officers did not appear until after 1900, established largely through the reforms of secretary of war Elihu Root, who created the Army General Staff, a unified personnel system, as well as a series of advanced professional educational institutions for military officers. The Rogers Act of 1924 instituted what we now know as the professional foreign service, but the dominance of quality foreign service professionals such as George Kennan and Charles Bohlen throughout key State Department slots did not emerge until after World War II.

Likewise, the professional control of state and local agencies in many regions began at roughly the turn of the century with the formation of small, fledgling professional associations such as the International Association of Chiefs of Police (1893), the International Association of Fire Chiefs (1893), the American Society of Municipal Engineers (1894), the Municipal Finance Officers Association (1906), the National Recreation Association (1906), the National Association of Public School Business Officials (1910), the National Organization for Public Health Nursing (1912), and the City Managers' Association (1914). But, for the most part, until after World War II these professional groups were weak and ineffective voluntary associations exercising little control over the inner dynamics of local public bureaucracy. The postwar era, however, brought into grass-roots and higher-level government an influx of university-educated specialists with wide assortments of technical competence. The postwar era also brought about a new respect for and demand for these specialists to deal with a myriad of technical tasks from constructing highways, educating children, cleaning air and water, and administering complex regulating machinery—often spawned by the professionals themselves—for certifying and controlling the application of skills inside and outside government.

The story of the professionalization of U.S. bureaucracy is complex and has not been explained nor even understood fully by historians and political scientists. Yet the point is that there has been a silent revolution within U.S. government, as a result of which, as Samuel Beer and others observe, professionals decisively determine much of what government does or doesn't do. In some locales, the revolution toward grass-roots control of bureaucracy proceeded swiftly. Particularly in "clean reform states," such as California, professional groups have gained control of even the upper reaches of bureaucracy over the past several decades. In poorer, rural areas, such as Mississippi, trends in professional dominance have been slower, but even there they are occurring because of federal mandates and other laws that have aided the growth and dominance of professions and professionals. Wherever bureaucracy operates today, in the words of Corinne L. Gilb, these groups constitute "the hidden hierarchies of government."[10]

Professionals in government today, however, by no means make up a monolithic group or a homogeneous mass of experts; indeed, they differ considerably from one another. First, there are the *general professionals*, who practice their calling within *both* government and the private sector. They tend to exhibit all the trappings of what traditionally are viewed as the qualities of "classic" professionals, such as advanced training beyond the college level, high status as perceived by the general public, as well as a fairly clear-cut occupational specialty with lifetime career opportunities and adequate (sometimes huge) financial rewards. General professionals occupy prominent posts in government and include physicians in local public hospitals or the National Institutes of Health; lawyers staffing DoJ or local district attorneys' and county counsels' offices; civil engineers in state highway departments or local public works offices; and accountants within the governmental affairs office or state auditing agencies. *Public professionals*, by contrast, are those whose sole employment is in government service, but whose characteristics are similar to those of the traditional general professional groups. Foreign service officers, public health officers, army, navy, air force and marine corps officers, urban planners, and city managers fall into this category. For various reasons *emerging professionals* have not obtained full-fledged professional status, pay, or career development opportunities as general or public professionals, but they have certainly been moving in that direction, as a fulfillment of their own "occupational ideal," for a number of years. Police officers, computer specialists, firemen, corrections officers, and environmental specialists are a few in the impressive array of specialists within public bureaucracy today. *Paraprofessionals* are among the newest groups of government workers; they are also striving for professional status and recognition. Paraprofessionals provide vital assistance to professionals in their work. They occupy the twilight zone between emerging professional groups and skilled workers in the public service. Paralegal assistants, various types of health and medical technicians, warrant officers in the military, and executive secretaries fall into this occupational group.

Whether or not individual professions fit into one or more of the above-mentioned typologies is certainly a moot question, but evidence supports the contention that most public organizations at every level of government today are controlled by one or more of these professional groups, which are most closely identified with that level's central missions, activities, and products. They make up what Burton J. Bledstein calls "the culture of professionalism,"[11] where the "regard for professional expertise compels people to believe the voices of authority unquestionably." If one could X-ray the insides of a typical public bureaucracy, one would see that the arrangement of professional dominance looks something like figure 4.4.[12]

Note that directly under political appointees, *professional elites* comprise the core group of experts. These are the senior and most prestigious and respected members of the profession. They give not only internal direction to the profession but also to the entire agency by controlling the important positions and advancement to those positions and by setting recruitment and entrance requirements as well as overall personnel policies and priorities for the organization. Rising to these posts is achieved only through long-term career investment in the field, attendance at the "right" schools for basic and advanced training in the field, and advancement through progressive levels of responsibility and prominence in areas closely identified with the central concerns of the agency. Pilots in the air force, line officers in the navy, doctors in the U.S. Public Health Service, foresters in the U.S. Forest Service, senior staff lawyers at DoJ, and top-ranking educators in local school systems or in state departments of education tend to fill the elite slots within their respective agencies.

There are some exceptions to this pattern of elitist control. Some agencies

FIGURE 4.4
Varieties of Professionals in a Public Agency

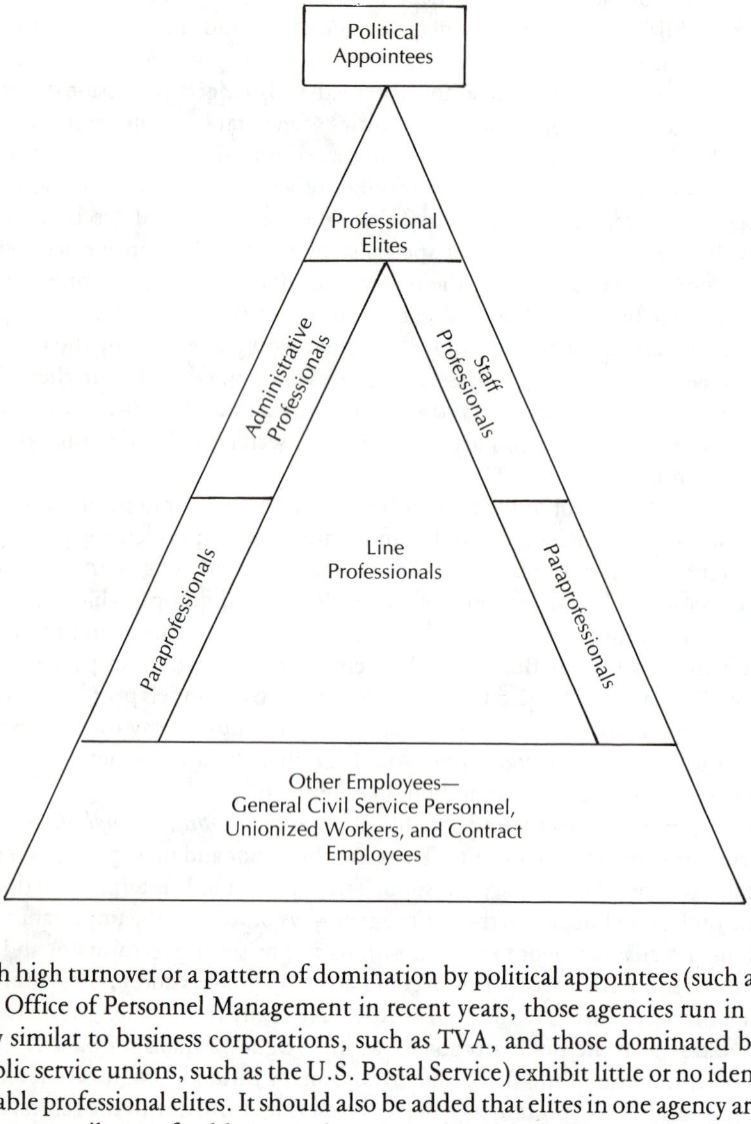

Political
Appointees

Professional
Elites

Administrative
Professionals

Staff
Professionals

Paraprofessionals

Line
Professionals

Paraprofessionals

Other Employees—
General Civil Service Personnel,
Unionized Workers, and Contract
Employees

with high turnover or a pattern of domination by political appointees (such as the Office of Personnel Management in recent years, those agencies run in a way similar to business corporations, such as TVA, and those dominated by public service unions, such as the U.S. Postal Service) exhibit little or no identifiable professional elites. It should also be added that elites in one agency are not necessarily transferable to another. A psychiatrist may be considered one of the elite at the National Institutes of Health but may well be a second-class citizen in a military hospital or in a local public health clinic in which MDs generally dominate the staff positions.

The pecking order of elites may indeed be multilayered within any public agency. A physician who is a general practitioner might be in charge of running a large Veterans Administration hospital, but a psychiatrist might head the mental health section of that same hospital because he or she is more specialized in that field. The psychiatrist holds an M.D. degree and can thus prescribe drugs, whereas the psychologist (who holds "only" a Ph.D.) who works for the psychiatrist in the same unit generally has less status because he or she lacks an M.D. degree and therefore cannot prescribe drugs. Occupying several rungs under these elites may be social workers, nurses, and medical technicians.

The registered nurse is considered an elite within that cluster of professionals. And not only is certification as an RN increasingly important to a nurse's elite status today, further certification within a very narrow specialized field within which she or he works, such as emergency room, orthopedic care, or surgery room practice, is also desirable. The continuous specialization of those who are already specialists within government is staggering. The professionals' pecking order therefore moves on down the line of clusters of professional groups in a unit where length of education, type of educational certification, quality of schooling, degrees of responsibility, and status in the eyes of the community and of the profession itself are sources for determining who is or is not in the nucleus of the particular professional elite.

The elites, in turn, within these various strata of professional clusters provide the leadership as well as set the work standards, the qualifications for entrance and advancement, and the overall values for the profession. Much of the critical tensions and conflicts between clusters of professional elites are over policy questions and control of turf—between doctors and nurses in hospitals or between air force, army, navy, and marine corps top-ranking officers within DoD. Much of this conflict is hidden from public view. Rarely does it become public, because it can most often be settled between the competing parties or by political superiors. But at times internal dissent can become so strained that work production slows and the mission of the unit becomes jeopardized.

Line professionals, who fall just below the level of the senior elites, actually carry out the day-to-day functions of the public agency. Whereas a few dozen three- and four-star generals compose the army's top professional elite, more than 200,000 army officers from second lieutenants to generals direct much of the real work of the army in a wide variety of combat and noncombat jobs. Some, given their West Point training and combat duties in the infantry, armor, or artillery (combat sections that are considered "ideal" rungs in the ladder to the level of the elite) may become part of the professional elite; others in the line may have neither the interest nor the proper backgrounds to attain those high level assignments. The line officers are essentially the "doing" and "implementing" functionaries of bureaucracy and are most directly associated with the central missions of an agency. Although most public professions, such as the foreign service, have no "West Points" to train recruits, Foreign Service Officers (FSOs) have a wide assortment of civilian backgrounds—economics, law, political science, and so on—but FSOs work as line professionals when they are assigned as political representatives abroad, which remains even today the central mission of State Department employees. They serve as staff or administrative professionals when they assume narrow special roles within the department.

Staff professionals in public agencies include a wide assortment of specialists and technical assistants who have unique and specialized expertise that may not be directly connected with the central tasks of the agency but are nonetheless critical to carrying out its assigned functions. Today almost every public bureaucracy employs a wide array of these individuals. In such diverse public organizations as the General Accounting Office at the federal level,

TABLE 4.3
Types of Professions and Their Elites in Several Public Organizations

Public Organization	Key Profession	Professional Elite
National Level		
State Department	Foreign Service Officers	Senior FSO 1 & 2 Level Career Ambassadors & Staff
Army, Air Force, Navy & Marines	Career Officers in Armed Service	General or Flag Rank Officers from Combat Arms in Senior Policy/Line Position
Justice Department	Lawyers	Senior Careerists in Key Litigating Divisions
Forest Service	Foresters	Career Foresters in Highest Policy and Line Posts
National Institutes of Health	Scientists	"Name" Scientists Heading Major Research Projects
Federal Reserve Board	Economists	Prestigious Economists Heading Key Analytical or Policy Units
Local & State Levels		
Auditing or Accounting Agencies	Accountants	CPAs Who Are Careerists Heading Major Auditing or Accounting Divisions or Units
Public Hospitals	Doctors	Senior MDs in Charge of Major Units or Depts.
Highway and Public Works Agencies	Engineers	Civil Engineers with Seniority in the Agency
Elementary and Secondary School Systems	Teachers	Principals, Asst. Superintendents, Superintendents
City & Town Government Administrations	City Managers, Chief Administrators	Senior Career Managers
Welfare Services	Social Workers	Ranking Career Social Workers in Top Level Agency Posts

where accountants staff the elite and the line jobs, or at a state highway office, where engineers are generally in charge, or a local social work agency, where social workers are the principal professionals, these and sundry staff professionals such as lawyers, computer specialists, public relations experts, and legislative relations officers, cluster around their headquarters' operations and are essential to fulfilling the agency's missions. They assume the critical advisory roles within an agency and in some government offices also frequently assume large and powerful policy roles, even though they are not directly in either the line or the elite ranks. In every federal department, the legal counsels, for example, not only can command high salaries, large staffs, exemptions from civil service hiring rules, and the ear of the top brass in the agency, but also frequently exercise enormous yet quiet influence over central policies of an agency through knowledge and expertise in the law (and frequently this advice is quite conservative in nature—more "don'ts" than "dos"). The top political and professional cadre often yield to such legal policy advice on technical matters because no one else can supply this knowledge. One only need attend a city council or county board of supervisors' meeting to watch the frequency with which elected members turn to legal counsel for assistance or to view federal organization charts to discover the strategic positions legal counsels occupy in most departments.

Administrative professionals comprise an assortment of budget officials; program officers; planning personnel; and finance, purchasing, auditing, and supply officials found in every public organization (the G–1 through G–5 jobs in the U.S. military). These men and women are critical to the activities of the agency because they essentially serve as "the directing brain" of the organization ("the directing brain" is Elihu Root's name for this group in his 1902 proposal for the creation of a general staff in the U.S. Army, which was a pattern copied by other public agencies and business corporations).

In some agencies these administrative staffs are quite large; for example, the Department of Health and Human Services employs several thousand individuals in this category. But in many places the staffs are quite small, as in small towns where a city manager may perform all these administrative support tasks. In larger organizations some of these slots are temporarily held by line professionals, but many are filled by permanent careerists from emerging professional groups, such as budgeting, personnel, and purchasing specialists. While these do not as yet rank as full-fledged professionals, they are increasingly taking on all the trappings of professionals, having their own associations, journals, "ideal career tracks," and educational requirements. Some even command higher salaries and status than their professional superiors. Municipal budget officers, for example, today are sometimes paid higher salaries than their bosses, city managers, or chief administrative officers, mostly because of the critical roles budget and finance expertise play in municipal decision-making processes in the 1980s.

In the uncertain environment within which agencies must operate, staff professionals must be adaptive and inventive in coping with the changing needs of their agencies. Much of their work is simply "fire-fighting" in order to maintain their structure amid turbulence, but much also is directed at thinking about the future of the organization, even if this planning is only incrementally achieved through short-term budgets, ad hoc personnel recruitment and selection, and partial programmatic design or redesign.

Finally, paraprofessionals make up another group increasingly seen within public agencies. These people receive substantially lower remunerative rewards for their work, although many units of government simply could not perform their assigned tasks without them. Many of these "paras" aspire to becoming full-fledged professionals in the field and use the experience as apprenticeship training. Others see this line of work as a rewarding lifetime career and seek no higher positions. From the standpoint of government, however, these workers are taking on increasing responsibility in various offices because of the rising costs of hiring fully qualified professionals. In other words, using paras is an effective governmental strategy for keeping down rapidly escalating personnel costs. In many cases paras perform the work as well as, if not better than, their highly paid counterparts. In this respect, their primary roles inside public organizations may well be an important economic function.

On the whole, what can be said about the influence of all the professional subsystems upon the activities and outputs of public bureaucratic institutions?

First and foremost, they are essential to the performance of the central missions of virtually every public agency. They define its mission, decide how it should be accomplished and who should accomplish it, as well as when it should be accomplished and where. As noted by Professor Beer, professionals in an age of "technocratic politics" play major roles from the conceptualization of a policy through to its implementation.

Second, by comparison with top-level political appointees, professionals by and large have longevity within agencies, thus giving them an enormous edge in the policy-making processes. They simply outlast their rival superiors. A classic example is the TFX decision. In the mid-1960s, defense secretary Robert McNamara, over violent objections by the individual services, rammed through approval for a joint-service tactical fighter aircraft, the TFX, which could be utilized by the combined commands of the air force and navy. By the 1970s, however, McNamara had left DoD and TFX died quietly as the navy and air force each went ahead and developed its own separate tactical fighter. Ultimately, the separate service professionals also had *their* way over that of the political appointee.

Third, professionals are not a single, unified group. They are part of a well-established pecking order, from elites down to paras, that is based on education, skills, seniority, levels of responsibility, and general competence and experience. Each level of professional brings different capabilities, policy roles, and political influences to the shaping of agency outputs. Elites occupy the highest level of policy-making roles; line professionals shape actions mainly through implementation practices; staff professionals fill advisory roles; administrative professionals prepare and plan tasks; and paraprofessionals carry out lower-level and lower-cost work. Each, therefore, is essential to the performance of the bureaucratic process. As a whole, though, professionals shape government agencies by controlling recruitment, selection, and other personnel actions as well as the overall organizational structure within many agencies.

Fourth, continuing political strength and popular support of professionals ultimately rest upon their recognized expertise and competence as well as on their ability to exercise these skills in a regular, uniform manner in the public interest. The widespread popularity of city-manager government rests fundamentally on its ability to apply systematic expertise to urban issues at the local level. Since expertise is professionals' stock in trade and is a source of authority and of legitimacy within government, a great deal of their efforts are directed at higher education. Professionals look to institutions of higher learning to sustain and enrich their knowledge base through training programs that give the professionals their credentials, and nurture the fundamental ethos and values of the profession. If political appointees draw support from their elected chiefs, professionals in government conversely derive their legitimacy from expertise acquired through higher education. The content and perspectives of these sources of learning influence the long-term priorities and fundamental value of professions. Hence, professions pay enormous attention to the shaping of professional education programs, examinations, accreditation, and licensing processes that help to determine the nature and content of professional work, as well as the knowledge and skill it requires.

Fifth, professionals influence policies not only by contributing a substantial share of the public work force and its top leadership cadre but also by moving upward and outward beyond the contours of their roles within agencies. As noted in the discussion of political appointees, they frequently assume temporary assignments at this level. Half the Cabinet in both the Johnson and Carter administrations was made up of former professors and of "in-and-outers" from various professional callings. Similarly, the influence of professionals is moving increasingly outward into legislative staff assignments or related nonprofit or business firms that directly and indirectly influence the course of bureaucratic policies. For example, retired military officers have for many years moved into prominent defense contracting firms with influential ties to the Pentagon.

Finally, the most serious tensions and conflicts within public organizations are generally hidden from view, since they arise mainly from policy disputes *between* clusters of key professionals or in some cases from disputes between professional elites and political superiors, though from these disputes important public policies often emerge. Fights between the army, navy, and air force over defense appropriations and priorities are a permanent part of the Washington landscape, but it is within these professional service battles that defense policies for DoD develop. Likewise, the typical controversies that occur at the grass roots between police and firefighters over annual budget appropriations, length of work day, and salary increases figure equally prominently in determining the directions of local public safety policies.

The General Civil Service Subsystem: Ladders of Bureaucratic Specialists, Generalists, and Workers

The classic professional career subsystem is characterized by long-range progressive career planning, a clear-cut occupational field of expertise, rank inherent in the individual, separate, self-governing personnel systems con-

FIGURE 4.5
Within Each Classified Grade Level the Salaries and Duties and Employment Standards Are Clearly Outlined According to Civil Service Rules

PERSONNEL ANALYST I
$19,407—28,674

Definition
Under close and instructional supervision, to perform a variety of technical duties in one or more phases of the personnel program; and to do related work as required.

Typical Tasks
Conducts on-the-job position audits to determine level and kinds of duties and responsibilities, makes analyses of information obtained, and recommends allocation of positions to classes as a result of analyses, assists in conducting wage surveys by compiling and recording data supplies on questionnaires and preparing simple analyses of data; assists in developing training materials by assembling resource material; preparing outlines of information to be covered, and researching material for data or information to be used; receives, reviews for accuracy and conformity with appropriate rules and regulations, and recommends approval of personnel action forms submitted by departments to reflect hirings, dismissals, transfers, promotions, reclassifications, and other personnel changes, assists in the positive recruitment program by interviewing applicants to determine interests, aptitudes, and qualifications, advising applicants of job opportunities to specific departments for interviews with operating officials, and works with departments in locating applicants for specific job openings; assists in the construction of examinations and administering examinations to applicants; assists in gathering data for use in developing or revising fringe benefit programs.

Employment Standards
Graduation from a four year college or university

Upon completion of the training program, employees must be promoted, transferred or dismissed.

Knowledge of the principles of public personnel administration; knowledge of statistical methods; ability to prepare graphs, diagrams, and organization charts; ability to interview effectively; ability to analyze data and reach sound conclusions; ability to develop and maintain effective relationships with officials and other employees.

Source: George Mason University Personnel Office, 1985.

trolled by the professional elite, higher educational requirements, and requirement of credentials as prerequisites for entrance into lifetime careers with opportunities for increasing responsibility and financial rewards.

While bits and pieces of the "ideal professional model" are being incorporated gradually into the general civil service, the bulk of government personnel are members of civil service and do not share in the professional model. Civil service is founded on the merit system, whereby positions are assigned on the basis of open, competitive examinations (written and/or oral) and candidates are evaluated and ranked in relationship to particular task requirements of a specific job. Generally, selection is made from among the top three scorers. Unlike the professional subsystem, civil service has no progressive job planning or control by elites but has, rather, a laissez-faire approach in which each individual seeks out and designs his or her own path within the system. Advanced training may or may not be essential. Rank is inherent in the job, not the person. Meeting the specific task requirements of the job is what counts most in landing a slot in civil service. Status, in turn, is derived from the specific job. A GS–9 civil servant, for instance, is a GS–9 because he or she holds that slot. If the employee leaves it, he or she is no longer a GS–9, unlike an air force colonel, who is a colonel wherever he or she serves. In the professional subsystem, conversely, rank inheres in the person, not the job.

In the words of O. Glenn Stahl, perhaps the foremost authority on this subject, the general civil service, at least in its ideal format, is "a personnel system in which comparative merit or achievement governs each individual's selection and progress in the service and in which the conditions and rewards of performance contribute to the competency and continuity of the service.[13] Of course, the merit ideal is not always achieved in practice, but it does serve as the basic driving ideological idea behind this subsystem.

The civil service subsystem was grafted onto U.S. bureaucracy somewhat haphazardly almost a century after the creation of the Republic. Even today its "fit" into government seems somewhat awkward and unsure. For the most part, this uncertainty about its place in U.S. public bureaucracy is caused by, as many scholars have noted, the growth of the general civil service out of a reaction to the excesses of the nineteenth-century spoils system, in which employment in public service was based largely, though not entirely, upon party loyalty and political patronage. In other words, it was built on a negative moral reaction to what was perceived as "evil" rather than on a positive and deliberate design.

The story of its growth is long and complex. To sum it up, in the late 1860s and throughout the 1870s a small band of reformers waged aggressive moral and political campaigns on behalf of civil service reform and against incompetence, graft, favoritism, and partisanship within the public service. Merit, they argued, should be the basis of appointment. Substantially modeled on the English civil service system, which had been in operation for nearly a half-century and was adapted to special pragmatic U.S. needs and concerns, the Civil Service Act (Pendleton Act) was enacted in 1883 mainly as a national reaction to the shooting of President James Garfield by a political supporter who had been refused a small patronage post.[14]

Pendleton became the classic model for "good personnel practices" throughout the nation. Extended gradually through executive order to cover increasing percentages of federal workers, it was also copied almost word for word by numerous states and localities. Localities borrowed from it their basic structural arrangements and concepts of merit processes, such as notions of a nonpartisan commission appointed by the chief executive to oversee the system, requirements of open, competitive examinations, probationary period prior to tenure, strict provision against political interference within civil service activities, classification of positions, and equal pay for equal work.

Today 91 percent of the federal civilian workforce, or 2 million workers, are covered under civil service personnel rules. While several structural and procedural adaptations over time have been added, such as the Civil Service Reform Act of 1978, its essential concepts of "merit," "open, competitive examinations" and "equal pay for equal work" remain intact. Today at the local level thirty-six states have comprehensive merit systems, while others have either fragmentary or partial systems. All cities with populations of over 250,000 operate with comprehensive merit systems as well as 90 percent of those with more than 25,000 people. However, as Jay Shafritz has observed, "All statistics concerning merit systems' coverage are inherently deceptive."[15] For the most part this is because of the wide discrepancies between legal mandates and actual operations of the civil service in various locales.

Even though a considerable diversity in civil service laws is found across the United States, in those areas of the public service covered by its practices scholars have discovered several common characteristics: First, the U.S. civil servant is largely representative of the general population. Repeated studies have indicated that civil service members—unlike political appointees or upper-level professionals—are broadly reflective of the American people's education, income, social status, age, and geographic backgrounds. Though these representational attributes appear in the aggregate—i.e., when the entire public service is viewed statistically—they tend to break down in the various particular units or levels of government. Women are predominant in the bottom ranks as well as in certain fields such as nursing and teaching but are small minorities in police, fire, or other traditionally male occupational roles. Blacks and other minorities have made impressive gains in recent years in all areas of the public service, but the upper ranks still tend to be heavily representative of white males. In the higher ranks, as Kenneth J. Meier points out, greater advanced educational degrees and professional backgrounds are apparent.[16] The fathers of one-half of the higher federal civil service workers were professionals or businessmen, while only 14 percent of Americans in the general population reflected this characteristic; this unrepresentativeness is also apparent in the higher ranks of business and professional fields outside of government.

The compositions of the workforces of individual agencies look particularly unreflective of the general population. The Bureau of Land Management in the Interior Department and the Bureau of Alcohol, Tobacco and Firearms within Treasury, and state and county agricultural departments tend to be composed overwhelmingly of males drawn from rural, agricultural, and land-grant colleges. Many enjoy hunting, fishing, and outdoor hobbies. Few are liberal arts graduates of large, urban institutions; most were trained in various narrow technical specialities pertaining to their fields.

By contrast, civilians at the Departments of Justice and Defense are drawn largely from urban, eastern, and ivy league colleges.

Even within departments, sharp differences in backgrounds can be discovered. As Kenneth Smith observed recently, within the State Department, Foreign Service Officers still are drawn heavily from upper class, eastern, prestigious universities and have a "generalist" liberals arts orientation, while those who work for the Agency for International Development tend to be drawn from less prestigious schools and socioeconomic backgrounds and have a wide diversity of occupational specializations and geographic backgrounds.[17] In other words, the personnel of AID is more heterogeneous, "middle class," and specialized than State's. In large part, these socioeconomic differences are caused by the fundamentally different needs of the agency itself. State's task demands are diverse and the FSOs' generalist backgrounds fit their representational duties abroad. On the other hand, the function of AID is mainly to provide specialized technical expertise to third world nations. Hence more heterogeneous sorts of specialists predominate in that agency.

Anyone who has worked in government or seen it from the inside knows quite well that moving from agency to agency—even within the same department—can be like traveling into another country with sharply different customs, language, traditions, practices, rituals, and backgrounds. Each agency is unique. Understanding the peculiarities of each territory requires the skill of an anthropologist; at the very least it takes time to appreciate the unique qualities of the organizational culture, adjust to the people, and acclimate to the peculiar flora and fauna of the landscape.

Members of the general civil service subsystem generally lack the cohesiveness and unity found among professionals. Marver Bernstein notes that "there are more differences among career jobs than there are between a career job and that of the immediate political boss, an assistant secretary.[18] Today there are more than 2,000 job titles in the federal civil service and undoubtedly an equal number of occupational specialities in state and local bureaucracies. The diversity of work leads to few similarities among the personnel of a particular agency beyond the statement that describes their work.

When asked what she or he does, the typical bureaucrat will say, "I work at the Office of Education" or "I'm with the County Sheriff's Department." Few are likely to see themselves in broader terms and to say, "I'm a bureaucrat" or "I work for the civil service." Whether because of the pejorative connotations attached to government work or the more personal attachment to a particular assigned task, most bureaucrats lack common ties with government as a whole or with the broad *public orientation* of their work. This phenomenon no doubt exists in the private sector as well, where few business people see themselves as dedicated to the free market, but rather perceive themselves as real estate agents, autobody repairmen, or retail sales clerks. Most are like civil servants, who identify with the agency or skill at which they work or with the people with whom they work. The grand design of the organization or the broad purposes of their occupation generally elude their interests or understanding.

This lack of common ties to the broad aspects and purposes of government may in large part be caused by the general lack of mobility within the civil service. In theory, the civil service subsystem provides for open, competitive exams that permit advancement into every level or part of government (though restricted to particular federal, state, or local jurisdictions). In practice, however, most civil servants spend their working lives within one agency. Eugene B. MacGregor, Jr., who studied the mobility of civil servants at the GS–14 level and above, discovered an average of seventeen to twenty-five years of service in the same agency or department.[19] Civil servants' depth of policy understanding, long-term views of issues, and particular expertise in an agency is therefore unmatched by comparison with those of transitory political appointees, who last in a post a mere twenty-two months at the federal level. Their longevity in an agency, expertise, sheer numbers, and longer time perspectives also make civil servants the core of modern bureaucracy. The first Hoover Commission Report (1949) put it well:

> It is the function of . . . careerists . . . who must serve whatever responsible officials are in office, to provide the reservoir of knowledge, managerial competence based upon experience, and understanding of the peculiarities of government administration. It is their job to keep the Government operating as effectively as possible at all times. They are essential to maintain the . . . administration. They can put political executives in touch with the large background behind most important issues, and help them to understand the probable consequences of alternative courses of action.[20]

While there was a series of noticeable examples of political appointees from the Nixon, Carter, and Reagan administrations who disregarded this "pool of expertise," nonetheless, civil servants perform most of the work in government and provide much of its leadership. In the words of Hoover, the civil service is the great reservoir of "knowledge, managerial competence, . . . and understanding."

So far, this discussion has pointed up several salient features of the civil service subsystem—its representational attributes as a whole, yet its uniquely unrepresentative elements in agencies or levels within the hierarchy: its lack of cohesiveness; its absence of mobility; its emphasis on rank inherent in the job; its diversity of jobs; the long-term career perspectives of its members; and its function as "the reservoir" of government expertise. Given these attributes, it is especially difficult to generalize about its influence on "bureaucratic outputs." As one veteran of government service says, "Civil servants don't really have mutual bonds or ties. There's nothing in particular in common except that these are people who know all the angles about how government works."[21]

Such seasoned cynicism, however, may obscure some of this subsystem's fundamental influences on bureaucratic activities. For one thing, as has already been emphasized, civil servants generally take the longer view of issues, problems, events, and actions, at least by comparison with political appointees (though they share this attribute with professional careerists). Their tenured positions make them somewhat more immune to the need for "quick fixes" or "instant results," compared with their politically driven bosses, who often see no further than the next election. For the most part, permanent bureaucrats realize that much that passes for "instant success" is ephemeral and that any real achievements in government come only in the long haul, after much struggle and persistence. Their view of what constitutes real, enduring change is therefore fundamentally different from the view of political appointees and leads to a much more realistic, conservative approach based upon recognition of the worth of incrementalism; namely that small steps taken over a long period of time will lead to permanent, solid achievements. This strategy of gradualism can be the source of exasperation and deep conflicts between civil servants and endless successions of political appointees, who normally want government to accomplish this or that task immediately, even yesterday. In particular, appointees in recent administrations who are fired up to make speedy changes and who have had little exposure to the realities of government find this philosophy of incrementalism frustrating. It quickly becomes the butt of their jokes about those "damn bureaucrats." These negative references symbolize the radically different time zones within which each subsystem operates. Their different "internal clocks" influence the basically different approaches to handling issues.

Also unlike political appointees, civil servants are restrained by the Hatch Act, and various "little Hatch Acts" that operate on state and local levels, from going public with their political opinions or policy views. Occasionally it may happen that dissent leaks out in the press, but active campaigning is expressly forbidden by law. Hence, civil servants generally must be discreet and work behind the scenes in dealing with the development, formulation, and implementation of policy questions. They realize that a head-on frontal assault on policy issues will only get them into needless political controversy. Experience over the years has taught them that those sorts of political firestorms are to be avoided at all costs; they waste time and energy and lead to few tangible results. As a result, on the whole they favor quiet discretion in handling problems. In the words of Louis Brownlow, they have "a passion for anonymity" (the famous title of the second volume of his autobiography). As with soldiers at the front, a "heads-down" attitude prevails most of the time.

This cautious posture comes not merely from pragmatism in effecting programmatic change but also from fear about long-term personal survival. In a world of endlessly shifting political appointees, the civil servant, at least in the top ranks, knows quite well that job security depends on his or her not being too closely allied with any one political party, else he or she become "politically tainted" and shunned by the next group taking office. The desire to stay neutral from the political appointee subsystem and to work quietly from the inside, at least for most top-level civil servants, springs from a very fundamental interest in long-term survival.

Unlike the professional careerist, on the other hand, the general civil servant operates *without* the control of a professional elite and without an extensive mutual support network of peers with status in the subsystem ("the ring knockers," in West Point parlance). In the civil service subsystem, every employee charts his or her own way through the bureaucracy. The hazards are many and the minefields often hard to locate. Thus much of their time is spent networking outward and downward into the bureaucracy, building personal bridges and personal friendships inside and outside agencies in order to develop the myriad horizontal and vertical contacts that are necessary for gaining information, accurately assessing the landscape, and making alliances in this hazardous, uncertain, and lonely bureaucratic world.

Such contacts are essential for creating the mutual support groups necessary for personal advancement and for making policy impacts in a world without clearly defined professional career ladders or professional elite controls over internal personnel systems and programmatic policy-making machinery. In this confused, fragmented, and shifting institutionalized world, networks of "friends" are valued not merely as potential sources of information, policy alliances, and assistance to later career advancement but also as social support groups—"shoulders to cry on" or "good partying company"—perhaps fulfilling the most elemental human need of communal companionship. In turn, these clusters of civil servants influence public policies through the social networks they have established over long periods, running in strange and uncharted pathways that run through an agency and outside into other unlikely agencies and even beyond government where information is swapped informally and ideas are traded within social contexts. When presidents complain about government leaking like a sieve, this is why. The informal group, as Elton Mayo and the Hawthorne researchers discovered long ago, operates with a similar potency in government and in business settings, though it is well hidden in the civil service.

In his book *Inside Bureaucracy*, Anthony Downs gives a typology of civil service officials that outlines the key types of bureaucratic behavior found in public agencies. It is probably a correct assessment of these officials' fundamental motivations. Downs's model is useful even today, except that these days the civil servants he describes in his "ideal typology" tend to cluster together and operate in networks of likeminded persons rather than as individuals. Following is a short description of Downs's basic types.[22]

Climbers consider power, income, and prestige as almost all-important in their value structure.

Conservers consider convenience and security as almost all-important. In contrast with climbers, conservers seek merely to retain the amount of power, income, and prestige they already have rather than to maximize them.

Zealots are loyal to relatively narrow policies or concepts, such as the development of nuclear submarines. They seek power both for its own sake and to effect the policies to which they are loyal. We shall call these their sacred policies.

Advocates are loyal to a broader set of functions or to a broader organization than zealots. They also seek power because they want to have significant influence upon policies and actions concerning those functions or organizations.

Statesmen are loyal to society as a whole. They desire to obtain the power necessary to have a significant influence upon national policies and actions. They are altruistic to an important degree because their loyalty is to "the general welfare" as they see it. Therefore, statesmen closely resemble the theoretical bureaucrats of public administration textbooks.

The *formal* structure of civil service makes a significant impact on policy outputs in government as well. Civil service structure remains perhaps "the bottom line" in determining the type, intensity, role, and variety of bureaucratic outputs performed by any individual civil service employee. Federal civil service, like state and local civil service (though they frequently use different titles), is based upon the classified General Schedule (GS) for all personnel—clerical, administrative, and managerial. As table 4.4 illustrates, the General Service schedule ranges from grades GS–1 through GS–15. Each grade indicates the level of responsibility required in a job. Further, within each grade level are steps one through ten, which indicate seniority or time-in-grade. On the basis of these categories, salaries are assigned based upon the concept of equal pay for equal work. Generally, the lower four grades are composed of nonpolicy personnel, who perform the more menial tasks in government. These are custodians, typists, clerks, and aides. Grades GS–5 through GS–9 are generally considered professional entry levels for college graduates—GS–5 for typical entrants and GS–7 and GS–9 for those with exceptional test scores and/or master's degrees. GS–6, 8, and 10 are grades nor-

TABLE 4.4
General Schedule*
January 1, 1988

Grade	Annual rates and steps									
	1	2	3	4	5	6	7	8	9	10
GS-1	$ 9,811	$10,139	$10,465	$10,791	$11,117	$11,309	$11,631	$11,955	$11,970	$12,275
GS-2	11,032	11,294	11,659	11,970	12,103	12,459	12,815	13,171	13,527	13,883
GS-3	12,038	12,439	12,840	13,241	13,642	14,043	14,444	14,845	15,246	15,647
GS-4	13,513	13,963	14,413	14,863	15,313	15,763	16,213	16,663	17,113	17,563
GS-5	15,118	15,622	16,126	16,630	17,134	17,638	18,142	18,646	19,150	19,654
GS-6	16,851	17,413	17,975	18,537	19,099	19,661	20,223	20,785	21,347	21,909
GS-7	18,726	19,350	19,974	20,598	21,222	21,846	22,470	23,094	23,718	24,342
GS-8	20,739	21,430	22,121	22,812	23,503	24,194	24,885	25,576	26,267	26,958
GS-9	22,907	23,671	24,435	25,199	25,963	26,727	27,491	28,255	29,019	29,783
GS-10	25,226	26,067	26,908	27,749	28,590	29,431	30,272	31,113	31,954	32,795
GS-11	27,716	28,640	29,564	30,488	31,412	32,336	33,260	34,184	35,108	36,032
GS-12	33,218	34,325	35,432	36,539	37,646	38,753	39,860	40,967	42,074	43,181
GS-13	39,501	40,818	42,135	43,452	44,769	46,086	47,403	48,720	50,037	51,354
GS-14	46,679	48,235	49,791	51,347	52,903	54,459	56,015	57,571	59,127	60,683
GS-15	54,907	56,737	58,567	60,397	62,227	64,057	65,887	67,717	69,547	71,377
GS-16	64,397	66,544	68,691	70,838	72,500	73,660*	75,765*	77,870*	79,975*	
GS-17	73,958*	76,423*	78,888*	81,353*	83,818*					
GS-18	86,682*									

*The rate of basic pay payable to employees at these rates is limited to $72,500, the rate that would be payable for level V of the Executive Schedule.

Source: The White House.

mally reserved for executive secretaries and high-level clerical personnel. GS–11 through 13 designate middle managers in the government service with responsibilities for minor offices and units of government or important staff responsibilities. The GS–14 and 15 slots are reserved for those with high-policy making and/or management duties. They are just below the executive senior service groups, which are composed of the highest-level cadre of government executives.

Generally, then, the higher the GS rating, the more responsibilities and influence the civil servant has. Thus the realities of the policy-making apparatus within the civil service subsystem is circumscribed at least to some degree by the formalistic assignment of GS job classes, with those at the higher levels having significantly greater expertise and seniority and more responsible policy assignments and making significantly broader inputs than those on the bottom GS rungs by virtue of the offices they hold.

Combining the Downs typology of informal bureaucratic networks and the formal GS rating scale, table 4.5 depicts graphically where various informal networks of bureaucrats are located and the outputs from this subsystem to the bureaucracy.

The Unionized Subsystem: Cadres of Workers Inside Bureaucracy

Most texts on government or bureaucracy ignore an important policy-making subsystem of public agencies that over the past two decades has grown rapidly into one of the most potent forces determining the internal directions and external outputs of bureaucracy: namely, unionized public service workers. As David Stanley observes, ''A whole new ball game has started since unions in the public sector have begun to operate''[23] Like the aforementioned subsystems, unionization has increasingly gained its own share of power and a role in shaping the inner dynamics of public bureaucracy—i.e., its rules, regula-

TABLE 4.5
Downsian Bureaucratic Types by Grade Levels in the Civil Service

	Climbers	Conservers	Zealots	Advocates	Statesmen
Top Political Managers (SES)	O	O	X	XX	X
Top Civil Service Managers (GS 14 & 15)	O	O	X	XX	X
Middle Managers (GS 11–13)	XX	XX	XX	X	O
Entry Levels (GS 5, 7, 9)	XX	XX	X	O	O
High Level Clerical Staff (GS 6, 8, 10)	XX	XX	X	O	O
Low Level Workers (GS 1–4)	X	X	O	O	O

XX—Highly likely to be found in this GS range
 X—Likely to be found in this GS range
 O—Less likely to be found in this GS range

tions, operating procedures, and structural relationships. Unions also exercise external controls over bureaucratic performance and influence upon society—i.e., its productivity, enforcement practices, political relationships, and policy agendas.

Much like the professional careerist and civil service subsystems, the union subsystem was not a planned innovation. It just grew inside government, evolving particularly rapidly since the 1960s. If the Pendleton Act was the landmark piece of legislation creating the civil service, the explosion of union involvement within bureaucracy did not begin in earnest until John F. Kennedy signed Executive Orders 10987 and 10988 in 1962. These two orders for the first time gave unions the right to bargain collectively with federal management representatives on a limited range of items. They stimulated similar measures in numerous states and localities throughout the 1960s and 1970s. And while the unionization movement in government has slowed perceptibly during the 1980s because of cutbacks and the weakening of unions generally, the collective bargaining processes now in place are based largely upon legislation of the 1960s and 1970s and are accepted institutional practices within many jurisdictions throughout the United States.

Though the phenomenon of significant union influence over the activities of public bureaucracy is relatively new, some deep pockets of union activity date from the turn of the century. Indeed, in 1912 the Lloyd-La Follette Act gave federal workers the right to unionize, and for a number of years several large unions represented most of the U.S. postal employees as well as employees in certain fields of civilian defense and in several government corporations such as the Tennessee Valley Authority. States and localities with large urban and industrial populations, which had traditionally strong private sector unions, also saw unionization in limited areas of their public bureaucracies, such as in New York, Michigan, and California. Yet these public service unions were, for the most part, economically weak, poorly organized, and had few legal rights to bargain collectively with representatives from the agency's management.

Why did the 1960s usher in a new era of union influence inside government? The historical reasons are still not clear. Certainly the election of John F. Kennedy in 1960 was a critical factor. Throughout Kennedy's campaign he pledged union recognition and collective bargaining at the federal level. Shortly after his election, he appointed a task force headed by Arthur Goldberg to make recommendations on how to handle union-management relations within government. In turn, this task force study led to the two executive orders just cited. But other factors were also at work behind the scenes. Statistics show that private sector unionization reached its high point in 1955 with one-fourth of the national workforce belonging to unions. This percentage of national union membership has been declining gradually ever since (now standing at 16 percent). With the "drying up," so to speak, of the private sector, major union leaders as early as the 1950s recognized that the public service was the last major untapped pool of nonunionized workers, and so they pressed their demands on Kennedy and subsequent administrations for the extension of union rights and prerogatives within this governmental sector. Particularly through the aggressive leadership of individuals such as the late Jerry Wurf, who for many years headed the American Federation of State, County and Municipal Employees (AFSCME), and others, numerous public servants at the grass roots were brought into the rank and file. AFSCME and other groups were instrumental in lobbying state legislatures for the right to organize and bargain collectively with state and local jurisdictions on behalf of public workers. Today only six states remain right-to-work states and prohibit union activity in government.

Much of this union intrusion into the ranks of bureaucracy resulted from a more tolerant, even perhaps permissive, public attitude toward unions in government. By the 1960s unions were no longer considered entirely "evil" and antithetical to the public interest. No doubt, very real economic forces were at work as well. The promises of higher paychecks, shorter work weeks, and better working conditions lured many government workers, principally blue collar employees but increasing numbers of white collar employees as well, into public service unions. Certainly the postal strike of 1970 and the New York City transit strike of 1966—two early key disputes—stimulated union membership. Finally, union growth was fostered by legislation such as the Civil Service Reform Act of 1978, which formalized union-management collective bargaining procedures by federal statute. In a few states, such as Massachusetts, union membership became a requirement for attaining a public job. In order for workers to have a job and a voice that would represent them at the bargaining table and involve them in the determination of their agency's activities, they joined public employee unions.

Whatever the causes of growth—and there are undoubtedly many—a sporadic but continuous climb in union strength has been apparent within public organizations. Today three-fifths of all federal civilian employees belong to unions (not including the 600,000 postal workers, who are almost entirely unionized); 35.5 percent of state and local workers are union members. Levels of unionization, however, range significantly from agency to agency and locale to locale. Thus, in practice the political clout of union members inside bureaucracy varies considerably. The postal service, made up largely of blue collar workers, is almost entirely unionized, whereas the employees of the Federal Reserve Board and the State Department are mainly white collar professionals, largely (though not altogether) untouched by unions. Urban industrial states and large metropolitan communities are heavily unionized, and public unions play major policy-making roles within their various public bureaucracies. On the other hand, rural, poorer, and less-industrialized regions contain fewer union members, who therefore have less policy involve-

FIGURE 4.6
Sample Outline of an Agreement between a Public Employee Union and a Government Agency (effective until Jan. 1, 1985)

Excerpts from *'Agreement between The Board of Education of the City School District of the City of New York and United Federation of Teachers - Local 2 American Federation of Teachers—covering Teachers'*:

Article 1: Union Recognition—"The Board recognizes the Union as the exclusive bargaining representative of all those assigned as teachers . . .

Article 2: Fair Practices—a) Non-discrimination policy of Board and Union. b) "The Board agrees that it will not require any teacher to complete an oath or affirmation of loyalty . . .

Article 3: Salaries and Benefits—a) As of 9/83, a person holding a BA with no experience receives approximately $14,500 annual salary; a person holding an MA plus 30 credits and 15 years of experience receives approximately $31,000 annual salary. b) Extra pay for additional college credits, industrial experience, nursing experience, special ed. c) Choice of Health Plan with shared payment.

Article 4: Pension and Retirement Program—a) For the first 20 years of service, a retirement allowance equal to 1/2 the salary of the final year; further work years add to that; retirement at age 55. b) Disability and death benefits.

Article 6: Hours—a) School day is 6 hours and 20 minutes and 'such additional time as the by laws provide. b) Work Year begins the Wednesday after Labor Day and does not exceed the last weekday in June.

Article 7: Working Conditions in Schools—a) Number of teaching periods b) Number of students c) Coverage of classes/substitutes d) Relief from non-teaching chores e) Not responsible for maintaining or repairing equipment.

Article 8: Statement of Policy—a) A programming preference for the following year is submitted by the teacher 60 days before the end of the school year; 10 days before the end of the school teachers are notified of their assignments for the following year. b) Every teacher should have one unassigned period each day.

Article 9: Procedure for Handling Special Behavior Problems—The child is referred to the principal. If the principal cannot solve the problem and the situation continues, the teacher may appeal to the assistant superintendent.

Article 10: Safety—a) Legal Services are offered in cases of assault. b) The principal has the responsibility for the School Safety Plan.

Article 16: Leaves—a) Sick Leave is granted at a rate of one hour for every 20 hours of work, up to 200 days. b) A sabbatical leave granted for one year at 70% pay, after 14 years of service.

Article 17: Layoff Policy—'The teacher with the latest date of appointment will be the first to be excessed.' Teachers shall be assigned to appropriate vacancies.

Article 18: Transfers—a) Teachers must list six choices; transfers are based on district need, seniority, etc. b) Hardship transfers are considered after three years of service.

Article 19: Union Activities, Privileges and Responsibilities—a) 'No teacher shall engage in Union activities during time he is assigned to teaching or other duties.' b) Special times are allotted for Union activities. c) Every school will have a bulletin board for Union business.

Article 21: Due Process and Review Procedures—a)Explanation of teacher files. b) A teacher summoned for disciplinary action has the right to be accompanied by a union representative.

Article 22: Grievance Procedure—Step 1 is at the school level; Step 2 case brought before the assistant superintendent; Step 3 case brought before the Chancellor; Step 4 Union submission to arbitration.

Article 23: Special Complaints—In the case of 'harassing conduct, acts of intimidation' directed against the employee in the grievance process a special Fact Finder will report to the City School Board for a determination.

Article 25: No Strike Pledge

Source: City School District of New York

ment in their regions of the public sector. Some functional areas, such as education, transportation, and refuse collection, show a much higher level of union activity than other fields.

Today there are three prominent and powerful public service unions (and numerous lesser ones) that speak for many, though certainly not all, public employees: the American Federation of State, County and Municipal Employees, the American Federation of Government Employees (AFGE), and the American Federation of Teachers (AFT). The National Education Association is technically *not* a union but rather a professional association of primary and secondary schoolteachers, yet it looks and acts like a union, often aggressively by representing its rank and file in collective-bargaining negotiations in various school districts across the country. NEA has been especially active within the Democratic party, substantially assisting President Jimmy Carter's election in 1976 and his bid for reelection in 1980. AFSCME, AFT, and AFGE have grown rapidly in power and prominence within the AFL-CIO labor council over the last decade, extending their activism well beyond traditional union concerns into national political circles of the Democratic party by aiding the party financially as well as through considerable campaign manpower. Public service unions are active at the state and local levels as well, particularly where there are large concentrations of public workers (such as in state or county capitals) and strong Democratic party organizations.

However, the actual conduct of negotiations between unions and man-

FIGURE 4.7

The Actual Conduct of Union
Negotiations Is a Highly Decentralized
Process Governed by Specific Federal,
State or Local Laws, but Generally,
Specific Steps Involve . . .

As Contract Nears End, Union
Representatives Initiate Process by
Outlining Demand for New Contract

Management Responds

No Agreement

Agreement

If no agreement is reached, then the parties may turn to:
1) *Fact-finding*—An independent third party is appointed to investigate and lay out the facts of the situation for both parties to review;
2) *Mediation*—A third party is agreed upon to mediate the dispute;
3) *Arbitration*—A third party is asked to hear and review the case; the verdict will be binding on both sides;
4) *Deadlock, Work Stoppage, Strike.*

If management agrees, contract is concluded with union and then ratified by the required political body; i.e., the city council, schoolboard.

agement within government—the principal source of union inputs into bureaucracy—remains a highly decentralized process, with local representatives of public employee unions conducting agency-by-agency or local jurisdiction-by-jurisdiction negotiated agreements. In other words, while the public employee unions have grown into the "big three" (or four, depending on how one counts NEA), no one person or group speaks for "the entire management side" of government. Separate bargains must be made with roughly 80,000 governmental jurisdictions in the United States and with many more "suborganizational" units within these separate governments that recognize the union right of negotiation. Not only is the process decentralized, but who actually speaks for the employers or management is also a highly complex and unsettled issue in many areas. Some governments use the civil service as spokescommission for management (Office of Personnel Management at the federal level); others have teams of top-level executives from *both* legislature and bureaucracy that speak for management. Highly diverse institutional arrangements for representation and the conducting of the actual negotiations are found across the United States, largely because the process still remains somewhat new, experimental, and undeveloped.

Equally unsettled is the scope of the bargaining that is allowed. In most jurisdictions, wages and hours—the two principal bargaining concerns in private industry—are legislatively determined and beyond the scope of public sector negotiations. These negotiations, therefore, mostly center on working conditions, grievance procedures, and other less major subjects. But even here, working conditions, grievance procedures, and "fringes" are often precisely prescribed by legislation, leaving little room for negotiations, even over these seemingly mundane matters. Further, laws on the books often stack the deck in management's favor. For example, according to the 1978 Civil Service Reform Act (CSR), management officials are authorized "to determine the mission, budget, organization, number of employees, and internal security practices of an agency . . . to hire, assign, direct, lay off and retain employees . . . or to suspend, remove, reduce in grade or pay, or take other disciplinary action."[24] In short, the CSR's tilt clearly favors management prerogatives over union rights, although through court decisions and legislative amendments unions have chipped away at these restrictions.

Another important condition of the union subsystem in government is that the actual means for enforcing their views at the bargaining table remain drastically restricted because of the ban on strikes by public employees at every level of government. The basic weapon used by private sector unions to enforce their demands in negotiations is illegal in the government setting. As Theodore Kheel writes, "The strike enables employees through their representatives to participate in the decisions setting wages, hours and working conditions. In the absence of the right to strike, an alternative system of determination is required when negotiating parties reach an impasse."[25] However, no such technique has yet been found for breaking public sector impasses. In reality, however, strikes do occur in the public sector; sometimes they are called "the blue flu" or "sick-outs," or they are actual walk-outs, such as the air traffic controllers' strike in 1981, which meet with varying degrees of success and failure. In the extreme case, the air traffic controllers, who went on strike over pay and fringe benefits, lost their jobs and their union as well. The union was fined and decertified, and its leaders were jailed for a short period. At the other extreme, some public workers who have walked off their jobs not only got them back but were well rewarded for them to the point of almost bankrupting the community. Such was the case in the New York City transit strike in 1966, which was quickly settled by Mayor Lindsey with ample wage hikes and fringes, well beyond what the city could afford in the long run.

If strikes are forbidden, so are picketing, compulsory arbitration, and a whole range of typical weapons used by private sector unions to enforce their demands. But this does not mean that labor is totally powerless in the public sector, for as Wellington and Winter point out, labor's real leverage is through the use of "institutional power of public employee unions in a way that would leave competitive groups in the political process at a permanent and substantial disadvantage.[26] To be more precise, public unions know very well how to play the inside political game. During negotiations they regularly make "end runs" around management to outside supporters, such as sympathetic legislators on city councils, in state assemblies, or in Congress. These potent friends of public unions frequently enable them to cut deals and achieve their priorities through the back door, thus undercutting management's position or dividing it so badly that its official bargaining position crumbles.

How then can the union subsystem's influence over policy outputs in bureaucracy be summarized vis-à-vis the other previously mentioned bureaucratic subsystems?

The first and perhaps the most striking aspect of union involvement with what happens inside U.S. bureaucracy is its variety. Some unions strive for nothing less than complete control from top to bottom of public bureaucracy. They want the options to select a public agency's top-ranking political cadre; to determine its internal structural arrangements, procedures, and rules as well as its methods of promotion, hiring, and firing; to specify its relations with other external groups; and most of all to call the shots as to what the agency will or will not do for the public. In general, those agencies are characterized by weak political executive oversight, an absence of a controlling professional elite, a strongly unionized rank and file, a degree of institutional autonomy, and traditions of union assertiveness, such as in the federal postal system and in large "weak-mayor" cities such as New York and San Francisco, where public service unions exert powerful long-term influence. At the other extreme, public sector unions are dormant or ineffective in right-to-work states, where public sector unions are outlawed entirely, and in agencies in the tight grip of professionals (strong city manager communities and the military) or under strong, united antiunion political executive leadership (similar to what the air traffic controllers faced in 1981 under the Reagan administration, particularly in the person of former secretary of Transportation Drew Lewis). Most situations in which unions operate, though, are at neither extreme, and so unions end up jockeying with other internal bureaucratic subsystems— political appointees, professionals, and civil servants—for varying degrees of autonomy and control over bureaucratic policies and outputs.

Second, the growth and intrusion of unions within bureaucracy have added new levels of complexities and complications to an already complex bureaucratic world. The procedures, rules, and requirements for labor management practices at the federal level fill twenty-three pages of the Civil Service Reform Act of 1978, which set up new units of bureaucracy, such as the National Labor Relations Board, to administer and oversee these operations. New varieties of specialists, such as mediators, contract specialists, labor-management training instructors, and the like, are now needed to implement these tangled legalistic processes. Whether such complexification of government has slowed down its institutional outputs or made it more productive is unclear and unmeasured, but it is apparent in many instances that new personnel and attendant rules and procedures have been added to administer this new subsystem and that relationships between labor and management have therefore become more formal and legalistic. Ironically, the union subsystem has spawned a whole new growth of job specialties in the professional career subsystem within government, hence furthering professionalization within bureaucracy's ranks.

Third, in cases where the union subsystem has developed fully within public bureaucracies but has not become the dominant subsystem, it has brought with it new bipartisanship management practices. Collective bargaining forces management to sit down at regular intervals with union representatives to discuss grievances, working conditions, and other matters of concern to both parties. In other words, unions and their memberships have a formal role and stake in the management processes of public agencies, whereas before employees had no formalized role (though certainly their informal influence was and always has been considerable). While the range of what is permissible for negotiations remains sharply limited in most cases, the collective process does circumscribe the previously unbounded prerogatives of management and offers workers some formal, regular channel for making inputs into the governance of their workplace.

Fourth, in many cases public service unions have won positive reforms that have long been advocated by public administration specialists to enhance, on the whole, the cause of "good government," such as better wages, working conditions, training programs and staffing levels, and organizational reforms promoting institutional productivity. Most union concerns, in other words, focus on internal issues rather than on external policies, but with important indirect spinoffs for bureaucratic policy outputs that are sometimes distinctly economic in nature. Certainly there have been union demands and victories notable for their fiscal excess: for example, San Francisco streetsweepers, who earn salaries above $40,000 annually, and New York City police, fire, and transit workers, who have earned fringes and early retirement packages purchased at the price of the entire city's fiscal solvency. But these instances generally are rare and confined to locales where unions dominate local politics (an increasingly rare phenomenon today, even in big cities). The specific "true effects" of public service unions on U.S. bureaucracies make highly varied patterns—neither totally negative nor wholly positive but falling somewhere in between, depending on the particular agency, the strength of its public employee unions, the leadership of their top-ranking members, and the politics of the locale within which a bureaucracy operates. Much depends on the many factors composing the external environment discussed in chapter 3: the level and degree of socioeconomic support and the political configurations and institutional patterns within which public service unions find supporters or allies for their goals. Public agencies, depending on their political environs, can either be "pushed to the extreme" by unions, or union demands can be tempered by the surrounding socioeconomic realities and interest group interplay.

Finally, the real loser with the advent of public service unions into the internal dynamics of bureaucratic policy making has probably been the underlying philosophy and practices of the century-old civil service subsystem. Concepts such as merit selection, open competitive exams, nonpartisan civil service boards, and "color blind" promotions based upon individual competence have yielded in many areas to union concerns about seniority, "closed shop" union membership, and neutral third-party mediation of disputes by those outside civil service. Indeed, in many instances the old neutral civil service commission has been replaced by highly partisan and political oversight agencies such as the Office of Personnel Management at the federal level. This is not to argue that the civil service subsystem will soon fade into a distant memory and its controlling procedures, rules, and personnel become history. To the contrary, it is alive and well today in many bureaucratic institutions, but it certainly has changed, or given ground to the influx of unionization over the last two decades inside the public service.

Contract Employment: The Newest, Fastest-Growing Bureaucratic Subsystem

At the federal, state, and local levels, public agencies up to roughly 1950 did most, if not all, of the tasks assigned to them in-house, using their own personnel and resources and the facilities allocated by legislatures and political executives. Hence much of the theory of bureaucracy, as well as the managerial approaches to public enterprise put forward by public administration experts and scholars, were based upon assumptions, increasingly erroneous, that bureaucracies controlled their own operations, did their assigned work inside, with neat, clear lines of managerial control running from top political executives down to the workers who actually carried out the agency's assigned missions.

The reality of internal bureaucratic life today, however, is far different. In the 1980s the federal budget tells another story about how government agencies actually function. Roughly 14 percent of the national budget goes for its own internal personnel services and benefits (excluding pensions). This means that only slightly more than one-eighth of the total federal budget is spent on directing activities that the government performs itself, such as law enforcement, food and drug regulation, forestry service, air traffic control, and so on. However, the category of "other contractual services" indicates the roughly 16 percent of the total annual operating budget that is spent for sundry activities performed by others who are contracted to render services from *outside* the federal bureaucracy.

In other words, close to 60 percent of the total obligation for goods and services produced by the federal government is contracted out (excluding funds for grants-in-aid to states and localities, direct transfer payments to individuals, debt servicing, and so on). The percentages run much higher for some agencies, such as NASA and the Department of Energy, which have traditionally contracted out most of their work. The development of most major weapons systems is contracted out to private businesses, as is the construction of large capital projects such as dams, roads, bridges, and sewer systems. Three-fourths of research and development funding at the federal level is contracted out to universities, think tanks, consultants, and private industry.

At the local level there are no comparable figures on the levels of contracting-out by governmental bureaucracy, though they probably mirror the federal pattern, with some communities going to extremes, such as Lakewood, California (originators of the Lakewood Plan), which contracts out all its municipal functions, including police protection. City Hall consists of little more than a city manager and a secretary, who principally act as contract-managers for the city council. While most localities do not go to the extreme degree of contracting for municipal services, most do draw upon private vendors and business enterprises in many ways for the construction of capital projects as well as for a variety of ongoing services, such as data collection, medical facilities, computer services, refuse disposal, as well as for accounting, auditing, and payroll functions. Today, most government agencies house varying mixes of full-time employees and temporary or long-term contract employees working side by side. The regular public employees and contractual employees are often difficult to differentiate from one another.

The story of the rise of contract labor inside bureaucracy is a complicated one. As was pointed out in chapter 2, early in the history of the U.S. government, mail delivery and canal projects were contracted out. However, until 1950 the use and application of contractual arrangements were drastically lim-

FIGURE 4.8

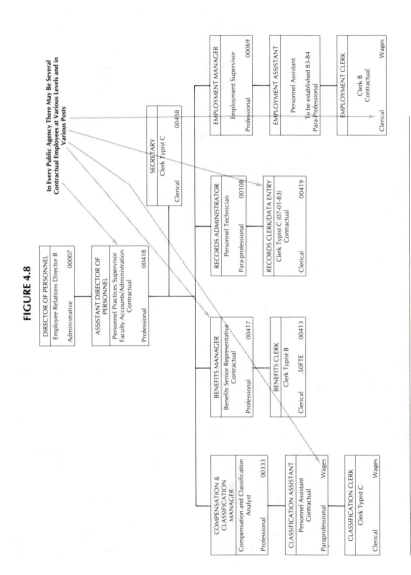

In Every Public Agency There May Be Several Contractual Employees at Various Levels and in Various Posts

DIRECTOR OF PERSONNEL	
Employee Relations Director B	00007
Administrative	

ASSISTANT DIRECTOR OF PERSONNEL	
Personnel Practices Supervisor Faculty Accounts/Administration Contractual	00418
Professional	

SECRETARY	
Clerk Typist C	00458
Clerical	

COMPENSATION & CLASSIFICATION MANAGER	
Compensation and Classification Analyst	00333
Professional	

CLASSIFICATION ASSISTANT	
Personnel Assistant Contractual	Wages
Paraprofessional	

CLASSIFICATION CLERK	
Clerk Typist C	Wages
Clerical	

BENEFITS MANAGER	
Benefits Senior Representative Contractual	00417
Professional	

BENEFITS CLERK	
Clerk Typist B	.50FTE 00413
Clerical	

RECORDS ADMINISTRATOR	
Personnel Technician	00108
Para-professional	

RECORDS CLERK/DATA ENTRY	
Clerk Typist C (07-01-83) Contractual	00419
Clerical	

EMPLOYMENT MANAGER	
Employment Supervisor	00069
Professional	

EMPLOYMENT ASSISTANT	
Personnel Assistant To be established 83-84 Para-Professional	

EMPLOYMENT CLERK	
Clerk B Contractual	
Clerical	Wages

Source: Commonwealth of Virginia.

155

FIGURE 4.9
On the Other Hand, Some Public Organizations
Go to the Extreme and Contract-Out All or Most of Their Work,
as in Lakewood, California

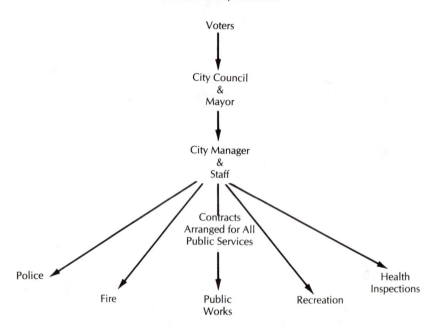

ited in most public agencies. All this changed, as chapter 2 explained, with the hot and cold war demands of the postwar era, when government increasingly needed highly skilled scientific and engineering talent from universities, private enterprises, and consulting firms to conceptualize, build, and implement numerous weapons programs. The Rand Corporation and the National Science Foundation were created by the federal government as outside sources for accomplishing in-house missions of DoD.

The growth of contracting-out for government services since then has been unprecedented in size, scope, and intensity. Government has been driven into contracting willy-nilly in so many fields because it has been asked to perform greater numbers of tasks of ever-greater complexity within shorter time frames, tasks for which it has neither the expertise nor the capacity to acquire it on a short-term basis. At the state and local levels, contractual employment accelerated in the 1970s and 1980s as a device for accomplishing programmatic goals while avoiding rising costs of hiring permanent civil servants (today a permanent civil servant costs government roughly twice the worker's *actual* salary, largely because of "hidden fringes" such as retirement programs and health and other benefit packages). Contracting-out is also a method of doing complex work in which states and localities have little expertise. But it has broad implications, for as Clarence Danhof, a prominent authority in this field, has written:

> The contractual system is . . . more than a device to get work done for a government agency. An agency's program is built upon contributions from many sources, public and private. There are numerous channels through which interested and knowledgeable groups may suggest courses of action to accomplish broadly defined objectives. A formal contract is merely a step in a process of interaction between private and public groups with an interest in a scientific or technical area. In this process the government agency assumes responsibility for preparing programs and seeing them through the normal authorization and budgeting routines. It also chooses from among the proposals made to it those which it will include as contractual projects in its approved programs. In both the formulation and the execution of its program the agency is heavily, and sometimes wholly, dependent upon the initiative of outside institutions in developing the expertise necessary to prepare the proposals and do the work.[27]

As Danhof correctly suggests, contractual relationships become extremely complex interactions between the purveyors of goods and services and public agencies, and as such they evidence a staggering array of formalized relationships, informal behavior, and complex ethical and institutional problems. However, the important point is that, as Bruce L. R. Smith has stated, the contracting phenomenon is "one of the most striking features of America's postwar public organizations."[28] The contractual subsystem has grown haphazardly and largely out of the public view. The implications of increasing reliance upon "outsiders" to perform the inside work of public bureaucracies are still not fully understood or appreciated, even by experts in political science, public administration, and government, and certainly not by the general public or by most public officials.

Some effects on public agencies and their outputs are fairly obvious. First, the growth of the contractual subsystem makes it increasingly hard to tell where government bureaucracy begins and ends. Is the permanent public agency that relies on the expertise of a single outside contractor *really* independent of that outside private enterprise? Or is the private contractor who relies on a public bureaucracy for all or most of his annual income *really* private, and not merely an extension of a public bureaucracy? Increasingly, the worlds separating government agencies and private sector businesses, universities, and consulting firms are dissolving into an area where boundaries overlap or are unclear and difficult to define.

What is clear, however, is that these "outside" groups perform much of the bureaucratic work of government. If their personnel were counted as government employees, the size of government bureaucracy would probably be twice as large as it is. Contracting-out, then, enables politicians to gain ser-

FIGURE 4.10
At the Federal Level, OMB Circular No. A–76
Has Been Particularly Instrumental in Expanding the Use
of Contracting-Out of Public Services

EXECUTIVE OFFICE OF THE PRESIDENT
OFFICE OF MANAGEMENT AND BUDGET
WASHINGTON, D.C. 20503

March 29, 1979

CIRCULAR NO. A–76
Revised

TO THE HEADS OF EXECUTIVE DEPARTMENTS AND ESTABLISHMENTS

SUBJECT: Policies for Acquiring Commercial or Industrial Products and Services Needed by
the Government

1. *Purpose.* This Circular establishes the policies and procedures used to determine
whether needed commercial or industrial type work should be done by contract with private
sources or in-house using Government facilities and personnel. This Circular replaces OMB
Circular No. A-76, dated August 30, 1967, and all subsequent amendments.

2. *Background.* In a democratic free enterprise economic system, the Government should
not compete with its citizens. The private enterprise system, characterized by individual freedom and initiative, is the primary source of national economic strength. In recognition of this
principle, it has been and continues to be the general policy of the Government to rely on
competitive private enterprise to supply the products and services it needs.

This policy has been expressed in Bureau of the Budget Bulletins issued in 1955, 1957, and
1960. In 1966, Circular No. A-76 was issued and, for the first time, prescribed the policy and
implementing guidelines in a permanent directive. The Circular was revised in 1967, by
Transmittal Memorandum No. 1, to clarify some provisions and to lessen the burden of work
by the agencies in implementation. Transmittal Memorandum No. 2 was issued in 1976, providing additional guidance on cost comparisons and prescribing standard cost factors for Federal employee retirement and insurance benefits.

In 1977, a comprehensive review of the Circular and its implementation was initiated. Transmittal Memorandum No. 3 was issued on June 13, 1977, announcing the review and temporarily reducing the Government retirement cost factor. This revision is the result of that review
and careful consideration of comments from all interested parties.

3. *Responsibility.* Each agency head has the responsibility to ensure that the provisions of
this Circular are followed. This Circular provides administrative direction to heads of agencies
and does not establish, and shall not be construed to create, any substantive or procedural
basis for any person to challenge any agency action or inaction on the basis that such action
was not in accordance with this Circular, except as specifically set forth in Section 11
below. . . .

vices for their constituents *and then* claim that they have "kept the lid on
government personnel costs." Such a claim is clearly untrue and leads to further confusion—and deception—about the realities of the size and true nature of government.

Second, some sectors of government have clearly become "captives" of
their contractors. The purveyors of many large DoD weapons systems, such
as Hughes, Boeing, Rockwell, and McDonald Douglas, not only design and

develop these multibillion dollar, multiyear systems but by proposing new weapons systems are also actively involved in establishing DoD and individual service priorities, budget requirements, personnel needs, and even the broad global strategic priorities of U.S. defense policy. And once the weapons are sold, these firms become the sole-source suppliers virtually dictating the costs—often overrun by huge amounts—to the contracting agency. Top executives move back and forth with ease between these firms and top policy-making posts within DoD. Harold Brown (DoD secretary under President Carter), William C. Foster (Brown's research and development specialist), Caspar Weinberger (the present DoD secretary), and John Lehmann (the current secretary of the Navy) are all products of the contract world surrounding DoD. This is not meant to suggest that these individuals or others who serve "in-and-out" at high DoD policy-making levels have acted unethically or dishonestly; it simply means that their backgrounds and skills are utilized in *both* government and business at various managerial and staff levels and that they therefore significantly influence policies and administration in *both* sectors.

Another effect of the increasing rise and reliance upon the contractual subsystem within public bureaucracy is that there is less and less use for traditional bureaucratic techniques, such as standard in-house work rules, for direction and control of personnel and resources. More emphasis is now placed upon contract negotiations, formal agreements, legal sanctions, economic rewards and penalties for inducing compliance by contractors, and auditing and management information systems for "tracking" completion dates. All these procedures are essential for quality control and to make the contractors and subcontractors perform their services according to schedule. Bureaucrats at all levels increasingly are becoming contract managers as opposed to fulfilling their traditional line management roles.

Also, as suggested before, with the growing numbers of public personnel "off the books" because of their nontenured status, the traditional sorts of personnel work rules, personnel oversight controls, and procedures governing employee behavior have diminished in importance. Thus the problems of imposing public accountability on contract workers grow as the numbers of third-party agents and subcontractors grow. Proper policy performance and implementation in regard to legality, honesty, competence, correctness of action, and effective completion of projects become increasingly difficult to ensure as the number of private businesses, universities, and others who perform the work of public agencies increases. Recent leaks of highly sensitive national security information by Hughes employees and the massive fraud cases of General Electric subcontractors working on various navy projects illustrate these enormous problems of public accountability and oversight. Indeed, *should* bureaucracy impose its public standards of accountability on such "private" groups and citizens? The difficult and uncharted ethical dimensions of the problems loom large.

Finally, the traditional tools for managerial oversight, such as budgets for integrating, controlling, and directing bureaucratic activities, are of decreasing importance and usefulness as the pressures of the contractual subsystem force new commitments and expenditures of funds years ahead of time and in turn become legally and politically "untouchable." As many scholars and budget experts now observe, not only is the federal budget out of control but also no one even knows how much is really being spent annually, largely because of the pressures of the growing contractual subsystem. Many contractors simply operate independently of the budget process—off the books and out of sight—developing independent accounting, auditing, and budgeting systems along with separate personnel rules, regulations, and procedures that are well beyond public scrutiny and oversight mechanisms.

Summary of Key Points

If public bureaucracy is the core system of U.S. government today, certainly the core of that core is composed of critical groups within bureaucracy. Bureaucracy's inner dynamics, or, in the words of Aristotle, its "real constitution," are made up of five subsystems, each in its own way determining what happens to bureaucratic activities in government. These subsystems decide what public agencies can and cannot do, and how and when they will perform tasks. The "balance" or "imbalance" of these groups within every agency is fundamental to its character, policies, and performance. The three basic patterns of distribution of these internal subsystems' power and authority within public bureaucracies are depicted by figure 4.11.

In an agency dominated by political appointees, as in the case of the local county commission, short-term goals, interest in broad political issues, responsiveness to the general electorate or to special pressure groups, and attention to the immediate requirements of the elected chief official become paramount. An agency dominated by professional careerists, on the other hand, tends to be more removed from the public, views the world in much longer time frames, and is motivated by professional norms, goals, and criteria for action. Status, credentials, rank-in-person, narrow expertise career ladders, and control over careers by professional elites—all are deemed critical within such a public bureaucracy. Thus these agencies tend to become more remote, more isolated, even unresponsive and conservative vis-à-vis immediate public pressures, which inspires both *criticism and respect* for the professions and is the root of their popular support as well as of hostility toward them. It is the basis of both their constitutional legitimacy and their institutional difficulties within government.

The civil service subsystem operates without distinct career ladders or professional elite controls. Rank is gained from the job. Less status and credentialism is evident. Hence, this subsystem is much more laissez-faire. It is a more "open" subsystem that comprises a broad range of specialists and gen-

TABLE 4.6
Summary of Key Aspects of Five Subsystems

	Political Appointees	Professional Careerists	Civil Service	Union Workers	Contract Employment
Position Inside System	Occupy top levels of system	Mid to upper levels	Throughout government	Blue collar, increasing white collar workers	Activities vary significantly by agency
Purposes & Goals	Provide top level policy direction	Key policy, management, expert roles	Generalists & specialists doing many jobs	Largely non-professional & para-professional work	Hired for fulfilling specific technical & general tasks within a limited time
Time Frames	Short term	Long term	Long term	Short/medium/long term	Mostly short term
Sources of Recruitment	Largely upper class	Largely middle class	Largely middle class	Largely blue collar	Largely from major corporations or small businesses or universities
Ladders for Promotion	Tend to be "in & outers"	Clearly defined hierarchy	Less clearly defined than careerists due to "rank in job"	Seniority system	Open competitive bidding for employment
Dominant Motivations Adhered to	Political responsiveness	Professional norms & values	Mixed motives	Based upon union contracts	Profit motives of the business—"the bottom line"
General Responsiveness to Public or Special Interests	Can be high to public &/or special interests	Generally low responsiveness to both	Mixed	Mixed	Oriented to mainly private business
Major Dilemmas Posed for Government	Lack of expertise and short tenure	Conservatism, monopoly on expertise and long tenure	Slow responsiveness due to emphasis on gradualism and fragmented oversight	Desire to "work to rules" in contract & seniority emphasis	Pressures of the "bottom line" subverting "the public interest"
Example of Agency Dominated by This Group and Impacts on Agency's Policies, Structure, and Character	U.S. Attorney's Office in Dept. of Justice—staffed by pol. appointees & highly responsive to local interests with limited control from above at D.J.—thus decentralized, highly political, & uneven program operations	U.S. Marine Corps—highly skilled at performance of limited military roles; centralized, hierarchical, expert and mission-oriented	Veterans Administration—large, complex, varied work force, linked to VA Groups and legislative allies, with autonomy from Pres. oversight.	U.S. Postal Service—Activities based upon negotiated contracts and support from unions, bilateral decisions between union & management.	NASA—highly technical, complex space activities draw upon services from many large contractors, who shape agency goals, priorities, political support, budget organization, etc.

FIGURE 4.11
**Three Basic Patterns of Distribution of Subsystem Power and Authority
within Public Bureaucracies**

Dominance of an Agency
by *One* Subsystem

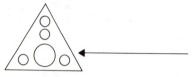

One is dominant over other four and hence
controls virtually all agency actions; e.g.,
lawyers at the Department of Justice or
medical professionals at the National
Institutes of Health create a stable & highly
powerful source for agency direction.

Dominance of an Agency
by *Two or Three* Subsystems

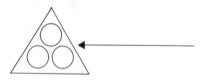

No *one* group gains control, but two or three
powerful subsystems compete for influence
in an agency, creating a stalemate *or* shared
power with healthy checks and balances
between competing groups, e.g., army, navy,
air force professionals within the Department
of Defense can create a stable or an unstable
agency.

No Subsystem Dominant
within the Agency

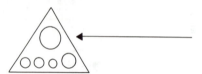

No group or groups dominate, but rather
several roughly equal subsystems share
power and authority through often unstable
and shifting arrangements (e.g., the Agency
for International Development), thus creating
weak and unstable agencies.

eralists. Like professional careerists, these tend to share the attributes of
longer time perspectives and to be conservative and gradualist in dealing with
issues. But, unlike professional careerists, they also tend to look less to their
immediate peers or to the values and knowledge of higher educational institutions for direction and more to individualized networks of like-minded
friends up and down the bureaucracy for support and alliances.

The union subsystem, by contrast, is made up of blue collar workers and
increasing percentages of white collar employees, such as teachers, who look
to their particular unions to represent their interests in periodic contract negotiations with government representatives. The subsystem's impacts upon bureaucratic operations range from wholesale takeovers to limited or no involvement with bureaucratic policy outputs. But, on the whole, the union
subsystem has added new dimensions of complexification, bipartisanship,
and formalistic worker-management relationships inside government organizations.

Finally, the contractual subsystem is rapidly blurring distinctions between public and private organizations by introducing a crazy quilt of private
workers within public agencies and public bureaucratic involvement deep
within private sector, profit-oriented and nonprofit firms. Where its processes

FIGURE 4.12
Summary of Key Historic Dates in the Development of Five Subsystems

Political Appointees	Civil Service	Career Professionals	Union Workers	Contract Employees
1789 First Cabinet Secretaries, Key aides, Ambassadors appointed by Pres. Washington	1871 First civil service law passed as a rider by Congress and then dies for lack of appropriations	1802 West Point est. as first public professional training school in U.S.	1857 National Teachers Assoc. formed	1860 Act of Congress est. "open competitive bidding"
1829 President Jackson introduces "spoils system"	1879 Dorman Eaton writes *Civil Service in Great Britain* and founds the National Civil Service Reform League	1902 General Staff and Army War College created for advanced professional planning & training	1912 Lloyd-La Follette Act gives federal workers right to join unions	1940 "Cost-plus-fixed fee" contracts approved
1936 Brownlow Report advocates civil service should be an "Arm of the Presidency" (rather than a neutral position)	1883 Civil Service Act enacted	1908 First city manager hired in Stanton, Ohio	1959 Wisconsin passes first law allowing local collective bargaining	1940–45 Manhattan Project creates atomic bomb and est. prototype of large-scale postwar government contracting with businesses and universities
1952 Schedule C positions introduced	1906-8 NY Bureau of Municipal Research develops first efficiency ratings and position classifications	1914 Professional assoc. of city managers begun	1962 Pres. Kennedy signs Ex. Orders 10987 and 10988 permitting federal collective bargaining.	1948 RAND Corporation created as first gov. "think tank"
1955 2d Hoover Report advocates a senior executive service	1912 Chicago adopts the first personnel classification system	1922 GAO created as 1st prof. staff for Congress	1969 Federal Labor Relations Council created	1948 NIH develops first large scale "domestic" contracting-out
1978 Civil Service Reform Act creates SES and OPM as a management arm of the White House	1916 The Model City Charter advocates local civil service systems	1924 Rogers Act creates the foreign service	1978 Civil Service Reform Act gives first statutory approval to labor-management collective bargaining on federal level	1950 NSF established
	1923 Classification Act adopted	1936 Brownlow Report recommends increasing professional staff for President		1961 BoB Circular A-49 approved use of management & operating contracts
	1939/40 Hatch Acts approved	1939 Reorganization Act creates BoB as staff arm of President		1967 BoB circular A-76 (revised in 1976, 1979, 1981), governs federal contracting policies
	1940 Social Security Act Amendment requires states to est. merit systems to receive federal funds	1939 ASPA created		
	1944 Veteran Preference Act approved	1955 Federal Service Entrance Exam est. (later changed to PACE)		
	1978 Civil Service Reform Act	1969 FEI established		
		1970 Intergovernmental Personnel Act passed		
		1978 Civil Service Reform Act creates more training and research opportunities for public service		

dominate an agency, as in DoD weapons acquisitions, an agency may well become entirely a "captive" of its business suppliers.

Most bureaucracies in the public sector are, however, dominated not by any one subsystem but by several; indeed, all these subsystems normally are found within their structures. Hence, policy outcomes frequently result from their jockeying for position, influence, and power over public bureaucratic actions. Conflicts between various subsystems are common. Sometimes the competition for power and control over the policy-making apparatus can become quite severe and intense, as in conflicts between professionals and political appointees, or among professional elites, or between union and management representatives. This can result in *either* healthy competition *or* a stalemate. More often than not it also is well hidden from public view and surfaces in the press only rarely. Finally, in some agencies *no* subsystem dominates but rather several roughly equal subsystems share power and authority through often temporary, unstable, and shifting arrangements. In many cases, this situation can, in turn, create weak, fragmented, and unstable agencies that can accomplish little or nothing. How government agencies accomplish their tasks and responsibilities will be the subject of the next chapter.

Key Terms

political appointees	GS rating
sub-Cabinet officials	rank "in person" vs "in job"
general professionals	Kennedy's Executive Orders 10988
public professionals	and 10987
SES	public service unions
"inner" vs. "outer" Cabinet	contract employment
Pendleton Act	line vs. staff personnel

Review Questions

1. What are the five major subsystems in public agencies that decisively influence bureaucratic policy? Briefly describe the characteristics of each one.
2. Where are political appointees situated in the bureaucracy and what functions do these individuals serve in U.S. government? Can you name a few current political appointees in government?
3. What are the essential differences between the professional careerist subsystem and the general civil service subsystem? What are the sources of each one's influence and authority?
4. How do general professionals, public service professionals, emerging professionals, and paraprofessionals differ from each other? Can you offer specific examples of each type of professional group in government?
5. Why have both the union and contractual subsystems emerged so rapidly within public bureaucracy in recent decades? Why are they important to setting public policies?

Notes

1. Hugh Heclo, *A Government of Strangers* (Washington, DC: Brookings Institution, 1977), p. 103.
2. These characteristics of political appointees have been true for some time. See David T. Stanley, Dean E. Mann, and Jameson W. Doig, *Men Who Govern* (Washington, DC: Brookings Institution, 1967).
3. For data on the backgrounds of city managers that tend to show a high degree of heterogeneity, read Richard J. Stillman II, "Local Public Management in Transition," *The Municipal Year Book 1982* (Washington, DC: International City Management Assoc., 1982), pp. 161–73.
4. Thomas P. Murphy, Donald E. Nuechterlein, and Ronald Stupak, *Inside Bureaucracy: The View from the Assistant Secretary's Desk* (Boulder: Westview Press, 1978).
5. Frederick C. Mosher, *Democracy and the Public Service*, 2d ed. (NY: Oxford University Press, 1982), p. 183.
6. Chester A. Newland, "The Reagan Presidency," *Public Administration Review*, vol. 43, no. 1 (January/February 1983), pp. 17–18.
7. See Samuel H. Beer's presidential address befrore the American Political Science Association, "Federalism, Nationalism and Democracy in America," American Political Science Review, vol. LXXII, no. 1 (March 1978).
8. Zbigniew Brzezinski, *Between Two Ages: America's Role in the Technetronic Era* (NY: Viking, 1970); Don Price, *The Scientific Estate* (Cambridge: Harvard University Press, 1965); Daniel Bell, "Notes on the Post-Industrial Society," *The Public Interest,* vol. 6 (Winter 1967), pp. 24–35; and Guy Benveniste, *The Politics of Expertise* 2d ed. (San Francisco: Josey Bass Publishers, 1983).
9. Frederick C. Mosher, *Democracy*, p. 142.
10. Corinne L. Gilb, *Hidden Hierarchies: The Professions and Government* (NY: Harper and Row, 1966).
11. Burton J. Bledstein, *The Culture of Professionalism* (NY: W. W. Norton, 1976), p.x.
12. Much of the following discussion is drawn from the research on professions in government contained in Frederick C. Mosher and Richard J. Stillman II, *Professions in Government* (New Brunswick, NJ: Transaction Books, 1982).
13. O. Glenn Stahl, *Public Personnel Administration*, 7th edition (NY: Harper and Row, 1976), p. 42.
14. The best account of the development of civil service remains Paul P. Van Riper's *History of the United States Civil Service* (Evanston, Ill.: Row Peterson, 1958).
15. Jay M. Shafritz, *Public Personnel Management* (NY: Praeger, 1975), p. 33.
16. Kenneth J. Meier, "Representative Bureaucracy," *American Political Science Review* (1975), pp. 535–53.

17. Unpublished data prepared by Kenneth Smith, DPA candidate, George Mason University, Fairfax, VA.

18. Marver Bernstein, *The Job of the Federal Executive* (Washington, DC: Brookings Institution, 1958), p. 49.

19. Eugene B. MacGregor, "Politics and Career Mobility of Civil Servants," *American Political Science Review* 68 (1974), p. 24.

20. *Task Force Report on Personnel and Civil Service, The Organization of the Executive Branch of the Government* (First Hoover Commission Report), pp. 1–2.

21. As cited in Hugh Heclo, *Government*, p. 142.

22. Anthony Downs, *Inside Bureaucracy* (Boston: Little Brown, 1967), p. 103.

23. David T. Stanley, *Managing Local Government under Union Pressure* (Washington, DC: Brookings Institution, 1972), p. 136.

24. PL 95–45, October 13, 1978, Section 7106.

25. As quoted in Harry H. Wellington and Ralph K. Winter, Jr., *The Union and the Cities* (Washington, DC: Brookings Institution, 1971), p. 30.

26. Ibid.

27. William Danhof, *Government Contracting* (Washington, DC: The Brookings Institution, 1968).

28. Bruce L. R. Smith, "The Future of the Not-for-Profit Corporation," *The Public Interest* (Summer 1967), p. 77.

Further Readings

A number of excellent books deal with the origins, growth, and operations of these various types of bureaucratic subsystems discussed in this chapter. The best account of the rise of the U.S. Civil Service remains Paul Van Riper's *History of the U.S. Civil Service* (1958). For a history of the European civil service, read Brian Chapman's *The Profession of Government* (1959). For an account of professionalism in the civil service, read C. L. Gibb's *Hidden Hierarchies* (1966), Don Price's *Scientific Estate* (1965), and Frederick C. Mosher's *Democracy and the Public Service*, 2d ed. (1982). O. Glenn Stahl's *Public Personnel Administration*, 8th ed. (1983) remains the best guide to current civil service practices. For an account of the interplay between political appointees, professionals, and civil servants, read Frank J. Thompson's *Personnel Policy in the City* (1975) and Hugh Heclo's *A Government of Strangers* (1977). The best review of the impact of the 1978 Civil Service Reform Act is found in Patricia Ingraham and Carolyn Davis's *Legislating Bureaucratic Change* (1984). For useful current perspectives on professional careerists, see Frederick C. Mosher and Richard J. Stillman II's (eds.) *Professions in Government* (1982), and on unions, A. Lawrence Chickering's (ed.) *Public Employee Unions* (1977) and David T. Stanley's *Managing Local Government under Union Pressure* (1972). For an overview of several of these groups see Lester M. Salamon and Michael S. Lund's *The Reagan Presidency and the Governing of America* (1984) and Eugene B. MacGregor's (ed.) "The Public Service as an Institution," a symposia, *Public Administration Review* (July/August 1982), and, particularly, Norton Long's "SES and the Public Interest," *Public Administration Review* (May/June, 1981). Even though the contractual subsystem has emerged as a powerful and significant force within public bureaucracy today, few scholars have examined the subject in recent years. This is both surprising and regrettable, though Clarence H. Danhof's *Government Contracting* (1968), although somewhat dated, is still useful for its history. Though polemics, both Gordon Adam's *Iron Triangles* (1981) and John D. Hanrahan's *Government by Contract* (1983) contain interesting data on this topic. Two recent books dealing with political appointees include John W. Macy, Bruce Adams, J. Jackson Walter's (eds.) *America's Unelected Government: Appointing the President's Team* (1983) and G. Calvin MacKenzie's *The Politics of Presidential Appointments* (1981). Also helpful on this topic are several first-hand "insider" views, including Alexander Haig's *Caveat* (1984), Joseph Califano's *Governing America* (1981), Elliot Richardson's *The Creative Balance* (1976), Ben W. Heineman and Curtis A. Hessler's *Memorandum for the President* (1980), andThomas P. Murphy, Donald E. Nuechterlein, and Ronald J. Stupak's *Inside the Bureaucracy* (1978).

5
Outputs of U.S. Bureaucracy

Police catch crooks, firefighters put out fires, social workers help the needy, the military defends the nation. No public organization is created, funded, and sustained for very long without some prescribed legal purpose to fulfill for the public. Whether it performs its mandated missions well, or even at all, is another matter. Many perform their goals in cooperation with other public, private or nonprofit units. Many agencies fall far short of performing their explicit goals. Many of bureaucracy's actual goals are not even explicitly defined. Yet, to whatever degree bureaucratic goals are publicly stated or in practice imprecisely defined, government agencies are ultimately purposeful entities, i.e., they are made up of people who are organized around the execution of some task or activity to be accomplished for someone, some interest group, or the public at large.

Legislators give much time and attention to framing these agency missions in enabling legislation as well as to continuously overseeing bureaucratic activities through budgetary approval, personnel authorization, and so on. Agency administrators, from first-line supervisors to top-level leadership, are actively involved in ongoing processes that clarify, modify, revise, and achieve various organizational goals. And certainly government workers are on the firing line, making whatever happens in any organization actually happen. Much of public organizational life therefore centers around the struggle over deciding what should be done and then carrying out that task or tasks within specific time frames and budgetary limits and despite tedious, tangled hierarchies, procedural routines, and numerous other complexities.

Ironically, though, when a governmental employee is asked, "Precisely what work does your agency perform for society?" the response is frequently ambiguous. The reply may be, "Legally we are responsible for undertaking this or that job, but let me tell you there is a lot more we do (or a lot less)." In other words, questions about precisely what public bureaucracy does normally lead to less-than-precise statements, even embarrassment or qualifications, and few clear-cut answers.

Part of the reason for this inconclusiveness was cited in chapter 3. Most public agencies have more than one purpose. Some agency missions are vague or ill defined in the enabling legislation. It may be of very little value to consult the law books to determine what activities a public organization performs (or fails to perform). The 1789 enabling legislation that created the State Department (first called a Department of Foreign Affairs) said that the department

> . . . shall perform and execute such duties as shall from time to time be enjoined on or entrusted . . . by the President of the United States, agreeable to the Constitution, relative to correspondences, commissions or instructions to or with public ministers or consuls, from the United States, or to negotiations with public ministers from foreign states or princes, or to memorials or other applications from foreign public ministers or other foreigners, or to such other matters respecting foreign affairs, as the President of the United States shall assign said department.[1]

Such an open-ended statement of purposes hardly gives even a glimmer of insight into the complex, multifunctional roles of the current State Department, many of which were outlined in chapter 2. Like Topsy, most of State's missions just grew.

Further, such lack of clarity in defining the purposes and goals of public organizations may be due to various groups—i.e., administrators, legislators, and citizens—wanting it that way for many reasons. Vague purposes often give administrators more flexibility in deciding on issues or managing programs. Legislators creating a new department may not themselves be very sure of the future duties it might someday acquire or of how they will be developed. Some fields, such as national security, require a degree of secrecy, hence its goals are unspecified. Certainly the CIA's charter as contained in the National Security Act of 1947 (with 1949 amendments) articulates its functions in the broadest, haziest language: "advise the National Security Council"; "make recommendations to the National Security Council"; "correlate and evaluate intelligence relating to the national security"; "provide for the appropriate dissemination of such intelligence within the Government"; and "perform for the benefit of the existing intelligence agencies, such additional services of common concern as the National Security Council determines."[2]

Imprecise objectives may in reality stem also from the inability of even the most gifted minds to comprehend all the ramifications of governmental actions. The Federal Reserve Board's responsibility for changing the discount rates periodically in order to "fine tune the economy" now have so many ripple effects on the country's and the world's economies and societies that its actions become deeply intertwined with a broad variety of public purposes (stated and unstated). Disentangling the *actual* objectives of this agency's actions as the country's central banker from *symbolic* ones can be difficult indeed. Stated purposes, in other words, may sometimes have nothing to do with the actual purposes of organizational actions, *and* the agency itself may not even know the difference.

Given all the complexity in fathoming the purposes of public organizations, this chapter will study such questions as: first, how can we conceptualize bureaucratic outputs? Second, how are these outputs then produced by public agencies? Finally, what, therefore, is a realistic way by which to comprehend overall the output processes of public organizations? Or, what is a valid model of the output process?

The Varieties of Bureaucratic Outputs in Government

Chapter 4 examined the interdynamics of public bureaucracies and observed that they revolve primarily around the interplay of five key subsystems: political appointees, professional careerists, general civil servants, union workers, and contract employees. Depending on its place in the bureaucratic hierarchy, each group plays an important role in shaping bureaucratic outputs and produces a unique type of "service," "product," or "result."

As figure 5.1 indicates, elected and appointed political officials occupy the very highest echelons of public bureaucracy. These political leaders as well as their Cabinet and sub-Cabinet officials formulate the overall political missions of agencies and forge public policy for these programs. As chapters 3 and 4 underscored, these political officials often work closely with the legislature, their committee staffs, the courts, other executive offices, and important interest groups outside government in developing policy goals through such means as initiating legislation, framing budgets, issuing political recommendations, informing the public by press releases and speeches, and devising new programs or revisions of old ones. What should U.S. policy be toward South Africa? Should the United States build a new "Star Wars" defense system? Can the present state highway system meet future transportation needs? These and other large questions occupy much of the time and attention of appointed officials. In a word, these officials produce outputs that *formulate policy directions and public goals for their agencies.*

The next level, occupied by lower-level political appointees, top career professionals, and civil servants, is also involved with the policy-making process but in a different way. The expertise at this level is generally narrower and more focused on *translating the broad policy mandates into operational programs.* This expertise is sought and valued by elected officials because it can

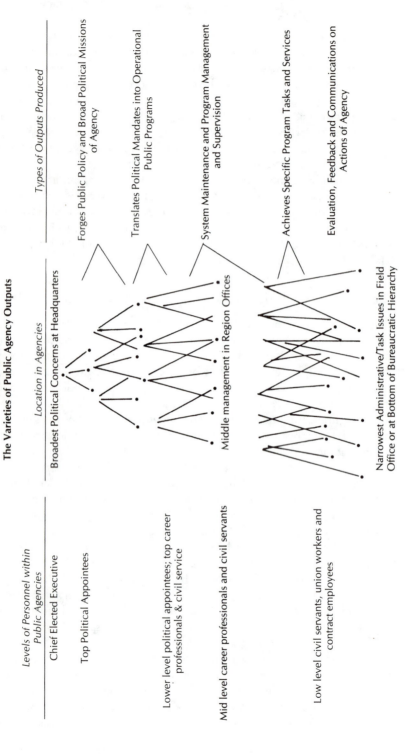

FIGURE 5.1
The Varieties of Public Agency Outputs

Levels of Personnel within Public Agencies

Chief Elected Executive

Top Political Appointees

Lower level political appointees; top career professionals & civil service

Mid level career professionals and civil servants

Low level civil servants, union workers and contract employees

Location in Agencies

Broadest Political Concerns at Headquarters

Middle management in Region Offices

Narrowest Administrative/Task Issues in Field Office or at Bottom of Bureaucratic Hierarchy

Types of Outputs Produced

Forges Public Policy and Broad Political Missions of Agency

Translates Political Mandates into Operational Public Programs

System Maintenance and Program Management and Supervision

Achieves Specific Program Tasks and Services

Evaluation, Feedback and Communications on Actions of Agency turn large and often vague political promises into functioning programs within agencies. When a president launches a space shuttle program, or a governor promises to upgrade the quality of education in public schools, or a mayor announces a new drug treatment program, it is often the "pros" inside government (top scientists/engineers at NASA, education specialists within a state, or public health officials in a city) that the political officials ask to design and initiate such new policy directions. Again, this "translation product" is not accomplished by these individuals alone; normally they act in cooperation with various other parties, e.g., clients to be served, political officials who initiated the idea, as well as a variety of individuals inside and outside government.

The middle levels of the civil service and professional career cadre, the next tier down, are largely concerned with still another product of public bureaucracy, namely, *system maintenance* (often not viewed as a "service" or "product"). By exercising various skills of management, supervision, control, and personnel and fiscal oversight, they see to it that the system runs as designed. These men and women are the managers and supervisors who ensure the social security checks are processed in a timely manner and that air quality standards are monitored and enforced according to the law and that local firefighters are prepared to fight fires. These administrative tasks involving system maintenance cover a wide array of activities, including collecting and analyzing data, issuing reports and orders, enforcing orders, developing policy alternatives for superiors, budgeting funds, awarding contracts, hiring personnel, and negotiating with citizens' and interest groups and other units of government.

Lower levels of the civil service, union members and contract employees in field offices or at the bottom of bureaucratic units, are largely concerned with *actual program implementation and service delivery*. Here is where the rubber meets the road, so to speak—the city police direct traffic, teachers instruct students, the IRS agent audits a taxpayer's 1040 form, and a postal worker delivers the mail. These men and women actually do the work of the agency or department. However, as chapter 4 pointed out, the rapid growth of contract employment in government in recent years had made it increasingly difficult to tell who *really* performs government services. Not all the work of government today is done by government employees in-house. Many private sector firms are largely "contract agencies" for the government.

All these groups share in still another important output of public bureaucracy, namely, *evaluation of the entire process*. Communications, i.e., positive and negative feedback, from all elements of any public agency can serve to shape and reshape policy agendas and political directions. Sometimes the evaluation is quite complex, formalized, and specialized, taking the form of evaluation reports prepared by bureaucratic staffs with the agency or outside of it (such as reports of the government affairs office). More than seventy units of the federal government alone are involved in producing these evaluations. At other times, the evaluation may simply be word-of-mouth gossip passed along from the ranks of the agency to the outside. Both formalized and informal communications can have significant effects upon agency actions. Figure 5.2 points out how these five bureaucratic outputs are produced in a typical federal program.

But how are these various outputs *actually* produced by public agencies? How does public bureaucracy *really* make things happen? First, let us examine three traditional ways of achieving bureaucratic outputs, including their shortcomings. Then let us propose an alternative, more realistic model to explain this process.

Making Bureaucratic Outputs Happen

Woodrow Wilson's famous observation may be pertinent here. In 1887 he perceptively observed in the first essay ever written by an American on U.S. public administration that "it is getting harder to run a constitution than to frame one."[3] Wilson's insight is even more true—and critical—today, for it is

FIGURE 5.2
In Typical Federal Programs, Outputs Vary by Bureaucratic Levels and Are Often Complex

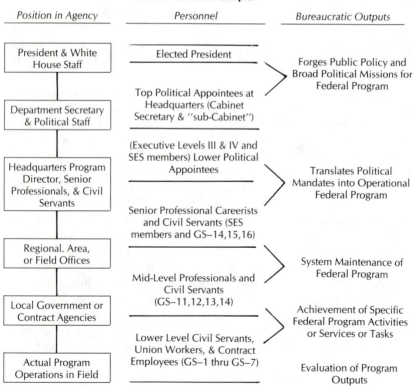

Position in Agency	Personnel	Bureaucratic Outputs
President & White House Staff	Elected President	Forges Public Policy and Broad Political Missions for Federal Program
Department Secretary & Political Staff	Top Political Appointees at Headquarters (Cabinet Secretary & "sub-Cabinet")	
Headquarters Program Director, Senior Professionals, & Civil Servants	(Executive Levels III & IV and SES members) Lower Political Appointees	Translates Political Mandates into Operational Federal Program
	Senior Professional Careerists and Civil Servants (SES members and GS–14,15,16)	
Regional. Area, or Field Offices		System Maintenance of Federal Program
Local Government or Contract Agencies	Mid-Level Professionals and Civil Servants (GS–11,12,13,14)	Achievement of Specific Federal Program Activities or Services or Tasks
Actual Program Operations in Field	Lower Level Civil Servants, Union Workers, & Contract Employees (GS–1 thru GS–7)	Evaluation of Program Outputs

comparatively easy to frame laws and devise policies pertaining to what an agency *ought to do* (constitution-making) in contrast to seeing to it that programs are *carried out* in a wise, efficient, and timely manner (constitution-running). What Wilson was arguing for was a science of administration to assist in the development of the accomplishing side of government—its performance of public activities. Grover Starling has called it "all those activities involved in carrying out the policies of elected officials and some activities associated with the development of those policies . . . in short, all that comes after the last campaign promise and election night cheer."[4]

With the growth of government and its increasing breadth of activities, these performance problems have become immensely more complicated *and* central to the government as a whole as well as to that of individual agencies. Indeed, the subject of implementation of government actions and programs has grown into a major preoccupation (perhaps "cottage industry" is the more correct term) of public administration experts and policy specialists. How should bureaucratic operations be carried out? Efficiently? Economically? Promptly? Fairly? Honestly? And in the public interest? Such questions have occupied the attention of a vast number of theorists, and their responses range from Frederick W. Taylor's scientific management principles to Peter Drucker's management by objectives concept.

Perhaps the classic formulation of "good" practices for accomplishing the basic purposes of government is found in *Papers on the Science of Administration* by Luther Gulick and L. Urwick (1937). These authors envisioned "the best" execution of public programs by means of the acronym POSDCORB, standing for a series of executive functions that presumably should be done in the following order:

Planning: goal-setting techniques/methods applied by executives as a means of preparing future courses of organizational action;

Organizing: arranging the organizational structure and processes in an appropriate manner essential to achieving these ends;

Staffing: recruiting and hiring personnel to carry out the essential agency work;

Directing: supervising the actual processes of doing the assignments;

Coordinating: integrating the various detailed elements of these tasks in cooperation with other units and people in government;

Reporting: tracking and communicating the progress of the work within the organization;

Budgeting: fiscal and financial activities necessary to economically support the completion of these programs, services, or activities.[5]

Various additions, changes, amendments, and refinements to the Gulick-Urwick sequence have been made over the years by other noted man-

agement authorities, such as Bertram Gross in his fivefold approach to producing organizational outputs:

> *Decision making*: defining the problems, setting out alternative courses of
> action, and choosing the best one;
>
> *Communicating*: getting out the information about the decision in oral
> and written form to those involved in its implementation and monitoring
> feedback and responses;
>
> *Planning*: developing purposeful actions toward the organizational future
> and correcting and adjusting these plans as they progress;
>
> *Activating*: through persuasion, pressure, controls, and so on, getting spe-
> cific action from the organization, its subunits, and its members;
>
> *Evaluating*: readjusting, correcting, and revising plans for the future and
> adjusting changes in the outputs, both qualitatively and quantitatively, as
> may be required for organizational survival and growth.[6]

Recently Graham Allison attempted to synthesize these varied lists of
"good" practices into one "grand" functional listing of eight generic processes:

Strategy

1. *Establishing objectives and priorities* for the organization (on the basis
   of forecasts of the external environment and the organization's capacities).
2. *Devising operational plans* to achieve these objectives.

Managing Internal Components

3. *Organizing and staffing*: In organizing, the manager establishes structure (units and positions with assigned authority and responsibilities)
   and procedures (for coordinating activity and taking action); in staffing
   he or she tries to fit the right persons in the key jobs.
4. *Directing personnel and the personnel management system*: The capacity of the organization is embodied primarily in its members and
   their skills and knowledge; the personnel management system recruits,
   selects, socializes, trains, rewards, punishes, and exits the organization's
   human capital, which constitutes the organization's capacity to act to
   achieve its goals and to respond to specific directions from management.
5. *Controlling performance*: Various management information systems—including operating capital budgets, accounts, reports, statistical systems, performance appraisals, and product evaluation—assist
   management in making decisions and in measuring progress toward objectives.

Managing External Constituencies

6. *Dealing with external units* of the organization subject to some common
   authority: Most general managers must deal with general managers of

other units within the larger organization—above, laterally, and below—to achieve that unit's objectives.

7. *Dealing with independent organizations*: Agencies from other branches or levels of government, interest groups, and private enterprises that can affect the organization's ability to achieve its objectives.

8. *Dealing with the press and public*, whose action or approval or acquiescence is required.[7]

Problems with Generic Output Models for Understanding How Bureaucratic Purposes Are Achieved

Most of the aforementioned lists of the "best" management practices by Gulick-Urwick, Gross, Allison, and others are drawn heavily from "generic management" thinking or the notion that "good" management is "good" wherever it is practiced—in business, nonprofit organizations, or government. Thus most tend to focus on "system maintenance" or "implementation" aspects of bureaucratic work and overlook other critical aspects of bureaucratic output actualities (cited earlier) such as policy formation or evaluation.

Such a point of view is not so much wrong as it is simply incomplete when it attempts to explain accurately the carrying out of programs and policies by public agencies. As the late Columbia University political scientist Wallace Sayre so aptly remarked, "Public and private management are fundamentally alike in all unimportant respects."[8] Or, as Paul Appleby put it, "Government is different."[9] Appleby might have added that the process of making public outputs happen is a lot different (in organizational structure, activities, purposes, and internal components) from the process of making private outputs happen. Several unique attributes make government agencies fundamentally *dissimilar* to business or other organizations.

Lack of a Bottom Line

Often (though not always) businesses operate with one clear priority, making a profit. Some, of course, do better than others at achieving this goal, but at least businesses *have a single goal*—profit making. As chapters 2 and 3 emphasized, few public organizations operate with such clear, singular objectives. Most pursue multiple goals and objectives to which simple quantitative measures regarding their outputs for society are frequently, though certainly not always, difficult to apply. Who can really tell whether a new ruling of the Nuclear Regulatory Commission (NRC) is appropriate and fair? Whether it is cost-efficient? Equitable? Whether it will impose undue burdens or additional costs to nuclear industry? Or whether it will prevent some future technological mishap such as that at Three Mile Island? How can one assess those "preventive" costs and benefits for society as a whole? The NRC, like most public agencies, is constantly juggling *many bottom lines*—e.g., social, political, economic, technological—and there are often no simple, quantitative ways of judging the worth of its actions.

Diversity of Institutional Arrangements

Again, as chapter 2 outlined, there is a wide array of public organizations in the United States. Some, such as the Defense Department, are larger than any business firm. Some, such as the small town with only one full-time employee, a village clerk of the council, to keep the doors of the city hall open and to pay the bills, are ''mom and pop'' operations. Some are organized like businesses, such as the more than one hundred government corporations operating on the national level or the 30,000 special district units rendering a multitude of special services on county and municipal levels. As a result of such institutional diversity, these public entities are enormously varied in their institutional and managerial infrastructure. Some utilize highly sophisticated technology, advanced professionalized managerial expertise, and quantitative measures in shaping, directing, and controlling their outputs that rival those at General Motors. Many do not use much more than pencil, paper, table, chair, and telephone to fulfill their assignments, simply because they have neither the need nor the finances to develop any high degree of managerial sophistication.

Fragmentation of Public Organizations and Their Authority

Business enterprises usually operate with one person ultimately in charge of seeing to it that things get done. But as chapter 3 stressed, the U.S. Constitution created a political environment within which every public bureaucracy must operate, thus fragmenting authority in many possible ways, breaking it up horizontally through a federal design and vertically through a division of power among separate, coequal branches of government. As a result of this scatterization of authority (intended by the founders to ''preserve individual liberties''), executives in every public agency must work with, in, and through many other units and levels of government—courts, Congress, and so on—to accomplish their assignments. It is this quality that has led Harvard professor Richard Neustadt to comment that the U.S. government is one of ''separated institutions sharing powers.'' Government administrators must constantly work with others beyond the boundaries of their own organizations in joint cooperative endeavors to reach collective decisions and achieve results for the public at large.

Public Agencies Operate in Goldfish Bowls

To complicate matters further, all these activities have to be done in the open with full public disclosure and accountability to legislature, media, and other oversight units such as independent auditors, subcommittees, hearings, and inspectors general. What is done in the business firm's boardroom can be decided largely in secret and without public scrutiny. Few public agencies enjoy that luxury or autonomy from such oversight today. The 1974 Freedom of Information Act at the federal level and "sunshine" laws enacted in recent years at the local level give the public press wide access to agencies' internal activities. Even the Central Intelligence Agency and Federal Bureau of Investigation have opened up their files and internal processes in unprecedented ways during the last decade. Both employ large full-time public relations offices to handle such external public "interface." Managers in every public agency know full well that what they say or do may hit the newspaper's front page tomorrow or local television news tonight. Most learn to act accordingly and to gauge their actions in light of the possible glare of public opinion.

Special Sensitivity to Broad Socioeconomic Changes

Business firms respond to changes in the particular markets they serve—autos, steel, housing, and so on. However, as chapter 3 stressed, public bureaucracies respond to broad socioeconomic trends within society in very immediate and practical ways—a rise in the unemployment rate may mean an immediate increase in workload for a local welfare agency or state unemployment office. A war or armed conflict abroad necessitates immediate national defense preparedness on a large scale. Large corporations may often, on the other hand, be entirely oblivious to changing local socioeconomic conditions and voter demands. A local Ford Motors auto plant or General Electric assembly plant or K-Mart may function in a community regardless of its changing broad socioeconomic patterns of life. Regional recession or prosperity may or may not have much to do with a multinational firm's decision to locate in a certain region. Further, private firms can and often do run their affairs without reference to local popular pressures, legislative concerns, and special interests (though, again, some do not).

Complexity, Rigidity, and Diversity of Internal Professional–Civil Service Subsystems

Chapter 4 of this book outlined the five competing subsystems that operate within most public organizations and that decisively shape bureaucratic policy and programmatic outputs. Each of these internal bureaucratic subsystems reflects an incredible degree of complexity, diversity, and rigidity. Unlike the private entrepreneur who can for the most part hire and fire his employees at will, government managers in professional and civil service subsystems are bound by an enormous quantity of detailed rules, procedures, and laws governing recruitment, selection, and promotion of personnel. No public manager can willy-nilly get rid of the professional–civil servant staff he or she inherits in an agency and hire entirely new personnel. Unlike managers of private firms, public managers have limited authority over personnel. This is also true for budgetary and most procedural routines inside government.

Differing Time Perspective of Each Subsystem

Whereas businesses and nonprofit organizations can and frequently do plan five, ten, even twenty years ahead, as chapter 4 pointed up, each of the five competing subsystems that operate inside public bureaucracies operate with their own time frame or "internal clock." The political appointees know that their time in office is limited to twenty-two months on an average, and so they must act accordingly in selecting and effecting short-term changes. The sights of the professional careerists and civil servants, in contrast, are mostly on the long term, and their activities are paced accordingly. The contract system's personnel look toward the built-in time frame involving the duration and completion of the specific project dates they are assigned by government.

Growth of the Contractual Subsystem Brings a Special Complexity to Public Management

As outlined in chapter 4, the proliferation of the contractual subsystem in government over the past few decades is fundamentally changing the jobs of public managers in areas of service delivery and program implementation. More and more government managers no longer are responsible for overseeing tasks performed in-house, but rather the work of bureaucracy is increasingly performed through contracting out for services by long chains of private and not-for-profit vendors. This change drastically shifts traditional tasks and responsibilities of public managers from managing line operations in-house to out-of-house demands of contract negotiations, contract management, oversight, auditing contractor performance, and so on. Complex ethical and accountability issues are furthermore involved that have little or no counterpart in private sector management practices. More will be said about this in the next chapter.

Constitutional Limits on Methods and Means of Service

Public agencies do not have the flexibility in targeting their audiences that businesses do. Rather, they must serve the public equally, fairly, and according to standards set forth in the U.S. Constitution, such as requirements for due process and equity and observance of the laws created by Congress. Fundamental constitutional values create radically different criteria for administrative action in the public sector than for that in the private sector. Concerns about equity, for instance, often, though not always, must outweigh considerations of efficiency in determining managerial choices for public agencies. For example, public schools *must* by law admit every child of school age (even illegal aliens), whereas private schools can base their selection of students on ability to pay, religion, sex, and mental or physical abilities. The comparative openness of public institutions, while making them considerably more heterogeneous and democratic, imposes special burdens, demands, and problems upon those responsible for making them operate.

FIGURE 5.3.
Summary of Unique Attributes of *Public* Organizations

*Lack of a bottom line
*Diversity of institutional arrangements
*Fragmentation of public organizations and their authority
*Public agencies operate in "goldfish bowls"
*Special sensitivity to broad socioeconomic changes
*Complexity, rigidity, and diversity of internal professional–civil service subsystems
*Differing time perspectives of each subsystem
*Growth of contractual subsystem brings special complexity
*Inability to select target audience
*Constitutional and legal limits on methods/means of service

And here perhaps is the most basic difference between private and public management practices, which Justice Louis Brandeis pointed out long ago, namely, that the goal of government is "not to promote efficiency but to preclude the exercise of arbitrary power."[10] This basic point had already been made by James Madison in his arguments for the checks and balances of the U.S. Constitution. In "The Federalist Papers, 51," he wrote: "The great security against a gradual concentration of several powers in the same branch, consists in giving those who administer each branch the constitutional means and personal motives to resist encroachment of the others. Ambition must be made to counteract ambition."[11]

The founders' tough-minded realism regarding human nature thus built into U.S. government—and especially into its public bureaucracy—a variety of internal and external checks on the activities of its officials that decisively constrains the myriad activities of public administrators at all levels today. The Constitution through its scatter of authority and built-in system of intricate checks and balances works to set up every possible institutional provision to *prevent* swift, decisive managerial action. Protection of individual liberty rather than promotion of effective management was truly the founders' "bottom line." *And* by and large it remains today as they conceived it in 1787. A remarkable success story *but* one that creates huge problems for modern public management for government bureaucracies.

Gamesmanship: The Reality of Making Bureaucratic Outputs Happen

If public agencies are created to accomplish certain tasks, but if the various generic models do not explain very well *how* these tasks are accomplished, what approach does? What best explains how bureaucratic activities are really performed in government? If U.S. public bureaucracies operate within a fluid, loose-jointed environment, surrounded by continually shifting socioeconomic forces and polycentric power structures, and if they are assigned multiple, often unclear missions by legislatures, and if, further, they are designed with severe constitutional limits that constrain actions, and if they are made up of competing, highly rigid, internal subsystems that prevent much managerial flexibility, how are outputs achieved in practice, given all these unique features? Indeed, how can *anything* be accomplished, given all these constraints?

While there are numerous approaches to understanding this process, as Richard E. Neustadt has observed, the hard reality of bureaucratic life is that administrative actions involving implementation of programs and policies are "a great game, much like collective bargaining, in which each seeks to profit from the other's needs and fears. It is a game played catch-as-catch-can, case by case. And everybody knows the game, observers and participants alike."[12]

Viewing the operations of bureaucracy as essentially gamesmanship may make it seem that the work of government is not very serious or purposeful, but as Laurence Lynn has written, "Public management . . . is neither all substance nor all process; it is a complex blend worked out over time in concert with others with whom one shares power and interests."[13] Lynn continues, "Thus the game metaphor can have immense practical value to executives attempting to orient themselves to new issues and circumstances involving uncertainty, ambiguity, and conflict."[14]

Gamesmanship in accomplishing bureaucratic tasks runs the gamut from conceptualizing the job to be performed to actually implementing the means of accomplishing it. It begins at the time an individual or group advocates a change in the status quo and ends when the discourse ceases and the services or tasks are finished. Gamesmanship activities can involve purposeful actions by managers with all the groups and units of government *outside* its formal boundaries as well as with internal subsystems within bureaucratic entities. What differentiates gamesmanship in government is often the level at which it is played: high, middle, or low. At each of these three levels public managers strive to obtain different sets of goals using different strategies; the gamesmanship at each level, too, involves different stakes.

High-Stakes Games

Focused on bringing about big, decisive public outcomes, high-stakes games influence the basic purposes and roles of government. These outcomes bring major impacts to the community or nation as a whole. At the federal level, high-stakes questions involve the type of problems that the Department of Health and Human Services confronts over whether or not to fund abortions or the Defense Department faces in deciding whether or not to place troops in the Middle East or Latin America. At the local level, some high-stakes games are: Should a city create a new master plan for the year 2000? Should the state government develop a comprehensive system of higher education? Such issues involve the most fundamental questions of society as well as shape the future directions of governmental programs to fulfill critical public needs.

This level of gamesmanship in government normally involves only the top-level political appointees, senior professional careerists, and civil servants. These high-ranking officials play these broad policy games well beyond the confines of their particular agencies, working and interacting with various elected officials, legislative committees, media representatives, pressure groups, and even the judiciary. High-stakes games involve the broadest possible strategies for mobilizing external support from various interest groups, jockeying with and outsmarting the opposition, gaining the backing of public opinion, and obtaining political influence and policy objectives through various agencies and branches of government. Many of the high-stakes strategies utilized at this level of "gaming" involve the broadest aspects of persuading, trading favors, arm-twisting, negotiating, and even issuing threats aimed at effecting purposeful change at the highest policy levels of government.

Middle-Stakes Games

At this level, games involve accomplishing more concrete, narrower bureaucratic goals: Should an agency act or not act in a specific manner, spend or not spend monies in particular ways, change or not change the methods by which it renders services. At the state level, middle-stakes games translate into such choices as: Should a new welfare program be devised to aid the elderly? Or, at the municipal level, should the park authority charge tennis players for using the lighted tennis courts at night? At the federal level these games might include the question of whether mandatory airbags should be required on new automobiles.

In the words of the late Columbia University sociologist C. Wright Mills, "American policies, as discussed and voted and campaigned for, have largely to do with these middle levels and often only with them. Most political news is news and gossip about middle level issues and conflicts."[15]

Broad ranges of bureaucratic subsystems inside government organizations shape these issues—from top-level political appointees to low-level unionized workers—not to mention the myriad external political and institutional forces surrounding every agency, such as the media, interest groups, the courts, and legislative bodies. Since the stakes are normally narrower, more expertise is required to "play" effectively at this level, and the "play" is not always carried out in full public view.

A good deal happens "sub rosa" in middle-stakes games, where personnel of more technical experience debate and resolve problems before they gain wide public attention. Middle-stakes games also generally require more long-term familiarity with the political, social, and economic environs of the public organization. Also mid-level gamesmanship generally is played out within the fine points of legislative drafting, program implementation, or over budgetary appropriations. There is less need to "play at" or "play to" a national audience and the larger public opinion. More managerial attention is directed at narrower ranges of bargaining, persuading, maneuvering, horse-trading, and swapping-off between particular key players who can influence decisively the outcomes of these middle-stakes games.

Low-Stakes Games

These games focus on the implementation and execution of public programs and policies and thus involve almost entirely the lower echelons of bureaucracy—professional careerists, general civil servants, union workers, and contractual employees. Low-stakes games concern "the workers in the vineyards of bureaucracy." This is not to say that these low-stakes games cannot create *big* headaches for top-level managers. At times the minor obstacles involved in low-stakes gamesmanship can mushroom into controversies of major significance throughout all of government. But most of the time low-stakes games are played out of the narrow confines of bureaucratic expertise and within the corridors of an intraagency or interagency arena. They concern issues like how the specific job should get done, when, how much effort should be made, and who is in charge—in other words, issues that come up *after* the program is in place and work begins.

Within a county government, a low-stakes game might involve the question of how to get rid of a problem employee who is slowing up road maintenance or snow removal schedules. At the state level it may involve a programmatic issue of a state revenue collection agency, such as what information should be added on the state income tax form to ensure higher compliance rates. At the federal level the Agency for International Development may wrestle with a low-stakes issue such as the construction dates for a new hydroelectric project in a third world nation that is funded and administered largely through AID sources. Such questions normally involve the operational aspects of carrying out the missions of a government agency. In low-stakes games larger policy choices and questions of program development and appropriations have already been settled. The disputes and conflicts that can and frequently do arise are usually internal problems involved with putting the program into action. Gamesmanship at this level is normally confined to a very narrow range of specialists—technical, scientific, and staff experts within the programmatic area, and these disputes are mostly, if not entirely, hidden from public view.

Participating at this game level usually requires long involvement with the particular agency and field of policy as well as a thorough understanding of the technical language and detailed operating substance of the particular program and its policies. Here, fewer issues of "pure politics" are involved (i.e., the typical broad political questions that Harold Lasswell described as "who gets what, when, how"), and more technical bureaucratic expertise is valued (i.e., traditional sorts of public administration concerns over matters of efficiency, economy, and effectiveness—the three E's). Given the types of issues involved in low-stakes games, it may be surprising to note that, as Francis E. Rourke has observed, "The sustained attention which bureaucrats can devote to specific problems gives them a decided advantage in framing such decisions over political officials who deal with a wide variety of problems and confront each issue of public policy only at sporadic intervals."[16]

While these are called low-stakes games, no top policy maker can safely assume they will remain lowly or out of sight. A simple problem of inadequate snow removal by a local public works department on a night of a big snowstorm could explode suddenly into a massive public controversy and "bad press" for top-level political executives. In other words, low-stakes implementation questions can and frequently do become high-stakes games of survival for the top echelons in public agencies. Thus, distinguishing the features between high- and low-level games can sometimes be quite difficult. They can overlap one another's turf and are not all that clear-cut in practice.

At times, also out of necessity, top-level executives must get involved in low-stakes games and, conversely, low-level bureaucrats can suddenly find themselves in the midst of high-stakes controversies. Both situations are awkward and rarely work out very well. When President Carter got involved in the specific details of scaling back western irrigation projects—or allocating tennis court times at the White House—he found himself entering a firestorm that was best left to the specific policy analysts and policy makers in this field. Similarly, when bureaucrats far down inside the bureaucracy try to establish broad policy agendas, they frequently do not have the breadth of policy vision nor the political capacity to carry them through. Many of the difficulties, for instance, that arose in establishing Zero Based Budgeting in the Carter administration or Program Planning Budgeting Systems in the Johnson administration resulted precisely from the fact that instituting both new types of budgetary systems required that fairly low-level budget specialists decide upon major policy choices. These choices frequently involved middle- or high-stakes games, well beyond the competence or capacity of these personnel to resolve.

As Laurence Lynn sees it, bureaucrats must be game players. "Game playing is the nature of their job."[17] Indeed, they may have little choice concerning which games they play, with what objectives or even with what intensity. But though deciding which game to play, if they do have a choice, may be their most critical problem. Given the limitations on time and resources, unlimited gamesmanship is impossible, so selecting what level to play at and what resources to utilize is critical for shaping bureaucratic outputs. *Internal* and *external resources* are two varieties of resources that can be summoned by bureaucrats to play these various levels of games. These resources are used to gain organizational cohesion and cooperative action for producing bureaucratic outputs.

Internal Resources for Gaining Organizational Cohesion and Cooperative Action

As already emphasized in this chapter, the constitutional framework within which every public organization must operate was not created to promote cohesion, unity, or purposeful, efficient actions on the part of government agencies. The founding fathers built into the system every conceivable device to do precisely the reverse, to promote division, disharmony, disarray, and disunity. Public organizations are constantly being pulled and tugged apart from the outside by media, pressure groups, and legislative oversight and from the inside by various competing organizational subunits and personnel subsystems. Government agencies swim with a vortex of fragmenting pressures that threaten programmatic integrity, organizational alignments, personnel allegiances, and even the survival of the basic organization itself—what Herbert Simon, Donald Smithburg, and Victor Thompson call "the struggle for organizational survival."[18] Gaining organizational unity and cooperative action and surviving at the same time are therefore a challenging, ongoing, full-time process (and preoccupation) within bureaucracy. In playing at their various levels of gamesmanship, however, bureaucrats can summon four basic types of resources from within their agencies to achieve programmatic direction, cohesiveness, and cooperation—and survival. Their ability to use these internal resources determines how the overall organization performs and what outputs a bureaucracy can or cannot achieve (and affects their own advancement and prestige).

Legal Resources

Used to create the agency in the first place, legal resources define its missions and its powers, and provide its independence from other units. These resources are provided for in the basic enabling legislation and in amendments to these laws and statutes. Legal resources can be highly potent vehicles for exercising control over bureaucratic activities and outputs. J. Edgar Hoover provides the classic illustration of their use. He saw to it that the FBI was granted legal authority to create a highly professionalized personnel system that operated independently of the civil service system, thereby giving the director vast discretionary powers over hiring, firing, and promotion of personnel. Even though the FBI operated within the Justice Department under the attorney general, Hoover made certain that the statutes governing the FBI gave the director a considerable degree of independence from both Justice and the attorney general. He saw to it that the statutes governing the FBI's central missions excluded involvement in law enforcement fields that were difficult, such as drug enforcement, and included those that made the bureau look good, such as recovering stolen autos and capturing bank robbers. Further, Hoover worked hard throughout his nearly fifty-year career as head of the FBI to ensure that administrative oversight of his agency was always delegated to "friendly" subcommittees in Congress and then did everything possible to curry the favor and support of these congressional figures. Furthermore, he attained the authority to create a vast, effective intelligence-gathering and information network that kept his friends "friendly" and his enemies at bay. In short, few individuals in government have ever exceeded Hoover in his ability to craft legal resources that benefited his own agency. The concrete results gave the FBI legal autonomy, the responsiveness of professional careerists, high funding, achievable agency missions, overall organizational unity, and long-term "friendly" congressional oversight (as well as autonomy from attorneys general and even presidents). These factors made the bureau a highly cohesive, potent instrument for implementing programs and policies it decided to undertake (though by the late 1960s and early 1970s, just prior to Hoover's death, his grasp upon effective control of the bureau's enforcement programs and policies had waned significantly).

Structural Resources

These are the formal elements of bureaucracy that managers utilize to coordinate, control, and direct agency activities. The range of structural resources varies considerably from office to office, but as Jeffrey Pressman observed, at the local level several of the following structural resources are critical for effective managerial gamesmanship:

1. sufficient financial and staff resources . . . ;
2. programmatic jurisdiction over social programs—such as education, housing, development, job training, etc.;
3. administrative capacity within city government to implement programs within these various policy fields;
4. a salary for (the official) which would enable him to spend full time on the job;
5. sufficient staff support . . . for policy planning, speech writing, intergovernmental relations . . . ;
6. ready vehicles for publicity such as friendly newspapers or television stations;
7. internal and external groups . . . to help achieve particular goals.[19]

The sufficiency or lack of such structural resources can make or break officials' abilities to carry out their duties. As Graham Allison observes, "The fact that the fixed programs (equipment, men and routines that exist at the particular time) exhaust the range of buttons that leaders can push is not always perceived by the leader. But in every case it is critical for an understanding of what is actually done."[20] President Carter's daring yet abortive helicopter raid to rescue American hostages in Iran during April 1980 failed precisely because Carter exhausted "the range of buttons" he could push to implement foreign policy in this case. The United States simply lacked the long-range mobile transports and combat personnel to carry out effectively such a complex, long-

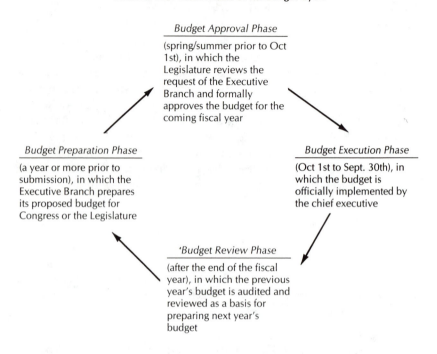

FIGURE 5.4
Control over Budgetary Processes Is an Especially Potent Process Resource and Annually Involves Four Basic Phases of the Budget Cycle

Budget Approval Phase

(spring/summer prior to Oct 1st), in which the Legislature reviews the request of the Executive Branch and formally approves the budget for the coming fiscal year

Budget Preparation Phase

(a year or more prior to submission), in which the Executive Branch prepares its proposed budget for Congress or the Legislature

Budget Execution Phase

(Oct 1st to Sept. 30th), in which the budget is officially implemented by the chief executive

'Budget Review Phase

(after the end of the fiscal year), in which the previous year's budget is audited and reviewed as a basis for preparing next year's budget

range rescue operation inside Iran. Jeffrey Pressman and Aaron Wildavsky's *Implementation* (1973) records a similar tragic tale at the local level (complete with Rube Goldberg cartoons) regarding the failure of the Economic Development Administration (EDA) to implement federal programs and public policies in Oakland, California, mostly because of the insufficiency of the basic structural resources necessary for the delivery of such community services. They point out how complexity of structures, short time frames, and an excessive number of missions defeated EDA's implementation plans in Oakland.

Process Resources

Such resources include managerial controls over hiring and firing, access to decision makers, opportunities to develop budgetary and fiscal resources, utilization of and access to computer data and management information systems, and freedom from audit controls or direct oversight from other agencies and branches. Process resources are also essential for shaping various levels of bureaucratic games. Officials' control of process resources is critical for flexibility, discretion, and exercise of bureaucratic actions.

Francis Rourke has particularly stressed how informational processes of bureaucrats contribute significantly to their power and influence: "Nothing contributes more to bureaucratic power than the ability of career officials to mold the views of other participants in the policy process. Bureaucracies are highly organized information and advisory systems and the data they analyze and transmit cannot help but influence the way elected officials perceive political issues and events. Herbert Simon has emphasized the importance of being able to shape the value or factual premises of decision makers as a means of insuring control over decisions themselves, and it is precisely in this way that bureaucratic information and advice commonly functions in the policy process."[21]

Rourke gives two prominent examples of how such elements contribute mightily to what happens in bureaucracy: George Kennan's postwar advisory role heading the policy planning unit at the State Department and his access to the ears of the secretary of state, the president, and the wider foreign affairs community decisively fashioned fundamental U.S. cold war programs and policies. Henry Kissinger in the late 1960s and early 1970s likewise significantly shaped U.S. Vietnam and China policies through his prominent National Security Council advisory role. Access to top decision makers, namely the president, as well as to astute minds that marshaled and controlled foreign policy information and determined where and when decision makers got the information, was instrumental to both Kennan's and Kissinger's success stories. At the state and local levels, officials' advisory roles also serve as potent sources of bureaucratic power. Sometimes this is offered quietly in back channels and other times it is offered up front in official briefing reports. By whatever manner, such process resources are critical to the shaping of ongoing outputs within every governmental jurisdiction.

Personal Resources

Individual qualities are equally important in shaping bureaucratic outputs, or what Yale's eminent political scientist Robert Dahl refers to as the individual attributes "to increase or combine resources through personal skills and abilities."[22] In essence, it is the person's own leadership capacity to combine and manipulate the resources of his or her bureaucratic office to achieve purposeful actions. As Bollens and Ries have noted, such personal leadership capabilities vary widely in city managers operating at the local level: "Depending upon their personality, individual managers will make more or less use of the resources attached to the position. Invariably managers are asked to present their views before civil and private organizations, that is, they are provided with many platforms for educating the public to municipal problems and can take the initiative in proposing programs for coping with them. A manager's sense of timing and tact will determine the extent to which he builds coalitions in support of his politics which, in turn influence council's response to them."[23] Ronald Loveridge[24] and others have classified four types of local-level leadership capacities and skills in bureaucracy at the grass roots: (1) *community leaders* who take the broadest, most creative view of their bureaucratic responsibilities and see themselves not merely as officials within government but as "doers," "change agents," and "activists" within the overall context of the community; (2) *chief executives* who confine their talents to executing in-house programs and policies and who prefer to work actively "behind the scenes" rather than up front in achieving actions within government agencies; (3) *administrative innovators,* managerial types found in local bureaucracies, who apply their administrative skills to technical and narrow roles in shaping the program outputs of an agency, especially in ways that improve its basic efficiency, effectiveness, and economy; and (4) *administrative caretakers* who exercise hardly *any* personal leadership capabilities at all, deferring to others' leadership, seeing their roles as simply to keep the doors of an agency open and the routines of government moving along, but little else.

Much of the exercise of personal leadership resources of course depends upon a manager's latitude of discretion within an agency. As chapter 4 pointed up, the mix of competing internal subsystems within any given agency determines the scope, quality, and size of governmental outputs. This mix of subsystems also invariably determines the type of personal resources required by any manager to induce cooperation and cohesive direction within an agency. A bureaucracy dominated by political appointees requires personal leadership resources involving party loyalties, political influence, patronage, and even a large amount of salesmanship and charisma. Professional careerists respect, by contrast, personal leadership built upon expertise, education, experience within the agency, and "the right schools and assignments," plus a long-term "corporate identity" with the central missions, values, and perspectives of the dominant professional elite within the agency. General civil servants are a more heterogeneous group of individuals, who in part respond to the qualities professionals admire in civic leadership but also are driven by more complex sociopolitical-bureaucratic-economic motives of task, salary, grade, and position. Union and contractual subsystems demand bureaucratic managers with still different leadership traits and skills, namely those who are able to negotiate well, persuade strongly, often in lawyerlike ways, and who can drive hard bargains in contract negotiations and then see to it that these contracts are fulfilled in the best interests of their union members or agencies *or both.*

While the necessary leadership skills therefore vary immensely depending on the mix of agency subsystems and the capabilities of individual managers, a good sense of timing as well as initiative, drive, creativity, tact, honesty, general good sense, and specific knowledge of the job area are all critical personal resources at every level of bureaucracy. These attributes make things operate, *even at the very lowest levels.* As Kenneth C. Davis points out about police officers on the beat,

The police are constantly confronted with problems of fairness to individuals and such problems are often intertwined with problems of policy. When should they not make an arrest that can properly be made? When should they stop and frisk? When should they say, break it up? When should they make deals with known criminals as the addict informers? What minor disputes should they mediate or adjudicate? These are tough questions which those on the lowest rungs of a police organization are asked to resolve everyday. No rule book holds the answers for each specific case. The individual patrolman must normally rely upon his own personal resources—i.e., experience, good judgment, common sense, etc.—for making such "calls."[25]

External Support for Bureaucratic Action: The "Windows of Opportunity"

Many of the important concepts administrative theorists have generated over the years have focused on the internal sources for cooperation and cohesion within organizations. According to Chester Barnard's notion of "the economy of incentives,"[26] for example, much of the executive's functional role is to juggle and calculate many of the aforementioned internal resources of an organization in order to achieve purposeful actions. Herbert Simon added the useful concept of "the zone of indifference"[27] as an equally important aspect to achieving organizational goals; i.e., individual members of any organization willingly accept authority within various degrees of personal compliance. According to Simon, it is within these ranges of indifference that employees are willing to go along with directives for achieving the overall administrative missions of an agency.

These *internal* administrative attributes may be important and certainly cannot be overlooked. Yet seasoned bureaucrats know that something else is even more critical and necessary for achieving programmatic and policy outputs. Sometimes they refer to it as "windows of opportunity" or the chance "to move" on an issue, policy, or program that for a long time had remained "on the back burner." Machiavelli called it *fortuna;* for others it is simply "good luck." By whatever name, opportunities to take or not to take action are an essential ingredient—the other half of bureaucratic gamesmanship, one might say—of making things happen and of accomplishing purposeful activity.

Therefore, in playing bureaucratic gamesmanship, much of bureaucrats' time is spent looking around at the *external bureaucratic landscape:* judging other players and the politics of the situation; finding out where potential outside sources of power lie; and discovering how to gain access to these power sources and how to avoid the pitfalls and traps of "enemy players." Karl von Clausewitz, the great nineteenth-century German military strategist, emphasized that in warfare "the situation is everything." In other words, where the soldier finds himself—the geography, terrain, climate, population, deployment of both enemy and friendly forces—fundamentally determines the outcome of every battle.

Consequently, in the tradition of Clausewitz, modern U.S. army officers who are destined to command battalions, regiments, divisions, and groups are sent to the U.S. Army Command and General Staff College at Fort Leavenworth, Kansas, for six months of intensive schooling directed primarily at case-by-case analyses of battlefield situations and strategies. Here future military leaders learn basic tactics through war games. They study how to quickly analyze "the lay of the land" and how to take the best defensive position and to devise offensive strategies and strikes against the enemy. Knowing how to exploit the other's weak points and how to strengthen one's own position in the field under stressful, trying, and constantly shifting battlefield conditions in which information, logistical supplies, and time for analysis are frequently inadequate are a few of the practical skills acquired by officers in these war games. Essentially, fake battles are used to sharpen military leadership skills for the real battle. Top-flight business, medical, and law schools put their students through many of the same rigors of case-method analysis. They encourage students to analyze concrete situations in business, medicine, and law in order to foster their ability to grasp quickly the essentials of a situation and then to take action on it in the boardroom, clinic, or courtroom.

The distinguished administrative scholar John Gaus argued in one of his important books, *Reflections on Public Administration,* that public administrators as well should analyze "the ecological factors" in the administrative landscape—i.e., the people, place, physical and social technology, wishes of the population, ideas of the times, catastrophes of the moment, and personalities of the "players" in order to properly undertake any effective bureaucratic activity. In his words, these ecological factors decisively determine "the ebb and flow of the functions of government."[28]

Louis Brownlow, one of the most outstanding city managers ever, certainly discovered this to be true in the field of local government. In his autobiography, *A Passion for Anonymity,*[29] he recounts how in the first community he managed, Petersburg, Virginia, his work had wide popular support. He consequently was able to accomplish many new capital works projects and to initiate many social programs for the city. This situation was a "bureaucrat's dream come true" (Brownlow was not only given a big salary but also a house to live in as part of his "fringes"). His next managerial post was Knoxville, Tennessee, at a time when the city was being torn apart by competing political factions. As the new city manager, Brownlow found himself in the midst of political turmoil from the moment he stepped inside the city limits. Several rival courthouse factions made his every action a subject of heated political controversy. It was a no-win situation, and eventually it broke Brownlow's health. Under the circumstances he was forced to resign and move elsewhere.

Astute bureaucrats, therefore, size up situational possibilities and impossibilities quickly and use their evaluations as the basis for their actions.

They learn when to move on projects and when not to move, depending on other events and other players in the bureaucratic game. Indeed, bureaucrats' very survival, as Brownlow's case in Knoxville illustrated, turns on how well or poorly they recognize and act upon the unique elements and configurations of any social, political, or organizational landscape. Much of their time, therefore, is spent scouting the landscape. Learning who's who and what's what is essential to building support for an agency's administrative programs and missions. Bureaucrats learn how and when to tap the various "input factors" to public organizations, which were discussed in detail in chapter 3. In other words, successful bureaucrats know that finding out and then working with the socioeconomic, political, and institutional factors that surround all public officials and their organizations are fundamental to effective administrative action. Sometimes this knowledge is acquired in a few weeks or months. Sometimes it takes many years and is a continuous process of learning and relearning about the fluctuating environments within which bureaucracies swim. For all successful bureaucrats it is a long-term inductive course of study.

However this knowledge is acquired, it is critical for the success of bureaucratic work anywhere. Paul Volcker, head of the Federal Reserve Board, spent a lifetime learning to read the economic and political "pulse rates" of the environment surrounding the Fed, i.e., the people, personalities, institutions, and critical economic forces that shape the board's missions and priorities. Consequently, he is generally credited today with being a highly successful board chairman. By contrast, President Jimmy Carter, although well intentioned and fired by lofty aims for his presidency, placed in top policy-making slots in the White House individuals who were largely inexperienced in the ways of Washington. These individuals did not have the background that would have enabled them to read either the highly complex Washington scene or the various players with whom the president had to work in building political bases of support. More than anything, Carter's loyalty to his own staff tended to isolate his administration from the significant political connections so essential for presidential leadership.

Furthermore, knowing the lay of the land helps any official not only to achieve purposeful actions but also to realize what *not* to do. In other words, recognizing fully the nature of the external situation is essential to understanding where the political land mines or roadblocks are located. Recognizing these limitations in any given situation helps the bureaucrat to set priorities for the best utilization of limited time and energy. Time and energy are always limited, and therefore understanding what *not* to do or what is simply impossible to achieve may well be as necessary to the accomplishment of purposeful actions as knowing what to do. Learning when to retreat can help avoid numerous disasters as well as personal frustration, wasted effort, and wasted lives, either on the battlefield or inside bureaucracy.

No one has yet invented the calipers that would accurately gauge the possibilities of any given situation. Yet seasoned bureaucrats know that windows of opportunity appear that enable them to take action within the shifting political landscape. These windows determine the scope, degree, and intensity of what they do or cannot do in performing agency missions. These windows come in various shapes and sizes and can be classified as follows.

Firm, Deep, and Broad Windows

Public agencies and their officials in small, homogeneous cities or large national organizations that operate during periods of strong national consensus involving their basic missions (as occurs during world wars and protracted national emergencies) have comparatively broad windows for bureaucratic action. Windows of this type are created by fundamental long-term socioeconomic-political commitments by the electorate and by groups within the society that support the agency and its actions. Officials of a small-town police force or fire department often operate at their own discretion principally because of the backing of a stable, homogeneous council and of solid community support. Similarly, some of the great innovative bureaucratic achievements on the national level have been accomplished because of just such firm, deep, and broad windows for action. Admiral Hyman Rickover, who fathered the U.S. underwater atomic navy in the 1950s, and James Webb, who organized and headed NASA in the 1960s, when the United States landed men on the moon, accomplished their programmatic mission largely because of long-term popular acclaim and solid congressional–White House backing. The Manhattan Project, which built the first atomic bomb during World War II, was also successful largely because of this broad window for bureaucratic action, which gave it the funding, secrecy, and leadership necessary for rapid development. Most rapid, innovative, and highly productive actions in the public sector are based upon such instances of broad national support.

At the grass roots, enthusiastic, homogeneous backing from a community, as Brownlow found in Petersburg, Virginia, offers enormously broad windows of opportunity. Aaron Wildavsky's *Leadership in a Small Town* reports that city manager Richard Dunn found himself in just such a situation in Oberlin, Ohio.[30] The community was fairly small and homogeneous and gave strong backing across the board to Dunn, its full-time local administrator. As a result, Dunn achieved a great deal, according to Wildavsky, and had broad involvement with most local decisions as well as with the public policy-making and bureaucratic outputs across the spectrum of community affairs. Much of this success was caused by his expertise in municipal matters, which filled a void in which no one else cared or was quite as well informed.

In such situations where broad support exists, wide windows of opportunity frequently provide a great deal of discretion to an agency and its officials in conceptualizing, formulating, and implementing programs. Further, an agency operating under these conditions finds it can hire able professionals to staff and implement programs, devise complex, efficient service-delivery systems, and even perhaps extend and broaden services and overall mandates for public actions. General Eisenhower, for instance, was given staggering amounts of discretionary powers and logistical support for the World War II D-Day landings, as was General MacArthur for his island-hopping campaigns in the Far East and postwar occupation of Japan. Eisenhower and MacArthur, on the national level, and Brownlow and Dunn, on the local level, though, were operating under unusual and rare conditions that maximized the breadth of windows for bureaucratic action.

Shallow, Temporary Windows

By contrast, many agencies and bureaucrats have comparatively shallow, temporary windows for action. That is, they may have broad popular and interest group appeal, or they may have opportunities that are fleeting. Frequently national, state, or local catastrophes bring about such opportunities—or necessities—for fast bureaucratic actions. A classic case involves the 1942 Coconut Grove fire in Boston, in which 490 people died, largely because the club's fire doors opened inward rather than outward. This tragedy caused outrage and immediate legislative reaction across the country. It brought about quick but very fundamental changes in fire codes and building requirements (bringing them into the twentieth century). Thus a tragedy that results in mass popular reaction gives bureaucrats broad but temporary windows for bureaucratic action and enables them to move on matters that may have been blocked for many years. The recent Mothers Against Drunk Drivers (MADD) campaigns to rid the highways of drunk drivers, the Three Mile Island nuclear mishap, the Iranian hostage crisis, and the Mount Saint Helens eruption brought similar long-term, intense popular demands for major bureaucratic responses to serious public problems and catastrophes. Creating limited delivery systems, temporary personnel, and short-term coping strategies are the norm for bureaucrats and their organizations in dealing with such issues. In these cases bureaucrats operate with the assumption that the window for action may close at any time, and so they must act fast.

Firm, Narrow, Long-Term Windows

Much more commonly, a federal, state, or local level of government has one sizable block of supporters that closely scrutinizes that bureaucracy and takes intense interest in its general affairs. Examples of such narrow, strong, continuous clientele backing include farmers' support of Agriculture Department programs; veterans and the Veterans Administration; unions and the Labor Department; educators and the Education Department. These powerful, well-placed, and well-connected groups carefully watch over and cultivate their "captured" units of government. They carefully scrutinize the key political appointments (as was pointed out in chapters 3 and 4, many of the appointees may in fact come from such pressure groups); secure favorable congressional programmatic and fiscal support (their representatives usually sit on the key legislative oversight subcommittees); gain favorable media and popular backing; and run interference on its behalf against external enemies and threats from other agencies or institutions. When an occasional critic does appear from within the ranks of "the protected agency," these support groups quickly see to it that the offending bureaucrat is removed or silenced. Robert Nimmo, who served from 1981 to 1982 as President Reagan's first head of the Veterans Administration and who began to modestly criticize many of the VA's excessive expenditures, was quickly sent packing to his home in California after one year in office mostly because of various veterans group pressures (though, of course, the official reasons for his dismissal were quite different).

Defense contractors have played similar roles in silencing DoD whistle-blowers within the ranks of the civil service. Such whistle-blowers learn quickly that special interests allied to the departments can play very hard ball and exercise enormous clout when they perceive the slightest threat to the status quo. After all, millions, indeed billions, of dollars may be jeopardized by such critics. So woe to the individual who runs afoul of such groups and who fails to nurture their support and blessings. On the other hand, with their backing, officials can often accomplish a wide range of bureaucratic activities that might include expanding their programmatic responsibilities; bringing on more and better-trained personnel to run those programs; inventing and implementing new effective service delivery systems; and possibly achieving a very high success rate of "favorable" customer support and clientele satisfaction for services rendered by the agency.

At the state and local levels, a stable clientele group such as the local business community as represented by the Chamber of Commerce can frequently generate similar long-term, narrow special-interest backing for a state economic development corporation or a municipal downtown urban renewal project. Such firm, powerful pressure groups can often give managers wide latitude for undertaking creative community-wide actions. L. P. Cookingham, the highly successful city manager of Kansas City for nineteen years, was installed by a reform group of business leaders who had ousted the old political machine. These business reformers retained control of city government for a number of years and kept Cookingham in office, thereby giving him enormous latitude for action and influence over most aspects of community life. His work there is something of a classic case history of how solid, enduring support from a sizable, well-placed faction in the community can offer a community-level bureaucrat widespread influence and programmatic discretion.

Tightly Closed Windows

On the other hand, bureaucrats know that some games are impossible to play because of widespread public opposition or narrow, intense interest group pressure that will block any initiatives in a policy or program area. Previous chapters have discussed such examples as the National Rifle Association's continuous efforts to keep the Bureau of Alcohol, Tobacco and Firearms poorly staffed and financed and with limited oversight roles (indeed, in 1981 the NRA came close to closing down ATF entirely). Western ranchers play the same role vis-à-vis the Bureau of Land Management and antiabortion groups vis-à-vis the Department of Health and Human Services' abortion funding programs. Various transportation interests have over the past twenty years eroded much of the Interstate Commerce Commission's regulatory authority in this field. Mexican-American groups in Congress and elsewhere have largely stopped legislative efforts to reform immigration laws and strengthen the Immigration and Naturalization Service's ability to cope with the flood of illegal aliens. In such agencies, bureaucrats are often in a state of shellshock from protracted battles with their enemies and must keep their heads down and learn to conduct holding actions or even strategic retreats because of the overwhelming strength, size, and intensity of their opponents. In such agencies morale is often low, and ranks may have been thinned because of a steady string of defeats and declines. These are often unpleasant places in which to work, since little usually is accomplished beyond the most mundane work routines.

Limited Openings in the Windows

In some situations public agencies operate within an even split between opponents and allies. Such a standoff can sharply curtail agency actions and allow bureaucrats only narrow latitudes for taking new initiatives. If the division between the two groups is somewhat unstable, support for or opposition to the public organization can swing back and forth at any moment, and so agency directors must be very careful not to alienate either party, since each could one day gain the upper hand. The bureaucrats confronting these situations must constantly balance two contending interests, ensuring that neither is slighted or overlooked in terms of goods, services, policies, and other organizational outputs rendered to these groups by the agency. Indeed, given their limited room to maneuver, bureaucrats frequently retreat to mundane, perfunctory tasks that will not alienate either party and upset the balance of forces surrounding the agency.

Many county and city bureaucracies work with just such evenly divided interests. They may be called the "uptown" and "downtown" gangs or the "east" and "west" groups. Handling such contending forces can be a ticklish problem for local bureaucrats, giving them only limited leeway for action, as

Frank Sherwood's classic administrative case study, "A City Manager Tries to Fire His Police Chief,"[31] illustrates. A small suburb of Los Angeles was divided roughly between "the Lemon Street gang" (long-time community residents) and newcomers (Hispanics, Catholics, and commuters to the center city). As Sherwood recounts, a controversy developed between the city manager and his newly appointed police chief, pitting one faction of the community against the other. The conflict soon became intense, protracted, and bitter, largely because both the manager and the chief mishandled matters. A stalemate ensued, and city government activities virtually ground to a halt until the chief was forced to resign at considerable cost and pain to everyone involved.

John Curry, a long-time city manager of Cambridge, Massachusetts, on the other hand, was a master at working out relations between Cambridge 39 (the blue collar, working-class section) and Cambridge 38 (the professional university crowd). He himself came from the Irish working-class background of Cambridge 39 yet also held a Harvard Ph.D. in linguistic philology, which placed him in good standing with Cambridge 38. He worked hard to antagonize neither group, keeping the lines of communication open to both sides and giving both groups the municipal services they wanted—i.e., safe streets, good snow removal, and decent parking for the Cambridge 38 crowd and public employment, welfare, and recreation and the like for Cambridge 39. He balanced quietly, neatly, and conveniently the needs of each community group.

At the federal or state level some agencies also find themselves surrounded by evenly divided blocks of allies and opponents, which often gives them only marginal room for bureaucratic maneuver. As with a divided situation arising at the local level, the same situation at higher levels can lead to bureaucratic indecision or limited activity in favor of either competing party. The story of U.S. foreign policy efforts concerning the Shah of Iran as recounted recently by Scott Armstrong[32] reflects even splits between backers and opponents of the shah inside the Carter administration. Both groups repeatedly pressed opposing sides of the policy debate with equal intensity. The protracted policy struggles within the foreign affairs community over U.S. responsibilities in regard to the shah resulted in indecisiveness over what actions to take to protect U.S. national interests in the region, ultimately leading to the shah's downfall and to reduced U.S. power in the Middle East.

Unpredictable, Constantly Opening and Closing Windows

Many public bureaucracies in large, urban settings or in industrial states or at the national level work within a context of multiple shifting factions where numerous social, economic, and political groups compete for power and influence over their activities. These pluralistic, polycentric, political situations have been described and analyzed carefully by various community power studies. Noted political science scholars such as Wallace Sayre and Herbert Kaufman in their book *Governing New York City* observe that "no single ruling elite dominates the political and government system of New York City. . . . New York's huge and diverse system of government and politics is a loose-knit and multi-centered network in which decisions are reached by ceaseless bargaining and fluctuating alliances among major categories of participants in each center and in which the centers are partially but strikingly isolated from one another."[33]

Hugh Heclo made much the same point recently regarding the diversity, openness, and instability of pluralistic interests operating at the national level, which he termed "issues networks." As Heclo writes, "Unfortunately, our standard conceptions of power and control are not very well suited to the loose-jointed play of influence that is emerging in political administration. We tend to look for one group exerting dominance over another, for subgovernments that are strongly insulated from other outside forces in the environment, for policies that get 'produced' by a few 'makers.' "[34]

Rather, as Heclo points out, "Looking for the few who are powerful, we tend to overlook the many webs, or what I will call 'issues networks.' "[35] These issues networks are open, shifting groups with numerous, temporary participants who move in and out of their circles, getting involved for a time and then "dropping out" of policy activities. They may suddenly "drop in" again on the policy-making processes quite unexpectedly. All this instability of surrounding interests tends to "complexify" matters for bureaucrats and their organizations. As Heclo points up, issues networks tend to complicate issues rather than simplify them: the spawning of zealots who are advocates of narrow programmatic and policy perspectives rather than of broad-minded compromise and conciliation produces further debate and argumentation.

Such diversity of opinion, shifting influence, and instability of people, policies, and their priorities create an extremely volatile, demanding situation within which public organizations formulate and implement their activities. Bureaucracy and bureaucrats caught in these turbulent, unpredictable environments must tread very cautiously, dealing with problems carefully, issue by issue, group by group. They must be able to put together coalitions on an ad hoc basis and be willing to compromise and entirely shift their organizational positions and activities quickly, even in the opposite direction, as new conditions arise. Managers of agencies operating under this uncertainty must be careful not to move ahead too quickly or to be too slow in adjusting to volatile shifting public policies and public opinion. Tact and sure-footedness are critical. Knowing when to move or not to move to take advantage of situations, positions, and opportunities is important. There is little wonder that lawyers abound in government bureaucracies today, for their training in the arts of bargaining, circumspection, compromise, negotiation, and deal making is precisely along these lines. In rapidly changing, pluralistic environments, public organizations in particular require these types of lawyerlike skills in their leaders in order to survive and prosper. In Robert Dahl's outstanding analysis of the pluralistic context of New Haven, Connecticut's, political life, *Who Governs?,* he describes precisely these leadership capabilities in its highly able former chief executive, Mayor Richard Lee: "He rarely commanded. He negotiated, exhorted, beguiled, cajoled, pressed, appealed, reasoned, promised, insisted, demanded, even threatened, but most he needed support and acquiescences from other leaders who simply could not be commanded. Because he could not command, he had to bargain."[36]

Bureaucratic Feedback Mechanisms: The Critical Link with the Environment

No bureaucratic unit in the United States is oblivious to its general environment. All have links, some quite elaborate, for assessing and responding to the changing social-political-economic conditions in which they function. As the previous section emphasized, survival may well depend on these links to the outside. These feedback mechanisms range from informal receipt of citizen complaints about their performance to formal, complex procedures for public budget hearings or legislative oversight of agency affairs. The range between the small and informal to large-scale formal feedback mechanisms is normally quite broad and diversified in most public agencies. Procedures include such techniques as citizen survey questionnaires, ombudsman offices, inspector general units, "complaint hotlines," and various special offices and personnel devoted to obtaining and giving out general citizen information. Today the press and media play a major role in this feedback process.

Increasingly, as well, various elements of public organizations are required to respond to rapidly fluctuating economic conditions through modern use of a variety of contractual arrangements discussed in chapter 4. OMB Circular A-76, for example, now requires competitive bidding for a broad range of federal contracts, which in turn makes many federal agencies highly dependent upon and responsive to private firms' costs and pricing requirements. Formulas and entitlements, which increasingly drive public budgets today at the federal level and which will be discussed more fully in the next chapter, "lock in" agency programmatic needs and demands directly and automatically to specific requirements. United States public bureaucracy is now so intertwined with and directly responsive to changing economic conditions that it is often hard to separate the public and private dimensions of economic life today.

As table 5.1 shows, communication factors play an important role in influencing the effectiveness of the feedback process. Also, the various windows within which bureaucratic action happens or fails to happen, which were discussed earlier in this chapter, shape the special nature and scope of the feedback mechanisms employed by any given agency. Within stable, homogeneous settings, much of the public agency feedback may be conducted entirely

TABLE 5.1
Bureaucratic Feedback Mechanisms Can Be Helped or Hindered
by Various Factors of Communication

Factors	Helping Feedback	Hindering Feedback
Language	Use of understandable and shared vocabulary	Use of language that is incomprehensible to parties involved
Perception of problems/issues discussed	"On same wavelength"	Mental perceptions of sender and receiver different
Geographic or status distance	Sender and receiver in close proximity	Geographic distance with many chains of intermediaries
Communication techniques	Face-to-face interchange	Impersonal exchange highly dependent upon inadequate technology that can break down
Volume	Adequate for needs	Excessive or insufficient volume for needs
Freedom to communicate	Free flow of ideas and information	Institutional censorship or personal self-protection of initiator distorts communication
Pressures of time and work	Adequate time and work load to receive, "digest," and comprehend communications	Time pressures & overload of work distorts or destroys effective communications between sender and receiver

on the basis of quite informal relationships between the citizenry and bureaucrats. Warner Mills and Harry Davis captured well this informality in the small town of Beloit, Wisconsin, in which city manager Archie Telfer "knows from long experience that city councils do not always know their own will. This is likely to occur with a problem whose political dimension is not clear. In such a case councilmen may either ignore the issue in the hope that it will go away, or offer some informal authorization for action to avoid going officially on record. Telfer knows that a nod of the head from a key councilman, or an oblique remark in informal conversation, may (or may not!) be as significant a clue to action as a formal resolution."[37] Similarly, where there is a shallow, temporary window for bureaucratic action, the game signals from the citizenry and feedback employed may be entirely informal and improvised, responses to the immediate demands and conditions of the moment. Certainly this is the case in bureaucratic responses to disasters, such as a downed aircraft or a railway accident. Such community disasters force public agencies to cope as best they can within the limits of their resources and personnel. Their responses to such mishaps are frequently haphazard and catch-as-catch-can.

Firm but narrow long-term windows are different. Since well-placed and strong clientele groups serve as the basis for agency survival and prosperity, gauging and responding to these groups' interests undoubtedly must be the principal bureaucratic concern. Hence, many of the feedback mechanisms employed by the agency are targeted and directed at its specific clientele groups. Usually quite a full range of such techniques is utilized to gauge consumer satisfaction, from informal speaking engagements to citizen surveys to formal public hearings. The opposite, of course, is the case where public agencies are opposed by large, overwhelming pressure groups. Neither side communicates with the other very much, and if it does, it is only via the most antagonistic, formalized routes.

Public organizations operating within either evenly divided interest groups or constantly fluctuating, pluralistic groups are prone to be highly communicative with their publics. Their leaders need to keep an attentive eye on the changing needs, demands, and requirements of such interests and then to respond as needed. Under these conditions, as exemplified by Robert Dahl's portrait of Mayor Lee, a full range of feedback mechanisms must be

TABLE 5.2
Key Factors Maximizing or Minimizing Bureaucratic Output

Factors that Influence Bureaucratic Outputs	Maximize Outputs	Minimize Outputs
Specific Assigned Tasks for Agency	well defined & within scope & competence of staff	poorly defined & outside scope & competence of staff
Gamesmanship Abilities	managers committed, well-trained, experienced, & capable of selecting and playing games at *correct* levels	managers untrained, uncommitted, inexperienced, and unable to select game level for play
Internal Resources	adequate for fulfilling assigned tasks	inadequate for needs or demands on agency
External Conditions	optimal conditions for discretion, flexibility, & action	little or no opportunities for discretion, flexibility, action
Feedback Processes	immediate, supportive, and clear, with adequate information for program improvement	slow in forthcoming; hostile, and/or fuzzy information for program managers
Overall Time Frame for Program	adequate for fulfilling assignments	inadequate for fulfilling assignments
Institutional Autonomy for Agency's Program Operations	public agency exercises institutional, political controls overall or most program operations and its authority equals responsibility for program operations	public agency must share authority with many units, jurisdictions, interests, and therefore authority and responsibility is highly fragmented

FIGURE 5.5
Public Bureaucracies Produce Five Varieties of Outputs

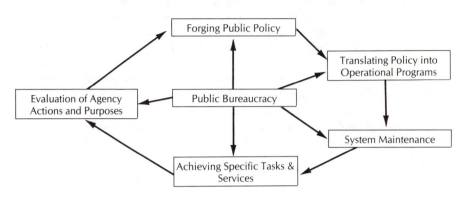

employed by bureaucratic agencies to keep their programs responsive to shifting, or potentially shifting, conditions. Perhaps these agencies will even employ a sizable staff of public relations experts and policy or program planners, whose job is to stay alert to these changing trends and respond accordingly. Much also depends on the special leadership abilities of the managers of these agencies. Often they need to be highly verbal, mobile, and adept at adjusting and shifting their priorities according to changing social contexts.

Summary of Key Points

Every public bureaucracy in the United States is created and sustained to perform some task or tasks. What these missions and duties are may be clearly evident or very hard to define. Generally, though, "the products" of every public agency depend upon the composition and activities of its internal subsystems (discussed in chapter 4): political appointees forge the broad political missions; bottom-level appointees along with top-level career professionals and civil servants translate these missions into operational programs; mid-level civil servants and professional careerists perform system maintenance; and the lower cadres of civil servants, union workers, and contractual employees are largely involved with implementing specific agency tasks. All groups communicate with the outside environment and thus share equally in producing the evaluation outputs that shape and reshape agency missions and goals. The processes by which these governmental outputs are performed vary significantly from private enterprise practices, and therefore traditional generic models for understanding public agency outputs are inappropriate.

Rather, the bulk of this chapter presents a conceptual approach for understanding the dynamics of how outputs from public agencies are performed. As figure 5.6 indicates, the achievement of public organization outputs involves five components: first, the specific tasks of the agency; second, its gamesmanship capacities: third, its *internal resources*—i.e., the agency's legal, structural, process, and personal resources; and fourth, the *external conditions* within which agency operations take place. These *external conditions* were identified as essentially six varieties of windows for bureaucratic action, ranging from wide-open, long-term windows to tightly shut windows of opportunity. Finally, feedback mechanisms are equally diverse as well as important to public agencies to aid in their response to changing environmental needs and conditions. However, the type of feedback mechanism used by any given agency depends largely on the external and environmental conditions within which it operates.

Key Terms

bureaucratic outputs
generic output models
POSDCORB
fragmented authority
"goldfish bowl" environment
legal statutes
high-stakes games

low-stakes games
internal resources
windows of opportunity
bureaucratic feedback mechanisms
bureaucratic routines
process vs. structural resources

Review Questions

1. Can you summarize some of the basic tasks public bureaucracies perform for society? What distinguishes these jobs from business or nonprofit organization tasks?
2. In what ways is the actual accomplishment of these public sector jobs performed differently than it would have been by private enterprise organizations?
3. What is meant by the argument that public agencies carry out their duties through the use of gamesmanship? Do you agree?
4. Discuss the internal types of bureaucratic resources that public organizations can bring to the accomplishment of agency missions. Why is each resource important to bring about direction, cohesion, and cooperation in organizations?
5. What are bureaucratic feedback mechanisms and why do they have a place in the overall bureaucratic system?

Notes

1. An Act for Establishing an Executive Department to Be Denominated the Department of Foreign Affairs, July 27, 1789 (1 Stat. 4).
2. Organization for National Security, Title I, Section 102, 61 Stat. 343 (1947) and 63 Stat. 412 (1949).

FIGURE 5.6
**Achieving Public Agency Outputs Involves Five Components
That All Work Together at the Same Time**

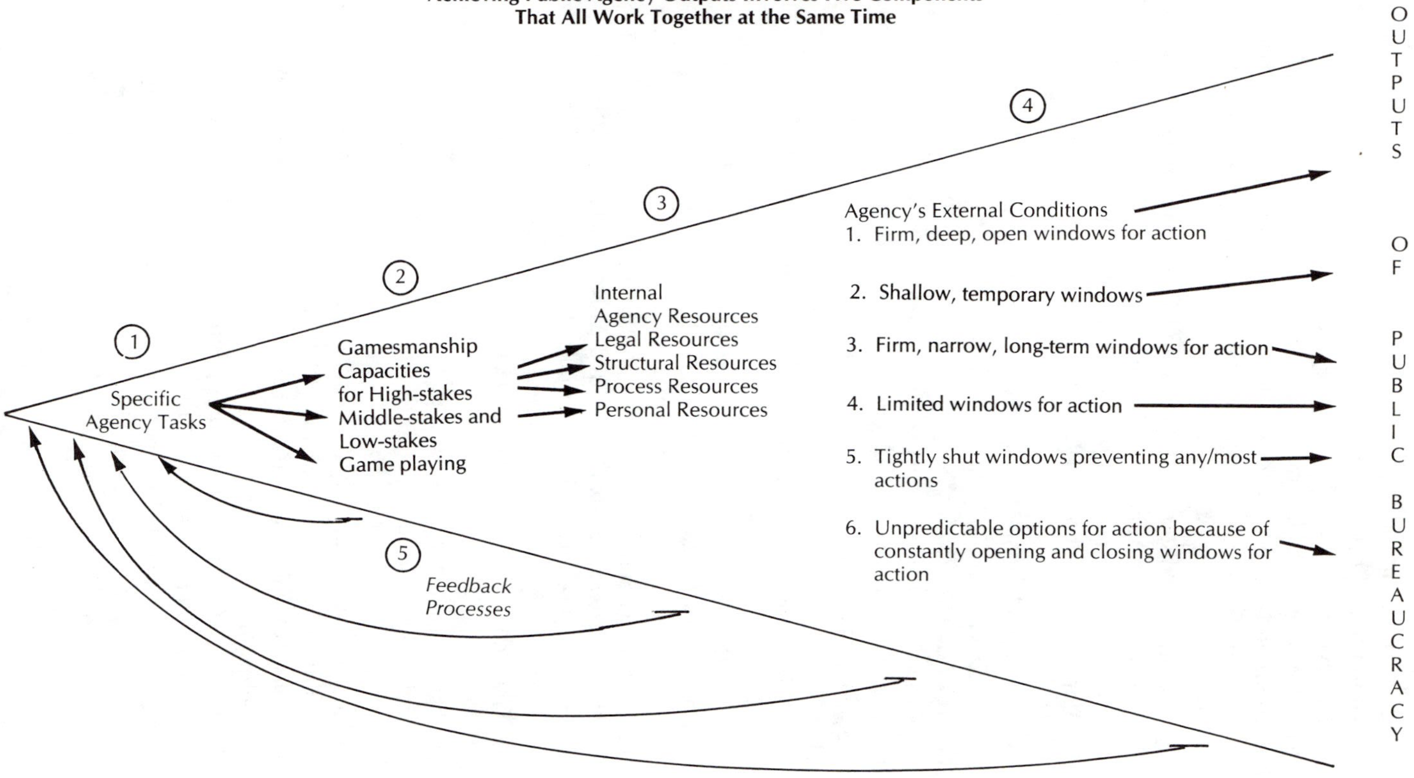

Specific Agency Tasks

Gamesmanship
Capacities
for High-stakes
Middle-stakes and
Low-stakes
Game playing

Internal
Agency Resources
Legal Resources
Structural Resources
Process Resources
Personal Resources

Agency's External Conditions
1. Firm, deep, open windows for action
2. Shallow, temporary windows
3. Firm, narrow, long-term windows for action
4. Limited windows for action
5. Tightly shut windows preventing any/most actions
6. Unpredictable options for action because of constantly opening and closing windows for action

Feedback Processes

OUTPUTS OF PUBLIC BUREAUCRACY

3. Woodrow Wilson, "The Study of Administration," *Political Science Quarterly* 2 (June 1887), pp. 197–220.

4. Grover Starling, *Managing the Public Sector,* 2d ed. (Homewood, Ill.: Dorsey Press, 1982), p. 1.

5. Luther Gulick and L. Urwick (eds.), *The Papers on the Science of Administration* (NY: Institute of Public Administration, 1937), p. 13.

6. Bertram Gross, *Organizations and Their Managing* (NY: Free Press, 1964).

7. Graham T. Allison, Jr., "Public and Private Management: Are They Fundamentally Alike in All Unimportant Respects?" in *Setting Public Management Research Agendas* (Washington, DC: Office of Personnel Management, February 1980), pp. 27–38.

8. Ibid., p. 27.

9. Paul Appleby, *Big Democracy* (NY: Alfred A. Knopf, 1945), p. 1.

10. As cited in Allison, "Public and Private Management."

11. *The Federalist Papers,* No. 51.

12. Richard E. Neustadt, as cited in Laurence E. Lynn, Jr., see note 13.

13. Laurence E. Lynn, Jr., *Managing the Public's Business* (NY: Basic Books, 1981), chapter 6.

14. Ibid.

15. C. Wright Mills, *The Power Elite* (NY: Oxford University Press, 1956), p. 245.

16. Francis E. Rourke, *Bureaucracy, Politics, and Public Policy,* 2d ed. (Boston: Little, Brown, 1976), p. 15.

17. Laurence E. Lynn, Jr., *Managing.*

18. Herbert A. Simon, Donald W. Smithburg, and Victor A. Thompson, *Public Administration* (NY: Alfred A. Knopf, 1950), chapter 19.

19. Jeffrey L. Pressman, "Preconditions of Mayoral Leadership," *American Political Science Review* 2 (June 1972), p. 512.

20. Graham T. Allison, *Essence of Decision* (Boston: Little, Brown, 1971), p. 79.

21. Francis Rourke, *Bureaucracy,* p. 19.

22. Robert Dahl, *Who Governs?* (New Haven: Yale University Press, 1961), p. 225.

23. John C. Bollens and John C. Ries, *The City Manager Profession* (Chicago: Public Administration Service, 1969), p. 16.

24. Ronald O. Loveridge, *City Managers in Legislative Politics* (Indianapolis: Bobbs-Merrill, 1971), p. 17.

25. Kenneth C. Davis, *Discretionary Justice* (Baton Rouge: Louisiana State University Press, 1969), p. 212.

26. Chester I. Barnard, *The Functions of the Executive* (Cambridge: Harvard University Press, 1938), pp. 139.

27. Herbert A. Simon, *Administrative Behavior* (NY: Macmillan, 1947).

28. John Gaus, *Reflections on Public Administration* (University: University of Alabama Press, 1947), p. 43.
29. Louis Brownlow, *A Passion for Anonymity* (Chicago: University of Chicago Press, 1955), pp. 105–203.
30. Aaron Wildavsky, *Leadership in a Small Town* (Totowa, NJ: Bedminister Press, 1964), p. 215–35.
31. Frank Sherwood, *A City Manager Tries to Fire His Police Chief,* ICP #76 (Syracuse: Inter-University Case Program, 1960).
32. Scott Armstrong, "The Fall of the Shah," *The Washington Post* (Oct. 25 through Oct. 29, 1980), p. 1.
33. Wallace S. Sayre and Herbert Kaufman, *Governing New York City* (NY: Russell Sage, 1960), p. 710.
34. Hugh Heclo, "Issue Networks and the Executive Establishment," in Anthony King (ed.), *The New Political System* (Washington, DC: The American Enterprise Institute for Public Policy Research, 1978), pp. 87–124.
35. Ibid.
36. Robert Dahl, *Who Governs?*
37. Warner Mills and Harry Davis, *Small City Government* (NY: Random House, 1962) p.32.

Further Readings

Several of Norton Long's insightful essays on bureaucracy first developed this notion of bureaucracy as gamesmanship. His book *The Polity* (Chicago: Rand McNally, 1962) is useful as well, as is the more recent book of Laurence Lynn, *Managing the Public's Business* (NY: Basic Books, 1981). Harold Seidman's *Politics, Position and Power* 3d ed. (1980) develops these themes more fully. The best sources of gamesmanship ideas are found in biographical sketches of several of the masters of this art, including: Joseph A. Califano, Jr., *Governing America* (1981); William Manchester, *American Caesar* (1978); Norman Polmar and Thomas B. Allen, *Rickover* (1982); Robert Caro, *The Power Broker* (1974); and Louis Brownlow, *A Passion for Anonymity* (1958). John Gaus's *Reflections on Public Administration* (1947) remains the most sensitive treatment of the external environment within which public agencies must work in order to implement their programs.

In recent years an impressive array of new books on program implementation has appeared. Especially useful are Jeffrey L. Pressman and Aaron Wildavsky's *Implementation,* 2d ed. (1978); Walter Williams' *The Implementation Perspective* (1980); Walter Williams and Richard F. Elmore (eds.), *Social Program Implementation* (1976); Eugene Bardach's *The Implementation Game* (1977); Richard F. Elmore's *Complexity and Control* (1979); Martha Derthick's *New Towns In-town* (1972); Beryl Radin's *Implementation,*

Change and the Federal Bureaucracy (1977); and Robert Fried's *Performance in American Bureaucracy* (1977).

Also useful are more general texts on public management, such as Elizabeth K. Keller's *Managing with Less* (1979); Brian Rapp and Frank Patitucci's *Managing Local Government for Improved Performance* (1977); Martha W. Weinberg's, *Managing the State* (1977); Joseph L. Bower's *The Two Faces of Management* (1983); James L. Perry and Kenneth L. Kraemer (eds.), *Public Management* (1983); and Wayne F. Anderson, Chester A. Newland, and Richard J. Stillman II's *The Effective Local Government Manager* (1983).

6
Trends in the Bureaucratic System

Following is a quick recap of the major ideas presented in this book so far: Chapter 1 outlined a systemic approach to comprehending U.S. bureaucracy and gave an overview of its inputs, outputs, internal subsystems, and feedback mechanisms. Chapter 2 summarized the growth of this dynamic bureaucratic system over the past two hundred years and argued that bureaucracy has evolved into a highly fragmented, malleable, diverse, and jerry-built set of structures that adapt to popular needs of the moment rather than to long-term national requirements. In short, U.S. public bureaucracy is not a monolithic and permanent organization, nor is it impervious to inputs from the outside. In reality it is 80,000 entities, most of them local and highly differentiated in design, scope, purpose, and origin.

Indeed, as chapter 3 outlined, U.S. bureaucracy is made up not only of diverse institutions but also of a vast array of sociopolitical-economic and institutional forces that continually reshape those various public agencies by feeding their various inputs into the bureaucratic system through a variety of methods and adapting these units to changing external conditions. These rapidly changing external inputs, made up of powerful and diverse forces, serve to create a set of continuously changing bureaucratic institutions that operate on an ad hoc basis.

Chapter 4 looked inside public bureaucracy and discovered that it is far from being a lifeless, static machine. Instead, the internal dynamics of every public agency are composed of fluid subsystems composed of individuals competing for power, authority, and position; i.e., political appointees, professional careerists, civil servants, unionized workers, and contractual employees. Each internal subsystem embodies a distinct view of the world. Depending upon which group gains the upper hand within a public organization, the values, policies, and overall directions of that public agency are correspondingly shaped and revised.

Chapter 5 focused on how bureaucratic outputs are accomplished, i.e., how public agencies make things happen. The central thesis of this chapter was that bureaucracies are fundamentally purposeful entities; their functional tasks give them their reasons for being, for continuing, for their funding and personnel assignments—indeed, these tasks provide their basic, ongoing institutional legitimacy. The practical aspects of fulfilling bureaucratic missions are built upon five components—the tasks themselves, bureaucratic gamesmanship, internal agency resources, external windows for action and feedback mechanisms. The unique mix of five factors in every public organization significantly determines the level, scope, and intensity of agency outputs, which may range from a very few activities and services performed by a small town, a special district, or a local governmental unit to a vast array of activities and services by large national bureaucratic organizations, such as the Defense Department, the Department of Health and Human Services, and the Veterans Administration.

Making sense out of this immense administrative complex, now so central to U.S. governing processes and the functioning of society, is difficult (figure 6.1). Indeed, generalizing about some of the major features of the bureaucratic system in the 1980s may well be risky, since exceptions can always be found that contradict any rule about bureaucracy—precisely because its entities are so vast and diverse. Further, change is so rapid within the system that what is apparent today may well disappear before the ink is dry on the page that attempts to describe it.

At the risk of misperceiving some of the current trends—or missing others entirely—this chapter will scan the bureaucratic horizon and speculate on the major changes shaping and reshaping the bureaucratic system today, particularly on three levels: first, how does today's turbulent socioeconomic-political environment influence the directions of public bureaucracy? Why does it raise profound problems for bureaucratic institutional operation? Second, what redirections and adaptations are actually taking place today within public bureaucracies, given the surrounding environmental turbulence? In other words, how are the external environs reshaping the internal bureaucratic processes and makeup? More specifically, how does the socioeconomic-political environs of the 1980s strengthen public bureaucracies as well as foster their decline? Third, in what ways do various types of popular and scholarly ideological reactions to bureaucracy manifest themselves in the 1980s? And how are these contemporary ideas important to what happens within contemporary public agencies? In brief, this chapter will look at three critical dimen-

FIGURE 6.1
U.S. Public Bureaucracy as a Complex System: A Summary Overview

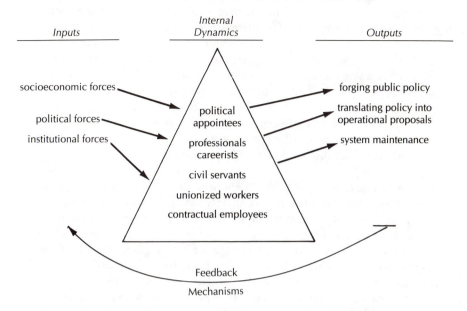

Total Environment within Which Agency Functions and Operates
(functional needs of society, national values, and constitutional structure)

sions of modern changes in regard to U.S. bureaucracy: its environment, internal design, and ideological impacts in the 1980s.

Environmental Turbulence in the 1980s: Or, the Shocks to Modern Bureaucracy

Public bureaucracy has been rocked by several significant traumas and social trends during the past decade that profoundly affect U.S. public institutions and their performances. Some are obvious; others are not as apparent. Certainly no complete "photo" of all these socioeconomic-political forces is possible, but the following may provide an overview of some of these major forces and illustrate the profound dilemmas they raise for the modern bureaucratic system as a whole:

The Aftershocks of the 1970s.   Major events and traumas shook the confidence of the nation during the 1970s: Vietnam, Watergate, the energy crisis, double-digit inflation, the Iranian hostage crisis, to name only a few. It seemed that whatever government did during the 1970s not only was wrong but also seemed to make matters worse. Periodic socioeconomic-political crises, in turn, caused widespread public distrust and dislike of government at all levels. Various public opinion surveys and voter polls showed how many shared this apathy and hostility toward government. This hostility and criticism still inspire mistrust of the institutional legitimacy and fundamental purpose of U.S. bureaucracy. Furthermore, these aftershocks translated into very real new constraints and controls within which public bureaucracy must operate in the 1980s, such as the Freedom of Information Act, the Privacy Act, sunset laws, property tax limitations, and balanced-budget revenue limitations. These were enacted precisely as a consequence of voter distrust, apathy, and hostility to government. These new constraints also produce a difficult, unstable, and erratic socioeconomic-political environment for public agencies. Some of the specific effects of legal constraints upon U.S. public bureaucracy will be discussed more fully later in this chapter.

Reformist Presidents and "New Reforms" in the Bureaucratic System. Throughout the 1970s, voters have sharply swung from one extreme to another in electing a succession of one-term presidents—Nixon, Ford, Carter— all of whom were highly critical of government and full of promises to reform bureaucracy if elected. Indeed, all ran *against* Washington, D.C.—and won largely because they were "outsiders." This is particularly true of Ronald Reagan, even in his 1984 reelection campaign. These elected chief executives, in turn, often appointed short-term office holders who were themselves hostile to bureaucracy (as chapter 4 pointed out) to initiate and develop new reforms. Hence, we have witnessed a succession of new, short-term initiatives to change, reform, and overhaul bureaucracy from *within*—from Nixon's Ash Commission to Carter's zero-based budget to Reagan's Reform 88. The high turnover at the top, combined with the urge to come up with new reforms of bureaucracy, continues into the 1980s. This constant turnover and flux at the top—combined with the inexperience and hostility of the appointees—have further promoted environmental instability, indecision, and lack of long-term, consistent, and capable direction in many public agencies.

The Rise of a Hostile, Entrenched, Permanent Opposition to Government: Issue Networks, the Media, and PACS.   As chapter 3 discussed, three groups in particular have emerged in the past decade that are a permanent source of hostility toward government in general and public bureaucracy in particular. Issue networks, for one, have evolved into thick webs of hostile critics surrounding every public agency. As Hugh Heclo noted (and which was discussed in chapter 3), for the most part they serve *their own* interests by fueling debate and conflict over policy priorities, rather than promoting closure, compromise, and consensus. The media as well have become a major power in public affairs. Ratings of television news programs depend largely on how well they stimulate controversy, promote argument, expose corruption, and uncover wrong-doing within the public sector. Indeed, entire news shows, such as "60 Minutes," one of the highest-rated programs on the networks in the

1980s, as well as popular newscasters such as Dan Rather and journalists such as Bob Woodward, have gained popularity precisely because of the incisive investigative reporting with which they uncover scandals inside government and especially within bureaucracy.

In addition, Political Action Committees (PACs), narrow in policy focus and rich in resources, have largely replaced political parties as the source of campaign financing and candidate support. The National Conservative Political Action Committee (NCPAC) alone spent $14 million in the 1984 election supporting various candidates committed to its particular conservative political agenda. Altogether, PACs spent one-third of a billion dollars in 1984. PACs, in turn, promote candidates that are frequently tied to this or that single issue and, if elected, can be trusted to speak for, lobby for, and defend PAC supporters vis-à-vis the bureaucracy. Finding broad popular consensus and clear public mandates for action is therefore increasingly difficult for governmental bureaucracies, who are surrounded by a thick maze of powerful issue networks, media, and PAC forces and who are for the most part dedicated to promoting criticism and controversy.

America's New Interdependence on the Global Economy. No longer is the United States self-sufficient in natural resources. This stark fact was brought home to most Americans with dramatic force when long lines snaked around gas stations during the energy crises of the 1970s. Today, more than half of the oil used domestically comes from abroad, mainly from the highly volatile Middle East, whose often-unfriendly nations are racked by political turbulence. Such is the case with many other natural resources Americans now consume. Even basic "Americana" such as baseball mitts are no longer American-made but come mainly from the Far Eastern industrial nations of Japan, Korea, and Taiwan, as do television sets, refrigerators, washing machines, and other commercial goods.

Further, cheap labor from abroad, especially the several million illegal immigrants arriving yearly because of higher wage rates, helps keep labor costs low in poorly paid service industries. For U.S. public organizations, this new interdependence with the global economy means that public sector agencies must now depend on the vagaries of the global economy, with its often wildly fluctuating prices for raw materials and finished goods, its cheap labor costs, and its uncertainties of supply and unpredictable quality of finished goods. For governmental organizations, these new economic uncertainties—such as rapid shifts in the money supply, interest rates, global demand for resources, prices for finished goods, cheap labor, sudden inflation or depression of costs—create enormously complex problems for long-term planning, efficient allocation of resources, and effective management of mandated programs. These new economic uncertainties also add profound insecurities for Americans, in turn promulgating profound distrust and lack of confidence in government's ability to cope adequately with the problems at hand.

The Emergence of New Influential Social Groups—the Old, Women, and Minorities.   The demographics of the nation are rapidly changing in the 1980s. New groups exercising considerable political power have come to the forefront in recent years. Americans are living longer; life expectancy is now seventy-four years plus. In 1970, 9.9 percent of the population was over sixty-five; by the end of the 1980s this figure will rise to 11 percent. A decade ago two-thirds of the work force was made up of white males; today less than half are male (49 percent). By the end of the 1980s, 64 percent of the work force is expected to be female, while at the time of the 1984 election slightly more than half of the voters were women. Women and the old constitute potent new political and social forces in U.S. society. Geraldine Ferraro's candidacy for Democratic vice president in 1984 symbolized the new power and strength of women in the electorate. Furthermore, the ethnic composition of the United States is rapidly changing as well. Asian-Americans from Vietnam, China, Korea, and other Asian countries make up highly visible ethnic communities in most U.S. cities. Italian-Americans make up a newly recognized influential bloc of voters in the Northeast, and Mexican-Americans are now the fastest-growing ethnic group in the Southwest. California alone has 4.5 million Hispanics, and Texas has 3 million. There are over 16 million in the country as a whole. These demographic shifts have resulted in various new pressures upon public bureaucracies for services, job opportunities, and the protection of human rights. These newly emerging social groups strongly assert their rights for *their* share of public services. These groups' demands for equity and equality help shape the practical operations of public bureaucracy in the 1980s.

The Decline of the Political Center and the Rise of the Polarized Electorate. Many of the traditional stabilizing institutions have declined in importance over the past decade—i.e., political parties, labor unions, mainline churches, home town industries, and the family. No longer can these basic societal institutions be counted upon as the consensus-producing and stabilizing organizations within U.S. society. These mainline establishment groups have in recent years been replaced in many locales by far different groups. PACs have largely eclipsed political parties as chief funding and organizing sources for election campaigns; the global firm has now overtaken the home town industry as the potent economic force throughout the United States; nonunionized workers have replaced unions as the dominant group in the labor force; fundamentalist sects and television preachers are drawing many away from mainline churches; singles and childless couples are replacing the traditional family unit as the norm.

It is hard to foresee what these fundamental shifts in the basic social fabric will bring for the nation. Perhaps the increasing mobility, detachment, and disaffiliation with institutions that were once the "centrist glue" of U.S. society are also fostering the increasing movement toward the right and left of the political spectrum, the hardening of ideological lines, and the polarization of the electorate.

Whatever the cause of the decline in the center and rise of the left and right on the political spectrum, this trend portends increased problems for public bureaucracy. Polarized electorates in particular make it difficult for public agencies to establish the political consensus and mandates for action necessary to design and implement programs. Many public agencies are based upon the notion that there is *a public* to be served. But what if there is no *one* public, but, rather, increasingly fragmented, diffuse, *and polarized publics on the left and right?* How can *public* bureaucracy function adequately—or at all—if THE PUBLIC is no longer there or has little relevance or importance?

Perhaps nothing better illustrates how this sharp polarization can reach directly into public bureaucracies' operations than the 1984 Republican and Democratic party platforms on several issues of central importance to public agencies:

Federal Income Taxes
Republicans: "We therefore oppose any attempts to increase taxes."
Democrats: "We will . . . enhance the progressivity of our own personal income tax code. . . . We will partially defer indexation. . . . We will close loopholes."

Deficits:
Republicans: "We favor reducing deficits by continuing and expanding the strong economic recovery."
Democrats: "The Democratic Party is pledged to reducing these intolerable deficits. We will reassess defense expenditures, create a tax system that is both adequate and fair . . . and eliminate other unnecessary expenditures."

Federal Reserve Board
Republicans: "The Federal Reserve Board's destabilizing actions must stop."
Democrats: "The task of the Federal Reserve Board will be critical. Monetary policy must work to achieve stable and real interest rates, the availability of capital for long-term investments, predictable long-term policy, and stable prices."

Nuclear Power Plants
Republicans: "We will work to eliminate unnecessary regulatory procedures so that nuclear plants can be brought on line quickly, efficiently, and safely."
Democrats: "The Democratic Party strongly opposes the Reagan administration's policy of aggressively promoting and further subsidizing nuclear power. . . . We will expand the role of the public in Nuclear Regulatory Commission procedures."

Environmental Protection Agency
Republicans: "We must remember that quality of life means more than protection and preservation . . . [it] means development as much as it does protection."
Democrats: "The Environmental Protection Agency should receive a budget that exceeds in real dollars the agency's purchasing power when President Reagan took office."

Federal Role in Education
Republicans: "The federal role in education should be limited."
Democrats: "We call for the immediate restoration of the cuts in funding of education programs by the Reagan administration and for a major commitment to education."

Social Security
Republicans: "We will work to repeal the Democrats' Social Security earnings-limitation test."
Democrats: "The policies and operations of the Social Security Administration must be carefully and fully investigated to reform its operations."

Civil Rights Enforcement
Republicans: "We pledge to do even more during the next four years."
Democrats: "The next Democratic administration will offer unwavering support for the following: a strong, independent Civil Rights Commission. Strengthened civil rights enforcement. Equal educational opportunity."

Foreign Affairs Involvement and National Defense
Republicans: "We shall keep the peace by keeping our country stronger than any potential adversary." "Technological superiority and qualitative superiority" (over the Soviet Union is promised) "with its globalist ideology and its leadership obsessed with military power." "We support the democratic freedom fighters in Nicaragua."
Democrats: (We pledge) "a strong defense" but "unequivocal support to reduce tensions between the Soviet Union and the United States." "We must terminate our support for the contras and other para-military groups fighting in Nicaragua."

Regional Shifts in Affluence and Economic Decline. The early 1980s witnessed the rise of the sunbelt states and decline of the frostbelt because of many factors: the exploding growth of retirement communities in Florida and the Southwest; the energy boom in the West; the rise of energy costs in the Northeast; the growth of new high-tech firms in the South and West coupled with a massive decay of the traditional smokestack industries in eastern and midwestern regions. These rapid regional economic changes have provoked equally rapid and powerful population shifts. In 1980 for the first time more Americans were living in the West (118 million) than in the East (108 million). Since the 1970s northeastern cities have experienced large out-migrations of people: New York City SMSA lost 853,370 people; Philadelphia, 107,292; Cleveland, 128,304; Detroit, 81,639, while sunbelt cities such as Houston gained 905,637; Miami, 357,988; Phoenix, 627,824; and San Diego, 503,892. As a result, northeastern states lost congressional seats in the 1980 reapportionment (New York losing five, for example), and many southern and western states gained seats (Florida gaining four, for example). Again as noted in earlier chapters, these sociopolitical-economic shifts have caused many difficulties for state and local public bureaucracies, including problems of adjusting public services to the new influx or out-migration of populations; dealing with a rapidly shifting demographic composition of local populations and clientele groups for those public services; coping with the strains of a growing or declining tax base and revenue structures; and meeting the new challenges of long-term resource and physical planning under conditions of rapid cutbacks in federal expenditures and local restraints on public revenues such as property tax limitations and balanced-budget requirements. Whether or not these massive regional dislocations will continue throughout the 1980s is difficult to predict, but coping with their aftershocks certainly will be a task of long duration for various governmental agencies, especially on the local level.

The Growth of Service-Sector Jobs and the Decline of Traditional Industries. Underlying these economic changes and population shifts is a fundamental realignment of the industrial base. Many of the aging smokestack industries are no longer competitive with third world nations in Latin America and the Far East. Because of their significantly lower labor costs, these nations can produce industrial goods far more cheaply and efficiently in virtually every market sector from automobiles to television sets than the United States can. Hence, since the 1970s jobs and industry in goods-producing fields have declined, often moving outside the country to cheaper labor markets, and the service sector, particularly information-producing jobs, is now among the rapid growth areas of employment and industrial productivity in the United States. These jobs normally require considerably more skill, education, and technological expertise, as illustrated by the following list of the fastest-rising and -declining occupations since 1970:

Fastest-growing Occupations (% +)
computer operators (346.2)
teachers' aides (190.2)
social scientists (155.0)
health administrators (150.0)
sales personnel (139.7)
real estate agents (122.1)
bank tellers (113.7)
restaurant and bar managers (108.9)
receptionists (106.9)

Fastest-declining Occupations (%–)
tailors (61.2)
stenographers (50.0)
newspaper vendors (39.6)
barbers (35.3)
textile operators (24.9)
telephone operators (22.5)
tool and die makers
file clerks (10.0)
sewers and stitchers (9.3)

If these trends persist throughout the 1980s, as many experts expect they will, the U.S. work force will require increasingly skilled, educated, and technologically competent workers. These economic and labor trends place enormous demands upon public bureaucracies at every level—i.e., preparing students for high-tech careers; retraining older individuals in high-tech skills; providing unemployment compensation and welfare support; and responding to the problems and pressures of those who for a variety of reasons cannot cope with or adapt to these rapid shifts in employment markets. Offering educational, welfare, and other vital human services that assist the job changes in the 1980s will no doubt be important roles of public agencies in this era of rapid technological transformation.

New Technologies: Challenges and Problems for Public Agencies.   Underlying both the sudden regional and occupational shifts in U.S. industry is a profound explosion of new technologies. Strikingly new developments in computers, word processors, telecommunications, integrated information systems, space shuttles, robotics, genetic engineering, undersea exploration, microchip processors, and space exploration—to name just a few—are examples of scientific and technological discoveries that are fundamentally altering the way Americans live, work, and even think. For public bureaucracies, the impact of these discoveries and inventions is staggering. They create new, profound ethical questions (when can hospitals "pull the plug" that terminates a life?); diplomatic problems (should new high technology be exported to the Soviet Union and elsewhere?); regulatory issues (can the public ensure safe and proper experimentation with genetic research?); international security and defense issues (how shall we cope with star wars technology, which makes wars in space a new possibility?); economic problems (who should profit from the taping of television programs by home video machines?); and complex internal management problems of bureaucratic services and resources (how can computers best be used by social service agencies to control costs and extend human services?). These and many more new questions raised by the unprecedented speed of scientific and techological change are being confronted by public agencies. Indeed, public agencies in many fields find themselves on the cutting edge of *both* scientific *and* ethical complexities of new and profound importance to the survival of the nation and the human race.

The Increase in the Number of Lawyers.   In 1960 there were 250,000 lawyers in the United States; in 1970, 355,000; in 1983, 622,000; and in 1987, about 750,000. In other words, while the total population since 1960 increased by roughly 50 percent, the number of lawyers almost tripled. While the causes of this "legal explosion" are numerous, the impacts upon government are equally numerous, for argumentation, the promoting of causes and cases, debate, and the "complexifying" of issues are lawyers' stock in trade. Rather than promoting closure, improving productivity, and securing results, lawyers tend to find methods of delaying procedures, slowing down action, and reducing outputs of organizations; in short, of making them less-effectively managed. As the number of lawyers has grown, so have the issues involving government liability for actions, once thought to be beyond the bounds of court involvement. Court actions involving the military's use of Agent Orange in Vietnam and the fallout from nuclear tests conducted in the Nevada desert during the 1950s are only two recent examples of the broadening scope of legal liability and lawyer/judicial activism affecting public bureaucracies.

Courts themselves have fostered the widening scope of litigation and liability. Society as a whole has become much more willing "to take legal action" against government for perceived or real wrongs inflicted by bureaucracy. The specific impacts of the litigiousness of society upon public bureaucracy are many, but on the whole the trend in this area has probably made public agencies more cautious and less prone to take initiative, even if those actions by public agencies benefit the majority of citizens. Fear of legal action, often involving large sums of money and public criticisms, is a sound reason for such inaction.

More Households: Smaller and Less Self-Sufficient.   Americans tend to live longer, divorce more frequently, delay marrying or remain single more often, as well as have fewer children or no children at all in order to pursue a two-career marriage. The result is both a marked increase in the number of households and smaller household size. Between 1970 and 1980 the number of households jumped from 63.4 to 80.8 million, for an average growth rate of 1.7 million annually. By the end of the 1980s there should be another 20 million households. The average household size declined substantially during the same period, from 3.14 to 2.72 persons, and the number of persons living alone nearly doubled from 10.9 to 19.4 million. The number of one-parent families doubled from 3.3 million in 1970 to 6.6 million in 1981, when these comprised 20 percent of the nation's 31.6 million families. Ninety percent of one-parent families were headed by women, and 51 percent were black. For public agencies, the changing composition and size of households in America are significant, particularly from the standpoint of increasing dependency upon and need for government services by growing groups of elderly living alone and single parents, especially poor, female-headed, minority households, which require public assistance in order to survive. The continued decline of the self-sufficient family unit places enormous burdens and strains upon public bureaucracies. The declining size of households also means shifting demands for public services in a variety of areas such as education, welfare, and recreation.

Shifting Fundamental Values.   The revolution in personal morality that began in the 1960s, spread in the 1970s, and continues in the 1980s has many important ramifications for public bureaucracies. Attitudes toward drug use,

FIGURE 6.2
Summary of Twelve Environmental Trends in the 1980s
Influencing Directions of Public Bureaucracy in the U.S.

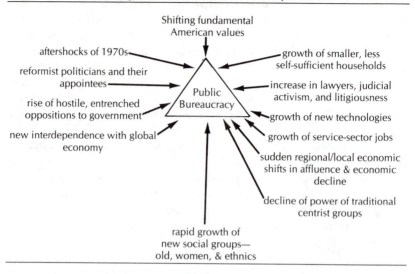

pornography, homosexuality, and premarital and teenage sex are considerably more tolerant today than they were two decades ago. Surveys point up that on the whole Americans are also more tolerant toward minorities, the poor, the handicapped, and women than they were two decades ago. As a result, important advances have been made among these groups in social legislation and in economic and political status. Yet strong moral reactions from the political right and religious fundamentalists are also evident in the 1980s in regard to these changing national mores and morals. In other words, concepts of the American Dream and the Good Society are being hotly debated today. Should the Good Society include a much broader spectrum of activities and groups than it did only a few decades ago? Should it reflect the ideals only of white, Anglo-Saxon, male protestants and of traditional Americans? Or should it become more pluralistic in scope, encompassing many new groups and life styles?

U.S. society today includes a rich texture of multiple subcultures from communities like San Francisco or West Hollywood, which are dominated by gays, to cities in south Florida where a Spanish-speaker can pass a lifetime without speaking English. As futurist John Naisbitt writes, we've moved from ''an either/or'' society to a society of ''multiple options.''[1] Or, from one that offers only chocolate and vanilla to one that offers thirty-one flavors. This new diversity of cultures and subcultures—and its many definitions of morality and of THE GOOD— is no doubt a two-edged sword in regard to the activities of public bureaucracies. Like the fragmented electorate discussed earlier, increased societal diversity often makes collective action on the part of public agencies more difficult to undertake on behalf of *the public*. What is good and correct public action in a society of increasingly diverse interests, views, and values? This multiple-option society, on the other hand, may be an important force in making public agencies more tolerant and open to the various groups that surround their activities. Competing claims of pluralistic demands and values pressing in on every public organization today may well be a powerful, perhaps the most powerful, check on their activities and behavior. Again, more will be said about this subject in the next chapter on bureaucratic accountability.

The Changing Public Bureaucratic System in the 1980s

More socioeconomic-political trends no doubt could be added to the aforementioned list of twelve (see figure 6.2). This list is nowhere near complete. Yet the more critical issue, at least for this book, is the effects of many of these societal trends upon the contemporary bureaucratic system. If the broad socioeconomic-political environment within which U.S. bureaucracy operates in the 1980s is turbulent and in flux, what are the effects upon public bureaucracy as an institution? As a system? As a group of public officials? As a central activity of government? The turbulent sociopolitical-economic environment of the 1980s is reshaping and redirecting the system of public organizations, their institutions, their people, and their activities in many new, profound, and significant ways. In particular, some aspects of the aforementioned trends of the 1980s serve on the whole to strengthen public bureaucracies by promoting clear organizational direction, institutional cohesion, managerial effectiveness, swift action, and decisive exercise of administrative authority. On the other hand, some aspects promulgate precisely the reverse: i.e., indecision, fragmentation, ineffectiveness, inaction, and limits on administrative authority. In short, its institutional decline. First let us review those that tend to promote the latter.

Forces Fostering Institutional Decline and Fragmentation

Rising Bureaucratic Governance by Temporary Amateurs. In many areas of the federal government as well as in state and local agencies, there is an increasing reliance upon staffing bureaucracies not just at the very top level but at two, three, four, or more levels down the bureaucratic hierarchies with temporary political amateurs. In turn, this generally has meant a declining support for and dependence upon professional expertise within agencies for long-term planning, personnel efficiency, innovative ideas, institutional memory, and managerial effectiveness. Many of these amateurs not only lack the necessary long-term commitment, skills, and experience in government but also exhibit a strong distrust of and even hostility to professionals and a disdain for their values and their competence. As Frederick C. Mosher recently observed: "This is no new phenomenon in American governmental life, but the recent attacks by candidates and political office holders upon the civil service, the foreign service, the military services, and other systems built up over the years to assure merit, loyalty and institutional memory have been particularly extreme. They are unfortunate, not only in their effect on the morale of public servants and the future attractiveness of government as a career, but also for the political appointees themselves who must ultimately depend upon the career people to help them make policy and carry out their directions."[2]

At the federal level in the 1980s, governmental units such as the Office of Management and Budget, the Office of Personnel Management, the Department of the Interior, indeed most major federal departments, have witnessed politicization in their career ranks to a far greater extent than ever before (though the trends of politicization began long ago in the Johnson, Nixon, Ford, and Carter administrations). Throughout all units the Reagan administration staffed S.E.S. with the maximum number of political appointees planned by law. The 1985 edition of the Plum Book, which shows federal executive branch jobs open to political appointees, lists, for example, six times more positions in the State Department than the 1980 version. Not only are there more jobs for those belonging to the "right" party at the State Department and elsewhere, but also close identification with the Reagan wing of the Republican Party has become essential in the 1980s for appointment to posts. Often these backgrounds show government inexperience, personal political ties, and frequent changes in positions.

This politicization of policy levels, in turn, affects professional and civil service subsystems in many ways. First, many "pros" are leaving government service. Half of the S.E.S. careerist members who joined in 1979 left by 1981. Aside from the obvious problems of reducing managerial and policy expertise when senior and mid-level policy posts are staffed largely by politicians or newly promoted careerists, more profoundly it is increasingly hard to separate the "pros" from the "pols" inside bureaucracy. Today, for example, "the heads-up-get-ahead" officers of the army, air force, and navy know that they must not only have "their tickets punched" as field commanders and staff officers to succeed in their respective career services, they must also be adept at using the jargon of systems analysis, Pentagon bureaucratic infighting techniques, and playing politics on the hill with the various armed services committees, subcommittees, and staffs. This mingling of politics and professionalism may well foster greater degrees of political responsiveness, but it may also incite greater activism among officers, as the recent example of Vice Admiral James (Ace) Lyons points up. His outspoken criticism of the War Powers Resolution at the Naval War College during the summer of 1984 raised a storm of congressional and media criticism,[3] which was repeated during the summer of 1985 when military professionals, housed at National Security Council, were used to gain conservative political support for Latin American conservative causes. This mixing of "pros" with "pols" raises other more profound problems. As Henry Kissinger recently suggested, "On some levels it has eased civilian-military relations, on a deeper level, it deprived the policy process of the simpler, cruder but perhaps more relevant assessments needed when issues are reduced to a test of arms."[4]

Increasing Complexity of the Entire Bureaucratic System. Once upon a time not very long ago, U.S. public bureaucracy at the local level came in essentially two varieties—a mayor-council and a council-manager form (with a few commission-type governments as well). Despite their institutional differences, their local functions were fairly clear-cut, i.e., to provide the basic public services at the community level, such as police, fire, welfare, and public works. Other services were left to private or nonprofit agencies. Federal and state intervention was limited. The revenue base—property taxes—for supporting these local activities was similarly well defined and largely separate from other levels of government. Thus functional and support responsibilities were fairly evenly divided among local, state, and federal agencies. Each had its own specific tasks, public organizations to carry out these tasks, and revenue bases for support. This may be called "the layer-cake model of federalism."

As prior chapters in this book have explained, such simple institutional arrangements have disappeared from U.S. government. Particularly in the 1980s, the layer-cake conception of federalism with its neat division of functional assignments has given way to a system of great complexity. Public organizations at every level of government are deeply intertwined and interrelated with one another. They are often hard to differentiate at any level of government. A state public health department, for instance, often secures 90 percent of its funds from federal sources and in turn depends entirely upon local agencies to actually administer its programs. Its personnel and buildings may be located in the state capital, but this state bureaucracy may be little more than a transfer point for federal funds that flow downward to local sources. The state agency may thus serve as an extended arm of federal and local bureaucracy—i.e., as a regulatory checkpoint for ensuring that local authorities indeed comply with state health codes and procedures. Numerous other examples abound. In practice, often not much distinction exists between federal, state, and local entities, because they are so operationally interdependent. Perhaps in legal fiction they remain different agencies, but certainly not in institutional practice. The same complex and intertwined interrelationships *between bureaucratic agencies* are the norm in virtually every policy field in the 1980s.

The complexification of the entire bureaucratic system generally works to make its actions more difficult, cumbersome, and problematic. Where more personnel, layers of hierarchy, units of government, vested interests, and regulations enter into the decisional and implementation processes, more opportunities for delay, indecision, and inaction occur. There are more points for "veto groups" to hold up action as the system "complexifies." Further, fixing responsibility for action or inaction becomes more difficult. Establishing who is at fault for a breakdown or delay becomes harder as more parties are involved and as the system grows in size and complexity. There are limits to what the human mind can comprehend and manage—even with the aid of supercomputers.

Too Many Promises and Ill-Conceived Demands on the Bureaucratic System. Elected officials today increasingly rely on television to get their messages across to voters. The thirty-second spot has become perhaps the most powerful vote-getter and source of political education for Americans in the 1980s. Heavy reliance upon simplistic commercials tends to make candidates exaggerate their claims. Furthermore, funding from various PACs and special interests, now so critical to the financing of these expensive campaigns, fosters a plethora of often very narrow and ill-conceived campaign promises, which often cause the electorate to make specific demands for bureaucratic action after the election. Again to cite Frederick Mosher:

> Candidates for the presidency are tempted, almost compelled, to make promises and commitments to those whose support they seek, long before the nominating convention is held. The pressure for promises increases right up to (and after) the inaugural address; pressure for jobs, for favors, for support on policies and programs. But once in office, things look a great deal different from their appearance outside. Commitments on programs and policies in particular, once seen as ideologically desirable and politically inviting, may later appear quite unwise, damaging, or downright impossible. If the successful candidate, once in office, abides by them, he may be doing himself and his country a grave disservice.[5]

In particular, as Mosher also observes, the pressure to put these demands into action is particularly acute during the first hundred days of a new administration, precisely at the time when it is least able to act with care and deliberation:

> There is no period when a president is as ill-prepared to launch a comprehensive program of legislation as during the months immediately following his first inauguration. He and his major advisers are still in the process of education. Unless he himself is a graduate of Congress his acquaintance with and channels to the appropriate fishing holes in Congress are still underdeveloped. The majority of his political appointees in various departments and agencies are not yet even named, let alone confirmed and in office. This means that contacts between top administration officials and the more knowledgeable career officers have not yet begun. It is hard to imagine a situation more conducive to mistakes—perhaps terribly damaging mistakes—than when a new administration, riding the crest of popularity, pushes through a program based on the ideological rhetoric of a heated

political campaign without benefit of the wisdom and the skepticism of officials who have had prior experience in government.[6]

Privatizing Government Bureaucracy through the Contractual Subsystem.
As chapter 4 stressed, the contracting out of services at every level of government today results from a mixture of economic pressures to keep costs down; and political pressures to reward specific local commercial groups with lucrative government contracts. Contracting out for services also coincides with the general public sentiments that government be cut, squeezed, and trimmed. As chapter 4 underscored, the contractual subsystem is one of the hidden major growth areas today in government. Its growth has, however, tended to accelerate numerous problems and dilemmas of managerial efficiency, oversight, and accountability. One only needs to read the newspaper headlines to discover some of these major issues of accountability:

*Army Probes a Computer Firm on Charges of Contract Misconduct
*Local Cable Contractor Defaults on Contract with County
*GAO Finds Difficulties in Fast Food Contract Services
*Navy Sub-contractors Face Fraud Charges Due to Cost-Overruns
*FDA Cites Phony Evidence in Contracted Drug Experiments

As these headlines point up, serious ethical, managerial, and accountability problems arise as public jobs get done out of house rather than in-house. Long chains of not-so-interconnected private contractors and subcontractors, driven frequently by the pressures of only the bottom line rather than by the broad moral concerns of the public good, have raised enormous problems involving the legal use of funds, programmatic efficiency and effectiveness, and security safeguards for classified defense work. Contracting out stretches and lengthens enormously the size of the bureaucratic system as more people and firms are involved with government work. Indeed, pinpointing who is responsible for delays, cost overruns, quality controls, and other failures, becomes increasingly complicated and difficult to determine. This is especially true when multibillion-dollar contracts for highly sophisticated public programs are at stake.

External and Internal Legal Checks on Bureaucracy.   Since the 1970s many legal checks at every level of government have been "invented" to curb bureaucracy—and in the 1980s most public agencies labor under these constraints, which were originally designed and approved by legislatures to improve public accountability. Examples are numerous: the Legislative Reorganization Act of 1970 significantly increased congressional oversight capacities; the War Powers Resolution of 1973 placed important curbs on presidential war-making powers; the Congressional Budget and Impoundment Act of 1974 substantially increased congressional involvement within executive budget-making processes; the Freedom of Information Act as

1973 sharply expanded public access to executive department records and information sources; the creation of Inspector General offices in every major federal department in 1978 provided new internal institutional checks upon agency practices; the Ethics in Government Act of 1978 toughened and extended financial disclosure and conflict-of-interest laws involving government employees. Likewise at the state and local levels, new restrictions were placed upon public bureaucracy through "sunshine" and "sunset" laws as well as through strict revenue limitations brought about by constitutional changes such as Proposition 13, which was passed by voters in California in June 1978.[7]

Bureaucracy at every level lives in the aftershocks of these and many other influential and significant measures. Often they affect public agencies in unforeseen and unintended ways, even in ways that are contradictory to their framers' intentions.

A good illustration is the Freedom of Information Act (FOI). It was originally intended to open up government. By the mid-1980s it is apparent that this seminal piece of reform legislation may well be doing precisely the reverse—opening up government for *private interests, not the general public.* Eighty-five percent of FOI requests processed at the Food and Drug Administration in 1985, for example, came from businesses that it regulates. In 1983, of the 72,534 FOI requests DoD processed, 22 percent came from law firms, 18 percent from the press, 11 percent from business, foreign governments, research groups, and special interests; very few came from the general public. The estimated DoD costs for processing FOI requests were over $10 million in 1983. As Antonio Scalia observes, FOI and its amendments "were promoted as a boon to the press, the public, the little guy; they have been used most frequently by corporation lawyers."[8]

Whether present proposed changes in FOI legislation in the 1980s will result in curbing such "excesses" is hard to predict. In general, such laws have created more legal complications, operational dilemmas, personnel costs, new budget requirements, and institutional management problems. These laws have also led to an increase in the number and power of lawyers *inside and outside* public agencies, who interpret and contest these legal requirements. In many cases, more alarmingly, the laws have given special interests a wider influence over internal bureaucratic operations and policies.

This growth of legalization of the system also slows down bureaucratic actions. Figures 6.3 and 6.4, which are two flow charts comparing the National Ambient Air Quality Standards (NAAQS) rule-making processes of the Environmental Protection Agency in 1970 and 1984, illustrate this phenomenon. When originally established by the 1970 Clean Air Act, it took sixteen separate steps for NAAQS to reach decisions on such complicated subjects as setting standards for carbon monoxide, particulate matter, and oxides of nitrogen. Figure 6.4, by contrast, shows a seventy-step NAAQS decision-making process in 1983 that takes an average of forty-three months to complete. In the 1980s, in other words, NAAQS is a much more complex,

FIGURE 6.3
NAAQS Decision-Making Process, 1971

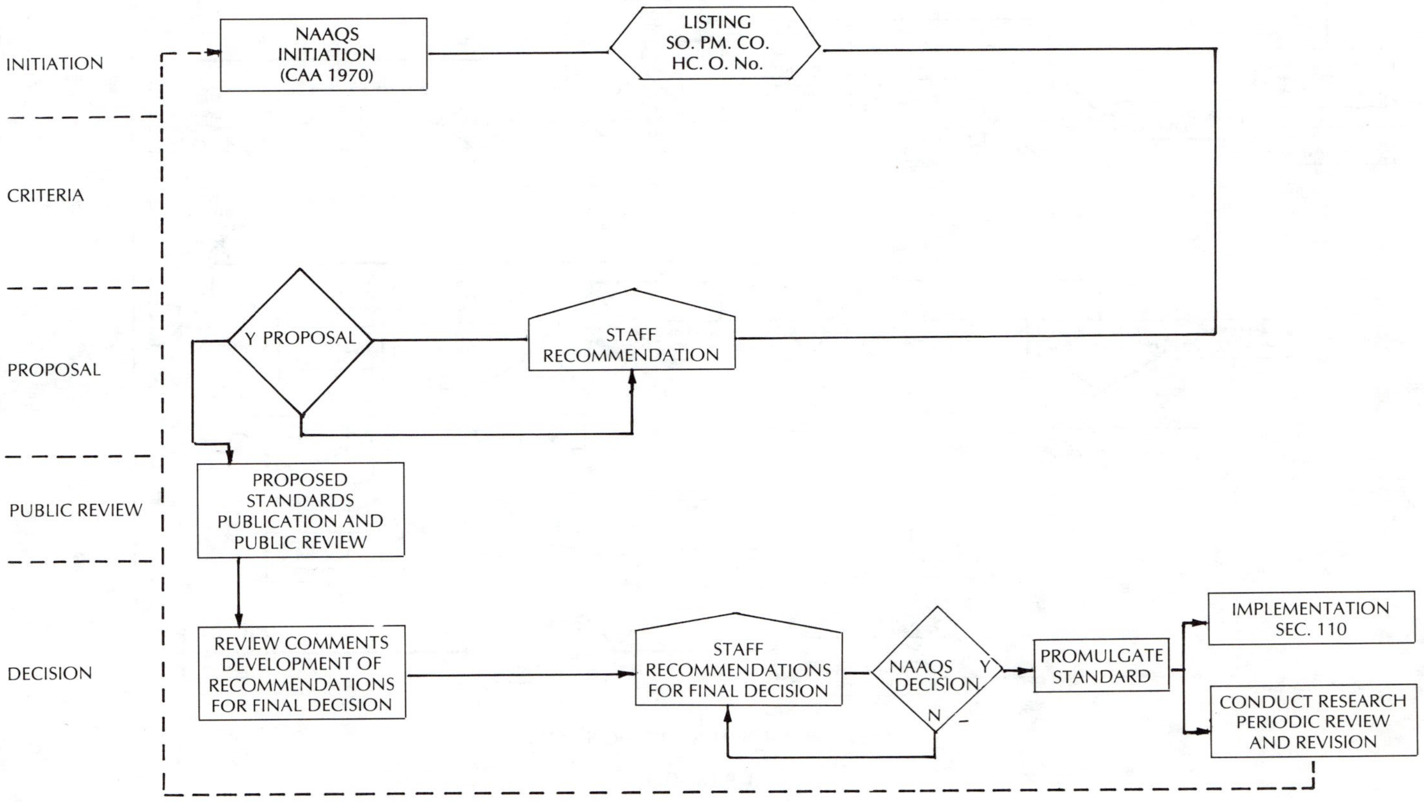

FIGURE 6.4

NAAQS Decision-Making Process, 1983

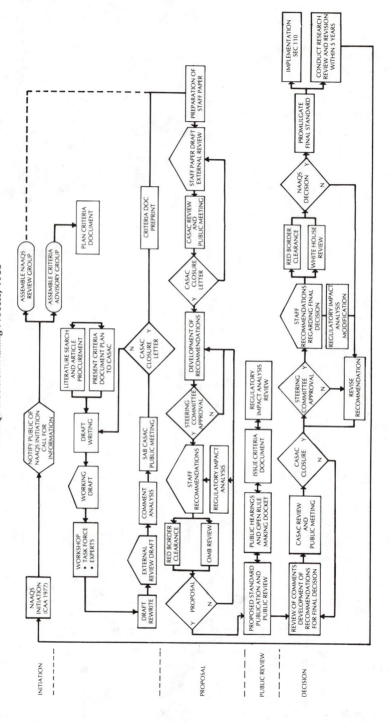

time-consuming, and costly regulatory process than it was in 1970, though it has not necessarily caused better air quality decisions.

Broad, Sustained Public Hostility Coupled with Effective, Narrow Special Interest Intrusion into Bureaucracy. The word *bureaucracy* in the 1980s, as in the past, conjures up notions of inefficiency, waste, and red tape. The press is filled daily with real-life examples of these problems. Moreover, although polls show a slight upturn in public support for government, the overall negative attitudes in the 1980s, toward government remain high as measured by the Michigan public opinion polls, with only 35% of the public saying "government in Washington can be trusted," down from 78% in 1964, 54% in 1972, but up from 28% in 1980. Such hostility not only engenders broad public opposition to bureaucratic activity, it also prevents governmental organizations from attracting capable individuals to staff their programs at all levels and from bettering overall agency morale and managerial effectiveness.

Along with broad and sustained public hostility to bureaucracy, in the 1980s we see the rise of well-organized, aggressive special interest groups. Increasing numbers of sophisticated hostile political interests surround many government organizations, thereby limiting public agencies' room to maneuver in many cases. These "issue networks" (to use Hugh Heclo's term) have continued to flower and grow in the 1980s. For example, in 1975 there were only 700 corporate PACs, but in 1984 there were 3,500—a 500 percent growth! They are well financed and highly influential. These political groups and other interests tend to complexify issues rather than simplify them; prolong debate rather than push for closure; and impede the implementation of programs rather than promulgate their effective and speedy administration. In short, they promote delay, not action. Further, they tend to push for particular interests rather than the general public welfare. Their sophistication, size, and influence over bureaucracy have tended to increase for many reasons—increased funding, more expertise, and advanced use of technologies, to name only a few.

Take, for instance, two of the most powerful pressure groups in Washington, D.C., in the 1980s: the Heritage Foundation and Gray and Company. Probably few Americans outside the nation's capital have heard of either, yet today they decisively influence the course of national politics and bureaucratic actions through spinning fine, invisible webs of influence around many public agencies. They tend to press for special interests rather than for the collective general welfare. Highly skilled lawyers and lobbyists in growing numbers tend to dominate, direct, and influence these groups.

The Heritage Foundation, a nonprofit conservative think tank, has been especially influential in the Reagan administration. It has succeeded in placing many of its key personnel in major political posts in the administration. It closely monitors the progress of various executive agencies in achieving conservative laissez-faire doctrines and openly criticizes any laxness in adhering to the conservative ideological line. Conservative lawyers and lobbyists who head this organization focus their efforts on educating the public and members of Congress about bureaucratic activities adverse to their point of view through frequent press conferences, testimony at public hearings, and brief, fact-filled reports passed out to the public and press. Heritage is well financed by wealthy individuals and businesses, highly sophisticated in public relations, well connected within the administration, and staffed with able specialists in various policy fields of foreign and domestic affairs that advocate and cultivate intensively the conservative view.

Gray and Company, a Washington D.C.-based lobbyist agency, is powerful, well connected, well financed, and extremely sophisticated in the arts of persuasion, media campaigning, computer capabilities, data analysis, and public opinion surveys. Gray represents 130 firms, foreign governments, and other groups and operates with an $11 million budget, making it the largest Washington lobbying firm (in 1984 Gray went public in order to raise an additional $4 million to expand its operations). Gray's personal connections run throughout the administration to Meese, Baker, and Weinberger. Gray uses many sources to acquire inside information for the gain of its clients (such as the Bendix Corporation, Republic of Turkey, and Zana Corporation). Much of its work is simply in opening the right doors, gaining access to information, and creating the right impression through public presentations and media campaigns aimed at influencing favorable bureaucratic decisions or outcomes. Sometimes Gray is not successful; for example, in its urging of the Justice Department to file a brief in favor of Reverend Sun Myung Moon in a recent Supreme Court case of tax fraud or in its support of American Express in opposing the Transportation Department's "scatter plan" for the Washington National Airport. Often, however, Gray is quite successful in pressuring Congress and the bureaucracy, as in a recent media effort to improve Turkey's national image in order to secure increased foreign aid for that country. In short, personal friendships, PR expertise, high speed computer capabilities, direct mailings, and ample finances make Gray and Company and other pressure groups potent forces that intrude into bureaucratic operations and influence public agencies on the federal scene.

The Rise of "The Uncontrollables" in the Public Budgetary Process. As Naomi Caiden pointed up recently in an excellent essay, "The New Rules of the Federal Budget Game," in the *Public Administration Review,* we no longer create government budgets by making annual authorizations through public managers, with incremental bargains struck between various bureaucratic and political players. Neither is budget making as isolated as it once was. Rather, budgeting has become "prey to the vagaries of assumptions about a fluctuating economy." Much of what is spent in the federal budget, which in turn fuels the size, shape, and purpose of public bureaucracy, is now tied to "uncontrollables"—i.e., formula-driven entitlements, long-term contracts with private enterprise, and interest payments on debt. These uncontrollable costs have become highly unpredictable and largely beyond the reach of traditional institutional budgetary controls. For the most part, their costs are driven by shifting groups/individuals qualifying for entitlements, by free market fluctuation of interest rates, by inflationary or deflationary trends affecting business contracts, and by sudden global shifts in the supplies of natural resources or finished manufactured goods used by government—all hard to predict or foresee. These same forces make governmental revenues hard to budget. As Caiden writes, even though "figures for budgetary allocations still march across the pages of the budget document in neat ranks by function and by agency to all appearances the results of conscious annual decisions," the reality is far different: "in seeking to control the economy, the budget has become its prisoner."[9]

The result is that not only the budget but also public bureaucracy in the 1980s—as a whole and as individual agencies—are now prisoners of economic forces beyond their control. Public managers must now *respond to* these forces, not exercise a measure of control over them. Bureaucratic functions and purposes are thus intermeshed, intertwined, and driven by complex global and national economic forces, which often are not easily seen or for that matter understood even by experts. No one knows for certain how these interrelationships work or influence society. Yet the interrelationships are there—*and are highly influential.* Here are some examples from recent newspaper stories:

- A slump in Detroit auto sales triggers slowing production, rising unemployment in primary and secondary-supplier industries, and an automatic surge of federal-state-local unemployment and welfare benefits to the jobless, in turn pushing up demands upon social service agencies;
- A one-cent increase in the cost of gasoline because of a cut in Saudi Arabian oil production automatically triggers a half-a-million dollar increase in a large metropolitan school district's annual operating budget, forcing, in turn, cutbacks in various extracurricular activities and sports programs in order to balance the educational budget;
- The Rural Electrification Administration, which makes low interest loans to a thousand small rural cooperatives for agricultural development, is going broke because the loans were negotiated at far below current market interest rates; hence program cuts are required;
- Chicago's Continental Federal Bank is saved by the Federal Savings and Loan Insurance Corporation because of bad loans made to failing third world Latin American nations that might trigger a crisis in the entire banking industry;
- Shortfalls in the social security's medicare program are expected in the 1990s as the number of retirees who are automatically entitled to social security payments climb steadily—lower benefits or higher payroll taxes therefore will be needed;
- One dollar in five now spent by the federal budget goes to pay for the

national debt. In 1985 $175 billion (approximately) was added to this debt. A 2 percent increase or decrease in the interest rates charged on this debt will automatically add or subtract $17.5 billion to the federal budget—which in turn will add pressures (or lessen them) on various other programmatic expenditures in defense and social programs;

- The number of World War II and Korean veterans, who are automatically entitled to free care at VA's 175 hospitals and 119 nursing homes, rises from 2.3 million in 1976 to 7.2 million in 1990, with an increased cost of $15.4 billion predicted by 1990 (see figure 6.5);
- As cheaper third world steel is dumped on U.S. markets, national production of steel slows, unemployment rises, and unemployment-welfare benefits to the jobless grow, thereby pushing up budget costs and social service demands.

Automatic economic-budget ratchets work on state and local levels with equally profound effects upon city, county, and state public bureaucracies and the people they serve. In 1978, for example, Prince George's County in Maryland overwhelmingly authorized the TRIM Amendment (Tax Reform Initiative by Marylanders) to its constitution. Much like California's Proposition 13, TRIM put a permanent freeze upon county property taxes—*without room for inflationary increases.* By the mid-1980s, local newspapers reported

FIGURE 6.5
How Socioeconomic Pressures Drive Agency Needs—
Future Trends in the Aging of the Veteran Population as a Case in Point

THE AGING VETERAN POPULATION

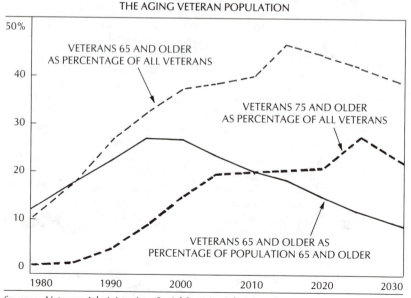

Sources: Veterans Administration, Social Security Administration

that county fire trucks were arriving understaffed at the scenes of fires; police cars were being used long after national standards required them to be replaced; road maintenance trucks and county roads were in disrepair; public schools had eliminated free driver education classes, free athletic events, and free textbooks, among other services; and that even student desks were in short supply.

In brief, the rise of these "uncontrollables" works to reduce bureaucratic authority, long-term planning, efficient use of resources, agency autonomy, and general public management effectiveness.

Temporary "Ad Hoc" Crisis Modes of Bureaucratic Operation. Many of the aforementioned trends—i.e., rise of political amateurs, too many ill-conceived demands on the system, rigidity of the system because of legal checks, intrusion of special interests, and "uncontrollables"—tend to lead to ad hoc crisis management of bureaucratic operations. In a few words, the system is fixed only when it breaks down and the public hue and cry is loud enough to merit political action. Rather than developing long-term planning capacities within governmental agencies to foresee problems well in advance and promulgate stable bureaucratic operations to prevent such problems, it often requires a nuclear mishap such as the one at Three Mile Island or an AMTRAK train derailment or a major air disaster such as the one at the Dallas–Fort Worth airport to secure more agency funding, capable personnel, adequate technology, and appropriate procedures to prevent such tragedies. In the 1980s, the urgency of THE PROBLEM often defines the nature and scope of agency response, rather than agency response controlling the problem-solving processes. Such ad hoc crisis modes of operational management are signs of institutional weakness rather than strength.

Forces Promoting Bureaucratic Cohesion and Effectiveness

Certainly the prospects for public bureaucracy in the 1980s are not all bleak. There is another side to the story, namely, forces at work supporting organizational cohesion, decisive agency direction, institutional effectiveness, administrative action, and the increased exercise of bureaucratic authority. At times these trends may be harder to see or at least are less obvious than those just outlined, but they are present nonetheless.

Insistent Demands for Effective "Multiple-Optioned" Governmental Action and Services. On August 13, 1985, voters in Miami rejected by an almost two-to-one margin a proposal to replace the current professional manager-council form of city government with a strong mayoral system. According to newspaper accounts, the strong-mayor plan "was opposed by black and Hispanic groups, who feared the measure would further politicize city government"[10] and reduce the effective delivery of public services. Perhaps the Miami election is symbolic of the enduring strong support of voters for effective public institutions—i.e., those that are professional, free of politics, well managed, and dedicated to the public interest—to deliver a wide variety of goods and services. The public expectation, not always realized, is that these public goods and services will be provided promptly, fairly, and efficiently. Like the larger U.S. society in the 1980s, U.S. bureaucracy has moved from offering only a choice of chocolate or vanilla to offering many choices of flavor. Bureaucracy comes in many forms and serves many purposes. Public organizations perform a staggering array of services that were not even dreamed of a few years ago: public libraries in some regions routinely rent out video games and do nationwide computer searches for virtually any kind of information; U.S. defense planners are preparing to fight warfare in space in the twenty-first century while working today to keep oil tankers in the Persian Gulf safe from terrorist attack; the Federal Emergency Management Agency offers enormous low interest disaster-relief loans while running all sorts of training programs for dealing with fire emergencies, nuclear attack, and other emergencies. Meteorologists of the National Oceanographic and Aeronautics Administration use sophisticated satellites, planes, and computers to map the weather all over the world. The list of programs and services could go on, but the point is apparent: public bureaucracy mirrors U.S. thirst for multiple options *and answers* to its problems. As John Naisbitt pointed up, just as U.S. society is now multiple-optioned, so too is its bureaucracy.

What multiple-option bureaucracy means in practice is that institutions must show a surprisingly high capacity for producing diverse goods and services, for diverse interests in society, in turn requiring increased professional competence by public agencies to deliver the goods. Increasing numbers of Americans are now also directly affected by public agencies and *expect* these public products to be delivered to them. Statistics show that in 1983 one-third of the U.S. population received direct personal benefits from the federal government (66 million persons in 36 million households). Much of government now touches citizens directly in ways heretofore unknown, heightening citizen demands for effective public services. They have, in other words, a greater vested interest than ever before in seeing to it that programs directly benefiting them are implemented well.

Bureaucratic Innovation Bubbling Up from the Grass Roots. While there remains broad, intense hostility toward bureaucracy, surprisingly strong support for innovation on the part of state and local governments is evident in recent surveys. For example, a 1984 ACIR survey (see table 6.1) asked, "From which level of government do you feel you get the most for your money—federal, state, or local?" Since 1972, the federal level has steadily lost popular support—from 39 percent down to a current 24 percent of the population—while at the same time both the state and local levels have steadily gained popular support, from 18 percent to 27 percent. As the ACIR report explains,

TABLE 6.1
From Which Level of Government Do You Feel You Get the Most for Your Money—Federal, State, or Local?

Percent of U.S. Public

	May 1984	May 1983	May 1982	Sept. 1981	May 1980	May 1979	May 1978	May 1977	March 1976	May 1975	April 1974	May 1973	March 1972
Federal	24	31	35	30	33	29	35	36	36	38	29	35	39
Local	35	31	28	33	26	33	26	26	25	25	28	25	26
State	27	20	20	25	22	22	20	20	20	20	24	18	18
Don't Know	14	19	17	14	19	16	19	18	19	17	19	22	17

Source: Advisory Commission on Intergovernmental Relations, U.S. Government Source, Survey Data, May 1984.

"In a period of high and continuing deficits, part of the sharp decline in public support for the federal government can be attributed to recent publicity highlighting wasteful spending by the federal government, as reported in the Grace Commission Report (1984). The increase in public support for state and local governments may also reflect public perceptions that states and local governments are doing a far better job of getting their budget acts together than is the federal government. In striking contrast to the massive federal deficits, states and local governments appear to have done whatever it took to avoid deficits during the severe 1982–83 recessions, including cutting back spending and raising taxes."

Furthermore, states and localities seem at times to be more directly responsive and innovative in handling immediate policy problems and public agendas. Many of the national policy solutions to pressing issues in the 1980s have seemingly bubbled up from experimentation at the state and local levels, e.g., preferred provider health care options to reduce health costs; recent campaigns to rid the roadways of drunk drivers; home day care for elderly; barring the use of nonreturnable bottles and cans; requiring nonsmoking sections in places of business and in public buildings; competency testing for teachers; placing moratoriums on the construction of nuclear facilities; workfare programs to reduce welfare costs. State and local bureaucracies also have been highly innovative in developing new nonadministrative devices to achieve their policy objectives, i.e., "down zoning" for stimulating new types of land use in communities; "targeted differential code enforcement" to promote business development; new sorts of tax differentials to promote investment; imaginative use of public procurement policies to increase internal efficiency; alternative uses of schools and public buildings to promote community activities; streamlining of permit procedures to expedite local construction. In short, the grass roots level of bureaucratic innovation and responsiveness compared with that at the federal level has been impressive in the 1980s and may account in large part for their differing images and levels of public support. Public agencies at the local level *seem* to the general public to be more innovative and responsive by comparison with their federal counterparts today. The reverse was true just a few decades ago when it was the federal level that was seen as more progressive.

Increasing Specialization and Professionalism in the 1980s. Despite the apparent intrusions of politics into the bureaucratic ranks and the attendant problems it poses for appointee and careerist subsystems, the drive for specialization, expertise, and professionalization at all levels of the public service and in virtually every policy field seems to continue unabated. Gifford Pinchot, for example, the first chief of the U.S. Forest Service, defined the job of a professional forester as simply "tree farming." That was in the early 1900s. Today, largely because of the National Forest Management Act of 1976 (which amended the Resources Planning Act of 1974), an ever-widening body of specialists is found in the ranks of the U.S. Forest Service. In order to run the nation's forests properly, the National Forest Management Act directs the Forest Service to use "a systematic, interdisciplinary approach intended to integrate the knowledge of the physical, biological, economic and social sciences and design arts." This legal mandate translates into a plethora of new specialists with advanced training in statistics, genetics, archaeology, petroleum engineering, chemistry, microbiology, and other fields—specialists who simply were not there a decade ago. Within the last decade, the growth rate of several selected professional specialities within the Forest Service has been as follows: hydrologists, + 86.4 percent; wildlife biologists, + 15.2 percent; soil scientists, + 10.5 percent; range conservationists, + 6.7 percent; and landscape architects, + 6.1 percent. During the same period, the number of general foresters ("tree farmers") increased by only 0.8 percent. The Forest Service reflects the broad trends of professionalization throughout government, favoring specialized expertise over administrative generalists.

The growth of professionalism can also be seen in a sample list of government-agency job openings and their requirements (see figure 6.6). Note the highly technical expertise required to fill these slots, which are mostly at the local level. Even grass roots bureaucracies in the 1980s demand highly specialized, diverse skills in order to function.[11]

The drive for professional specialization and expertise within public bureaucracy in the 1980s is stimulated by many factors: (1) legislation (as in the case of the Forest Service, which mandates the use of experts); (2) new technologies (for example, in health or defense fields, where new inventions spur the growth of new expertise to understand and cope with them); (3) new problems for social action (recent mandates to deal with acid rain, chemical spills, and unsafe landfills force agencies to hire a whole new set of experts); and (4) the professions themselves create new types of professions when they press to subdivide their ranks into clearly defined new varieties of subspecialties (teachers who today are "reading specialists" or "remedial teachers"—categories created in large part by the demands of professional educators).

Chief Accountant
Salary: $30,972

Regional planning agency seeks professional with accounting degree plus 7 years experience, 3 to 4 years in governmental fund and federal grant accounting. Automated accounting system experience also necessary. CPA desirable. Apply to: Atlanta Regional Commission, 100 Edgewood Avenue, Suite 1801, Atlanta, GA 30335, (404) 656-7750. EOE.

Deputy Director
PA Senate Republican Caucus Research Office

Must have PhD, or MA with 5 years experience in policy analysis; excellent editing skills; and a thorough knowledge of benefit cost-analysis. Salary negotiable. Send resume, transcripts, and writing samples to: Dr. Charles Greenawalt, Director, Policy Development and Research Office, Room 611, North Office Building, Harrisburg, PA 17120.

EOE/AA

Chief of Police
City of Seaside, CA

Salary $3146–$3772 per month (salary negotiations now in process), excellent management benefits including City paid PERS.

Under the administrative direction of the City Manager, the Police Chief is responsible for directing all activities of the Police Department. Department consists of 37 sworn positions and an annual operating budget of 2.2 million. Seaside, a beautiful coastal city, is seeking a progressive manager with proven leadership skills. Applicants must also possess excellent community relations skills.

Requires graduation from a four year college or university with a degree in Administration of Justice or comparable field of study. Five years increasingly responsible municipal law enforcement experience, including at least three years at the command level. Possession of Advanced and Management POST certificates. Apply to Personnel Department, City of Seaside, 440 Harcourt Ave., P.O. Box 810, Seaside, CA 93955. (408) 899-6250. City application form is required. Final filing date is *October 18, 1985* before 5 p.m.

EOE/AA

Community Development Supervisor

Private, non-profit, areawide housing agency seeks experienced person to undertake CDGB administration and to supervise staff engaged similarly. Candidate should have considerable CDGB experience in housing rehabilitation and ability to supervise a staff of four. Agency serves rural area in Adirondack-Lake Champlain region. Exceptional life-style/quality of life living conditions. Submit resume, references and salary expectations to Alan S. Hipps, Executive Director, Housing Assistance Program of Essex County, Inc., P.O. Box 157, Church Street, Elizabethtown, New York, 12932. Phone #: (518) 873-6301 ext. 256 or 257. *Resume must be received by 9/30/85.*

Director, Management Information Services
Pinellas County, Clearwater, FL

Salary open DOQ to low $50's. Excellent benefits. Reports to 6 member MIS Board comprised of heads of user departments. Responsible for comprehensive state of art control distributed

FIGURE 6.6 (continued)

DP system; 80+ employees; budget in excess of $5.5 M. Must have proven management and communication skills, experience with the knowledge of main frame, distributed system related. Local government MIS experience highly desired. Submit resumes *immediately* to: Korn/Ferry International, Attn: Robert E. Slavin, 1800 Century Park East, Suite 900, Los Angeles, CA 90067.

Legislative Fiscal Analyst
Oklahoma House of Representatives

Nonpartisan staff for appropriations process. Will work closely with Legislators and agency directors on policy and budgetary analysis. Requires MPA, MBA, political science or economics masters degree, and excellent analytic and communications skills. Salary range $21,400–$28,700. Send cover letter, resume, transcripts, and sample of written work to D. J. Enevoldsen, Director, House Fiscal Staff, 305 State Capitol, Oklahoma City, OK.

Community Development Director

City of Liberty, MO. (18,000). $42,000–$50,000 depending on qualifications. Requires degree in civil engineering, urban planning, public/business administration, or related field; MA preferred. Requires minimum of 5 years significant management experience with strong experience in public works administration. Department head responsible for engineering, capital improvements, economic development, housing, historic presentation; planning and zoning, building inspection, code enforcement, water/wastewater utilities, municipal buildings and CDBG/miscellaneous grant programs. Reports to City Administrator.

Historic full-service community expanding residential and commercial base located in Kansas City metropolitan area.

Send resumé, references and salary requirements to: Personnel Officer, City Hall, 101 E. Kansas, P.O. Box 159, Liberty, MO 64068 (816) 781-7100, ext. 202 *by 11/15/85.*
EOE

Chief Budget Officer
$32,366–$43,374

Pima County, located in Tucson, Arizona, is accepting applications for a Chief Budget Officer (Class Code 1376). A management position in the unclassified service reporting to the Director of the Office of Budget and Research, the incumbent performs work of considerable difficulty directing, coordinating and administering the budget activities of the County. DESIRED QUALIFICATIONS are a Bachelor's degree from an accredited college or university with a major in finance, accounting, or a closely related field and five years of experience in professional accounting and/or budget research including two years at the supervisory managerial level. A Master's degree from an accredited college or university with a major in finance, accounting or a closely related field may substitute for two years of the professional accounting and/or budget research experience. Four years additional professional accounting, financial and/or budget research experience may substitute for the required Bachelor's degree. Interested applicants should call Bob Curran, Selection Division Supervisor, for necessary application materials which Must Be Completed and Returned by 5:00 P.M., Monday, August 26, 1985.

Pima County Human Resources Department
4th Floor, 150 W. Congress St.
Tucson, AZ 85701
(602) 792-8176

FIGURE 6.6 (continued)

Transportation Planner

Houston-Galveston Area Council (H-GAC), metropolitan planning organization (MPO) for the Houston area is accepting applications for an entry-level transportation planner. H-GAC is actively involved in long-range planning for highways, transit, airport systems, and air quality for a region with one of the nation's most dynamic programs of transportation improvements. Position involves assisting in regional travel forecasts, development of area mobility plans, and reviewing proposed transportation improvements. Position requires a Masters degree in urban planning with emphasis on transportation planning, or equivalent experience. Salary Range: $19,000–$24,000.

Persons interested in applying should submit a resume to:

Jules Narcisse
Director of Internal Operations
Houston-Galveston Area Council
P. O. Box 22777
Houston, Texas 77227

Professional associations are particularly vocal in pressing for separate, identifiable status, high recognition, unique training programs, special certification, and new subfield identities. Every professional association involved in the public sector exhibits these tendencies in the 1980s. The 1980 Code of Ethics of the National Association of Social Workers, for instance, argues at the outset: "The social workers should strive to become and remain proficient in professional practices and proficient in professional functions." The emphasis throughout is upon uniquely differentiated roles, specialized expertise, advanced training, higher status, and *professionalism* as the unique hallmarks of the modern-day social worker.

New Technologies Outside and Inside Bureaucracy Strengthen Public Organizations. As has been said, much of the pressure for hiring new professionals and creating new professional subfields inside public organizations today is promoted by the technological imperative. As new problems confront U.S. government—i.e., fighting covert wars in Latin America, aiding refugees in Africa, or combating the medfly in California orchards—increasingly sophisticated technologies are needed by government agencies, which in turn necessitates the hiring of personnel who can "invent" and apply these technologies on behalf of the public. Government itself has become the spawning ground for new technologies on a vast scale within virtually every policy field. DoD's little-known Defense Advanced Research Planning Agency (DARPA) is today promoting the fifth generation of computers necessary to fight complex "star wars," and this will no doubt have important spillovers in industrial-economic-social development across the United States. The FBI has developed innovative uses for behavior research through its behavior science research unit at Quantico, Virginia, which can "profile" psychological portraits of serial killers with amazing accuracy. Further, the FBI has invented new high-speed automated fingerprint-reading devices that increase the speed with which police departments can "read" prints, enabling them to make arrests in cooperation with local police all across the country. Many large public university programs today, such as those at the University of California and the University of Texas, are developed and enhanced by state legislators to attract industrial and regional development. Through high-tech research, universities are becoming "magnets" for industrial growth. The Internal Revenue Service is using new supercomputers in its regional centers throughout the country to increase their collection rates, reduce their labor-intensive manpower costs, and achieve higher taxpayer compliance.

The application and use of new technologies by public organizations are reshaping public services in profound and important ways. Like their private enterprise counterparts, public sector agencies are using applied technologies to extend their range of services, reduce costs, improve the timeliness and efficiency of services rendered, and increase internal analytical and control capabilities. The complexities of these new technologies reshape the fundamental nature of the public work force by fostering increased specialization, expertise, and professionalization. The ethical implications are apparent, too. The computerization of the IRS, for example, has created enormous ethical and security problems for the agency.

Perhaps the White House organization in the 1980s best epitomizes these contemporary trends involving technological impacts inside government. For although the White House has always been a highly political entity, President Reagan, perhaps more than any other president, has structured the White House in ways that draw upon a wide range of hard and soft management technologies to extend his influence and control over his staff. Through numerous skilled assistants, the White House employs a highly sophisticated cluster of technologies for strategic planning through its Office of Policy Development, for evaluation through its Office of Planning and Evaluation, and for survey research through public opinion polling. Besides drawing on these technologies and specialized experts, the White House has innovatively utilized several unique organizational formats (or soft technologies) to implement its programs and policies, such as employing the cabinet council concept and temporary "outside" private commissions, such as the Grace Commission, and temporary internal task forces, such as Reform 88 (housed within OMB), to push through its various policy priorities and initiatives. The troika management team and the cabinet council concept are highly innovative managerial devices for policy planning and implementing.[12]

Application of New Expertise and Knowledge Bases from the Outside.   The negatives of contracting out government services were cited above. There are also positive aspects to the increased reliance upon the contractual subsystem;

namely, it brings into government fresh perspectives and new talent that could not normally be tapped for long-term governmental service or that government agencies could not afford to hire. It also tends to break up traditional professional relationships and create broader, more diversified and democratic pools of expertise for solving public problems.

In the words of William Bacchus, we may now have "professionals without professions."[13] His point: we now have many professionals in the public service whose formal links to particular professional groups or specific professional educational programs are tenuous at best. Indeed, many public professionals are not even housed in one place as a unified, identifiable group of people but are rather "nested" all over government, even outside government, in odd and curious places. Witness the professional intelligence community (see figures 6.7 and 6.8). The National Security Act of 1947 and 1949 set up the Central Intelligence Agency to unify all intelligence operations under one roof, and, consequently, during the 1950s a highly professional cadre of intelligence personnel grew up within the CIA. In 1953 the agency contained most government intelligence agents *within its own house* and within a highly structured professional career system, as depicted in figure 6.7.

By the 1980s, however, all that was changed, as figure 6.8 illustrates. Intelligence activities—and intelligence professionals—are spread out across the federal government, even outside the CIA because of contracts with major think tanks such as Brookings and Rand and with large companies, such as Hughes, that are involved with developing intelligence-gathering techniques and inventions. These intelligence "pros" today lack a common home, clear lines of advancement, "elite controls," the "right" schools for professional preparation, and a commonly agreed upon set of skills, values, and expertise—in short, an overall corporate identity. On the other hand, the CIA significantly influences the course of policy choices in this particular field, even though its informal ranks and operational activities cut across many organizational lines, subareas, and specialties—even beyond the traditional boundaries of government.

Such is also the case at the state and local levels, where the neat, precise boundaries and contours of public professions have faded or been erased entirely in the 1980s. The "pros" influencing the public sector have become fluid, hard-to-identify clusters of men and women (and women in recent years have grown in numbers and prominence in these ranks). For professionals in government, the route to success or to failure is increasingly difficult to pinpoint. There are no longer clear guideposts or road maps that direct individuals toward the one best way to succeed. But the diversity among employees that this ambiguousness fosters may well be a new source of institutional strength that promotes new perspectives, taps fresh talent, creates better research opportunities, and on the whole strengthens expertise in government agencies and their delivery capabilities.

FIGURE 6.7
**1953 CIA Organization Chart Shows That Most Intelligence Operations
Are Housed In-House**

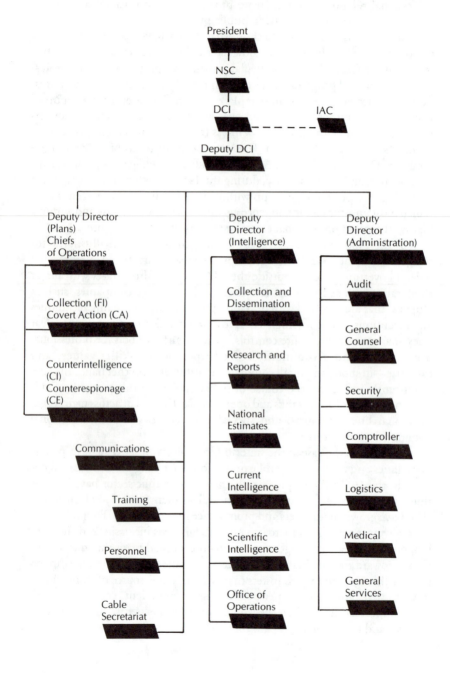

FIGURE 6.8
**In the 1980s the CIA Is Only One Among Several Major Federal Intelligence-
Gathering Agencies with Various Overlapping Duties & Functions
That Form the Intelligence Community**

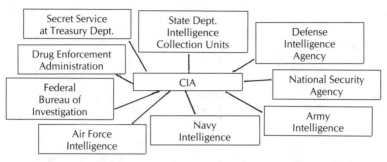

Small Is Beautiful.   Complexification of the bureaucratic system, as just observed, fosters several disfunctional attributes: indecision, inaction, unresponsiveness, and even irresponsibility and unaccountability. The Reagan administration since 1981 has initiated several policies, particularly in the area of domestic programs, to reverse these trends: i.e., the reduction of federal personnel in human services by 75,420 (excluding defense); deregulation of various sectors of the economy; the shifting of federal programmatic responsibilities to state, local, and private sector organizations; the reduction in federal grants, loans, and subsidies; the easing of federal regulations attached to intergovernmental aid programs to states and localities; and the accelerating of nongovernmental solutions to public problems through tax and private sector incentives (such as enterprise zones for industrial development of poor or depressed regions).

Such programs have tended to shrink significantly the size and scope of federal domestic (though not defense) programs since 1980. The effort has reduced federal aid to states and localities from 31.7 percent (1980) to 22 percent (1986), its mid-1960 level. Federal tax revenue dropped from 13.7 percent of the GNP (1981) to 11.3 percent (1984). Simplification and reduction of regulatory activities have shrunk the pages of the *Federal Register* from 87,012 (1981) to 63,554 (1984). Some regulatory units, such as the Civil Aeronautics Administration, were shut down entirely, and others such as the Interstate Commerce Commission have had their staffs and budgets dramatically cut back (see table 6.2) so that their functional capabilities have been severely limited. Cutbacks have been across the board in the domestic field. Specifically, the President's Private Sector Survey on Cost Control (the Grace Commission) made 2,478 recommendations for cost cutting and personnel reductions, and the Reagan administration had enacted 879 of these by mid-1985, for an estimated savings of $111,882,000. Business and nonprofit organizations were further actively encouraged to supplement, even replace in

TABLE 6.2
The Decline in Interstate Commerce Commission Appropriations
and Employment for Selected Years 1955–1984

Year	Appropriation	Average Employment
1955	$11,679,655	1,859
1960	19,650,000	2,344
1965	26,715,000	2,339
1970	27,742,660	1,802
1975	44,970,000	1,986
1980	79,063,000	1,946
1981	82,400,000	1,852
1982	70,150,000	1,540
1983	65,600,000	1,319
1984	60,000,000	1,160

Source: Interstate Commerce Commission, *97th Annual Report,* Government Printing Office, 1984.

some cases, governmental action to meet the needs caused by the cutbacks in employment, education, community development, and health care.

Aside from the question of the wisdom of such cutbacks and their efforts upon the clientele served, such cutbacks have the general effect of simplifying government bureaucracy. Thus, from an institutional standpoint, these recent trends can have healthy side effects, such as forcing an agency to clarify organizational goals; eliminating bureaucratic deadwood; focusing resources on priority areas; enhancing agency efficiency; exercising effective organizational control and oversight; and expanding accountability for action or inaction. In short, a leaner bureaucracy may well be a more responsive and responsible one.

Centralizing Political Control over Public Bureaucracy. Concomitant with the striving toward a leaner federal bureaucracy, the Reagan administration has imposed a greater centralization of political authority over federal operations than prior administrations by means of several avenues. First, it has exercised budget authority over other agencies to an unprecedented degree. Particularly during his first two years in office, David Stockman, Reagan's OMB director, centralized budget policies in accordance with the president's goals and program priorities with little regard for agency requests, interest group demands, or congressional opposition. The budget was put together and considered as a whole, rather than in incremental, piecemeal fashion, as was the norm before, through the inventive use of the reconciliation process established by the 1974 Congressional Budget and Impoundment Act.

Second, OMB exercised centralized controls over the regulatory process as well. OMB's Office of Information and Regulatory Affairs aggressively proposed new regulations, revisions, and cutbacks on regulatory agency actions, staffs, and budgets. Under Executive Orders 12291 (1982) and 12498 (1985), OMB applied cost-benefit analysis to a wide range of regulations and strongly and systematically influenced them to change their substance, directions, and processes. In short, these new executive orders allowed OMB to create a unified regulatory program in accordance with the president's agenda and goals.

Third, the administration, also through OMB, drastically reduced federal regulatory burdens on states and localities in a variety of intergovernmental grants-in-aid programs involving enforcement of affirmative action and occupational safety and environmental codes.

Fourth, the Office of Personnel Management, another political arm of the White House, tightly controlled the appointment of political officials who are thoroughly in agreement with the president's political agenda, establishing a cadre of political managers committed to the president. In some cases early in the president's first term, *not* appointing officials served to expand White House control over agency affairs, since no one was there at the agency who could defend the agency against OMB's drastic cuts.

Fifth, the bureaucratic information services were also pruned back—i.e., agency planning, analytical, data collection, and public information staffs—and the budgets for printing and statistics-gathering units were severely reduced between 1981 and 1985. This shrinking information base gave agencies fewer capabilities for gaining clientele support and for promoting individual agendas and personal programs, which, in turn, strengthened OMB and White House political controls over agencies.

Sixth, outside units to check and control bureaucracy in accordance with the president's policies were effectively used by the Reagan administration. The work of the Grace Commission, staffed largely by volunteer businesspersons, already has been cited. The appointment of aggressive inspectors general in every federal department to uncover waste, fraud, and abuse is another prominent example.

Finally, the Reagan administration, through Office of Personnel Management (OPM) first director, Donald Devine, articulated a renewed emphasis upon a clear division between "policy" and "administration" that put the president and his political appointees squarely in charge of policy making. As Devine stated:

> The distinction between policy and administration rests upon the broader distinction between the policymaking elected public official and the responsive civil servant, upon which democracy rests. This, in turn, rests upon the fundamental principle upon which Western culture is built, the distinction between a limited-power state and a free society. We in the new Administration want to get public administration back to its real job of administering the government. A reform of the system which cuts back on the size of government and the functions it performs, will help us in this task. A small federal establishment will be an easier one to manage and a more rational one.[14]

TABLE 6.3

How Key Trends Weakening the Bureaucratic System Affect Elements of the System in the 1980s

	Weakens External "Inputs" & Supports	Weakens Internal Subsystems & Cohesion	Weakens Effectiveness/ Efficiency of Outputs	Weakens Role, Scope, Authority, & Discretion in Society	Weakens Controls, Oversight, & Accountability
Governance by Political Amateurs		X	X		X
Complexification of System	X	X	X	X	X
Too Many Ill-conceived Demands	X	X	X		X
Privatizing Bureaucracy		X	X		X
External/Internal Legal Controls		X	X	X	
Public/Special Interest Group Hostility	X	X	X	X	X
Rise of Uncontrollables		X		X	X
Ad Hoc Crisis Management		X		X	X

Overall, what can we make of these twin trends within public bureaucracies in the 1980s—those enhancing its strength and those promoting its weakness and decline? Certainly, as we have already observed, the picture is mixed. Both trends are at work today, though as tables 6.3 and 6.4 indicate, each of these previously enumerated forces exhibits significantly different impacts upon various elements of the bureaucratic system. In reality, then, the 1980s have neither totally transformed U.S. public bureaucracy nor allowed it to remain a stable institution; rather, important elements of the system are simultaneously being weakened and strengthened by powerful forces of change.

One further point: probably no prior decade in U.S. history has witnessed such an intense outpouring of antibureaucratic literature and ideas that have profoundly shaped the institutional changes and trends just cited. Because of their uniqueness and prominence in the 1980s, the last section of this chapter will review the substance and influence of contemporary ideas about bureaucracy.

The Ideological Reactions to U.S. Public Bureaucracy in the 1980s: The Varieties of Ideas about Bureaucracy Today

For many years Americans have held largely negative views of government bureaucracy. The 1980s are certainly no different in this regard, as public opinion survey data (cited earlier) point up. What is new, however, is the flowering of so many ideological perspectives, largely hostile ones, regarding public bureaucracy, amounting to what Herbert Kaufman has described in the title of an essay as a "Fear of Bureaucracy: A Raging Pandemic."[15] The following discussion attempts to outline several of these prominent ideological perspectives on bureaucracy, their major values, their central arguments, and their proposals to reform bureaucratic institutions. Many of these ideas directly influence the shape and direction of public organizations in the 1980s. Indeed, no other decade in U.S. history has contained so many diverse ideas about bureaucracy and what should be done about it. Few decades have exhibited such a direct influence of ideas upon government agencies and their internal operations as the 1980s. The following listing of major perspectives is not complete but offers several important theoretical-ideological points of view now being debated and discussed.

The Businessperson as Hero and the Bureaucrat as Antihero

In the mid-1980s, a highly effective television commercial for Federal Express, a private overnight delivery service, showed a typical big city post office swamped by a growing avalanche of letters and packages. A voice states "The U.S. Post Office handles 300 million letters and packages every day. Now do you want to put *your* important mail in that mess?" The name Federal Express is next flashed on the screen. The message is none too subtle—the postal service is inept, and important mail is better handled by an efficient private sector company.

TABLE 6.4

How Key Trends Strengthening the Bureaucratic System Affect Elements of the System in the 1980s

	Strengthens External "Inputs" & Support	Strengthens Internal Subsystems & Cohesion	Strengthens Effectiveness/ Efficiency of Outputs	Strengthens Role, Scope, Authority, & Discretion in Society	Strengthens Controls Oversight, & Accountability
Popular Demand for Multi-optioned Services & Actions	X	X	X	X	X
Innovations Bubbling Up Front Grass Roots	X		X	X	
Increased Professionalism & Specialization		X	X		
New Technologies		X	X		X
Application of New Outside Expertise & Knowledge			X	X	
Small Is Beautiful		X	X		X
Political Centralization		X	X		X

Another recent example is an article that ran in a prominent business journal, "Washington's Red Tape Just Keeps Rolling Out."[16] The story catalogs numerous examples of waste, inefficiency, duplication, and bad management practices found in the federal government. Throughout the story the ineptitude and inefficiency of government are contrasted with the virtues, expertise, and efficiency of private enterprise. "If you ran a business like government, you'd be out of a job for sure," emphatically concludes its last line. Again, the message—bureaucracy is inefficient and business is efficient.

Such examples reflect Americans' strong, enduring attachment to business and the businessperson—the cultural heroes of the 1980s?—and conversely their persistent disparagement of public sector activities and civil servants—the cultural villains of the age? But there is another cause at work. They also reflect to a large degree the belief in the *practice* of business and businesspersons; that they, far better than government, can achieve the most returns (big profits?) from the least expenditure of labor, money, and materials (smart use of wealth?).

The belief in businesspersons as cultural knights in shining armor tends to value their worth in terms of economic accomplishment: i.e., they are best at achieving social efficiency and at creating widespread material wealth. Businesspersons' work, drive, initiative, thrift, and enterprise are viewed as the prime sources of U.S. wealth and greatness. Hence, *their ways* of doing things in the private sector are preferable to bureaucrats' ways in the public sector, and their practices should be emulated particularly by the bureaucracy and the bureaucrat.

It is unlikely that there will be another figure like "Engine Charlie Wilson," ex-president of General Motors and U.S. secretary of defense in the 1950s, who proclaimed publicly: "What's good for General Motors is good for America." Yet, the 1980s exhibit a fresh resurgence of faith in business and conversely a decline in enthusiasm for public sector activities.

Why this occurred in the 1980s is not clear, but during that decade there were many signs of public confidence in business—e.g., President Reagan's election in 1980 and reelection in 1984 on a strong anti-Washington-probusiness platform; the renewed interest in business classes by college students; an enthusiastic interest in books about being successful or making it "big" in business; support for popular businesspersons such as Lee Iacocca, who rescued a failing Chrysler Corporation from bankruptcy; and the passage of 1981 Tax Reform measures aimed at stimulating the economy through cuts in federal revenue and increases in private revenues for businesses. The concomitant cutback in funds for public services—roads, schools, hospitals, and a broad range of federal social programs—was in large part fueled by a belief that the private sector is far more able to deliver those public goods and services to the people. Somehow, bureaucracy always seems to waste and misuse public funds allocated to it and hence becomes THE social villain of our time.

The popular idealization of businesspersons and business, always strong throughout U.S. history, has also been fed in large part in recent years by the political ideas and activities of the neoconservative movement. This contemporary conservative movement in the United States is worth examining in more detail, particularly with regard to its views and ideas concerning U.S. bureaucracy.

Neoconservative Challenges to Public Bureaucracy: Hostility from the Right

American conservatives have never developed an explicit theory of bureaucracy. They simply opposed bureaucracy in whatever form. To the right, bureaucracy traditionally has been an anathema—a curse that must be stamped out or at least constrained as much as possible. American conservatives in the past have viewed bureaucracy as a special threat to both human and political values, not to mention the free enterprise system. Popularity elected conservative presidents such as Calvin Coolidge and Herbert Hoover and would-be presidents such as Robert Taft and Barry Goldwater shared this point of view; so have monetarist economic conservatives such as Ludwig von Mises, Friedrich von Hayek, Milton Friedman, and all of the Austrian economic school of monetarists, who have long championed limited bureaucracy primarily as a safeguard to human freedom, dignity, individual choice, and free enterprise. In the tradition of Adam Smith, they believed that government should be kept as small as possible and that the *real* work of society should be left to the unplanned and unpredictable working of the marketplace—i.e., "the invisible hand."

More recently, the 1980s have witnessed a fresh revival of the neoconservative movement. Its perspectives are those of a younger group of conservative thinkers, mostly trained in the monetarist school of economics but with more contemporary points of view on modern social problems. These thinkers' ideas have achieved increasing respectability and even fashionable notoriety in recent years. Indeed, their ideas buttressed many of President Reagan's campaign themes in the 1980s and his federal tax and budgetary initiatives in 1980–1982. This neoconservative resurgence had many sources—spanning both coasts, from the conservative think tanks at the Hoover Institution at Stanford University to the American Enterprise Institute in Washington, D.C.—and a diverse range of independent theorists—from clusters of writers associated with the *Wall Street Journal* to those at the *Public Interest*. Much of their thought cannot be compressed into a single idea but contains diverse points of view regarding government and its role in society.

Specifically, neoconservative ideas are largely "hard-line," laissez-faire ones that argue against bureaucracy. George Gilder's *Wealth and Poverty* (1981) popularized many of these themes. Essentially, Gilder's book is a tract against bureaucracy. "Its crippling regulations, restrictions and laws," he writes, "have served to undermine America's real source of wealth—individual incentive, creative geniuses, technological adventurers and personal risk-takers—which are the true source of America's productivity and growth."[17] Most of what government does, by contrast, believes Gilder, retards U.S. development; indeed, much of what government does, such as redistribute public funds to the poor, only serves to keep the poor dependent on welfare and victims of poverty. As Gilder concludes, ''All modern governments pretend to promote economic growth but in practice doggedly obstruct it.'' Material progress depends, therefore, not on bureaucracy, an institution in Gilder's view fundamentally inimical to progress, but on individual achievement, expansion of private opportunity, and unpredictable creative behavior in the free marketplace.

Many neoconservatives share Gilder's distrust and dislike of bureaucracy and several have pushed specific programs to shrink it. The drive to deregulate large sectors of industry was stimulated in the 1980s by this neoconservative philosophy. California's Proposition 13—as well as other local tax-cutting initiatives around the country—was supported by most neoconservatives precisely because it sought to cut the revenue sources of bureaucracy by imposing strict limits on property tax increases. At the federal level, the 1982 Kemp-Roth tax bill, fashioned largely by neoconservative theorists and passed by Congress, cut federal taxes in three successive years and indexed federal taxes principally to halt the further growth of government and public expenditures and to return more dollars to the private sector in order to stimulate its growth.

Of the variety of techniques and methods of limiting bureaucratic expansion, the balanced-budget amendment to the U.S. Constitution was the most popular with neoconservatives. Aaron Wildavsky, for example, in his book *How to Limit Government Spending* (1980) makes a strong case for this new constitutional amendment on the grounds that it would help redress the balance in ''public vs. private'' spheres, which Wildavsky believes are out of balance: ''Big government is no bargain. Doing what comes naturally, it will (without consent, to be sure) eat us out of house and home.''[18] The balanced-budget amendment would, in his view, limit the increase in federal expenditures to the proportional rise in the Gross National Product; hence, the size of the public sector would not be allowed to grow any faster than the private sector. Public consumption would be irrevocably tied thereafter to private production (except in emergencies, when a two-thirds vote of Congress could override the limitation for short periods). This proposed constitutional amendment has so far not been approved by Congress or by the required three-fourths of state legislatures. Its rationale is based upon microeconomic analysis, another method of evaluating bureaucracy that is worthy of closer examination.

Microeconomic Analysis: The Free Market as Hero and Bureaucracy as Antihero

The neoconservative challenge to bureaucracy draws heavily from microeconomic analysis, which is used to analyze the operations and decision-making processes of business firms and, to some extent, the methodology of policy analysis. Such microeconomic perspectives on bureaucracy are not new. Ludwig von Mises's *Bureaucracy* (1944); Gordon Tullock's *The Politics of Bureaucracy* (1965); Anthony Downs's *Inside Bureaucracy* (1967); and William A. Niskanen's *Bureaucracy: Servant or Master?* (1973) all draw heavily on the eighteenth-century writings of Adam Smith. The common perspective contained in these writings is that bureaucracy should operate much like a business firm does. In microeconomic writings, bureaucrats are assumed to be, like private entrepreneurs, motivated purely by self-interest. The notion of the public interest or the public good is missing entirely from their calculations.

Like managers in business firms, according to these microeconomic analysts, bureaucrats pursue the development of various products to satisfy their customers' wants, larger budgets, larger staffs, and personal promotions. The uniqueness of bureaucracy, according to these economists, is that bureaucracies, in large part financed by taxes or grants, have a "bilateral monopoly" between supplier and consumer—i.e., seller and customer have no alternative market or source of goods. Thus, government bureaucracies, like any industrial firm that has monopolized a market, tend to grow too large, too powerful, and too unresponsive to the needs of customers. Most microeconomic writers therefore argue in favor of disciplining public bureaucracies to encourage them to increase their responsiveness to consumers, improve efficiency of production, and lower the costs of goods through competitive practices. To accomplish these ends, they frequently suggest numerous ideas for "privatizing" bureaucracy.

E. S. Savas's *Privatizing the Public Sector* (1982) proposes a broad range of solutions to cure the problems of bureaucracy. Basing his ideas largely upon microeconomic analysis, Savas sees bureaucracy as being much like a business firm that delivers public goods to customers. However, bureaucracy's operations—unlike those of business—are largely wasteful, inefficient, and counterproductive because of their monopolies over certain areas of the marketplace. The alternative, according to Savas, is "privatization of government": i.e., either returning its activities as far as feasible to the private sector or operating those activities inside government as closely as possible to free market competition through a variety of arrangements such as load sharing, franchising, contracting-out for services, voucher systems, and the like. Much of Savas's book is devoted to exploring and elaborating upon each of these alternative proposals for privatizing bureaucracies. His explicit purpose is to push privatization as far as possible to promote freedom of choice for the consumer, maximize productive capacity and efficiency for the supplier, constrain the growth of bureaucratic government, and thereby expand freedom of choice for U.S. citizens. In practice, for public bureaucracy at all levels, these arguments have served not only to cut government programs but also to accelerate the trends toward contracting-out many public services to private firms.[19]

While Savas's microeconomic perspectives and solutions are spread over a variety of public bureaucratic issues, policies, and problems, several more narrowly focused books in the 1980s apply this perspective to single policy fields and develop specific recommendations for these policy areas. In the area of natural resources, for example, John Baden and Richard L. Stroup (eds.) *Bureaucracy vs. Environment: The Environmental Costs of Bureaucratic Government* (1981) is an important collection of writings of microeconomic analysts specializing in natural resource economics who strongly advocate free market solutions to problems involving natural resources: "The market based on the willing consent of individuals and operating through the mechanisms of prices . . . tends to move resources to the most highly valued uses. . . . The market will . . . provide socially optimal production of goods and services."[20] The problem with bureaucratic regulation and policies is, according to these writers, that they tend to underprice natural resources, generating excessive production and negative externalities such as the overuse of public lands, the waste of natural gas, and air pollution. According to their theories, public activity suffers from the "tragedy of commons"—everyone's property is no one's. And because the bureaucrats are for the most part interested only in expanding their own organizations, the size of their budgets, and the growth of their careers, little change can be expected from the inside. Rather, the answer, according to these authors, to the problems of protecting natural resources and ensuring their efficient employment lies on the outside—i.e., promoting greater marketplace discipline over environmental resources: "Most, if not all of the environmentally destructive practices . . . would not occur if the agencies were required to meet the standards of economic efficiency."[21] Many of their specific suggestions for reforms in this area were adopted by the Interior Department in the 1980s, based upon notions that the market and the free natural flow of material goods and services are the remedies for the ills of modern bureaucracy.

Neo-Marxist Perspectives: Hostility to Bureaucracy from the Left

If bureaucracy is anathema to the right and private enterprise—especially the free market—is a cure to its ills, the left has in the 1980s a similar distrust and strong hostility to bureaucracy, though for decidedly different reasons and with distinctly different prescriptions for bureaucratic reform. Neo-Marxist thinking is largely derived from academic theorists, leftist social scientists in political science, sociology, and kindred disciplines, who are avidly opposed to the political status quo and are especially critical of modern-day commercialism, consumerism, and lack of concern for the underprivileged. In the tradition of Karl Marx, these thinkers generally favor grand utopian schemes for change—radical transformations of the social order that would bring about a more humane, egalitarian world. They favor especially an ideal world free of traditional bureaucratic hierarchy, authority, and order, which most neo-

Marxists associate with the support of the present authoritarianism and the domination of the U.S. political and economic system. Thus, like traditional Marxists, these writers are inspired by visions of a new world order without bureaucracy and without government; one that is utopian, humane, egalitarian, and characterized by a new universal brotherhood of humankind.

Examples of such neo-Marxist writing in recent years include William G. Scott and David K. Hart's *Organizational America* (1979), in which the authors argue, "There are too many people, not enough resources, not enough space and not enough time for all nations to realize their material ambitions."[22] The culprit they see behind this greed for material wealth is the powerful, relentlessly driving bureaucratic organization or what they term "the organizational imperative": "The modern organization is the essential feature of totalitarianism because it is the primary means of control." This control has, in the authors' view, served to increase the uniformity, sterility, commercialism, inequality, and loss of personal freedom and dignity in our culture—it "is the root of our current national malaise."[23] Nothing short of a total social revolution to eliminate bureaucratic organizations, led by "a vanguard of professionals," would satisfy Scott and Hart—a sort of Marxist goal through Leninist means?—in order to smash all elements of "the organizational imperative" and bring to fruition their humanistic visions of a new world order without bureaucracy.

In a similar vein, Frederick C. Thayer's *An End to Hierarchy and Competition* (2d edition, 1981) sees the modern organization, specifically its bureaucratic hierarchy and related problem of competition, as a dreaded culprit, *the* source of social evil in the modern world. "Hierarchy," writes Thayer, "actually is the fundamental problem [of human society], competition merely the most unfortunate result of an attempt to escape from hierarchy."[24] We need to eliminate both hierarchy and competition, argues Thayer, in order to return to "the genuine community," "personal engagement," and "mutual dependence."[25] Thayer sees, as do Scott and Hart, bureaucratic organizations as artificial; hence the cry for their fundamental reform, indeed overthrow. Much like Marx, Thayer is in favor of radical redirection toward what is natural social order without bureaucracy, one that is, in Thayer's words, "cognitive, collective, and non-hierarchical . . . on a global basis."[26]

The most consciously avowed contemporary neo-Marxist social criticism of bureaucracy is, though, found in Robert Denhardt's *In the Shadow of Organization* (1981). It is consciously avowed because the author draws quite explicitly from the neo-Marxist sources of the Frankfurt School of Social Theory of Horkeimer, Habermas, Adorno, Marcuse, Fromm, and Sartre. Denhardt directly draws up these neo-Marxist "imports" as the basis for his arguments, which envision the individual as a good, creative person, desirous of personal growth, freedom, and development. "We are basically creative beings," writes Denhardt, but we are all trapped in "organized systems in order to accomplish those things which our surroundings and security demand. In order to master the physical world . . . we permit ourselves to submit to a certain amount of domination. . . . Our labor is no longer an expression of our needs; it is instead subjected to organizational rationalization."[27] Denhardt thus views bureaucratic organization as essentially corrupting and unhealthy because it is unnatural. It suppresses the "true" feelings, spirits, and aspirations of humans. According to Denhardt, the central question is no longer how the individual may contribute to the efficient operation of the system, but how the individual may transcend that system. Denhardt calls for a revolution that is therefore a very personal one that would free humanity—spiritually, mentally, physically—from the artificial constraints of bureaucracy. The natural person and natural organization, not the free market, therefore, are Denhardt's heroes.

Like other neo-Marxists, Scott and Hart as well as Thayer and Denhardt offer no explicit agenda for making their neo-Marxist prescriptions a reality (hence their ideas have had little or no impact upon government). They prescribe increased self-reflection, self-awareness, personal communication, and face-to-face contact as routes for change. "We might begin," writes Denhardt, "by shifting our focus to organization (or interpersonal) processes instead of technical tasks."[28] Freeing the natural person inside artificial bureaucratic worlds is Denhardt's real aim.

Neo-Marxists, in summary, like neoconservatives, are hostile to bureaucracy and seek its fundamental reform, even its overthrow. Both neo-Marxists and neoconservatives tend to favor a return to the natural social order and the natural person. For neoconservatives, that concept translates into the free marketplace where businesspersons—the natural people?—spontaneously create goods, services, and activities for consumers. Sometimes they fail and go out of business; sometimes they succeed and gain great profit. For neo-Marxists, by contrast, the individual—every individual—is naturally good and will cooperate with others "naturally," but only if the artificial constraints of bureaucratic organizations can be eliminated; their cry is therefore for smashing artificial, unnatural hierarchical organizations that constrain an individual's basically good instincts. Both the left and right thus stand on a common ground of social "naturalism," "natural order," "goodness of human beings," and hostility toward the artificial and rational qualities of bureaucracy, as well as hostility toward self-interested, calculating bureaucrats. In the 1980s, the neoconservative, not the neo-Marxist, line of reasoning has had considerably more practical impact(s) upon public bureaucracy and its operations.

The Neo-Jeffersonians: Home-Grown Reformers on the Left

Another important school of contemporary thought about bureaucracy draws its inspiration directly from sources native to this continent. Some academic theorists who study bureaucracy have philosophic roots in past U.S. ideas and ideals, principally stemming from Thomas Jefferson. For the most part, however, these roots are unconscious or at least not explicitly acknowledged (unlike those of neoconservatives or neo-Marxists). Yet the lineage is obvious to anyone who examines these perspectives on bureaucracy. These theorists, who are the living intellectual heirs of Jefferson, favor decentralization, popular participation, small-scale operation of government, and equality of opportunity inside public organizations.

Of the several books published on bureaucracy in the 1980s, H. George Frederickson's *New Public Administration* (1980) perhaps most vigorously expounds neo-Jeffersonian themes. Frederickson contends that equity should have a central role or be the core criterion for directing modern-day administrative choices and actions. Frederickson writes, ''Social equity emphasizes quality in government services.''[29] His emphasis upon equity is purportedly intended to aid the oppressed minorities in society: ''A public administration that fails to work for changes to try to redress the deprivation of minorities will likely eventually be used to repress those minorities.''[30] Unlike neoconservatives or neo-Marxists, who would like to eliminate or reduce bureaucratic organizations altogether, Frederickson is an institutionalist who supports them and believes in enlarging the scope of action of governmental organizations, principally because they can and should play vigorous roles in promoting a just, good, fair, and *equal* society.

Another important characteristic of Frederickson's book—one that clearly makes him heir to Jeffersonian beliefs—is his passion for decentralization. Public organizations, in his view, should be highly decentralized in order to ''push down decision making . . . in the bowels of the organization to be certain they are not blocked.''[31] He argues in favor of small, decentralized hierarchies with terminal dates for completing projects (sort of New England town governments with limited agendas and specific deadlines for projects). Flat, fluid, democratic organizational types, such as NASA's project management and local neighborhood centers for dispensing community services, are Frederickson's ideal models of bureaucracies.

Michael Harmon also favors decentralization along neo-Jeffersonian lines, but adds important participatory themes as well in his scholarly book about public bureaucracy in the 1980s, *Action Theory for Public Administration* (1981). Harmon argues that ''face to face interaction among interactive practices is the context in which all may simultaneously initiate proposals for cooperative action and hear and respond to the incentives of others. The dialectic between initiative and responsive action is facilitated by the interaction process that administrators *assist* rather than dominate or control. Responsibility for decision outcomes as a result is shared rather than individualized.''[32] Small, personal, face-to-face encounters are clearly preferred, in Harmon's view, as ways of improving modern-day bureaucrats and bureaucracies.

Many neo-Jeffersonians favor this participation to promote better decisions and decision making, but Deena Weinstein, in her book *Bureaucratic Opposition* (1979), suggests a different advantage; namely, it enhances personal freedom and democracy within organizations. She assumes, unlike Harmon (who sees people as basically cooperative by nature), that conflict and competition are built into the very existence of bureaucracy. She finds this opposition in and of itself to be a fundamental liberating and democraticizing force with organizations that are, in her view, frequently highly authoritarian and restrictive. While much of her book is devoted to studying the various forms, tactics, and strategies of bureaucratic oppositions in several organizations, she views oppositions within bureaucracies as necessary in order to ''respond to specific situations flexibly, show people that at least for a moment they can resist, sometimes create systems of shared powers, and keep elites aware that their employees are persons, not cheerful robots.'' In her belief, ''bureaucratic oppositions fulfill more closely than any other contemporary social phenomena the Jeffersonian ideal of human beings freely and periodically asserting their liberty against tyrannical structures.''[33] Much like Thomas Jefferson, Weinstein believes that people can find freedom, liberty, even democracy and some happiness within an established institutional order—if they work *against* it.

Dominant Insiders' Public Organizational Ideologies in the 1980s: The Professional/Managerial Ethos

While the 1980s so far have witnessed an outpouring of both popular and scholarly perspectives on bureaucracy—influential schools of thought such as those espousing business values, neoconservative thinking, microeconomic analysis, neo-Marxism, and neo-Jeffersonianism—the dominant ideas of good management and professionalism also continue to flourish and find support inside government agencies. Business and public administration largely support classical management doctrines, theories, and viewpoints on bureaucracy a là Alexander Hamilton, Frederick Taylor, and Leonard White. Here traditional centrist management concerns of strengthening organizational and institutional capacities of government and elements of government are emphasized. To achieve this aim, values of economy, efficiency, and effectiveness are stressed through a variety of methods and approaches. Their names and methodologies may differ, but their rationales are much the same and stem from a long tradition of management science that has flowered in many diverse forms during this century since Frederick Taylor's notions of scientific management. Many books, periodicals, and articles can be found espousing these good management practices for government enterprise.[34] Especially within particular public agencies, the dominant professional ideologies of lawyers, physicians, military personnel, and teachers are also critical to the shaping of the philosophy and the future of the entire spectrum of agency

FIGURE 6.9
Multiple Hostile Ideological Perspectives Toward Public Bureaucracies
in the 1980s on the Right and Left

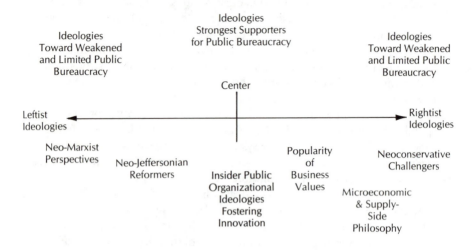

operations. The importance of the ideas and roles of these professionals as well as their particular viewpoints were already outlined in chapter 4.

The Dominant Mood and Metaphor of the 1980s: Toward a Supply-Side Public Bureaucracy?

How can we sum up the wide diversity of trends and ideas described in this chapter? Is there an overriding concept that aptly characterizes the era of the 1980s with respect to public bureaucracy as a core institution of U.S. government?

Perhaps there are too many trends and ideas around today to be summarized neatly in a single phrase. Perhaps we are too close to the 1980s to accurately gauge such matters. More distance from events may well be required for a clearer understanding of their lasting importance and significance for bureaucracy.

However, three prominent students of public bureaucracy, James D. Carroll, A. Lee Fritschler, and Bruce L. R. Smith, may well have captured the dominant mood of the 1980s in regard to public organizations by their apt use of the term *supply-side*. In their view, most economists use *supply-side* to denote an economic approach to stimulating economic growth and general prosperity through lowering public expenditures, taxes, and government involvement in the private sector. But as Carroll, Fritschler, and Smith argue, supply-side approaches to the governance and management of public agencies can be viewed as a prominent public-management tendency in the 1980s. Supply-side approaches are "a collection of precepts that fit together uneasily, and an operation code driven more by political necessity than by ideological orthodoxy."[35] In other words, *supply-side* may denote a mood or even a metaphor for the 1980s that varies remarkably in many ways from the older demand-side approach to public bureaucracy:

	Supply-Side (1980s)	*Demand-Side* (pre-1980s)
Size of Bureaucracy	Sharply reduced	Expanded to meet public/special interest needs
Federal Role	Sharply restricted and expanded state/local roles	Feds take lead in most policy fields
Regulation of Business	As much deregulation as possible to free up business	Strong public sector role in private sector on behalf of consumers and citizens
Source of Policy Direction	Top-down—from chief executive—with centralized controls	Bottom-up—from legislative and special interest groups
Operational Emphasis	Operating functions with "bottom line results"	Emphasis upon staff functions (planning, policy analysis, data collection, etc.) and critical of business practices
Key Personnel Staff	Reliance on temporary appointees drawn from business or "new-right" supply-siders	Career professionals committed to the public interest and application of expertise to public problems
Agency Policy Development and Management Approach	Tolerant of risk-taking, entrepreneurship, contracting-out for public services, and voluntary approaches	Emphasis upon consensus building, conciliation, "muddling-through" coupled with professionalism, planning, analysis, evaluation, etc.

Political / Administrative Relationships	Sharp split in roles of political policy making and careerist administrators	Cooperative relationships between political appointees and careerists
Reliance upon Ideology for Governance of Bureaucracy	Heavy reliance on supply-side theory and economic methodology	Little or none—pragmatic orientation most often used
Ideal Public Bureaucrat	David Stockman, Reagan's 1st OMB director	David E. Lilienthal, builder of TVA

On the whole, the three writers conclude that supply-side, while radically different from demand-side, may not permanently restructure because "it seems bound to fall short on many of its objectives, but it has brought to the forefront a renewed emphasis on governmental performance." They conclude: "Concern with improved performance will persist and even grow in importance until it collides with, and in turn, is modified by, competing values that also appeal to the American people." In this regard, supply-side may well be a passing mood or metaphor of the 1980s rather than a permanent reform that fundamentally changes public bureaucracy in the United States.

Summary of Key Points

U.S. public bureaucracy during the 1980s has been influenced in three important ways: first, the turbulent external environment in which government agencies operate has undergone rapid changes that have placed new and important demands upon public agencies at all levels of government. The twelve socioeconomic-political forces outlined at the beginning of this chapter work in many ways to "complexify," reshape, and enlarge the tasks and responsibilities of bureaucracy while at the same time working to make basic socioeconomic-political support for those tasks and responsibilities harder to achieve. The paradox is that today U.S. sociopolitical *and* economic responsibilities of a global nature require more diverse and complex actions from government agencies, but popular opinion on the home front offers, at the same time, significantly diminished political support for those public agencies.

As a result of these external forces, the internal dynamics of the bureaucratic system are rapidly changing to adapt to these severe pressures to do more with less in the 1980s. Some pressures serve to strengthen elements of the bureaucratic system by enhancing organizational cohesion, institutional effectiveness, administrative action, and authority. Some trends in the 1980s do precisely the reverse. The picture is mixed.

Also decisively influencing U.S. public bureaucracies in the 1980s are several new ideological perspectives, largely hostile to the activities and operations of government agencies and proposing a wide array of solutions and alternatives to their programs, designs, and organizational models. These normative ideologies range from neoconservative thinking on the right to neo-Marxist points of view on the left. Often they obscure or distort the reality of bureaucratic roles and operations in modern U.S. society. All have, however, flowered in the 1980s and have been pressed upon public agencies through different sources and channels. These ideologies have vigorously urged bureaucratic reform in profound and provocative ways, which has stimulated critical changes and important redirections within the bureaucratic system—both its particular parts and as a whole. Supply-side bureaucracy may indeed be the term that most aptly sums up these trends and ideas of the 1980s.

Key Terms

turbulence of external environment

complexification of bureaucratic system

privatization of bureaucracy

external/internal legal checks

PACs

think tanks

neo-Marxist perspectives

neoconservative challenges

new right political appointees

uncontrollables

multioptioned bureaucracy

grass roots innovations

professionals without professions

hard vs. soft technologies

Grace Commission

deregulation

crisis management

supply-side views

business values

Review Questions

1. Which of the dozen critical environmental pressures outlined in this chapter that impact upon the activities of public agencies strike you as being the most significant ones? The least significant? And why?
2. How are some of these pressures perhaps affecting you and your future? In what ways will they act in positive or negative ways in shaping your future career and personal development?
3. Given those critical and significant environmental pressures upon bureaucracy that you outlined in question one, think about how some of these might influence the design and structure of particular public agencies. Take a specific government agency you know or have had experience with (say, a public school or post office or motor vehicle department) and outline at least three effects these environmental trends might have today upon that unit of government.
4. What are some of the "unintended consequences" of several of these aforementioned trends on bureaucracy? For example, on the contractual

subsystem? Or on the newly imposed legal constraints upon public agencies?

5. Compare and contrast two of the ideological perspectives outlined in this chapter relative to public bureaucracy from the vantage point of their sources, their central values, their major criticisms of bureaucracy, and their prescriptions for its reform.

Notes

1. John Naisbitt, *Megatrends* (NY: Warner Books, 1984), chapter 10.
2. Frederick C. Mosher, "Presidential Transitions and Foreign Policy: The American Experiences," *Public Administration Review* (July/Aug. 1985), p. 470.
3. "Admiral Decries Military Restraints," *Washington Post* (June 23, 1984), p. 1 + .
4. "Can We Fight a Modern War?," *Newsweek* (July 9, 1984), p. 48.
5. Mosher, "Presidential Transitions," p. 471.
6. Ibid.
7. For a comprehensive collection and discussion of these seminal documents affecting U.S. bureaucracy in the 1980s, see Richard Stillman II (ed.), *Basic Documents of American Public Administration Since 1950* (NY: Holmes and Meier, 1982), section 4.
8. Antonio Scalia, "The Freedom of Information Act Has No Clothes," *Legislation,* vol. 6, no. 2 (March/April 1982), p. 16.
9. Naomi Caiden, "The New Rules of the Federal Budget Game," *Public Administration Review* (Nov./Dec. 1984), p. 643.
10. *PA Times* (September 15, 1985), p. 1.
11. For a discussion of the recent trends of increasing professionalism and politicization at the local level, read Richard Stillman II, "Local Public Management in Transition," 1982 *Municipal Yearbook* (Washington, DC: International City Management Association, 1982).
12. For an excellent discussion of these management innovations within the Reagan White House, read Chester A. Newland, "The Reagan Presidency," *Public Administration Review* (January/February 1983), p. 1 + .
13. William Bacchus, "Foreign Affairs Officials: Professionals without Professions?" in Frederick C. Mosher and Richard Stillman II (eds.), *Professions in Government* (NJ: Transaction Books, 1982), pp. 11–20.
14. Donald Devine, as quoted in *The Bureaucrat* vol. 11 (Spring 1982), p. 20.
15. Herbert Kaufman, "Fear of Bureaucracy: A Raging Pandemic," *Public Administration Review* (January/February 1981), p. 1 + .
16. *U.S. News and World Report* (April 4, 1983), pp. 62–63.
17. George Gilder, *Wealth and Poverty* (NY: Basic Books, 1981), p. 259.
18. Aaron Wildavsky, *How to Limit Government Spending* (Berkeley: University of California Press, 1980), p. 6.

19. E. S. Savas, *Privatizing the Public Sector* (NJ: Chatham House, 1982), p. 14.

20. John Baden and Richard L. Stroup (eds.), *Bureaucracy vs. Environment: The Environmental Costs of Bureaucratic Government* (Ann Arbor: University of Michigan Press, 1981), p. iii.

21. Ibid.

22. William G. Scott and David K. Hart, *Organizational America: Can Individual Freedom Survive within the Security It Promises?* (Boston: Houghton Mifflin, 1979), pp. 16–17.

23. Ibid.

24. Frederick C. Thayer, *An End to Hierarchy and Competition: Administration in the Post-Affluent World* (NY: New Viewpoints, 1981), p. A–1.

25. Ibid., p. 83.

26. Ibid., p. 133.

27. Robert B. Denhardt, *In the Shadow of Organization* (Lawrence: The Regents Press of Kansas, 1981), p. 123.

28. Ibid., p. 128.

29. H. George Frederickson, *New Public Administration* (University: University of Alabama Press, 1980), p. 6.

30. Ibid., p. 7.

31. Ibid., p. 91.

32. Michael M. Harmon, *Action Theory for Public Administration* (NY: Longman, 1981), p. 157.

33. Deena Weinstein, *Bureaucratic Opposition: Challenging Abuses at the Workplace* (NY: Pergamon Press, 1979), p. 125.

34. For a general collection of this thinking see Carol H. Weiss and Allen H. Barton, *Making Bureaucracies Work* (Beverly Hills: Sage Publications, 1980), or see Frederick V. Malek, *Washington's Hidden Tragedy: The Failure to Make Government Work* (NY: Free Press, 1978), p. vii.

35. James D. Carroll, A. Lee Fritschler, and Bruce L. R. Smith, "Supply-Side Management in the Reagan Administration," *Public Administration Review* (Nov./Dec. 1985) p. 807.

Further Readings

Some of the futurist literature, even though it may be popularly oriented and sometimes uneven, provides at times a good guide to socioeconomic-political trends influencing U.S. society. In particular, see such writings as John Naisbitt's *Mega-Trends*, Alvin Tofler's *Future Shock*, and Daniel Bell's *The Coming of the Post-Industrial Society*. Theodore White's *America in Search of Itself* is a keen historical insight into the present by a contemporary student of history and a respected journalist. Reading some of the outstanding national newspapers, such as the *New York Times*, the *Wall Street Journal*, the *Washington Post*, and the *Los Angeles Times* and thoughtful periodicals such as

Newsweek and *Time Magazine* can be helpful, as can some of the journals that are more focused on bureaucratic activities, such as the *National Journal, Administrative Science Quarterly,* and *Public Administration Review.*

Writings specifically focused upon trends inside public bureaucracy in the 1980s are: Lester M. Salamon and Michael S. Lund (eds.), *The Reagan Presidency and the Governing of America* (1984), John L. Palmer and Isabel Sawhill's *The Reagan Record* (1984); William G. Torpey's *Federal Management Initiatives* (1984); Hugh Heclo and Lester M. Salamon (eds.), *The Illusion of Presidential Government* (1981); Roland P. Watham's *The Administrative Presidency* (1983); Charles H. Levine (ed.), *The Unfinished Agenda of Civil Service Reform* (1985); Howard Rosen's *Servants of the People* (1985); and Bruce L. R. Smith and James D. Carroll (eds.), *Improving Accountability and Performance of Government* (1983).

Several outstanding essays should be reviewed: Chester A. Newland's "The Reagan Presidency: Limited Government and Public Administration," *Public Administration Review* (Jan./Feb. 1983); Frederick C. Mosher's "The Changing Responsibilities and Tactics of the Federal Government," *Public Administration Review* (Nov./Dec. 1980); Hugh Heclo's "A Government of Enemies?," *The Bureaucrat* (Fall 1984); Bernard Rosen's "Effective Continuity of U.S. Government Operations in Jeopardy," *Public Administration Review* (Sept./Oct. 1983); Edie N. Goldenberg's "The Permanent Government in an Era of Retrenchment and Redirection" in Lester M. Salamon and Michael S. Lund (eds.), *The Reagan Presidency and the Governing of America* (1984); and Jonathan Rouch's "Stockman's Quiet Revaluation at OMB May Leave Indelible Mark on Agency," *National Journal* (May 25, '85).

Particularly helpful in understanding prominent supply-sider views are: Victor A. Canto, Douglas Joines, and Arthur B. Laffer's *Foundations of Supply-Side Economics* (1983); Paul Craig Roberts's *The Supply-Side Revolution* (1984); William Greider's *The Education of David Stockman and Other Americans* (1982); David Stockman's "The Social Pork Barrel," *The Public Interest* (Spring 1975); and Stuart M. Butler, Michael Sanera, and W. Bruce Weinrod's *Mandate for Leadership II* (1984).

Several of the books cited in the notes to this chapter would be helpful as a review of the various ideological viewpoints toward bureaucracy of the 1980s.

7
The Future of the U.S. Bureaucratic System

What is the future of the bureaucratic system in the United States? Will it become more effective and efficient in delivering public goods and services for society? More equitable and fairer in distributing those goods and services? Will it be more accountable to the public at large as well as more responsive to individual and group needs? Will it retain its significant core functions in U.S. society? Will it grow or decline in influence? In short, what is tomorrow's role for public bureaucracy within America's democracy?

This final chapter will attempt to answer these and other critical questions by arguing that the future of public bureaucracy in the U.S. is fundamentally a normative value problem, one rooted in a unique, changing triad of historic national values. In other words, the central thesis of this concluding chapter is that our peculiar past national values will shape our future bureaucratic institutions. The chapter will be devoted to understanding these values and how they have influenced U.S. bureaucracy. It will begin by outlining the essential nature and content of these historic norms that are labeled Hamiltonianism, Jeffersonianism, and Madisonianism and explain how these values decisively influenced the course of American bureaucracy over the last 200 years. The chapter will conclude by stressing that the future role of U.S. bureaucracy will ultimately be determined by ''trade-offs'' among these competing values.

265

Three Founding Fathers' Normative Models for Bureaucracy in a Democracy

The U.S. Constitution largely ignored the existence of or *need for* a bureaucratic system. It was mostly silent on this subject. But three of the founding fathers did give some attention to the subject in their writings—Alexander Hamilton, Thomas Jefferson, and James Madison.

Alexander Hamilton: Maximizing Administrative Efficacy

Of all the founding fathers, none displayed more interest in and enthusiasm for administration and organization than Alexander Hamilton. Hamilton was a man of action from the time he was the brilliant twenty-three-year-old aide-de-camp to General Washington during the Revolution. Throughout his tenure as the first secretary of the treasury in President Washington's Cabinet, he demonstrated masterful planning, control, and organization of national finances. As Leonard White writes, ''In the Federalist Papers, Hamilton set out the first systematic exposition of Public Administration, a contribution which stood alone for generations. In his public life, he displayed a capacity for organization, system and leadership which after a century and a half is hardly equalled.''[1]

The role Hamilton saw for bureaucracy in government as well as in society was an expansive one. He was an ardent, enthusiastic nationalist who envisioned a big, bold, broad role for the American nation—politically, economically, and militarily. His writings are studded with glowing ideas for promoting ''the public interest,'' ''the public good,'' ''the good of the general society,'' and ''the national interest.'' Some say he valued the nation more than its people. At least there was nothing timid or modest about Hamilton's vision for the future of the United States, for he was a very early believer in positive government framed essentially to promote a strong nation and its interests. He argued for setting up a national bank, a national university, a professional army and navy, a public school system, and a variety of national public works projects, such as building roads, ships, canals, and dams and mining metals for industrial development. In short, he laid out a bold blueprint for the nation's future.

Hamilton favored a strong, energetic administration[2] based on maximizing the efficiency and effectiveness of public organizations to bring about his expansive vision of the future of the country. His normative model of the place of bureaucracy within a democracy thus contained these elements: (1) broad discretionary and activist roles for public agencies, characterized by strong, decisive leadership that evidenced ''energy'' and ''tone'' (words he repeatedly used); (2) unified public organizations with responsibility for administrative action undivided and preferably concentrated in one individual (as opposed to being divided among boards or committees); (3) administrative power allocated to individuals and governmental units commensurate with the responsibility for the tasks assigned; (4) adequate time in office to ensure administrative effectiveness, long-term planning, and operational stability for implementing public programs; (5) preference for paid, trained professionals (as opposed to part-time volunteers) in staffing governmental positions; (6) emphasis on national planning, sound fiscal management, and responsible exercise of creative public leadership; and (7) popular control of public organizations achieved by means of the election of responsible, capable chief executives with adequate political power and support in order to ensure that tasks are performed competently and well.

Thomas Jefferson: Maximizing Administrative Accountability to the Public at Large

If the values of nationalism fired Hamilton's conception of administration, Jefferson's values were shaped primarily by concerns for THE PEOPLE. His commitment to individual liberty, freedom for humanity, and the pursuit of personal happiness were evident throughout his writings, but never more forcefully than in the Preamble to the Declaration of Independence, which dedicated the United States to popular values of "life, liberty and the pursuit of happiness." Unlike Hamilton, Jefferson exhibited an abiding faith in human nature and its unlimited potential for growth and development unfettered by governmental authority. And unlike Hamilton, who repeatedly spoke of "administrative discretion," "energy," and "tone," Jefferson stressed "limits on government," "individual rights," "freedom," and "liberty." As he said, "I am for a government that is frugal and simple." The New England town meeting perhaps came closest to his ideal of a polity that *was* "simple" and "frugal" and maximized citizens' participation in governing their own affairs.

A Jeffersonian normative model regarding the relationship of bureaucracy to democracy therefore, as Lynton Caldwell observed,[3] placed a heavy emphasis upon numerous devices to ensure bureaucracy's strict accountability to the general public and included such elements as: (1) extensive popular participation, especially voluntary mass involvement in administration (as opposed to staffing administration with paid, full-time professionals); (2) maximum decentralization of functions in order to limit activities and bring public activities under close and constant popular scrutiny; (3) operational simplicity and economy—simplicity so that administrative activities could be easily understood by the average citizen, and economy so it would not be economically burdensome to the public; (4) strict legal limitations that clearly spell out organizational purposes and restrict administrative discretion and authority in order to protect human rights; (5) a weak leadership role for public administrators through defining them as narrow functional specialists and technicians rather than as broad-ranging general managers or educated professionals exercising wide discretionary powers; (6) lack of concern for promulgating national planning, long-term operational stability, and effective program implementation but rather a focus on developing voluntary citizen efforts, private initiatives, and the free market alternatives to the performance of public tasks; and (7) administrative power in public organizations that flows from the bottom up, not from the top down, in order to sharply limit administrative outputs and ensure public oversight.

James Madison: Balancing Administrative Interest Group Demands

James Madison shared many of Jefferson's concerns about protecting human liberty through limitations placed upon government, but he also held little enthusiasm for his fellow Virginian's idealization of the broad abstraction, THE PEOPLE, that served as Jefferson's basic value premise and upon which his normative conceptions of bureaucracy-democracy relationships were founded. Madisonian analysis of U.S. government and the exercise of political authority rested instead upon the faction (or in modern terms, the interest group), which he saw as the chief fount of government's authority.

Federalist 10 indicates that while Madison saw factions as the prime movers of U.S. politics, he had little liking for any sort of faction. He defined a faction as "a number of citizens whether amounting to a majority or a minority of the whole, who are united and actuated by some common impulse or passion, or of interests adverse to the rights of other citizens, or the permanent and aggregated interests of the community."[4]

Madison "fathered" a Constitution that employs numerous "checks and balances" to mitigate the pernicious influence of factions upon governing institutions. As he underscores in Federalist 51, while the root causes of factions can never be eliminated, a framework of government can be designed so that their harmful influence over government institutions and public decisions is reduced. His fundamental advice in Federalist 51 on the framing of a stable, enduring government is well known: "Ambition must be made to counteract ambition," so that "you first enable the government to control the governed; in the next place, oblige it to control itself."[5]

Madisonian analysis basically was oriented toward structuring a process that would reduce but not eliminate factional influence to enable government *both* to govern adequately *and* to ensure its public accountability. Hence, he sought a "mixed government" that would balance competing interest group demands. His genuine contribution to political philosophy was his conception of "an extended republic" that would broaden geographic size and diversity in order to balance competing interests and thus protect human liberty and promote social stability. Indeed, throughout his writings, unlike either Hamilton or Jefferson, Madison, as historian Ralph Ketchum indicates,[6] places a special premium on achieving the values of organic social balance, political equilibrium, and the Aristotelian "Golden Mean."

Yet, unlike either Hamilton or Jefferson, Madison says little *explicitly* about the role of administration in the context of U.S. politics. But from what he said about the executive branch, the execution of public policies, and his conceptions of faction-based politics, we can conclude that Madison conceived of a very different role for bureaucracy in democracy. The normative elements of this Madisonian model include the following elements: (1) public organizations that are involved in a pluralistic political process rooted in the divergent, changing factional interests of society; thus, their administration and relationship to politics can be neither static nor clear-cut but rather are dynamic, complex, intertwined, and interconnected with a diversity of organic social interests; (2) bureaucracies are political in that they share in the processes of exercising political authority with other branches of government—courts, executive, and legislature—and thus they should, like the other branches, engage in balancing social interests to promote consensus, stability, and representation of divergent points of view; (3) public agencies, though they may formally be separated bodies because of functional differentiation, in practice share power with executive, legislative, and judicial branches in order to undertake effective action and to operate within a continuous, complex *horizontal* system of checks and balances upon the other three branches; (4) public entities that operate in a continuous, complex set of *vertical* power-sharing arrangements between federal, state, and local units and acquire power to take effective action as well as to operate checks and balances upon one another; (5) in this fragmented world of political authority, public administrators that exercise the ''art of the possible'' in dealing with these competing interests. Their roles would principally entail political negotiation, compromise, and bargaining; (6) that social consensus and equilibrium between competing interest groups, not organizational efficacy nor accountability to an abstract will of THE PEOPLE, should be the primary aim of public officials; (7) that administrative power to drive actions come from neither the top down nor the bottom up but must be picked up piecemeal by public administrators from the top, bottom, and sides of government agencies within a politically fragmented, constantly fluid environment.

In sum, these three founding fathers produced three very different normative models of bureaucratic-political relationships. They can be summarized in table 7.1.

Historic Patterns of Balancing Administrative Efficacy, Public Accountability, and Interest Group Demands

Americans have never made up their minds throughout their two-hundred-year history as to which of the three normative models they prefer. They have remained uncertain about finding a place for their bureaucracy within their democracy. From time to time, the stress has been placed on promoting the values of administrative efficacy over the other two values; at other times, accountability to the general public has predominated; and at still other times, responding to diverse interest group demands has been clearly an overriding

TABLE 7.1
Three Founding Fathers' Normative Models

Topic	Hamilton	Jefferson	Madison
overall goal	strong organizational efficacy to promote national interests	strict public accountability to maximize personal liberty	organic balancing of interest group demands to promote social stability
key method	unified administrative processes	decentralized, participatory processes	horizontal/vertical checks and balances; an extended republic
degree of administrative discretion	broad	narrow	mixed and interdependent with other branches
degree of centralization	high	low	varied with the capacity to acquire power
organizational autonomy	high	low	interdependent
ideal public official	professional careerist—"a doer"	citizen volunteer—"a servant of the people"	negotiator and compromiser—interest brokers
sources of power	flows from top down	flows from bottom up	flows from all around—top down, bottom up, and side to side
agency outputs and capacity to shape future	strong	weak	mixed—driven by conflicting needs of special interests
degree of separation of politics from administration	sharp—to promote agency efficiency	sharp—to promote public control	complex, mixed and unclear, depending upon many processes
social status of bureaucrats	high status professionals	low status technicians	mixed status as interest brokers

priority. Yet within any single historic period where one value has held sway over the other two, the others have never been entirely neglected or ignored. Calibrating the proper emphasis has never been easy nor have the results ever been permanent, though four distinct eras where one value has tended to predominate over the other two can be discerned.

The Nineteenth-Century Dominance of Jeffersonian Values

As chapter 2 emphasized, during most of its first century the U.S. government operated with little bureaucracy (with the exception of the Civil War era). Hence its Constitution, erected upon republican ideals, was largely compatible with its limited bureaucratic institutions. Limited functions were demanded from government. Accident of geography had much to do with creating these conditions. High agricultural productivity made the nation largely self-sufficient, and continental isolation made a large standing army unnecessary. Further, there was virtually no popular demand for extensive social services. Rural farmers and small communities that dotted the landscape were relatively independent from public institutions for key support services. Only briefly, in the 1790s, did an activist (Alexander Hamilton) favoring rapid national modernization seriously press the case for an expansionist positive government, complete with a large professional army and a trained civil service to perform a broad array of nation-building tasks. The rapid decline of the Federalists and the rise of Jeffersonian-Jacksonian Democrats committed to the political dogma that ''government governs best that governs least'' ensured the continuation of the Jeffersonian ideals supporting negative government throughout most of the nineteenth century.

Ideology and geographic accident that sharply restricted administrative functions were external constraints on bureaucracy. They, in combination with three other important internal constraints in this era, maximized the Jeffersonian values favoring tight controls and public accountability of bureaucracy. First, direct popular controls over administrative machinery waxed because of the rapid growth of a party system that awarded administrative jobs based upon party loyalty and activism. Particularly after the election of Andrew Jackson, the spoils system grew and became a deeply ingrained institutional process. The belief that any job in government could and should be done by the average person was accepted as a given. Thus party affiliation was stressed over professional expertise as a central requirement for holding public office. Most of the federal government jobs were with the post office and required the performance of menial and repetitive tasks that could indeed be performed by the lay citizen, making bureaucratic expertise unnecessary. Further, the lack of serious external threats, except for those from Native Americans, meant that the United States could rely upon untrained citizen-soldiers in state militias for its primary defense. Even the top military posts in this era were largely filled by political appointees; of the thirty-seven generals appointed between 1802 and 1861, not one was a West Pointer and twenty-three were without any military education or experience.[7] Political appointment became common practice in most civil administrative offices as well (with citizen-volunteers providing most public services at the local level). Probably these personnel trends peaked in the 1860s when Lincoln used patronage more effectively than any previous president to run a government and to fight the Civil War.

Money, or more precisely tight fiscal constraint, was the second critical instrument ensuring the primacy of public accountability. Despite Alexander Hamilton's early efforts to develop a comprehensive executive budget in order to strengthen executive branch autonomy and managerial planning, Congress, not the chief executive, firmly grasped the reins of budgetary controls over public agencies. Surprisingly, presidents gave up this authority over the purse without much of a fight.[8] In his first annual message to Congress, Thomas Jefferson recommended that appropriations be made as ''specific sums to every purpose susceptible of definition[9]; and each public agency operated through a complex voucher system expending funds incrementally authorized by Congress in the absence of centralized treasury oversight. This fiscal pattern of legislative control made the nation's financial system unique by comparison with that of every other nation (both then and today) by giving Congress, not the president, authority over policy formulation and internal administrative matters of agencies. The multiplicity of fiscal controls over public agencies by legislatures at every level of government was further extended by dividing up responsibility for fiscal oversight among several special committees and subcommittees. Not only was it customary for several legislative subcommittees to exercise financial oversight over the same public agency—thereby serving to fragment bureaucratic fiscal integrity—but the process of financial oversight was further divided into two elements: first, legislative authorization to approve the programs, and second, appropriations to fund the programs.

A third critical strategy for extending public accountability over public organizations throughout the nineteenth century involved the structuring of their organizational designs so as to prevent organizational autonomy and enhance their dependency upon other branches in order to function. From the earliest period onward, public agencies, their organizations, and their procedures were subject to intense congressional scrutiny. Nothing was considered beyond the bounds of legislative concern. As Don Price notes, ''The term executive branch . . . is a misleading metaphor. Organization charts and television pundits to the contrary, there is no such thing as an executive branch of the U.S. government. The Constitution gives the President certain executive powers, but it does not mention the executive branch. Instead, it lets the Congress by legislation set up executive departments and control their organization and procedures to any degree it likes.''[10]

Beginning with Jefferson, Congress developed the habit of setting up governmental organizations through highly detailed legislative statutes that exhibited minute technical controls over their designs, purposes, internal procedures, and external relationships. The general thrust of these legislative mandates was not only to make these agencies creatures of the legislature but also to foster functional specialization. The military, for example, was, throughout much of the nineteenth century, organized around strong specialized bureaus—i.e., cavalry, infantry, engineers, and ordnance—rather than around a unified command structure staffed with military professionals who were servicewide generalists, not technical specialists. Officers identified with bureaus in which they served since they were not general military professionals with broad training and experience. Not until the National Security Act of 1921 was this preference for bureau specialists over military generalists altered. The same was true for civilian agencies where specialized bureaus rather than broad departmental interests were of paramount influence and concern. Institutional fragmentation served not only to inhibit unity of purpose and generalized public professionalism but also to divide and conquer. By creating small "bureau governments," staffed with political appointees in various specialized fields, Congress easily controlled these numerous small bureaucratic entities through detailed subcommittee oversight.

Throughout most of the nineteenth century, U.S. public agencies were creatures of Congress, not the president. President James Garfield in 1882, for example, could enumerate *all* of his presidential duties without ever mentioning "administration of the executive branch" as a significant responsibility. And the young Woodrow Wilson in 1885 wrote his political science Ph.D. dissertation, which became a best-selling book entitled *Congressional Government,* as a criticism of legislative control over most federal administrative machinery. The irresponsible actions that ensued from fragmented, haphazard political oversight by congressional subcommittees were Wilson's primary target. Indeed, most of the great leaders of federal departments during this period were lawyers and legislators—e.g., Albert Gallatin, Jefferson's secretary of the treasury; John C. Calhoun, Polk's secretary of war; and William Seward, Lincoln's secretary of state—who knew the workings of the law and Congress and gained most of their fame in legislative halls. Bureaucracy offered no opportunity for bolstering one's reputation in that century.

But were the other values—administrative efficacy and interest group demands—entirely neglected during this era? Hardly, but they were not predominant values. Flashes of concern for administrative efficacy appeared in various parts of government from time to time in the nineteenth century, such as during Amos Kendall's tenure as postmaster general in Jackson's presidency, described in Mathew Crensen's *Federal Machine,*[11] and during the Civil War, when professionals gained prominence in Lee's army, as described in Douglas Southall Freeman's *Lee's Lieutenants.*[12] The organization of special interests, such as farmers, who pressed their case for the first clientele department, the Department of Agriculture (1889), also began in the nineteenth century.[13] However, political authority was exercised by fairly homogeneous political communities, not by organized special interests.[14] There were, of course, sectional interests that loomed large over the entire century's politics, especially prior to the Civil War, but the organization of government services *around or directed at* particular special interest group demands had to await the twentieth century and a fundamental shift in the underlying nature of U.S. political authority.

The Dominance of Neo-Hamiltonian Values 1883–1939

The year 1883 saw the passage of the Civil Service Act. It also marks the beginning of a decisive shift in national values, away from the Jeffersonian ideal of limited government and its attendant emphasis upon strict administrative accountability to THE PEOPLE. Instead, stress upon neo-Hamiltonian values favoring administrative efficacy began to appear. Not that Hamiltonianism ever entirely eclipsed Jeffersonianism, only that new methods, outlooks, and perspectives tended to give priority during this period to improving overall efficacy of public institutions.

If Jeffersonianism favored limited functions, popular representation, fiscal constraints, and organizational dependency as the keys to "marrying" bureaucracy with democracy, Hamiltonianism sought to broaden the range of public action, enhance public professionalism, and strengthen executive management and organizational autonomy. This decisive shift in national values did not come all at once but grew gradually over time and was to a great extent caused by a rapidly changing sociopolitical and economic environment that required a new approach to national governance.

The nation itself was rapidly modernizing from an agrarian republic to a contemporary industrial society with significantly differentiated and expanded functions. A modernizing nation required a modernized government. Industry during this era replaced agriculture as the major employer, thus creating needs for new public regulatory agencies such as the Interstate Commerce Commission. Growing international responsibilities required a standing military and diplomatic presence abroad; and a vast influx of immigrants to the United States turned towns into cities, creating heterogeneous urbanized communities requiring effective local administrative services of many kinds. These new socioeconomic and political realities of life at the turn of the century made Jeffersonian values less relevant to the growing responsibilities of a modernizing nation. Jeffersonian values, for most Americans at the dawn of the twentieth century, just did not make sense or contain much meaning in a rapidly changing society that suddenly demanded that new tasks be performed with efficiency and dispatch (though some, such as William Jennings Bryan, clung steadfastly to the old Jeffersonian values). Effective public organizations were now required to carry out the myriad and expanding responsibilities of a modernizing nation–state.

This period witnessed not only the rapid expansion and differentiation of governmental services but also the development of skilled, specialized public personnel. Any effective public bureaucracy must contain, at its heart, a career service, with dedicated employees who are offered opportunities for career development and have advanced education, specialized expertise, and at least some degree of freedom from politics in order to exercise bureaucratic responsibilities. The Civil Service Act of 1883 was a first important step in that direction. Drawn largely from the British experience but adapted to American circumstances, the act developed merit criteria as opposed to political criteria for appointment to public office. While it took nearly a half-century to extend merit protection to most elements of government (helped by the passage of other such important laws as the Classification Act of 1923), the growth in the size and scope of skilled expertise inside government agencies was perhaps the most significant factor enhancing and extending administrative efficacy during this era. Also critical to strengthened public agencies was the establishment of various specialized professional groups, such as the foreign service, which was established by the Rogers Act of 1924. The extension upward, downward, and outward of professional expertise came gradually and piecemeal during this era with the growth of new specialists in various fields, such as public health, personnel, teaching, and city planning.

Along with growing expertise, professionalization, and specialization, modernization of key management institutions and techniques was also instrumental in furthering the goal of administrative efficacy. Among the important management reforms were the establishment of the general staff by Elihu Root in 1902 to improve management planning, coordination, and control of the military (later extended to most civilian agencies); and the development of an executive budget, first used by the New York Bureau of Municipal Research for the New York Public Health Department and later established in the federal government through the 1921 Budget and Accounting Act. Also, new staff offices such as the Bureau of the Budget (established by the Treasury Department in 1922) and the post of chief of naval operations, created in 1915, were important organizational devices for centralizing executive control. At the grass roots level, the reorganization of state government pursued by Governors Lowden in Illinois and Byrd in Virginia set new patterns for increasing executive management effectiveness and centralizing state-level functions. The council-manager government in cities and towns, spurred on especially through the 1916 Model City Charter of the National Municipal League, modernized, centralized, and rationalized local institutions by putting trained management expertise at the core of expanding municipal functions. City government with city managers in charge soon equipped cities with new financial management and with budgeting, planning, and civil service capacities.

Equally critical to the enhancement of overall administrative efficacy during this period was the increasing institutional autonomy of executive branch agencies at every level of government. Separation of politics and administration was advocated as good government practice by reformers and theorists. In practice, though, institutional autonomy from congressional subcommittee oversight was promoted by Congress itself. Independent regulatory agencies, beginning with the ICC in 1887, and the first government corporations, starting with Panama Railway Company in 1905, were designed as autonomous units that could do what Congress either could not do or did not want to do (see chapter 2). World War I particularly accelerated the trends toward organizational autonomy and centralization of authority in executive agencies. Wartime emergencies, as always, necessitated rapid troop mobilization, national economic planning, press censorship, and emergency nationalization, as well as regulation of various sectors of industry.

While peacetime in the 1920s saw the return of many of these administrative powers to private authority, the Great Depression and World War II saw another set of emergencies that created overnight new bureaucratic institutions with autonomous authority for dealing with these crises. Perhaps the strongest influences in achieving organization autonomy and administrative independence from congressional oversight were the Reorganization Act of 1939 and Reorganization Plan No. 1, which implemented several of the Brownlow Commission's recommendations.

Brownlow synthesized most forcefully the neo-Hamiltonian values in arguing for the creation of a strong, energetic presidency by means of (1) placing the president in charge of an independent executive branch; (2) establishing adequate staff assistance in the White House in order that the executive branch functions could be properly managed; (3) transferring authority for budgeting, personnel, and planning to the White House in order to strengthen the managerial capacity of the president; (4) professionalizing civil service personnel by extending upward and downward merit protection to cover all nonpolicy-determining posts; (5) reducing the president's control and the lines of authority by reorganizing the more than one hundred agencies reporting to him into twelve major departments; (6) giving the executive "complete responsibility for accounts and current financial transactions" while providing a genuine independent post-audit of all fiscal transactions by an auditor general reporting to Congress.

Here, in short, was the "high energy" model for the federal government that had been in the making since 1883—i.e., professional personnel, executive budgets, rationalized organizational span of control, "pre-audit" authority, autonomous executive units, general management and planning capacity, and political authority concentrated in political executives while leaving administrative work to the "pros" to allow maximum administrative efficacy. Brownlow, as Barry Karl observed,[15] transferred upward to the federal level many ideas that twenty years earlier had become the model for effective local government practices, especially as exemplified by the council-manager plan. And certainly long after the Brownlow Report, these neo-

Hamiltonian ideals favoring administrative efficacy echoed in many postwar recommendations for governmental reorganization, such as the two Hoover Commission Reports (referred to by Herman Finer as "Mr. Brownlow's children"), the continued growth of the council-manager plan, the Ash Commission Report (1970), and even most recently the National Academy of Public Administration's report, "A Presidency for the 1980s" (1981). But in the post-World War II United States, neo-Hamiltonian values were no longer in ascendancy, having given way to a very different amalgam of values for designing "ideal" political-bureaucratic relationships.

Madisonian Value Patterns in the Postwar Era

World War II proved to be another turning point in political-bureaucratic relationships. The crisis of wartime not only centralized political authority in the United States to unprecedented degrees, but the new postwar global responsibilities of an economic-political superpower also required the maintenance of a complicated international and military apparatus in order to carry out tasks imposed by free world leadership. Further, a welfare state largely created by the New Deal required numerous administrative agencies in order to carry out growing social tasks that Americans deemed essential.

The lives of millions of Americans in this period were directly touched for the first time by the activities of an expanded bureaucracy at every level of government; for payment of social security checks, auto licensing, FHA/VA home mortgages, regulating most sectors of the economy, and furthering new scientific developments, such as the atomic bomb. As a result, bureaucratic institutions became more numerous and more complicated. Their interconnections and relationships with politics likewise became more complex. Hence, the underlying American values associated with these relationships shifted as well. Compare, for example, two bureaucracies—both considered highly successful in accomplishing their particular missions during World War II—the Manhattan Project and the Selective Service System. By means of quite different institutional processes, both organizations achieved their objectives.

The purpose of the Manhattan Project was to develop an atomic bomb quickly. The complexity of this task (no one really knew if the bomb would work or even if it could be built in the first place), the diversity of personnel and material resources required for it (spanning a continent), and the requirements of speed and secrecy (only a chosen few, those at the very highest policy level, could know about its existence), forged a public entity that was unprecedented. U.S. bureaucracy showed remarkable inventiveness in designing this new public organization. The project was organized in such a way as to ensure tight control at the top by secretary of war Henry Stimson, chief of staff General George C. Marshall, and General Leslie Groves as operational director. A wide range of expert personnel and highly specialized material resources was pulled together from across the United States in the production of the bomb. Dispersion of resources prevented many individuals from knowing the overall extent and purpose of the operations. A highly restricted group composed of top scientists of that day, such as Vannevar Bush from MIT and James B. Conant of Harvard, and military officers such as navy Admiral Parnell and army General Styer, served as a joint sciences-military advisory policy committee for the project. Requirements for competitive bidding for contracts were eased to permit sole-source suppliers to build specialized parts of the bomb. The project maximized administrative efficacy—i.e., speed, secrecy, efficiency of implementation—through limiting, though not entirely neglecting, accountability requirements.

By contrast, the complex system for drafting individuals developed in World War II (which operated until 1973), the Selective Service System, created by Congress and directed by General Hershey, proved an equally effective bureaucratic instrument for inducting 12 million soldiers during World War II. Whether one agreed with its purposes or not, the draft system functioned well in World War II by maximizing public involvement at the grass roots. While there was a national headquarters, the bulk of its work was delegated to state headquarters and 6,443 local boards composed of three or more volunteer community citizens. In contrast with the highly centralized, scientifically driven institutional processes involved with the Manhattan Project, voluntary grass roots participation, coupled with federal- and state-level procedural controls, mobilized men rapidly and implemented the draft laws successfully and economically—it cost only $22.50 to draft a soldier during World War II.

The complexification and differentiation of bureaucratic processes continued in the postwar era, as described in chapter 2, with the establishment of large, unique entities for achieving the varied tasks of governance. Americans invented superdepartments at the federal level, such as the Departments of Defense and of Health and Human Services, as well as small but critical coordinative units, such as the Advisory Commission on Intergovernmental Relations, and units to control and extend scientific knowledge, such as the Atomic Energy Commission, and the National Science Foundation—each highly complicated, differentiated institutional processes deemed vital for servicing complicated, diverse national interests. As Herbert Simon, Dwight Waldo, and other postwar theorists stressed, simple pre-World War II principles of economy and efficiency (à la Brownlow) no longer applied to organizational life. The "one-best-way" gave way to "multiple-best-ways" of organizing and formulating political-administrative relationships.[16] Thus institutional complexity became the hallmark of bureaucratic operational processes after 1945.

The development and growth of postwar U.S. bureaucratic institutions, as "realistic" political scientists point out, involved numerous special interest groups. As administrative agencies touched more Americans in this era, more groups and individuals, out of self-interest, came to influence the course of administrative processes. In *The Governmental Process* (1951), David Truman depicted the reality of government as *a process,* a seamless web of competition and compromise between competing social interests, each pressing its claims on existing public institutions and creating new ones to service its needs. Like Madison, Truman analyzed in realistic and behavioral terms U.S. society as based upon interest groups and their interaction. According to Truman, ''The behavior that constitutes the processes of government cannot be adequately understood apart from groups, especially the organized and potential interest groups.''[17] Truman, echoing Madison, postulated that government provides social equilibrium through establishing and maintaining a ''measure of order between groups.'' Bureaucracy became but one of ''a multiplicity of points of access'' for groups seeking to influence public policies.

Like Madison, Truman and other political scientists of this period viewed the problem of governance essentially in terms of *structuring access* of groups to government so that none gains the upper hand and so that, overall, balanced points of view are heard. Public well-being therefore is served. Implicit within their writings was a faith that the processes of bargaining and compromise between interests over administrative goods and services would work out for the good of the total society or of *most of those within society.* As Truman writes, ''Government functions to establish and maintain a measure of order in the relationship between groups.'' We find this evidenced also in Robert Dahl's classic, *A Preface to Democratic Theory,* where he writes: ''The vast apparatus that grew up to administer the affairs of the American welfare state is a decentralized bargaining bureaucracy. This is merely another way of saying that bureaucracy has become a part of . . . the 'normal American political process.' ''[18] Most Americans probably concurred with this uncritical, benevolent view of the self-regulating pluralistic system of interest groups operating in, around, and through bureaucracy. Theodore Lowi coined the phrase ''interest group liberalism''[19] to capture the postwar mood of general support of these arrangements.

Perhaps no one has captured the spirit, attitudes, and faith in interest group liberalism as well as Charles E. Lindblom did in his famous 1959 essay, ''The Science of 'Muddling Through,' ''[20] Here, the bureaucrat is not a ''doer'' governed by the Hamiltonian values of promoting efficacy or efficiency, but rather an official, one of many, who practices ''the art of the possible'' in a complex world of competing interests. Negotiation and compromise are the tools of his trade, with which he tries to produce ''agreeable compromise to all parties concerned.'' He ''muddles,'' rather than manages. Yet in this difficult, confused act of incremental decision making, argued Lindblom, he produced the best pragmatic results for society as a whole. He produced social harmony and political equilibrium through compromises in a fluid, unstable sea of ever-changing interest groups. Here were Madisonian values stated in their clearest, most concise, and most persuasive manner in the postwar United States. In the relatively calm period of the 1950s, when the United States enjoyed both superpower status and industrial prosperity, these Madisonian values stressing balance fitted hand in glove with the social stability and conservativism of the times.

Hence, the debate over how best to control bureaucracy in a democratic society between Carl Friedrich and Herman Finer,[21] which dominated the thinking of political scientists and government specialists after 1940 (i.e., were internal or external controls the most effective instruments for controls?), was largely an irrelevant question. Both Friedrich and Finer's ideas were in practice used. Both at times were highly effective. Both at times were highly ineffective. In the postwar world of Madisonian institutional complexity, built upon a liberal faith in self-regulating interest groups, a wide variety of institutional controls were put into place and found to be effective *and* wanting at the same time. The prior examples of the Manhattan Project and Selective Service point out this diversity quite well. But there were others. The Veterans Preference Act of 1944 created the Veterans Administration as an independent agency built upon open access to single-interest veterans groups. The act catered to veterans' interests, often at the expense of the interests of others. Conversely, new postwar institutions were created, such as the Department of Defense at the federal level, which merged the army, navy, and air force under one superdepartment, and the Council of Governments (CoGs), which administers 701 grants to grass roots organizations that foster planning on a regional basis. These two organizations, which are decidedly important postwar bureaucratic innovations, promote diverse points of view on defense and metropolitan policy matters. But DoD did not prevent the rise of—and controls by—the military-industrial complex. Nor did CoGs solve critical political problems of postwar center-city decay. No absolute "objective" controls for bureaucracy by democracy seemed to exist; some only promoted certain values over others. The diversity of means *and* ends was quite relative and mixed. In short, Madisonianism thrived.

Table 7.2 sums up elements of bureaucratic-political relations in each of the three historic eras discussed so far in this chapter.

The Persisting Rivalry of the Three Value Traditions

In the words of Samuel P. Huntington, the late 1960s and early 1970s witnessed a "democratic surge"[22] that characterized past eras of Jeffersonian-Jacksonian democracy and progressive reform, in which there was a vital reassertion of democratic idealism in all phases of life in the United States. As Huntington argues, the era reflected

> a general challenge to the existing system of authority, public and private.
> In one form or another, this challenge manifested itself in the family, the
> university, business, public and private associations, politics, the govern-

TABLE 7.2

Basic Elements for Structuring Political-Bureaucratic Relations in Three Eras

	19th Century (Jeffersonian Era)	Late 19th/Early 20th Century (Hamiltonian Era)	Post-World War II (Madisonian Era)
socioeconomic setting	largely rural, stable, isolationist model	predominantly nation-building and developing model	basically mature welfare state with global responsibilities
political authority basis	family oriented and homogeneous community life	rapid sociopolitical-economic change	interest group liberalism, scientific changes, and international responsibilities
bureaucratic duties	limited	expanding	diverse
generalist/specialist personnel	general political personnel	growth of professional/specialized staffs	mixed internal subsystems—political, professions, civil service, union contractual type
fiscal element	sharp limits imposed by legislatures	increased executive control/authority through executive budgets	mixed controls on finances depend upon agency and policy area
organizational autonomy/dependency	highly dependent upon legislature	increasing autonomy	mixed organization autonomy, and dependence
use of external or internal controls	primarily external controls utilized, based upon laws	increasing reliance upon internal controls, based uipon public professions and their norms	highly complex mix of both external and internal controls
ideological basis of relationship structure	"best government governs the least"	politics—administrative dichotomy	interest group liberalism

mental bureaucracy and the military service. People no longer felt the same compulsion to obey those whom they had previously considered superior to themselves in age, rank, status, expertise, character or talents. Within most organizations, discipline eased and differences in status became blurred. Each group claimed its right to participate equally—and perhaps more equally in the decision making which affected itself. In American society, authority had been commonly based on organizational position, economic wealth, specialized expertise, legal competence, or electoral representation. Authority based on hierarchy, expertise and wealth all obviously ran counter to the democratic and equalitarian temper of the times.[23]

Was the reassertion of Jeffersonian idealism due to the Vietnam war? The rise of a "youth culture"? The demands for equal rights by women and minorities? The television age? The Great Society programs? The reactions to Watergate and the Nixon presidency? While the reasons for the sudden "democratic surge" were complex and are even now still unclear, Huntington points to a number of significant consequences of the "democratic surge":

1. Increase in the size and scope of governmental activity, though with a concomitant decline in governmental authority;
2. Increased public interest and concern about government, coupled with a sharp decline in public trust and confidence in government;
3. Increased public activism in politics, yet with a commensurate decay in the traditional two-party system;
4. A noticeable shift away from coalitions supporting government to those in opposition to it.[24]

Popular in this period was a philosophical treatise by John Rawls, *A Theory of Justice,*[25] which defined justice in egalitarian terms. In the fields of history and politics, Arthur Schlesinger's *The Imperial Presidency*[26] found a wide, enthusiastic post-Watergate audience for its criticism of the flagrant abuses of strong executive institutions in the United States. This book stood in sharp contrast to a popular text on the presidency a decade earlier by Richard E. Neustadt, *Presidential Power,*[27] which had praised the values of a strong chief executive. Egalitarian themes found their way into the literature of economics, particularly in E. F. Schumacher's *Small Is Beautiful,*[28] which proposed that the goods and services in society be distributed more equitably and, in the words of its subtitle, *As If People Mattered.* In public administration, books such as that of Frank Marini (ed.), *Toward a New Public Administration,*[29] and Vincent Ostrom's *The Intellectual Crisis in American Public Administration,*[30] though grounded in radically different methodological traditions, argued for the similar popular values of broader participation, decentralization of authority, and social equality.

Throughout the 1970s many of these Jeffersonian values were translated into institutional reality by means of new legislation directly affecting the internal operation of most public agencies.[31] First, there was a sharp increase in

formal and informal controls placed upon bureaucratic operations, as discussed in chapter 6, to improve public accountability. The Legislative Reorganization Act of 1970 began a rapid expansion of congressional oversight
staff and functions aimed at improving public accountability. New legislation, such as the War Powers Resolution (1973),the Freedom of Information
Act as amended in 1974, the Congressional Budget and Impoundment Control Act of 1974, the Ethics in Government Act of 1978 and Codes of Ethics for
Public Services (1983) sought to place important new external controls on executive branch activities. New internal procedural controls, such as the extension of the Office of Inspector General throughout the federal executive
branch, were approved in 1978, as were the various ombudsman offices and
''sunset'' and ''sunrise'' laws instituted with state and local bureaucracies
during this same period. Such legislation tended to reduce public organizational autonomy, flexibility, and discretion and to increase institutional
fragmentation and legislative oversight. Furthermore, efforts were made by
the late 1970s to limit sharply bureaucratic functions. At the local level, Proposition 13 in California (1978) and Proposition $2^1/_2$ in Massachusetts served as
''model legislation'' for those who advocated reducing the role of the public
sector through placing tight revenue-raising lids in state constitutions. On the
federal level, the movement toward deregulation of various economic sectors
begun in the Carter administration, combined with sharp cutbacks in federal
expenditures inaugurated by the Reagan administration in 1981, reflected
these popular Jeffersonian values favoring less government. Furthermore, the
scope of popular representation *within* public organizations at every level of
government was extended and enlarged during this era. Generally, the roles
of professionals and professional groups such as city managers, foreign service
officers, and public health officials were not enhanced or supported by the
public but rather gave ground to expanded groups of political appointees,
minority group representation, citizen volunteers, and contractual employees. Administration efficacy yielded to extended public accountability, on
many fronts, throughout the 1970s.

By the mid-1980s, however, the picture, as described in chapter 6, has
become mixed. Strong concerns about finding effective means of achieving
broader public accountability over bureaucracy are still expressed by many.
The dominant ideological environment, sharply hostile to public bureaucracy
and evidencing supply-side ideas, exhibits these values that favor squeezing,
cutting, and reducing bureaucracy and expanding public controls. However,
as chapter 6 also stressed, the competing demands of Madisonian interest
groups on governmental activities and its bureaucracy have hardly declined.
Indeed, as chapter 6 suggested, there is strong indication that PACs, issue
networks, and pressure groups have strengthened their influence throughout
the executive branch in the 1980s. Not infrequently, voices favoring Hamiltonian values for increased administrative efficacy have been raised to promote
defense preparedness and environmental protection, conduct international

diplomacy, enhance national competitive capabilities in international trade and economics, revitalize U.S. industry, rebuild local infrastructure, employ the unemployed, stimulate hi-tech industries, and improve educational opportunities. These and other insistent public demands for action by liberals, moderates, and conservatives turn on the capacity of some public agency to ultimately deliver the goods. The 1980s, again as chapter 6 emphasized, present a crazy-quilt pattern of contradictory assertions of all three values—administrative efficacy, public accountability, and interest group demands.

The Necessity for Recognizing the Value of Trade-Offs in Public Bureaucracy in the United States Tomorrow

Americans have never quite made up their minds about the place of bureaucracy in their democracy. Certainly this confusion over values is apparent today. As with numerous other unsettled constitutional issues, the genius of the founding fathers in writing the U.S. Constitution was precisely in allowing succeeding generations of Americans to determine the shape of their government. Throughout the nineteenth century, when Jeffersonian values predominated, institutional arrangements affecting bureaucratic-democratic relationships were fashioned to stress the value of public accountability. In the late nineteenth and first half of the twentieth century, when the United States was in a nation-building mode, administrative efficacy replaced accountability as the overriding priority. As a mature superpower and welfare state in the socially stable era after World War II, a benign Madisonian liberalism favored an interplay of interest groups stressing organic social balance and institutional equilibrium.

No single value for structuring political-bureaucratic relations is inherently right or wrong. Each of the three has worked successfully in its own time and place. Each of the three also contains inherent limitations and problems. The dilemma the United States faces today is that all three of these values have come to the forefront of national debate and attention. Strong ideological currents and political interests in society loudly press their cases for Jeffersonian, Hamiltonian, and Madisonian perspectives. The issue of which *one* historic value should predominate over the others remains unresolved in the 1980s. Americans run their government with a confusing amalgam of all three value-emphases, which creates a situation of enormous confusion and complexity—and frustration. Realistically, one cannot expect the United States to suddenly decide to adopt one value perspective and neglect the others entirely. The problem is a matter of emphasis and accent.

The U.S. system of governance throughout its history has given at least some attention and concern to all three values as a basis for fashioning bureaucratic-democratic relations. But throughout most of its two-hundred-year history, only one value approach at a time has tended to predominate over the other two. What is perhaps most important for the future of bureaucracy in U.S. society is a frank appreciation of the strengths and limits of each value and of what trade-offs or consequences ensue from the adoption of one value over the others. Understanding the trade-offs can help clarify the alternatives facing Americans today as they fashion tomorrow's bureaucratic-democratic relationships.

Hamiltonian Values Maximizing Administrative Efficacy

A modern system of public bureaucracy constructed upon Hamiltonian values is depicted as a generalized model in figure 7.1. The system focuses on producing high-energy outputs rather than on maximizing public accountability or interest group demands. A bureaucratic system reflecting these values (1) ensures the adequacy of economic and political inputs in order to undertake the required tasks; (2) permits clear political objectives and policy directions from the top; (3) contains a highly professionalized cadre of public officials to carry out the tasks; (4) possesses the essential tools of effective leadership, broad administrative discretion, institutional autonomy, and unified orderly procedures to deliver public goods with speed and dispatch; and (5) manages and restricts feedback, communications, and publicity in such a way as to enhance, not detract from, the efficient programmatic outputs. Table 7.3 depicts representative public agencies today that approximate this model.

FIGURE 7.1
Public Bureaucracy (Hamiltonian Model)

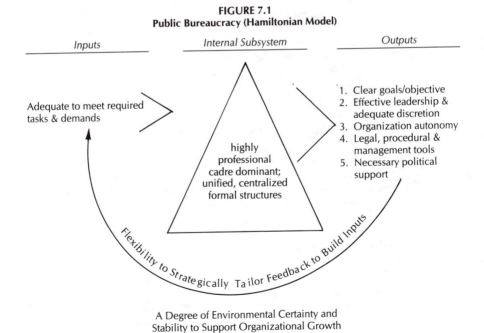

| Inputs | Internal Subsystem | Outputs |

Adequate to meet required tasks & demands

highly professional cadre dominant; unified, centralized formal structures

1. Clear goals/objective
2. Effective leadership & adequate discretion
3. Organization autonomy
4. Legal, procedural & management tools
5. Necessary political support

Flexibility to Strategically Tailor Feedback to Build Inputs

A Degree of Environmental Certainty and Stability to Support Organizational Growth

TABLE 7.3
Representative Public Agencies Approximating Hamiltonian Model

	U.S. Marine Corps	NY Port Authority
Clear purposes	combat missions & defense preparedness	metropolitan transportation projects
Organizational designs	centralized military hierarchy—power flows from top down	independent special district with autonomous funding/personal authority
Source of inputs	strong popular support and congressional backing	autonomy for revenue raising and fiscal directions
Internal subsystem control	highly professionalized military cadre of officers	highly professional engineering & transit planners
Outputs—the strengths	swift combat force prepared for demanding, single missions of national need	effective regional-wide transit planning & building
Outputs—the weaknesses	complex missions, with multigoals or political goals offer problems as in the case of Lebanon	single-mindedness in transportation development neglects other urban needs

The values that ultimately shape the overall design of this bureaucratic system, however, are not purchased without some costs:

1. Doing a particular job is given precedence over temporary popular concerns or individual group demands. This perspective assumes that there is a fixed task that can be understood and accomplished. It thus tends to be rigid and inflexible in its pursuit of these goals.
2. The emphasis upon achieving administrative efficacy, i.e., getting the job done effectively and quickly by focusing on achieving certain objectives, sometimes at any cost, tends to ignore other important, though possibly secondary, tasks. Adaptability to multiplicity of goals is thus sacrificed or reduced.
3. Hamiltonian values demand the attainment of adequate inputs of economic and political power to perform the required tasks. In other words, authority must equate with responsibility. This ideal is considered sound management practice for fashioning any high-energy bureaucratic model. Yet more often than not, public bureaucracy in the 1980s involves dealing with fragmented institutions, shifting interest groups, and radically opposing ideologies. Power to operate agencies usually must in real life be picked up piecemeal, and available input resources normally are never adequate to do any job.
4. The internal dynamics of this system place a premium upon maximizing professional expertise and limiting political oversight. Increasing the autonomy of professionals assumes a degree of faith in their competency to make important judgment calls. Ultimately, professionalizing bureaucracy involves increasing discretionary authority of experts over lay citizens.

5. A high-energy model achieves efficient output levels by building unified, stable administrative delivery systems with the necessary administrative discretion and staffing levels. The following elements are critical
for inducing high-level outputs: limiting the span of control, clear lines
of nonfragmented authority, authority for reorganization, internal systems for long-range planning, and tight hierarchical control. However,
such centralized management tools for speeding service delivery reduce
opportunities for political participation, decentralized community involvement, and intrusion of particularistic demands by interest groups.
6. Hamiltonian values also stress the importance of bold, creative, and decisive leadership as central to making things happen in order to maximize administrative efficacy. Robert Moses, General George Patton,
J. Edgar Hoover, and Alexander Hamilton exemplify this sort of high-
energy public leader. But this high-octane leadership frequently is purchased at the price of individual rights, due process, and the accommo-
dation of interest group demands.
7. Feedback mechanisms necessary to achieve administrative efficacy require that communication, secrecy, and news management be restricted
to a degree in order to gain agency publicity, popular support, future
resources, and political approval. Degrees of openness, access to information, and public scrutiny are, therefore, sacrificed in adopting Hamiltonian values.

Jeffersonian Values Maximizing Public Accountability

By contrast, a modern bureaucratic system constructed upon Jeffersonian values can be abstractly illustrated as in figure 7.2. Here the emphasis is upon
maximizing accountability to the public as a whole, often at the expense of
administrative efficacy or satisfying special interest group demands. Important elements of the model include (1) strict legal limitations placed upon
economic and political inputs; (2) a high degree of political oversight and
popular participation *within* the bureaucratic system; (3) emphasis on decen-
tralizing delivery of outputs as far as possible; (4) weak overall executive leadership; and (5) constant public scrutiny over the entire system. Public organizations exhibiting these features are outlined in table 7.4. Some of the costs
apparent in using this type of value-orientation to structure bureaucratic-
democratic relations are as follows.

1. Extensive popular participation, expanded oversight, and political involvement serve to lengthen the time needed to achieve agreement
upon organizational goals and create delay in the implementation of
services, thereby reducing the overall administrative efficacy of the organization.
2. This model assumes that there *is* a single, undifferentiated *public* to be
served, not many groups, or that the PEOPLE, not groups, are paramount in making democracy work. It is thus "blind" to the essential
requirements and problems of operating in a pluralistic society.

FIGURE 7.2
Public Bureaucracy (Jeffersonian Model)

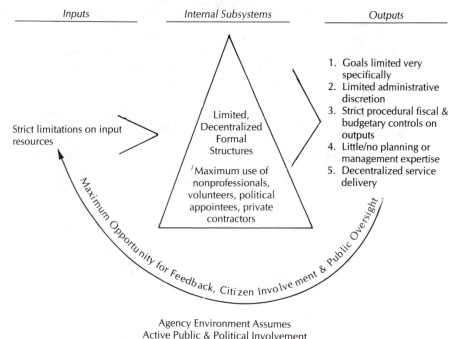

Agency Environment Assumes
Active Public & Political Involvement

3. Legal limitations on inputs, particularly economic resources, reduce the flexibility and ability of the governmental agency to meet changing and expanding demands, frequently leading to situations where responsibilities *exceed* the authority to act. This can lead to irresponsible, even corrupt, bureaucratic actions.

4. The internal dynamics of such a bureaucratic system emphasize expanding the roles for political appointees, citizen volunteers, and nonprofessionals, thus frequently reducing knowledge, expertise, skilled planning, and management competency, as well as rationality and operational consistency.

5. Decentralization of public services promotes flexibility and adaptability to different local and regional needs, but this also can create frequent opportunities for political intrusion by special interests as well as lack of uniform standards in services rendered and laws enforced.

6. Strict legal internal procedures to ensure public accountability related to program implementation, staffing, budgeting, and organizing service delivery can reduce the likelihood of bold, creative, and innovative public leadership.

TABLE 7.4
Representative Public Agencies That
Approximate Jeffersonian Model

	Executive Offices of the Mayor, Governor, President	*New England Town-Meeting Government*
Purposes	re-election of chief executive	representation of community interests
Source of inputs	voters selection	decisions of town meeting
Internal subsystem control	political appointees	citizen-volunteers
Outputs—the strengths	responsiveness to public opinion	mass citizen involvement in community life
Outputs—the weaknesses	little long-term planning/management capacity	little or no expertise in dealing with complex demands or problems
Organizational Design	fluid & changing according to chief executive needs	simple organizations with few employees

7. Public scrutiny, ample information, and media publicity enhance "honest" feedback to citizens about agency actions, but not without possibly jeopardizing national security, personal privacy, law enforcement, security, and the confidentiality that is necessary for frank appraisals and thoughtful deliberations within the inner councils of government. Economic costs to government might also be increased.

Madisonian Values Maximizing Balanced Interest Group Demands

A third alternative for modeling bureaucratic systems on Madisonian values is depicted in figure 7.3. Madisonian values stress attaining a social equilibrium through balancing interest group demands. The generalized elements of this system include (1) inputs principally based upon interest groups' demands; (2) bureaucratic outputs incrementally adjusted to meet special interest needs; (3) putting the principal focus of the internal bureaucratic subsystem upon "satisficing" the interest groups; (4) directing feedback toward promoting interest group satisfaction; and (5) devoting the bureaucracy not to efficiency, effectiveness, or to public service but to the promoting of social equilibrium. Some of the typical units of government that operate in this mode are depicted in table 7.5, but there are costs in adopting this bureaucratic model:

1. The goal of maintaining social equilibrium through satisfying interest group demands is an essentially conservative doctrine favoring the status quo over change and innovation. The model implicitly assumes that the present arrangement of social interests is adequate and that their "caring and feeding" at present levels are acceptable, *and* that nonincremental change upsetting the existing status quo is unacceptable.

FIGURE 7.3
Public Bureaucracy (Madisonian Model)

Inputs	_Internal Subsystem_	_Outputs_

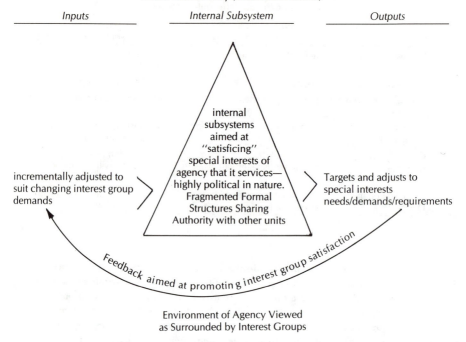

internal subsystems aimed at "satisficing" special interests of agency that it services— highly political in nature. Fragmented Formal Structures Sharing Authority with other units

incrementally adjusted to suit changing interest group demands

Targets and adjusts to special interests needs/demands/requirements

Feedback aimed at promoting interest group satisfaction

Environment of Agency Viewed as Surrounded by Interest Groups

2. The model thus favors the powerful and organized groups over the "voiceless," unorganized, and underrepresented ones.

3. The Madisonian system, by its very nature, is a complex, fragmented, interconnected system of institutions operating with numerous checks and balances upon one another, but it also induces a high degree of institutional fragmentation and dispersal of authority, thereby making bureaucratic accountability and responsibility much harder to establish. Whom does the individual citizen turn to for help or justice when administration becomes so complicated? Which institution or public agency can be held accountable when power becomes so fragmented, interdependent, and shared? Public accountability tends to be reduced as fragmentation increases.

4. Where inputs and outputs of the system turn largely upon "satisficing" special group demands, what ensures that _national_ needs are considered, international economic or global security needs accomplished, and long-term future policy responsibilities for such imperatives as the fiscal deficit or environmental problems met? The narrow perspectives and short-term agendas of particular groups tend to overtake the long-term broad agendas. The big picture, in short, is sacrificed often for the short-term immediate needs of special interests.

TABLE 7.5
Representative Public Agency Approximating Madisonian Model

	Veterans Administration	*State Road Dept.*
clear purpose	fulfill veterans needs	transportation functions
organization design	permits limited executive control; maximizes veteran group oversight	permits limited executive control; maximizes highway interests control over department
sources of inputs	large veterans organizations	powerful highway & transportation groups
internal dynamics	highly political	highly political
outputs—strengths	high amounts of social services for veterans	promotion of various state road-building & transit programs
outputs—weaknesses	largely ignores other interest group needs & requirements	promotes road building & major capital projects at expense of alternatives

5. The internal dynamics of agencies that maximize representation of special interests inside agencies tend to open up agencies to political fun and games, not to doing work. Representation of interests, political diversity, and participation are given primary emphasis.

6. Leadership of these public organizations, from top to bottom, is measured in terms of an individual's capacities to bargain, negotiate, and compromise effectively as opposed to his or her ability to make things happen and efficiently produce goods and services. Important institutional elements *necessary to lead* and deliver services are often overlooked. Gaining agreement, rather than achieving tangible goals, becomes an end in itself.

7. Feedback, and indeed all agency activity, is judged by essentially political perspectives—will it strategically enhance the short-term interests of the agency? Gain bargaining chips? How will it "play" to the media? Build political support? Enhance reputations? The general public welfare or institutional efficacy for the long term is down played.

The Future of U.S. Public Bureaucracy as a Value Problem: The Worth of a Systems Perspective

At the end of a recent book, Don Price recalls an incident that happened during his service as vice chairman of the Weapons Research and Development Board in the Pentagon.[32] Price was being flown in a navy plane out to Cape Hatteras (off the coast of North Carolina) to an aircraft carrier, where he was to watch the testing of new naval weapons. The weather was cloudy and the sea was rough. The navy lieutenant flying the plane had trouble finding the carrier. While cruising in search of the ship, he tuned in a radio station that announced the appointment of a new secretary of defense. While Price and others aboard expressed surprise at the appointee's selection, the navy lieutenant expressed little interest and then said, ''By the way, who is the secretary of defense now?'' Price tells how he felt a sense of outrage at a naval officer having so little comprehension of the broad governmental picture that he did not even know the name of his civilian superior. ''But then,'' explains Price, ''came a break in the clouds and far below—it seemed miles below—we could see the carrier on which we were to land. It looked about as big as a teacup, bouncing on the waves. And all of a sudden I did not want that navy pilot to have the slightest concern with the policies or the identity of his political superiors. I only wanted him to know how to land that plane.''

In real life, especially when *our* lives depend upon it, we, like Don Price, want public bureaucrats to do what they are supposed to do, when they are supposed to, as effectively as possible. Knowingly or not, we depend upon numerous public agencies to do such important jobs as inspecting the food we eat, the roadways we use, and the drinking water we consume, securing our

FIGURE 7.4
Significant Events in Shaping the 20th Century Values of U.S. Bureaucracy

Neo-Hamiltonian Values *Strengthening Administrative Efficacy*	*Neo-Jeffersonian Values* *Strengthening Administrative Accountability*
Est. of General Staff (1902)	Freedom of Information Act (1967)—FOIA
Taft Commission on Economy &	Amendments (1974)
Efficiency (1912)	Legislative Reorganization Act (1970)
Model City Charter (1916)	War Powers Resolution (1973)
Budget & Accounting Act (1921)	State "Sunset and Sunshine" Laws
Classification Act (1923)	(mid-1970s)
Brownlow Report (1937)	Privacy Act (1974)
Reorganization Act (1939)	Budget Impoundment & Control Act (1974)
Hatch Acts (1939 & 1940)	Civil Service Reform Act (1978)
Government Corporation Act (1945)	Inspector General Act (1978)
Employment Act (1946)	Proposition 13 (California, 1978)
First Hoover Report (1949)—Performance	Ethics in Government Act (1978)
Budgeting	
Organization for National Security Act	*Neo-Madisonian Values Strengthening*
(1947 and 1949)	*Special Interest Roles*
Second Hoover Report (1955)	
Kestnbaum Report (1955)	Veterans' Preference Act (1944)
Creation of ACIR (1959)	Administrative Procedure Act (1946)
PPBS Applied to DoD (1961)	Federal Labor-Management Program est.
BoB Circular A-95 (1969)	by E.O. 10987 and 10988 (1962)
Reorganization Plan No. 2 (1970)	Title VII of Civil Rights Act of 1964
ZBB est. (1977)	Equal Employment Opportunity Act
Civil Service Reform Act (1978)	(1972)
Reagan's Cabinet Councils (1981)	Legislative Reorganization Act (1970)
	Freedom of Information Act Amendments
	(1974)
	Budget & Impoundment Control Act
	(1974)
	Privacy Act (1974)
	Creation of Expansion of PACs by
	Campaign Reform Act (1974)

public safety, teaching the young, and protecting consumers in the market-place as well as workers on the job. In real life, also, we want these numerous agencies to be responsible to the public they serve, protect the rights of citizens, obey the law, follow legally prescribed due processes, allow for popular oversight of their actions, and, above all else, be responsive to the general welfare and needs of the citizenry. In short, we prize public accountability as well. *And* in real life, too, we form associations to press our claims upon government as groups of farmers, veterans, steel workers, teachers, and many others who lay legitimate claim to benefits and services from one or several public agencies. The right to associate and secure *our group's interests* from government is regarded as important and essential by most Americans.

The point is that in reality Americans are not pure Jeffersonians, Hamiltonians, or Madisonians. Rather, we take public action based on bits and pieces of all three value systems, often contradictory and confused, regarding public bureaucracy. And such has been true throughout the course of U.S. history. While one value may have predominated over the other two for long periods, the others have never been entirely neglected or ignored. All three are vital to knitting together democracy with bureaucracy.

But, as the foregoing analysis suggests, there are always important trade-offs associated with the pursuit of one value over the other two. In maximizing one, sacrifices are required from the other two. All three cannot be obtained at the maximum levels simultaneously—nor would we want them if they could be. How ghastly is the prospect of living with (or under) the perfectly efficient bureaucracy! Or under one that is perfectly accountable to the public! Or perfectly responsive to all interest group demands!

And in real life, too, public agencies must operate with the constant dilemma of adjusting and juggling these three competing values in the course of carrying out their affairs. As long as they operate within the U.S. governmental system, they must constantly balance concerns for administrative efficacy, public accountability, and interest group demands in order to govern justly and well. No one value can entirely eclipse the other two. Certainly so far no one has discovered a magic tool with which to fine tune the relationship among the three values.

What is most important for citizens and public officials to appreciate is that important costs and benefits are associated with each value. And here, taking the broad systems perspective, as this book does, can give a better understanding of what happens to any public organization, to its inputs, outputs, and feedback, and to the general environment when a certain value is emphasized over others. In the imperfect world in which we live, there always will be trade-offs, costs, and benefits resulting from actions based upon particular value orientations. Being conscious of the results of our actions before they are taken makes not only good horse sense but wise public policies as well.

Summary of Key Points

The U.S. Constitution of 1787 was largely silent on the subject of bureaucracy. Two hundred years later the United States operates with a large, complex public bureaucracy as its core system of governance. How to knit together our democratic ideals embodied in the written constitution and operational reality involving bureaucratic practices has been a recurring dilemma throughout U.S. history. No perfect "fit" between the two has yet been discovered. The issue involves a fundamental question of values: what is the place of bureaucracy in our modern democracy? Three value-approaches were outlined in this chapter—i.e., Jeffersonian, Hamiltonian, and Madisonian normative models—that have, in very different ways, served to answer this question. Throughout much of the nineteenth century, Jeffersonianism, emphasizing public accountability, dominated American bureaucratic-political relations. It fitted hand in glove with the largely rural, self-sufficient, isolationistic nation. The nation-building, expansionist forces of the late nineteenth and early twentieth centuries led to a strong assertion of Hamiltonian values reshaping fundamental democratic-bureaucratic relationships. The mid-century United States, with the creation of a mature welfare state and global international responsibilities, found Madisonian values, embodied in the interest group liberalism, formulating the design of democratic-bureaucratic relations. In the 1980s all three values gained prominence and support. The chief theme of this chapter is that the selection of *any one* value over the other two involves certain costs and benefits. A frank recognition of the trade-offs involving adoption of any one value over the other two is essential. A systems perspective can be an invaluable tool for improving our knowledge about these potential trade-offs.

Key Terms

administrative efficacy
public accountability
administrative interest groups
Brownlow Commission Report

value trade-offs
Hamiltonian values
Jeffersonian values
Madisonian values
systems perspective

Review Questions

1. What briefly are the nature and content of Jeffersonian, Hamiltonian, and Madisonian values?
2. Why is the problem of relating bureaucracy to democracy so complicated within the context of U.S. politics?
3. Can you describe the periods in U.S. history that were turning points in political-administrative relations?

4. Why does the author argue that the future of U.S. bureaucracy involves recognizing trade-offs associated with different values involving political-bureaucratic relationships?
5. Briefly, how did three founding fathers—Hamilton, Jefferson, and Madison—conceive of connecting bureaucracy and democracy?

Notes

1. Leonard D. White, *The Federalists: A Study in Administrative History* (NY: Macmillan, 1948), p. 478.
2. Clinton Rossiter, *Alexander Hamilton and the Constitution* (NY: Harcourt Brace Jovanovich, 1964), p. 162.
3. Lynton K. Caldwell, *The Administrative Theories of Hamilton and Jefferson: Their Contribution to Thought on Public Administration* (Chicago: University of Chicago Press, 1944), pp. 236–41.
4. James Madison, "The Federalist, No. 10," in Edmund M. Earle (ed.), *The Federalist* (NY: Random House, 1937), p. 54.
5. James Madison, "The Federalist, No. 51," ibid., p. 337.
6. Ralph Ketchum, *James Madison: A Biography* (NY: Macmillan, 1971), p. 301.
7. Samuel P. Huntington, *The Soldier and the State* (Cambridge: Harvard University Press, 1957), p. 206.
8. Don K. Price, *America's Unwritten Constitution: Science, Religion, and Political Responsibility* (Baton Rouge: Louisiana State University Press, 1983), p. 83.
9. Ibid.
10. Ibid., p. 86.
11. Mathew Crensen, *The Federal Machine* (Baltimore: Johns Hopkins University Press, 1975).
12. Douglas Southall Freeman, *Lee's Lieutenants: A Study in Command*, 3 vols. (NY: Scribners, 1942–44).
13. Refer to chapter 2 of this text for an extended discussion of this subject.
14. Robert H. Wiebe, *The Search for Order, 1877–1920* (NY: Hill and Wang, 1967).
15. Barry Karl, *Executive Reform in the New Deal* (Cambridge: Harvard University Press, 1963).
16. See especially Dwight Waldo, *The Administrative State* (NY: Ronald Press, 1948) and Herbert Simon, *Administrative Behavior* (NY: Macmillan, 1947).
17. David B. Truman, *The Government Process* (NY: Alfred A. Knopf, 1951), p. 501.
18. Robert A. Dahl, *A Preface to Democratic Theory* (Chicago: University of Chicago Press, 1956), p. 145.

19. Theodore J. Lowi, *The End of Liberalism* (NY: W. W. Norton, 1969), p. 37.

20. Charles E. Lindblom, "The Science of 'Muddling Through,' " *Public Administration Review* vol. 19 (Summer 1959), pp. 79–88.

21. Carl J. Friedrich, "Public Policy and the Nature of Administrative Responsibility," *Public Policy* (1940), pp. 3–24, and Herman Finer, "Administrative Responsibility in Democratic Government," *Public Administration Review* vol. 1 (Summer 1941), pp. 335–50.

22. Samuel P. Huntington, "The United States," in Michael Crozier, Samuel P. Huntington, and Joji Watanuki (eds.), *The Crisis of Democracy* (NY: New York University Press, 1975), pp. 74–75.

23. Ibid.

24. Ibid.

25. John Rawls, *A Theory of Justice* (Cambridge: Harvard University Press, 1971), p. 25.

26. Arthur Schlesinger, *The Imperial Presidency* (Boston: Houghton Mifflin, 1973).

27. Richard E. Neustadt, *Presidential Power* (NY: John Wiley, 1960).

28. E. F. Schumacher, *Small Is Beautiful: Economics as If People Mattered* (NY: Harper and Row, 1973).

29. Frank Marini (ed.), *Toward a New Public Administration: The Minnowbrook Perspective* (Scranton, Pa.: Chandler, 1971).

30. Vincent Ostrom, *The Intellectual Crisis in American Public Administration* (University: University of Alabama Press, 1973).

31. For a useful summary of these seminal pieces of legislation framing political-administrative relationships in the 1970s, refer to Part IV of Richard J. Stillman II (ed.), *Basic Documents of American Public Administration Since 1950* (NY: Holmes and Meier, 1982).

32. Don K. Price, *Unwritten Constitution*, pp. 177–78.

Further Readings

The historic problems associated with bureaucratic-political relationships have been discussed by scholars for some time.

The earliest and best discussion is between Carl J. Friedrich, "Public Policy and the Nature of Administrative Responsibility," *Public Policy,* 1 (Cambridge: Harvard University Press, 1940), pp. 3–24, and Herman Finer, "Administrative Responsibility in Democratic Government," *Public Administration Review* 1 (Summer 1941), pp. 335–50. A summary of both these essays can be found in Alan A. Alshuler (ed.), *"The Politics of Federal Bureaucracy* (1968). Also useful are Paul H. Appleby's *Morality and Administration in Democracy* (Baton Rouge: University of Louisiana Press, 1952); Frederick C. Mosher's *Democracy and the Public Service,* 2d ed. (NY: Oxford University Press, 1982), especially chapter 8; Arthur A. Maass and Laurence I.

Radway's "Gauging Administrative Responsibility," *Public Administration Review* 9 (Summer 1949), pp. 182–92. Some useful recent treatments include: Douglas Yates's *Bureaucratic Democracy* (Cambridge: Harvard University Press, 1982); Louis Fisher's *The Politics of Shared Power* (Washington, D.C.: Congressional Quarterly Press, 1981); Samuel Krislov and David H. Rosenbloom's *Representative Bureaucracy and the American Political System* (NY: Praeger, 1981); Richard E. Hartwig's *Roads to Reason* (1983); and Francis E. Rourke's *Bureaucracy, Politics and Public Policy*, 3d ed. (Boston: Little, Brown, 1984), especially chapter 7.

For several useful articles, see: Kenneth John Meier's "Representative Bureaucracy: An Empirical Analysis," *American Political Science Review* (June 1975), pp. 526–42; Herbert Kaufman's "Emerging Conflicts in the Doctrines of Public Administration," *American Political Science Review* (December 1956), pp. 1057–73; David H. Rosenbloom's "Public Administration Theory and the Separation of Powers," *Public Administration Review* (May/June 1983), pp. 213–27; Lynton K. Caldwell's "Novus Ordo Seculorum: The Heritage of American Public Administration" and Barry D. Karl's "Public Administration and American History: A Century of Professionalism," appearing in *Public Administration Review* (September/October 1975), pp. 476–505; Mark T. Lilla's "Ethos, 'Ethics' and Public Service," *The Public Interest* (Spring 1981), pp. 3–17, and in the same issue, Thomas C. Shelling's "Economic Reasoning and the Ethics of Policy," pp. 37–61. Several of Norton Long's insightful essays wrestle with the problems of bureaucratic oversight and accountability and can be found in a collection of his writings: *The Polity* (Chicago: Rand McNally, 1962).

The classic works on the influence of interest groups on administration are: Arthur F. Bentley *The Process of Government* (Cambridge: Harvard University Press, 1908); E. Pendleton Herring's *Public Administration and the Public Interest* (NY: Russell and Russell, 1936); David Truman, *The Governmental Process* (NY: Alfred A. Knopf, 1951); and Robert A. Dahl and Charles E. Lindblom's *Politics, Economics and Welfare* (NY: Harper and Brothers, 1953).

Serious students of the topic of administrative efficacy, accountability, and interest groups should also examine primary materials—executive orders, congressional acts, and official reports as contained in Frederick C. Mosher (ed.), *Basic Documents of American Public Administration, 1776-1950* (NY: Holmes and Meier, 1976) and Richard J. Stillman II (ed.), *Basic Documents of American Public Administration since 1950* (NY: Holmes and Meier, 1982).

Index

ABOUT THE AUTHOR

Richard J. Stillman II, Professor of Government and Politics at George Mason University, Fairfax, Virginia, teaches in that school's new doctoral program in public administration. He is the author or editor of books on various aspects of public bureaucracy and its management, including: *The Rise of the City Manager, Public Administration* (3d ed.), *Professions in Government* (with Frederick C. Mosher), *Results-oriented Budgeting, The Effective Local Government Manager* (with Wayne Anderson and Chester Newland), *Basic Documents of American Public Administration since 1950,* and *A Search for Public Administration* (with Brack Brown and Dwight Waldo). He serves on the editorial boards of *Public Administration Review* and *American Review of Public Administration.* Stillman has been a NASA Fellow, Public Administration Fellow, Research Fellow at the Institute of Governmental Studies, University of California at Berkeley, and Robinson Fellow at George Mason University.